TOMMASO CAMPANELLA

ARCHIVES INTERNATIONALES D'HISTOIRE DES IDÉES

INTERNATIONAL ARCHIVES OF THE HISTORY OF IDEAS

200

TOMMASO CAMPANELLA:
THE BOOK AND THE BODY OF NATURE

Germana Ernst

For other titles published in this series, go to
www.springer.com/series/5640

Tommaso Campanella

The Book and the Body of Nature

Germana Ernst

Università di Roma Tre

Translated by

David L. Marshall

Kettering University

 Springer

Germana Ernst
Dipartimento di Filosofia, Università di Roma Tre
via Ostiense 234, 00144 Roma, Italy
ernst@uniroma3.it

Translator
David L. Marshall
Department of Liberal Studies
Kettering University
1700 W. Third Avenue, Flint
MI 48504, USA
david.marshall@kettering.edu

The translation of this work has been funded by SEPS
SEGRETARIATO EUROPEO PER LE PUBBLICAZIONI SCIENTIFICHE

Via Val d'Aposa 7 – 40123 Bologna – Italy
seps@seps.it – www.seps.it
and
Department of Philosophy of the Third University of Rome

ISBN 978-90-481-3125-9   e-ISBN 978-90-481-3126-6
DOI 10.1007/978-90-481-3126-6
Springer Dordrecht Heidelberg London New York

Library of Congress Control Number: 2009943040

Printed on acid-free paper

Springer is part of Springer Science+Business Media (www.springer.com)

CONTENTS

PREFACE

I know that many will comment on what I say, they will mock me,
they will be after phrases and accents
without the spirit of God, judging me in their own way.
Campanella, *Lettere*, p. 48

And they want to fight against me with unjust officials, prisons,
handcuffs, bars, ropes, tortures and slayers, darkness and hunger,
whereas I cannot use such weapons against them,
nor do they want to fight with reason.
Ibid., p. 13

Even if one has studied an author for many years, perhaps precisely for this very reason, anything that is said about him or her appears inadequate and insufficient: an abyss opens up behind each word, every phrase recalls yet other phrases. With an author like Tommaso Campanella, the feeling of disorientation may turn into actual dizziness. Campanella was bold enough to address all fields of knowledge. However much his attempt can be better described as generous rather than pretentious, the whole enterprise was undoubtedly tricky, marked by all kinds of difficulties, with very diverse outcomes, which at times cause amazement and emotion, even as on other occasions they prove disappointing and almost irritating. This has led to so many contrasting evaluations of his thought, characterised as it is by the presence of both powerfully innovative visions and tenaciously persistent convictions. All these elements, however, result in a complex picture, which the author, striking out on tortuous and intricate paths, intended to present as unified by a coherent vision.

This volume is an attempt at offering a map of the biographical and intellectual journey of Campanella. Taking into account new findings about his life and works that enhance or correct the classic studies of the author, these pages try to present, through variations of recurrent motifs, the origins, development, and persistence of some of the fundamental themes of his philosophy. This map is necessarily a selective one. Needless to say, it can only barely touch upon monumental works such as the *Metaphysica*, the *Theologia*, and many others, while it draws the reader's attention to less known or forgotten texts. It is a map that offers itself as an introduction, with an eye to future research and a much-to-be-desired project of gathering and publishing all the works of the philosopher.

I truly hope that this translation of my monograph on Campanella will contribute towards a better understanding of the wide-ranging thought of one of the most original philosophers of the early modern period and that it will generate further interest in his complex oeuvre. With regard to the Italian edition (2002) and the subsequent translation into French (2007), I have limited myself to adding occasional bibliographical references and making a few minor changes to the text so as to render it more straightforward. I have also reorganized the material in some chapters in a way that makes the presentation more coherent.

I would like to express my heartfelt gratitude to all those who have contributed towards the realization of this initiative. I would like to thank, in particular, Sarah Hutton, who kindly suggested that I should publish the volume in the present series; Anita Fei van der Linden of Springer Publishers, Raffaella Colombo (SEPS – Segretariato Europeo per le Pubblicazioni Scientifiche, Bologna), and the publishers Laterza, who followed and supported the various phases of the production of the book. I would also like to express my gratitude to David Marshall, who took on the job of translating a demanding text with friendly enthusiasm and courage; special thanks are due to Jean-Paul De Lucca for his many suggestions and for compiling the subject index. I would also like to thank Guido Giglioni for his constant help, and all those whose affection and friendship have accompanied me throughout my work.

G. E.

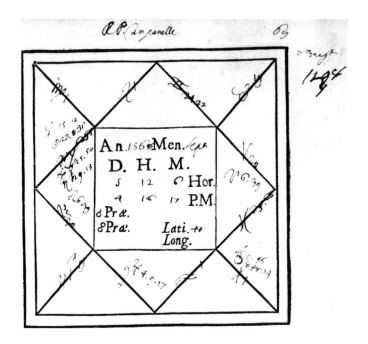

Natal chart of Tommaso Campanella (Rome, Archivio di Stato,
Tribunale criminale del governatore, Processi 1630)

F· THOMAE

CAMPANELLAE

CALABRI DE STYLO,

ORDINIS PRÆDICATORVM PHILOSOPHIA, SENSIBVS DEMONSTRATA,

In Octo Difputationes diftincta ,

Aduerfus eos , qui proprio arbitratu , non autem fenfata
duce natura , philofophati funt .

Vbi errores Ariftotelis , & affeclarum ex proprijs dictis , & naturæ decretis conuincun-
tur ; & fingulæ imaginationes , pro eo à Peripateticis fittæ prorfus reijciuntur cum
vera defenfione Bernardini Telefij Confentini, Philofophorum maximi , antiquorum
fententijs,quæ hic dilucidantur, & defenduntur,præcipuè Platonicorum confirmata:
ac dum pro Ariftotele púgnat Iacobus Antonius Marta , contra feipfum, & illum pu-
gnare oftenditur .

Ad Illuftrifsimum Dominum D. Marium de Tufo .

NEAPOLI, Apud Horatium Saluianum . 1 5 9 1 .

Frontispiece of T. Campanella, *Philosophia sensibus demonstrata* (Naples, 1591).

F. THOMÆ
CAMPANELLÆ.
APPENDIX POLITICÆ,
CIVITAS SOLIS
Poetica.

IDEA
Reipublicæ Philofophicæ.

Frontispiece of T. Campanella, *Civitas Solis* (in *Philosophia realis*, Paris, 1637)

AD DIVVM PETRVM
Apoſtolorum Principem Triumphantem.

ATHEISMVS TRIVMPHATVS
Seu
REDVCTIO AD RELIGIONEM
PER SCIENTIARVM VERITATES.
F. THOMÆ CAMPANELLÆ STYLENSIS
ORDINIS PRAEDICATORVM.

CONTRA
ANTICHRISTIANISMVM ACHITOPHELLISTICVM.

Sexti Tomi Pars Prima.

ROMÆ, Apud Hæredem Bartholomæi Zannetti. M. DC. XXXI.

SVPERIORVM PERMISSV.

*Dño Gabriel Nodeo pro amico
& Thomas Campanella
amoris testimonium dat
16 o Maji 1631.*

Frontispiece of T. Campanella, *Atheismus triumphatus* (Rome, 1631)
with dedication to Gabriel Naudé

1. TELESIUS ME DELECTAVIT

The Book of Nature

Having become worried because it seemed to me that one could not find
truth in the Peripatetic school and because falsehood had taken the place
of truth, I took up the task of examining all the commentators on Aristotle
– Greek, Latin, and Arabic – and my doubts with respect to their doctrines
were increased. I wanted therefore to discover also whether their assertions
could be verified in the world, which – as I learned from the doctrines of
the philosophers – is the living book of God. And since my teachers were
not able to respond to the objections that I raised to whatever they taught, I
decided to read for myself all the books of Plato, Pliny, Galen, the books of
the Stoics, those of the followers of Democritus, but above all the works of
Telesio, so that I might compare them with the book of nature and thereby
find out, from such a comparison with the original and autograph version,
how much truth and how much falsehood there was in the copies. In the
course of public disputes at Cosenza or in private conversations with fellow
friars, the replies of my interlocutors did not succeed in allaying my doubts.
Only Telesio replenished my spirit with joy, both on account of his liberty
of philosophizing and also because he derived his opinions from the natural
world, and not from the words of men.[1]

In this passage, from his *Syntagma de libris propriis* (written at Rome in 1632 in
response to repeated requests from Gabriel Naudé), Campanella expressed the
deep significance of his early studies in the years of his youth spent in the Dominican convents of Calabria.[2] The section just cited is preceded by a rapid sketch of

---

[1] *Syntagma*, I, 1, pp. 31–33. On book metaphors in Campanella, see Margherita
Palumbo, 'libri, libro della natura,' in *Enciclopedia*, vol. 1, coll. 257–265.
[2] The *Syntagma* would be published in Paris only in 1642, three years after the death of
the author. Even if a degree of inaccuracy and some incoherence have raised suspicions
of manipulation (probably minor) of the text by Naudé, the text immediately proved to
be an irreplaceable document for the purpose of reconstructing the human and intellectual development of the author. Campanella had also dictated a *Vita Campanellae* to
Naudé, the loss of which cannot be but deeply regretted. In the *Syntagma* scant and not

G. Ernst, *Tommaso Campanella,* International Archives of the History
of Ideas / Archives internationales d'histoire des idées 200,
DOI 10.1007/978-90-481-3126-6_1, © Springer Science + Business Media B.V. 2010

his childhood and early adolescence, characterized by a precocious, intensely felt desire to learn that was accompanied by a gifted memory together with a natural predisposition to poetic expression. Campanella composed his first verses at around the age of thirteen (even if they were mostly without great merit); at fifteen, in the village of San Giorgio Morgeto, during celebrations on the occasion of the visit of the lord of the place, he recited an oration in verse that he had composed himself, before a great crowd, which had gathered there from nearby villages.[3]

Campanella was born shortly after dawn on 5 September 1568 in Stilo, in Calabria, which was part of the Spanish viceroyalty of Naples.[4] On 12 September, he was baptized with the name Giovan Domenico. His family was of humble extraction: his father, Geronimo, was an illiterate cobbler; his mother, Caterina Martello, died just after her son had turned five years old. In a curious passage in the *Theologia*, Campanella would later remember that, in the course of a diabolical evocation in Padua (in 1593–1594), the devil, inhabiting the body of a possessed woman, had guessed the name of his mother (who had died at Stilo twenty years earlier), but was curiously incapable of recalling the first words of Plato's *Timaeus*.[5] Testament to his desire to learn and to his poverty is an anecdote relating that as a child he listened from outside the school (being unable to pay for lessons) and, when the schoolchildren did not know how to respond to the questions of the teacher, he would appear at the window and shout: 'Would you like me to tell you?' This was the first of many such anecdotes – more or less verisimilar – that recur throughout his autobiography.

During an outbreak of the plague (which was said to have been caused by infected cloth imported from Algeria to Messina and later to Calabria), his father Geronimo had managed to keep the disease under control.[6]

---

always perspicuous autobiographical notes are woven into a critical bibliography of the contents of his own books. For autobiographical information present in other books, see Germana Ernst, 'Autobiografia di Tommaso Campanella,' in *Laboratorio Campanella*, pp. 15–38.

[3] *Syntagma*, I, 1, p. 30.

[4] The hour indicated by Firpo ('six minutes after six in the afternoon') in *DBI*, XVII (Rome, 1974), p. 372, ought to be modified. A correct interpretation of the hour indicated within the nativity theme, which is included in the papers of the Abbot Orazio Morandi (for which see below, ch. 11.2), indicates twelve hours after the setting of the sun (the moment at which the new day was judged to have begun in the early modern period) and eighteen hours post meridiem on 4 September – that is, around six in the morning of the 5th. The nativity, preserved at Rome (Archivio di Stato, Tribunale Criminale del Governatore, Processi 1630, n. 251, c. 1298r) is reproduced in Ernst, *Religione,* p. 158; Campanella, *Opuscoli astrologici*, p. 62. For another nativity theme, which confirms these dates, see Germana Ernst and Giuseppe Bezza, 'Una natività manoscritta di Campanella,' *B&C*, 13 (2007), pp. 711–716.

[5] Tommaso Campanella, *Le creature sovrannaturali, Theologicorum liber V*, ed. R. Amerio (Rome, 1970), p. 104; the passage is highlighted by Romano Amerio, *Il sistema teologico di Tommaso Campanella* (Milan-Naples, 1972), p. 64, note 2.

From childhood Campanella had suffered from pains in the spleen and during a night of the new moon, he had been restored to health by a healer thanks to a magical formula.[7] At the age of fourteen and a half, against the wishes of his father (who had hoped to send him to Naples in the care of a relative, so that he might follow courses in jurisprudence), Campanella decided to enter the Dominican order. He had been fascinated by the eloquence of a preacher (from whom he had learned the rudiments of logic) and by the figures of Albert the Great and Thomas Aquinas. After entering the convent of Placanica and changing his birth-name to Tommaso, he was transferred to the convent of the Annunziata in San Giorgio Morgeto, where he studied scholastic texts on logic and physics, as well as Aristotle's *Metaphysics* and *De anima*.[8] On the occasion of the mentioned visit of the small town's baron, Giacomo II Milano, who had married Isabella del Tufo, he forged a relationship with the del Tufo, an important aristocratic family in whose palace he would later stay during his sojourn in Naples. In the autumn of 1586, Campanella was transferred to the convent of the Annunziata in Nicastro, where he struck up a friendship with the Ponzio brothers (Dionisio in particular), who would later play an important part in the Calabrian conspiracy of 1599.

Immediately, the reading of Aristotelian texts together with their commentators prompted dissatisfaction and a critical attitude in the young friar. At Nicastro, a teacher, referring to that polemical attitude, is said to have warned: 'Campanella, Campanella, you will not meet with a good end!'[9] Campanella explained the reasons for breaking with the doctrines of the schools in

---

[6] *Medicina*, p. 324. The reference is to the plague that struck Sicily in 1575–1576. A contemporary report on the plague by the physician Giovanni Filippo Ingrassia has recently been published in a modern edition as Giovanni Filippo Ingrassia, *Informatione del pestifero et contagioso morbo*, ed. L. Ingaliso (Milan, 2005).

[7] *Senso delle cose*, IV, 17, p. 215.

[8] There, he wrote a sequence of *Lectiones logicae, physicae et animasticae*, which has not survived. Regarding the organization of the Dominican convents and their library collections in Calabria, see L. G. Esposito, *I Domenicani in Calabria. Ricerche archivistiche*, ed. G. Cioffari (Naples-Bari, 1997); little is known concerning the earliest periods in Campanella's youth, but see Carlo Longo OP, 'Su gli anni giovanili di Fr. Tommaso Campanella OP, 1568–1589,' *Archivum Fratrum Praedicatorum*, 73 (2003), pp. 363–390; Idem, '"Thomas ille tertius." I Domenicani di Placanica e Campanella,' *B&C*, 12 (2006), pp. 137–144.

[9] Amabile, *Congiura*, III, doc. 278, p. 199. In the volume *Fra le letture del giovane Tommaso Campanella* (Vibo Valentia, 2002), Antonella De Vinci relates that there are autograph notes made by a very young Campanella in the margins of books that come from the convent in Nicastro; see also her subsequent paper, 'Postille del giovane Campanella in volumi della Casa del Libro Antico di Lamezia Terme', in *Laboratorio Campanella*, pp. 39–63.

the preface of his first published work, the *Philosophia sensibus demonstrata*. They are intense pages, that offer the reader a vivid autobiographical sketch and a passionate methodological manifesto.[10] Not by chance, this preface opens with the word 'truth,' which is represented, in the vignette of the frontispiece, as a sphere that floats on the water, while winds blowing from every quarter try to sink it and a young friar attempts to reach it by swimming. Truth can be obscured and attacked, begins the author, but in the end it emerges from the shadows and becomes once again resplendent. Campanella does not hesitate to add that one ought even to prefer the truth to life itself.

Tracing the fundamental lines of his first years of study, Campanella confessed that the reading of Aristotle's scholastic texts had raised in him more doubts than certainties. His teachers did not know how to respond to his questions and gave embarrassed replies, in which the young student found little solace. Thus, he came to find himself in a painful condition of fearfulness and loneliness, feeling himself completely isolated from the entire philosophical tradition. But in the end, there awoke in Campanella the intuition of a new philosophy taken not from books or from the intellect of Aristotle, but rather from things themselves and by means of the senses and experience. And nothing could any longer impede the powerful development of this perspective: 'thereafter the truth burned brightly and it was not possible to contain it within me.'[11] Accused of supporting doctrines similar to those of Telesio, Campanella could not help but feel joy at the judgment – which was meant as a reproach and a condemnation – because he had finally found an intellectual companion and guide.

Having moved to Cosenza so as to pursue the study of theology, Campanella was able to read the first edition of Telesio's *De rerum natura iuxta propria principia* (Naples, 1565). From the very first pages, he intuited the novelty and the coherence of a doctrine that, in accord with his own aspirations, 'derives the truth from things examined by means of sense and not by means of illusions.'[12] His desire to meet Telesio in person was, however, frustrated by the death of the philosopher at the age of eighty. Campanella could only admire his noble face and offer a reverent homage to the corpse as it lay in state at the cathedral of the city. He then affixed some verses by

---

[10] There is an Italian translation in Luigi Firpo, 'Il metodo nuovo (*Praefatio* alla *Philosophia sensibus demonstrata* di Tommaso Campanella),' *Rivista di Filosofia*, 40 (1949), pp. 182–205.

[11] *Phil. sens. dem.*, p. 7: 'Post haec incaluit veritas et intus cogi amplius minus poterat.'

[12] Ibid.: I appreciated Telesio 'tanquam veritatem ex rebus conspectis sensu elicientem, ut patuit, non ex chimeris.'

the casket.[13] This virtual encounter, in which the young Dominican seemed
to receive the spiritual inheritance of the new philosophy, fixed itself indel-
ibly in his mind, and would later reemerge with the same emotional intensity
more than forty years later, in a letter written from Paris to Nicolas-Claude
Fabri de Peiresc on 19 June 1636. Evoking once again this memorable Telesian period and recalling some of Telesio's exponents, such as the physician
Francesco Sopravia of Seminara (who 'glossed the opinions of Leucippus
and Democritus wondrously to everyone, when I was sixteen'), Campanella
did not fail to remember his own desire to go to Cosenza, as he described
the homage he paid to the corpse: 'then I went, growing in feeling and desire
to know, to where Telesio was in upper Calabria; I was not able to see him
except in death, when I composed for him an epigram and read his books.'[14]
The episode would strike later readers too, and in the second half of the
nineteenth century a poet from Cosenza, Vincenzo Baffi, would dedicate a
long elegy to the funeral vigil of the young Campanella next to the coffin of
Telesio, imagining that in the course of the night, during the breaking of a
violent storm, the young friar, asleep, foresaw in a dream the difficult trials
that he would later have to endure. But, in the morning, as he awoke, the fury
of the elements was stilled and when he came out of the church into the fresh
air he was able to contemplate the consoling image of a rainbow under a sky
that had once again become serene.[15]

Although the youthful verses attached to the casket have been lost, Campanella celebrated in a famous sonnet the philosopher who had defeated and
killed the tyrant of the intellects, emancipating man from the yoke of Aristotle and from every other philosophy that would presume to substitute itself
for the book of nature, so as to restore to man that *libertas philosophandi* that
is inseparable from the truth:

> Telesio, in the midst of the sophists' encampment
> An arrow from your quiver kills
> The tyrant of the mind without hope of escape;
> And conquers liberty, so sweet to truth.[16]

---

[13] Ibid.: 'me ibi [in Cosenza] existente defunctus est summus Telesius et ab eo suas
sententias audire non licuit, nec viventem videre sed mortuum, in templum delatum, cuius
vultum discooperiens admiratus sum, et in eius tumulo plurima de eo affixi carmina.'

[14] Germana Ernst and Eugenio Canone, 'Una lettera ritrovata: Campanella a Peiresc, 19 giugno 1636,' *Rivista di storia della Filosofia*, 49 (1994), pp. 353–366: 364; the text
of the letter is also in *Lettere 2*, p. 116.

[15] Vincenzo Baffi, *Una notte di Tommaso Campanella*, in *Versi* (Florence, 1858),
pp. 27–32.

[16] *Poesie*, p. 278: 'Telesio, il telo della tua faretra/uccide de' sofisti in mezzo al campo/
degli ingegni il tiranno senza scampo;/libertà dolce alla verità impetra.'

When Campanella sought to explain in the *Syntagma* why, after having searched through the entire philosophical tradition, his restless research had settled on the philosophy of Telesio ('sed Telesius me delectavit'), he emphasized two reasons: *libertas philosophandi* and adherence to natural facts instead of to the words of men. Campanella was among the first to use the expression *libertas philosophandi* in order to denote emancipation from all authority whatsoever and the right, which was also a duty, on the part of the scholar to read directly from the book of nature.[17] A third reason was that Telesio, animated by a disinterested love for the truth and unmoved by vain academic honors, also embodied in his own life, and not just in his thought, an authentic (and extremely rare) philosophical style. According to Campanella, in the entire history of thought one can enumerate only twenty-five true philosophers – and only four in modern times. Even if we do not know the names of those philosophers – or even whether, or how, Campanella might have responded to François La Mothe Le Vayer, who was curious to know them – at least two are absolutely certain: Socrates for antiquity and Telesio, an admirable example of true philosophical modesty, for modernity.[18]

Telesio's philosophy reestablished those connections between things and words that had been worn out and lost in the Aristotelian tradition. Even if in Aristotle (depicted in the *Syntagma* as one of the greatest geniuses of the human race) the importance of the relationship to the natural world was front and center, his followers, convinced that in the corpus of his writings the master had included, once and for all time, the whole truth, no longer recognized the necessity of verification by means of experience. Indeed, such verification was perceived as a disturbance and a menace. Denouncing the 'fictions' and sophistries of the Aristotelians, the young Campanella underlined their incapacity to distance themselves from the narrow confines of their own philosophy in order to go outside into the open air and observe things themselves:

> Never, by Hercules, have I succeeded in finding one of them looking upon
> things, going into the countryside – to the sea, to the mountains – in order to

---

[17] See John M. Headley, 'Campanella on Freedom of Thought: The Case of the Cropped Pericope,' *B&C*, 2 (1996), pp. 165–177; see also his important monograph on *Tommaso Campanella and the Transformation of the World* (Princeton, 1997); on the *Apologia pro Galileo*, see below, ch. 9.1.

[18] *Ateismo trionfato*, I, p. 18 (*Ath. triumph.*, p. 4); regarding La Mothe le Vayer, see Naudé's letter to Campanella sent from Urbino on 21 August 1632 (where, perhaps as a result of a printing error, 'twenty-four natural philosophers' of modern times are spoken of, whereas Campanella wrote 'vix quatuor'), in *Epistulae* (Geneva, 1667), p. 262. As for other ancient philosophers, one might imagine Pythagoras, Plato, Diogenes, Hermes Trismegistus, perhaps Seneca and Dante.

observe things, instead of remaining always squirreled away at home, studying only in the books of Aristotle, over which they are always poring.[19]

Campanella found in Telesio a response to the necessity of leaving the labyrinth
of paper and of words, in which books beget books and reason (forgetting its
relationship to things and to experience) degenerates into sophisms and merely
verbal disputes. As he would say in a passage from a later work addressed to crit-
ics who were accusing him of privileging sense over reason, he explained that he
did not deny reason in itself but rather held that, cut off from the senses, reason
lost itself in sophisms.[20]

In another famous sonnet, among those translated by Herder,[21] Campanella took up the metaphor of the book of nature, connecting it to that of the
living temple:

> The world is the book in which Eternal Wisdom
> Has written its ideas; it is a living temple
> Decorated from high to low with living statues
> Representing its own undertakings and its own example.[22]

From here he went on to deplore the human attitude of preferring 'dead
books and temples/copied by the living with many errors,' which cannot but
engender evils such as 'disputes, ignorance, great difficulty, and sorrow.' He
concluded with a vivid exhortation to return to the observation and study of
the original book of nature itself.

In Defense of Telesio Against Aristotle

In 1591, at Naples, in the publishing house of Orazio Salviano, the first of
Campanella's published works appeared – the previously mentioned *Philosophia sensibus demonstrata*. It was a massive volume defending Telesio's natural
philosophy and dedicated to Mario del Tufo, in whose palace the author was
residing. Campanella had written it in the first eight months of 1589, before
he was twenty, in the Calabrian convent of Altomonte, where he had been
sent by his superiors, perhaps as a punishment for his enthusiastic adherence
to Telesio's philosophy.[23] There he established friendships with physicians and

---

[19] *Phil. sens. dem.*, p. 5.
[20] See *Dialogo politico contro Luterani*, p. 42 (for this work, see ch. 3.1).
[21] See ch. 7, note 13.
[22] *Poesie*, p. 44: 'Il mondo è il libro dove il Senno Eterno/scrisse i proprii concetti,
e vivo tempio/dove, pingendo i gesti e 'l proprio esempio,/di statue vive ornò l'imo e
'l superno.'
[23] It is probable that material elaborated previously is woven into the work, and
perhaps others elements were added later.

local scholars[24] and was able to develop his own readings further. This nourished and fed an appetite for knowing so insatiable that in a sonnet (significantly titled *Anima immortale*, 'Immortal Soul,' as if in the measurelessness of
that desire to know there might be a sign of such immortality), he gave voice
to his own soul:

> I am held in a brain the size of a fist and I devour
> So much that all the books in the world
> Are not enough to satiate my vast appetite:
> I have consumed so much and yet I am dying of hunger.[25]

It was in fact his new friends who procured for Campanella a copy of the
Pugnaculum Aristotelis adversus principia Bernardini Telesii, in which the
Neapolitan jurist Giacomo Antonio Marta set himself up as a defender of
Aristotle's doctrines, deriding Telesio's. Indeed, these friends encouraged
Campanella to respond and return the attack and he did just that, quickly
and with confidence. He drew up the eight weighty disputations of the *Philosophia*, setting out a systematic critique of Aristotle's philosophy from physical,
cosmological, and metaphysical points of view in light of Telesian principles
combined with arguments derived from other philosophies and traditions
(including the pre-Socratics and the Platonists, as well as the Neo-Platonist
and Hermetic traditions). The text is not easy to read.[26] The very polemical
structure of the text makes the reader's journey tortuous and disjointed and
is illuminated only by flashes of vivid attacks on Marta, who is presented as a
presumptuous and arrogant pseudo-philosopher, a dog barking wildly in the
street. And then, when this pseudo-philosopher had the temerity to make a
joke on the connection between Calabrians and the sphere of fire, Campanella
replied proudly that Calabrians might be said to partake in that sphere with
good reason, on account of the subtlety and the purity of their minds, capable
of penetrating the heavens, while Marta – made up of dense and murky animal

---

[24] In the *Praefatio*, Campanella mentioned the physicians Giovan Francesco
Branca and Plinio Rogliano, Muzio Campolongo, baron of Acquaformosa, and the
jurisconsult Giovan Paolo Galterio.

[25] *Poesie*, p. 39: 'Di cervel dentro un pugno io sto, e divoro/tanto, che quanti libri
tiene il mondo/non saziâr l'appetito mio profondo:/quanto ho mangiato! e del digiun
pur moro.'

[26] The scholars who have analyzed the themes of this work the most are Antonio
Corsano, Nicola Badaloni, Pasquale Tuscano, and Luigi De Franco. On the relationship
between Campanella and Telesio, see Michel-Pierre Lerner, 'Telesio et Campanella:
de la nature *iuxta propria principia* à la nature *instrumentum Dei*,' *B&C*, 13 (2007),
pp. 79–97.

spirits – would merit being closed up in the bowels of the earth. Similarly, responding to one contemptuous line on the Calabrian origins of Telesio, he launched into a passionate speech on the illustrious Calabrian philosophical tradition, of which Telesio was a renowned exponent.[27]

Although the text proceeds in a minute and tedious manner, the work actually turns out to be important, both because it contains themes and problems that would later be much further developed and also on account of the extremely dense blizzard of citations, which serves to reveal the young Campanella's 'library' – in all its surprising extension and variety – in a way that would never be repeated. Campanella moved with great confidence within the Aristotelian texts themselves, as well as in those of his commentators and followers – the ancients (Themistius, Alexander of Aphrodisia, Philoponus), the medievals (the 'prince' Averroes is heavily cited, as is St. Thomas, and above all the 'divine' Albert the Great), and the moderns, such as Agostino Nifo. Campanella reevaluated the Pre-Socratics, suppressed and criticized by Aristotle. He knew well the physicians, from Hippocrates to Galen, Peter de Abano, Jean Fernel, and Vesalius. He had read the texts of the astronomers and those of the natural philosophers. A central role was reserved for Pliny the Elder and his *Naturalis Historia*, but Cardano's *De Subtilitate* is also cited.[28] Above all, there is Ficino, who is mentioned with some reserve but also with the strong will to connect his doctrines with Telesio's philosophy – Ficino the commentator on Plato (especially the *Timaeus* and the *Symposium*) and the *Enneads* of Plotinus, with whom the 'Platonic' Virgil is associated.

Other than proposing a new methodology, based on sensory categories instead on words or astractions,[29] the *Philosophia* is concerned with attacking Aristotelianism on all fronts: thus, in an examination both systematic and precise, Campanella discusses and rejects the doctrines of form and privation, of the four elements as principles of the sublunary world, of matter as privation, of the derivation of celestial heat from the friction of the spheres, and of the distinction between natural and violent motion. This is a systematic work of dismantling that finds its complement in a radical critique of traditional cosmology, both with regard to the nature of the heavens and to the trajectories and mechanisms of heavenly motions. Alongside the *pars destruens*, the work defends with passion and ample argumentation the constitutive principles of

---

[27] *Phil. sens. dem.*, pp. 473–474; *Praefatio*, p. 18.

[28] According to testimony from the trial following the attempted revolt in Calabria, Campanella recoursed to Pliny in order to identify God and nature: '...nel ragionamento [Campanella] diceva che non ci era Dio, ma solo è la natura, et noi a questa li avemo messo nome Dio, et allegava Plinio, quale teneva in mano' (Amabile, *Congiura*, III, doc. 393, p. 421; see also doc. 303, p. 245).

[29] *Syntagma*, I, 1, p. 34; *Phil. sens. dem.*, p. 363.

Telesio's philosophy, according to which every being derives from the modifications that follow from the acting of the two primary principles of heat and cold on matter, which is considered not as an abstract *ens rationis*, but as an inert, obscure, corporeal extension deprived of every particular form but capable of taking on any form. The sun and the earth are the first bodies and elements, seats of the two primary principles. Motion is the operation of heat. The sky has an igneous nature and the celestial heat is of the same nature as its terrestrial counterpart. With regard to the complicated mechanism of the celestial spheres, Campanella did not hesitate to reject the absurdity of mathematical fictions, together with the ambiguous role played by the motive intelligences, so as to propose a more coherent theory that, shared by Telesio, was derived from the Arab astronomer Alpetragius. With the spheres eliminated and with the uniqueness of the heavens asserted, the diversity of celestial motions and bodies is explained in terms of the different quantities of heat with which each is endowed.

Campanella's interests and studies in medicine manifested themselves above all in the second disputation, which was dedicated to the generation and constitution of the fetus. On this subject – very dear to him – Campanella broke decisively with Aristotle, who accentuated almost exclusively the active and formative function of the male seed. Instead, Campanella took up the positions of Telesio – who adopted, but also went beyond, the positions of Galen. With the role of the menstrual blood discounted (because it was considered to be simply an excrement to be expelled), important factors in the constitution of the embryo other than the male seed were taken up: the female seed, the mere existence of which Aristotle had denied, and above all the heat of the uterus, which (endowed with great understanding and art) had the capacity to awaken and organize the life contained in the seed. In this way, the uterus did not merely perform the function of a passive container, but, just the opposite, played a fundamental role in the development of the seeds, a role similar to that played by the 'fertile and fecund' earth, as is underscored with a reference to Fernel.[30]

With precise references to passages in the *Timaeus* and to the commentary by Ficino, Campanella underlined the powerful influence of the imagination on the complexion of the child, given that the *spiritus* takes in and transports the images impressed in itself that pass from the brain to the 'mirror' of the liver and can from there easily imprint themselves on the supple complexion of the fetus. And it is naturally for this reason that the bedrooms of Campanella's utopia – the City of the Sun – are furnished with 'beautiful statues of famous men, at which the women look intently.'[31] In confronting a problem so diffuse

---

[30] *Phil. sens. dem.*, p. 216.

[31] *Città del Sole*, p. 19. For a good English translation see T. Campanella, *La Città del Sole: Dialogo Poetico / The City of the Sun: A Poetical Dialogue*, ed. D.J. Donno (Berkeley and Los Angeles-London, 1981).

as that of the birthmarks, Campanella did not refrain from reporting popular beliefs, oscillating between skepticism and attempts to provide more plausible philosophical explanations. He insisted on continuity between the maternal spirit and that of the child, as well as the possible communication of strong passions. From such attention to the marvelous constitution of the fetus derives a decisive theoretical reappraisal of the role of the female in generation, a role that is no longer relegated to the categories of privation and passivity. Taking up Galen again, Campanella emphasized the fundamental similarity of the male and female sexual organs, which are differentiated only by the fact that the male sex organs are external while the female are internal, a difference that, in turn, reflects the greater or lesser heat with which they originated. On the basis of such a description, one could account for the possibility that a woman, in particular circumstances, could push out her own internal organs and become a man. In the *Quaestiones physiologicae* too, Campanella recalled a recent case (which he had observed personally in Naples) of a Spanish nun who became both a man and a soldier. He added a contemptuous dig directed at the *Disquisitiones magicae* of the Spanish Jesuit Martin Del Rio, who had maintained that the change of sex was a result of diabolical intervention, whereas according to Campanella this was a completely natural fact.[32]

The third dispute, dedicated to the heavens and to the cosmos, discusses the igneous nature of the heavens and the motions of the stars. Speaking of celestial heat, Campanella inserted a lengthy digression on astrology, directed against Marta, that recalls the astrologers' distinction between the cold bodies, such as the Moon and Saturn, and the hot ones. Campanella replied that all celestial bodies are hot, and that they are distinct only on account of a greater or lesser degree of heat. Moreover, he argued that all entities without exception, including the earth, must be hot in various degrees and proportions, since all originated in the action of solar heat on matter. After having responded to the objections of his adversary, Campanella took the opportunity to linger for a while on the problems of astrology. Some years later, in two famous passages, Campanella would recall his own youthful aversion to astrologers and relate that eventually, having considered the matter from a different point of view, he overcame this aversion.[33] In truth, in these dense pages of the *Philosophia*, Campanella is not so much an adversary of astrology as a Telesian reformer. Against those who argue that human events (both individual and collective) depend on the stars, he added nothing to what Picohad said on

---

[32] *Quaest. phys.*, p. 362; see Guido Giglioni, 'Immaginazione, spiriti e generazione. La teoria del concepimento nella *Philosophia sensibus demonstrata*,' *B&C*, 4 (1998), pp. 37–57.

[33] See ch. 9.3.

the matter. Campanella knew and valued Pico's *Disputationes adversus astro-logiam divinatricem*, and is in full agreement with him when he maintains that from the heavens comes only heat and light. Then, a long passage from Pliny is relayed, in which it is asserted (against Hermetic doctrines that seemed to institute a connection between particular terrestrial beings and specific astral bodies) that there are not stars for rich people and stars for poor people. In accordance with Plotinus, who in the third *Ennead* asserted that the heavens cannot act either for good or for ill, Campanella reaffirmed that from the heavens came only life, and never death. He showed himself, moreover, to be very critical of the vain predictive pretentions of astrology, going back once again to Pico's *Disputationes*.[34] Then, the deterministic and necessitarian aspect of astrology is decisively rejected. Since fate is understood as the general sum of all causes, which are of various kinds (some of them contingent), fate is not inexorable but can be avoided and changed. When he then went on to consider the occult powers, accepted by the hermetic tradition, Campanella intended to explain and specify them rather than reject them in a radical way, and he connected the variety of terrestrial beings with the almost infinite quantity of variations in heat.

Out of the subtle and minute argumentative structure of the eight hefty *disputationes* emerges a powerful unifying motive: the centrality, nobility, and primacy of solar heat, which operates at various levels to confer connectedness and life to all beings. It is in this context that the assimilation of solar heat with the soul of the world takes on a particular significance, and it is a theme that constitutes the beating heart of the third dispute. Campanella gathered together a series of authors and texts – the golden chain of Homer, the colcodea of Avicenna, hermetic excerpts – so as to call attention to a theme neglected in Telesio, but that is in fact similar and assimilable to Telesio's concept of solar heat. The author who most approximated this perspective was Ficino and Campanella transcribed verbatim the beautiful passages of the commentary on Plotinus's *Enneads* in which Ficino discusses the soul of the world and the 'vital and sensual breath' it expires and out of which the heavens are constituted.[35] Ficino compares such hot breath, which penetrates and is infused throughout the world, to a famous verse of the *Aeneid*, VI, 726 (*spiritus intus alit:* 'the spirit nourishes within'). Because it contains all things

---

[34] On the relationship between Campanella and Pico, see Luigi Firpo, 'Pico come modello dello scienziato nel Campanella,' in *L'opera e il pensiero di Giovanni Pico della Mirandola nella storia dell'Umanesimo* (Florence, 1965), II, pp. 363–371; Nicola Badaloni, 'L'influenza di Giovanni Pico sulla giovanile *Philosophia sensibus demonstrata* del Campanella,' ibid., pp. 373–388; now in Idem, *Inquietudini e fermenti di libertà nel Rinascimento italiano* (Pisa, 2005), pp. 363–375.

[35] *Phil. sens. dem.*, p. 322ff.

and because it flows smoothly 'like oil,' that breath can also be compared to the divine spirit of Genesis, 1:2 (*spiritus Dei ferebatur super aquas*: 'the Spirit of God was hovering over the waters') that moved on top of – or, better, 'hung over' – the water, communicating an occult, vivifying heat to all cold matter. The heavens are constituted out of this breath and divine word. It is the word of the soul extending out that vivifies and nourishes everything:

> From the Soul of the world, thus, pours forth always a kind of animal spirit, almost an offshoot of the interior life, and this is fire, almost an animal light stretched out towards dimension, a luminous hot spirit and a spark for the generation of all things; a sky, I say, not only surrounding, but also infused in all things and a sky of skies, a breath of the divine spirit in a certain form close to soul; celestial, igneous, luminous, hot, it flies away and expands in the air while it contracts in water and in earth.[36]

Thus, everything that grows on the earth has celestial origins: the heavens are infused in everything and 'everything lives by virtue of the occult heaven or heat inside it.'[37] In so far as they are humid, fecund, and generative of life, the heavens, living and life-giving, are analogous to animal spirits: that which in the soul is life is heat in the heavens, and it is thanks to such heat and to such life that the wondrous concord of all discordant things is realized. These are things that, in so far as they are all governed by a single cause, remain connected with each other, are animated by the same life, and are vivified by the same spirit. Specifying the relationship between God, soul of the world, and heat, Campanella insisted, however, on underscoring the fact that God is not identified, as Varro had it, with the soul of the world. Instead, one is to understand that God creates by means of heat, and Campanella proposes once again passages from Ficino, flanked, in order to show the agreement, by verses from Psalms.[38]

As for the relationship between theology and the Holy Scriptures, Campanella, though conscious of the risk and the danger of an attack on Aristotelianism, intended to argue in favor of dissociating Peripatetic philosophy and theology, so as to demonstrate how other philosophical traditions can be more suited to such a union. Holding fast to some points of Christian doctrine that were impossible to renounce (such as creation ex nihilo and divine providence) and that he reinterpreted in the light of Telesio, Campanella emphasized Aristotle's impiety instead. After all, Aristotle maintained the eternity of the world and the disinterestedness of God for human events (caring for such events would render him base), so as to demonstrate

---

[36] Ibid., p. 323 (the passage cited comes from Ficino).

[37] Ibid., p. 327: 'coelum esse infusum singulis entibus et occulto coelo seu calore vivere omnia.'

[38] Ibid., p. 523ff.

how the Christian Telesio permits a reading of many Biblical passages that is simpler and closer to the text than the reading one would get if one accepted the principles of the pagan Aristotle.[39] Notwithstanding such an effort at reconciliation, Campanella was completely aware of the delicacy and the possible risks of such a proposition. He was aware also of the insinuations – only just coming to light, but already very menacing – of possible conflicts between Telesio and the Bible. Marta warned that considering water as the dampness of the earth (and no longer as the 'great elemental body,' as had been the common opinion of theologians and Councils) could have implications for the sacrament of baptism.[40] Moreover, Marta had also suggested that reconsidering, or even eliminating, the role of the male seed in reproduction could have consequences for the doctrine of original sin and the miraculousness of Mary's conception of Christ.[41] To such objections and insinuations, Campanella replied by seeking to stabilize the division of competences between theology and natural philosophy, emphasizing the great difficulties that present themselves on the path of the search for truth.[42]

So as to render the dense pages of the *Philosophia* somewhat lighter, Campanella related some autobiographical anecdotes. Some were more certain and direct, as when the author recalls having seen the volcanic eruptions of Aeolian Islands with his own eyes from the convent of San Giorgio Morgeto. Others were less certain and more indirect, such as when Campanella, in a genuinely odd passage, while speaking of the similarities between children and parents, criticized the way in which many attribute dissimilarity in father and son to a sort of degeneration or an attenuating of the energy of the seed that would bring with it a weakness of spirit. Had this been the case, he objected, 'a Calabrian child of the Campanella family not looking like any of his relatives (nor even like a Calabrian) and instead looking like someone from a completely different family (that might even be Indian), ought to be of very low quality in mind and body.' He rejected this conclusion, because 'every day we have experienced just the opposite.'[43] Campanella also remembered – while speaking of mice and other animals whose eyes glow in the dark or of the fact that sometimes, having rubbed one's eyes at night, one sees a certain light being emitted – that a man 'when he woke up at night saw his own bed completely illuminated by the light from his own eyes, a light however that then vanished at once.'[44]

---

[39] Ibid., p. 522.
[40] Ibid., p. 519.
[41] Ibid., p. 282.
[42] Ibid., p. 447ff.
[43] Ibid., pp. 343; 240.
[44] Ibid., p. 662; see *Epilogo magno*, p. 401.

2. FROM NAPLES TO PADUA: ENCOUNTERS, CONFLICTS, TRIALS

Naples

At the end of 1589, the twenty-one-year-old Campanella, after a second brief stay at Cosenza, where he perhaps had the opportunity to frequent the Academy of Cosenza, the 'prize' of which is described in a passage in the *Poetica*,[1] left both Calabria and his affiliates there (who are remembered with affection in the sonnet dedicated to Telesio).[2] He headed for Naples and would not return for nine years. He may have been accompanied by a mysterious rabbi Abraham, necromancer and astrologer, to whom Campanella never made reference, but who, according to some reports and rumors, may have communicated to him the secrets needed to acquire extraordinary knowledge and who may also have predicted an exceptional destiny for him, tempting him to abandon the Dominican order.[3] As soon as he reached the capital, Campanella took part in a public debate. Relatively common in that time, such debates took place in churches, mostly on Sundays, before large audiences. They concentrated on arguments announced by posters affixed publically in the preceding days. The arguments of the young Dominican were so brilliant that he quickly put his adversaries to flight and was carried in triumph by his colleagues into the convent at San Domenico, where he lodged at first, transferring later to

---

[1] *Poetica*, p. 401. See Lina Bolzoni, 'Conoscenza e piacere. L'influenza di Telesio su teorie e pratiche letterarie fra Cinque e Seicento,' in *Bernardino Telesio e la cultura napoletana* (Naples, 1992), pp. 221–226: 224.

[2] *Poesie*, pp. 278–279.

[3] For testimony on Rabbi Abraham see Amabile, *Congiura*, III, doc. 328–329, pp. 281–283. The episode was noted by Ernst Salomon Cyprianus, *Vita Campanellae* (Amsterdam: Wetstenios, 1722), pp. 4–5, who recalled a passage from a letter by Carlo Cassa, which cited the testimony of one of Campanella's former peers, according to whom the young friar was quickly transformed from an initial condition of ignorance and roughness (*rudioris Minervae*) to the heights of an exceptional understanding thanks to the cabalistic teachings of a rabbi; on the life of Campanella by Cyprian, see Margherita Palumbo, 'Ernst Salomon Cyprian, biografo di Tommaso Campanella,' in *Laboratorio Campanella*, pp. 137–159.

the palace of the del Tufo family. Similar episodes had already been reported at Cosenza, as well as later in the Paris years when Campanella would astound people with his dialectical abilities.

At the age of twenty-three, Campanella was the victim of a severe attack of sciatica, from which he suffered for many months. He listed a series of factors as causes of the disease: first, having taken a horse-ride that was too long and hurried, second having eaten pig brains and, in general, too much rich food in the splendid kitchen of the lord with whom he was living, third having imbibed iced beverages.[4] On the question of using iced beverages, animated arguments had flared up between physicians and philosophers in the last decades of the century. It was asked whether, in order to satisfy thirst, it might be better (above all in summer) to follow the modern usage of adding 'snow' to drinks or alternatively to drink them tepid, as the ancients were accustomed to doing and as was the practice among Orientals in modern times. Campanella fell into line with those supporting the drinking of 'warm liquids,' writing also a small work, now lost, in defense of a treatise on this matter by the Telesian Antonio Persio, to whom he was linked by an affectionate and lasting friendship.[5] The sciatica would resolve itself only after a couple of years, thanks to a spell at the baths of Pozzuoli and to a radical change in eating habits.[6]

In the capital of the viceroyalty, the young Campanella had opportunities to frequent intense intellectual circles, especially the one centered on the palace of the brothers della Porta (which was a meeting place for scholars from all over Europe), as well as that centered on the group of scholars protected by Matteo di Capua, Prince of Conca.[7] In this way, Campanella was able to get to know, among others, scholars such as Ferrante Imperato, whose celebrated Museum of natural history he visited, and Colantonio Stigliola (the architect, astronomer, and philosopher who was an adherent of the

---

[4]The marquises del Tufo owned thorough-bred farms in Apulia, at Minervino, that without doubt Campanella was able to visit (ch. 4.1). He would dedicate a work on horses and the art of riding to Mario del Tufo, which has been lost, and the observation (*Città del Sole*, p. 10) that men pay greater attention to breeding dogs and horses than to the reproduction of men ought perhaps to be connected Campanella's acquaintance with such breeding.

[5]Antonio Persio had published the short work *Sul bever caldo* (Venice, 1593); see the anastatic copy in the appendix to the *Trattato sull'ingegno dell'huomo*, ed. L. Artese (Pisa-Rome, 1999); Campanella addressed the issue in *Quaest. phys.*, pp. 549–556.

[6] *Medicina*, p. 381.

[7]See Nicola Badaloni, 'I fratelli Della Porta e la cultura magica e astrologica a Napoli nel '500,' *Studi storici*, 1 (1959–60), pp. 677–711 (now in Idem, *Inquietudini e fermenti di libertà nel Rinascimento italiano*, pp. 93–125).

theories of Copernicus and Giordano Bruno).[8] Years later, some passages of the *Metaphysica* would echo conversations that he had had with Stigliola regarding a Pythagorean and Brunian vision of the universe. The young Campanella showed some reserve on these issues – especially regarding the basic structure of the stars and the possibility that they might be inhabited, a doctrine that he rejected in favor of an assertion of the igneous nature of the heavens and the stars, which were the seat of celestial spirits:

> Stigliola said to me (like the Nolan in a different way and the Pythagoreans have said in the past) that it seemed irrational to him that bodies so much larger than the earth and the space between the centre of the earth to the moon should be composed simply of idle fire, and not instead of all manner of elements and plants and animals and men, just as our countryman Philolaus held. But to me it seems easy to parry this argument. Indeed, I ask myself – stupefied – why on earth God should have made our system of earth, water, and animals, in which men are subjected to constant travails and are exposed to generation and decay. On that account, I hold that the stars are instead the composites of immortal things and the seats of the angels that know and praise God. In our system, in fact, ignorance, unhappiness, and deceit rule; God is blasphemed against, faith is not extended to him, nor is he recognized. Therefore if God did indeed make other systems unhappy in this way, then this would seem to be evidence not of his goodness but rather of his anger.[9]

But such disagreement on various specific points did not prevent a generally strong interest in Pythagorean philosophy, to which Campanella had dedicated a poem in his youth – the loss of which is to be greatly regretted. At Naples, he participated in the Academy of the Awakened (*Accademia degli Svegliati*), which soon thereafter in 1593 was closed by the Spanish authorities. The Academy counted among its members Ascanio Pignatelli, Paolo Regio, and Iacopo da Gaeta and had been founded (and then led) by Giulio Cortese, a learned man

---

[8] On Ferrante Imperato (circa 1550-1631), author of *Dell'historia naturale* (Naples, 1599), see Enrica Stendardo, *Ferrante Imperato. Collezionismo e studio della natura a Napoli tra Cinque e Seicento* (Naples: Accademia Pontaniana, 2001), and the entry by C. Preti, in *DBI*, LXII (Rome, 2004), pp. 286–290. Nicola Antonio Stigliola (1546–1624), was the author of works much appreciated by Campanella, such as the *Telescopio*. Of his principal work, *Encyclopaedia Pythagorica*, only a summary has survived. See Giuseppe Gabrieli, 'Intorno a Nicola Antonio Stigliola, filosofo e Linceo napoletano,' *GCFI*, 10 (1929), pp. 469–485, now in Idem, *Contributi alla storia della Accademia dei Lincei*, 2 vols. (Rome: Accademia Nazionale dei Lincei, 1989), I, pp. 889–905; Nicola Badaloni, *Tommaso Campanella* (Milan, 1965), p. 87ff; Idem, 'Il programma scientifico di un bruniano: Colantonio Stigliola,' *Studi storici*, 26 (1985), pp. 161–174; Saverio Ricci, *Nicola Antonio Stigliola, enciclopedista e Linceo*, together with an edition of the treatise *Delle apparenze celesti*, ed. A. Cuna (Rome, 1996).

[9] *Metaphysica*, III, p. 52.

whose striking similarity to and unmistakable echoes of Campanella (both on a philosophical and political level) have been pointed out. Campanella would later make him one of the interlocutors in the *Dialogo politico contro Luterani*.[10]

Of the brothers della Porta, Giovan Vincenzo, the eldest, was fascinated by every field of scientific inquiry, and had particular competence in medicine and alchemy. But he was above all 'divine in astrology, both in the theoretical part that measures the motions of the stars ... and in the practical part that foretells future events,' such that he was accustomed to saying of himself that the spirit of Ptolemy had transmigrated into him given the amazement he provoked in many because of the precision of his predictions.[11] Giovan Vincenzo had written many works, above all commentaries to Ptolemy's *Almagest* and *Quadripartite*, works that he hurriedly destroyed.[12] He had also collected an impressive number of nativities – and it is thus probably from him that Campanella derived his understanding of the technical aspects of astrological theory, once he had overcome his earlier diffidence. Yet the more productive exchange was with Giovan Battista, whose early *Magia naturalis* (in four books, published in 1558), beyond being an immediate success, had created quite a stir for the unscrupulousness of some of its remedies and for having revealed the ingredients of witch's ointment – something that had also not failed to attract the dangerous attention of the Inquisition.[13] But what made him famous in Europe was the new edition of the work in twenty books published more than thirty years later (1589). There the parts dedicated to the occult were eliminated and ample space was given to more clearly scientific and practical interests. In this way, the new text came to be configured as an encyclopedia offering recipes, advice, and explanations on various subjects, from domestic economy to cosmetics, from the art of distillation to optical

---

[10] See Lina Bolzoni, 'Le prose letterarie di Giulio Cortese: una fonte della giovanile *Poetica* campanelliana,' *GSLI*, 148 (1971), pp. 316–326; Ead. 'Note su Giulio Cortese. Per uno studio delle Accademie napoletane di fine '500,' *Rassegna della letteratura italiana*, 77 (1973), pp. 475–499; Maurice Slawinski, 'La poetica di Giulio Cortese tra Campanella e Marino,' *B&C*, 7 (2001), pp. 127–153; on Regio, see Anna Cerbo, 'La *Sirenide* di Paolo Regio,' ibid., pp. 77–106.

[11] Nicola Badaloni, *I fratelli Della Porta*, p. 679.

[12] A commentary on the *Almagesto* of Giambattista has recently been edited within the National Edition of the *Opere* of G. B. della Porta. See *Claudii Ptolemaei Magnae Constructionis liber primus cum Theonis Alexandrini commentariis Io. Baptista Porta Neapolitano interprete*, ed. R. De Vivo (Naples, 2000).

[13] Giovanni Aquilecchia, 'Appunti su Giovan Battista Della Porta e l'Inquisizione,' *Studi secenteschi*, 9 (1968), pp. 3–31, now in Idem, *Schede di Italianistica* (Turin, 1976); Germana Ernst, 'I poteri delle streghe tra cause naturali e interventi diabolici. Spunti di un dibattito,' in *Giovan Battista della Porta nell'Europa del suo tempo*, ed. M. Torrini (Naples, 1990), pp. 167–197 (and then in *Religione*, pp. 167–190).

phenomena, from magnetism to secret writings. Yet it retained a particular taste for stranger and more unusual phenomena and remedies. The Neapolitan magus inserted the vast range of his discoveries into the Neo-Platonic outlook that had been made popular by Marsilio Ficino, Pico della Mirandola, and Cornelius Agrippa of Nettesheim, according to whom the role of the magus consisted in combining terrestrial and celestial things. Moreover, Giovan Battista della Porta connected that tradition to the most successful vein of the literature on secrets, which, thanks to the collection of secrets made by the self-styled Alessio Piemontese (i.e. Girolamo Ruscelli), had been a success from mid-century on and was enjoying a growing diffusion.[14] The first draft of the *Del senso delle cose e della magia* originated precisely in conversations with Giovan Battista, who was also the author of several treatises, from the *Physiognomica* to the beautiful *Phytognomonica*, dedicated to highlighting and interpreting the variety of correspondences and analogies between the different levels of natural reality. The *Del senso delle cose* sought to offer a philosophically grounded interpretation of those phenomena of antipathy and sympathy, of attraction and repulsion between natural entities, the existence of which della Porta, faithful to an image of nature as *ludus* and spectacle, simply confirmed without attempting to offer any explanation.[15]

At Naples, however, suspicions and allegations regarding the young friar were also taking shape. In 1592, the 'first trial' took place, an event that was still obscure and uncertain in the treatment of Amabile and then later took on more precise contours in the studies of Giovanni Gentile and Luigi Firpo.[16] In the month of May, Campanella was imprisoned in the convent of San Domenico, on the allegation that his extraordinary knowledge had a demonic origin and that he had scoffed at excommunication. But the real issue, as would later be verified from the text of the condemnation, was adherence to the doctrines of Telesio. The suspicion that Campanella's knowledge had a diabolical origin resounds in his own writings. In the proemial letter of *Ateismo trionfato* addressed to Kaspar Schoppe, in which he confirmed having been 'called to judgment' five times, Campanella specified that the first accusations

---

[14] On the book of secrets, see William Eamon, *Science and the Secrets of Nature: Books of Secrets in Medieval and Early Modern Culture* (Princeton, 1994); by the same author, see also 'Natural Magic and Utopia in the Cinquecento: Campanella, the Della Porta Circle and the Revolt of Calabria,' *Memorie Domenicane*, n. s., 26 (1995), pp. 369–402.

[15] *Syntagma*, I, 1, p. 34.

[16] See Giovanni Gentile, 'Il primo processo d'eresia di Tommaso Campanella,' *Archivio storico per le provincie napoletane*, 31 (1906), pp. 623–31, then in *Studi sul Rinascimento* (Florence, 1923), pp. 165–73; Luigi Firpo, *I primi processi campanelliani in una ricostruzione unitaria* (1939), now in Firpo, *Processi*, pp. 44–95: 45–54.

concerned his alleged relationship with the devil: 'how can you know so much, if you never learned?' (*quomodo literas scis, cum non didiceris?*), 'you have a devil in you' (*demonium habes*); he replied to these charges by saying that his knowledge derived only from his own vigilance and incessant studies: 'and I showed that I had consumed more oil than they had consumed wine.'[17]

In the middle of May, Giovan Battista da Polistena (the former provincial for Calabria) attempted to shelter Campanella from persecution. He sent a note to the Grand Duke Ferdinand I, in which he asked him to take the gifted young man – who, he said, had been made the object of unjust accusations – under his protection. From Rome, the Florentine ambassador Giovanni Niccolini, in a letter dated 23 May, informed secretary Lorenzo Usimbardi that Polistena had confirmed that he had written to the Grand Duke, 'saying that he had been moved because this father had been falsely charged and because, being a man of great literary cultivation (particularly in philosophy but also in other disciplines), he wanted him to be embraced and favored in the protection of his Highness.' As referees for the young Dominican, Polistena suggested that at Naples 'Mario Del Tufo (with whom the said Tommaso had been residing) could speak to the issue, as well as the Regent Mardos[18] and Ascanio Pignatello and many other gentlemen who had taken part, according to Campanella, in the same Academy.'[19] According to Polistena, the most immediate assistance for the young man in difficulty would consist in having him come to Rome 'with some assurance of safety … for the purpose of clearing his name from the unfounded accusations brought against him, as he was offering and desiring.' Niccolini concluded that, if the young man were indeed virtuous and if it were confirmed that he was in fact innocent, then it would be possible to accede to the request. He raised, with some caution, the possibility of employing him 'to lecture on philosophy or theology at the university in Pisa or Siena; if, of course, that also seemed appropriate in this case.'[20]

The Tuscan agent in Naples, Giulio Battaglino (to whom, at Niccolini's indication, the Grand Duke turned) at first suggested that one ought not to 'involve oneself in that kind of bother,' considering the fact that Campanella found himself imprisoned 'for reason of religion;' but in a subsequent letter dated 4 September, once the suspect had been cleared, he expressed the greatest admiration for someone he called 'one of the rarest intellects that

---

[17] The Italian redaction of the letter is in *Ateismo trionfato*, I, p. 10; the Latin version, in *Lettere*, pp. 100–111: 107.

[18] The reference is to Alfonso Martos Gorostiola, to whom Campanella would address the *Monarchia di Spagna*, declaring that he had written it at his behest.

[19] Probably an allusion to the Academy of the Awakened: see note 10.

[20] Firpo, *Processi*, p. 50.

Italy has' and 'a gigantic mind' on account of his knowledge.[21] The verdict of the Order's internal inquiry had been handed down on 28 August. It determined that Campanella was to return to Calabria within a week, and was to adhere to the doctrines of St. Thomas, giving up those of Telesio.[22]

In Rome and Florence

With the intention, or the pretext, of punishing the person who in his opinion had denounced him, Campanella departed instead on 5 September for Rome, where he stayed for a couple of weeks. There he met with, among others, Cardinal Francesco Maria Del Monte, who had also been asked by the Grand Duke to report on the young friar and who sent a rather perplexing letter to Florence on the twenty-fifth of the same month. On the basis of impressions derived from meeting Campanella in person and from the judgment of learned men who had visited him (among whom the Dominican theologian Alessandro de Franciscis, a Jewish convert, and the political writer Fabio Albergati), he maintained that the young man was certainly endowed with a great mind, but was unfortunately taken in by Telesian fancies while also being a supporter of illusory doctrines based on ramshackle foundations:

> And at first Master Alessandro, a Jew, said to me that this Father had a beautiful mind. Yet, not being on the true path, he has no hope of a good outcome, since his doctrine is Telesian, and full of chimeras, madness, and things that apparently can sound good at table to the ignorant, but that possess neither substance nor foundation. The father commissioner says that many books of this Father are now seen as being full of trifles and vanities, and that it is still not clear whether there is something contained in those books that pertains to religion. Fabio Albergati says to me that this Father has a good but not extraordinary intellect, and that his contentions derive from Telesian caprices and do not proceed from good foundations – and he says that there are many ordinary things in it too. Finally, I spoke with him and I find him very bold; he reasons effectively enough as do all the subjects of the realm. He immediately started talking about his works, which are set against the doctrines of Aristotle, and I found him promising great things and expressing his conception fluently, but the foundations of his thought

---

[21] Amabile, *Congiura*, III, doc. 3, p. 12.

[22] The text of the verdict reads as follows: 'ut discedat ab hac provincia et ad suam se conferat infra spatium octo dierum, et sub poena gravioris culpae ut disputando, praedicando et legendo teneat doctrinas sancti Thomae et reprobet doctrinas Telesii' (Firpo, *Processi*, p. 52).

appear to me highly dilapidated. And this is as much as I am able to say after the sole conversation that I had with him.[23]

Resuming his journey, Campanella arrived in Florence at the beginning of October, where he resided in the convent of San Marco and where he was warmly received by the Grand Duke, to whom he dedicated the first version of *De sensu rerum*, following which he received compliments and a sum of money. On 13 October he visited the Biblioteca Medicea, a 'wonder of the world,' where he had philosophical discussions with two learned men in the presence of the librarian Baccio Valori, who had also been asked by the Grand Duke to look after the guest, for the purpose of reporting on his doctrines and the books he had already published or that he intended to publish – as we learn in a letter dated 2 October, which the Secretary Lorenzo Usimbardi had asked Campanella himself to deliver to Valori. The combination of exceptional gifts and adherence to Telesianism were once again emphasized in that letter:[24]

> His Highness has commanded me in his name to communicate to your Lordship the desire he has that you welcome openly the Dominican friar brother Tommaso Campanella, who is at San Marco on his way to Padua and who is held by his Highness to be a man of the greatest learning, an excellent philosopher, although a follower of Telesio. At Naples, he had been held in high esteem. He wishes to see the library of San Lorenzo. It would be most helpful to his Highness if your Lordship could use the opportunity of meeting with him in the presence of other learned gentlemen and to speak with him and evaluate his doctrine. Examine the works that are set for publication and relay how they seem; and see to it that he departs satisfied from Florence – as will come to pass, given the prudence of your Lordship, for which I kiss your hands.[25]

---

[23] Published for the first time by Cesare Guasti, 'Lettera del Cardinale Del Monte al Granduca Ferdinando I a proposito di frate T. Campanella,' *Giornale storico degli archivi toscani*, 3 (1859), pp. 159–160, the letter has been reproduced and commented upon in Zigmund Wazbinski, *Il Cardinale Francesco Maria del Monte. 1549–1626*, 2 vols. (Florence, 1994), II, pp. 421–422. Actually, in the months that followed, the Cardinal would demonstrate interest in Campanella's new philosophy of nature, sending the *Phil. sens. dem.* to the Duke of Urbino. Later, he would harbor real sympathies for the opinions of Galileo and Fabio Colonna (ibid., I, pp. 50, 51, 53). The "Father Commissioner" cited in the letter is the Cardinal of the Santi Quattro (Gio. Ant. Facchinetti, + 1606), who presided over the Commission of the Index. Regarding the encounter with Campanella, see Firpo, entry *Campanella*, in *DBI*, XIII, p. 375; Id., *Processi*, p. 57; Id., 'La proibizione delle Opere di Campanella,' ibid., pp. 317–318.

[24] The scholars were probably Ferrante de Rossi and the Florentine Dominican Giovan Battista Bracceschi: see *Lettere*, p. 389 and note 26.

[25] Florence, Biblioteca Nazionale Centrale, Rinuccini, 27, cass. 3 (lettere a Baccio Valori, T-Z), cc. 77–131, c. 113*r*.

In the course of the encounter in the library, the conversation turned to Machiavelli. When, many years later, he had to defend himself against the accusation of having been offensive and insulting in alluding (in the *Atheismus triumphatus*) to Machiavelli's illegitimate birth, Campanella indicated that he obtained the information in Florence, from a trustworthy source – namely, from Baccio Valori himself, the 'old knight' and librarian at San Lorenzo who had accompanied him in the visit: 'when he showed me secret books inside a small room into which no one could enter, he produced for me the works of Machiavelli written in his own hand and, speaking of him, he said that he was of noble extraction, but a bastard, and he narrated to me the story of his life.' This piece of information was said to have been confirmed by Giovan Battista Bracceschi, an old Dominican present during the conversation, 'who was able to remember Machiavelli and Leo X and Clement VII.'[26]

On 15 October, Campanella took his leave of Florence, writing two letters, one addressed to Usimbardi, a second to Grand Duke Ferdinand. While expressing gratitude and respect, these letters already reveal the bitterness of not having been at once accepted into service.[27] Later too he would often express a strongly felt regret at having failed to become established there, something that would have guaranteed him a more peaceful life, safe from persecution. The negotiations for a position in Tuscany did not succeed, and again on 15 October Valori deigned to write the letter that had been requested. He praised the gifts of a 'young man with a mature sense who possessed numerous and recondite ideas.' He argued that this was something one could appreciate both from the volumes that had been published and from those treatises that he intended to publish, as well as from his arguments and from the conversations in the library 'on quite arduous subjects, which astounded us even if they did not persuade us.'[28] Once again, however, even as he was praising Campanella for these reasons, Valori emphasized the risks posed by his adherence to Telesianism and by his break with Aristotle: 'it is true that some in Rome are currently trying to prohibit Telesio's philosophy, given that it seems to harm the scholastic theology founded on Aristotle, and he too runs the same risks because of his adherence to that [i.e. Telesio's] school.'[29] Campanella would later get to know about this judgment, and lamented it greatly, as one reads in a letter – somewhat embittered because his hopes were being

---

[26] *Risposte alle censure all'Ateismo trionfato*, in *Opuscoli inediti*, pp. 53–54.

[27] *Lettere*, pp. 4–5.

[28] Valori, emphasizing the interests of the young Dominican for Pythagoreanism, cites a *De sphaera Aristarchi*, a title that Campanella never actually cited; Firpo's reference (*Bibliografia*, p. 172) to the *Phil. realis* does not seem verifiable.

[29] *Opere di Tommaso Campanella*, ed. A. D'Ancona (Turin, 1854), I, p. LXXV.

dashed – that he wrote to the Grand Duke from Padua on 13 August 1593. In that letter, Campanella strongly defended Telesianism and the new philosophies, which as he put it do not harm but are rather 'useful, because they render the prince admirable and worthy of respect,' while the old and accustomed sciences 'render man less respectful.'[30]

Subsequent inquiries made by the Grand Duke did not turn out positively. The General of the Dominican Order, Ippolito Maria Beccaria, replied on 23 November with a letter in which the desire to accommodate Ferdinand – in the event that he might want to take the young man into his service – is accompanied by tones of great caution ('I have a somewhat different report of brother Tommaso Campanella'). Beccaria also gave the instruction, not completely reassuring, to 'review those works that he had prepared to give to the printer, as instructed by the Council of Trent and the Orders of the Religion – and, if it is found that they merit publication, then I will gladly order that they be printed.'[31]

Having reached Bologna, a very serious episode took place, one that foreshadowed future suspicion of and dangerous inquisitorial interest in his writings. In the city, the manuscripts that he was carrying with him were confiscated by those whom he called 'false friars.' Even if he would later tend to minimize the incident, the episode was the harbinger of serious future developments.[32] The writings underwent a close examination in July of the following year, in the context of the condemnation of Telesio's philosophy, and he would see his own writings again in the Roman Holy Office, where he would be called upon to clear himself of the doctrines contained in them. But he would claim, proudly, that he did not request the return of the papers, having decided to re-write them in a better form.[33]

Padua

From Bologna, Campanella went on to Padua, where he lived at the convent of Saint Augustine and enrolled himself at the university as a Spanish student.[34] Not even three days after his arrival, he was involved with others in a

---

[30] *Lettere*, pp. 6–7.

[31] See Luigi Firpo, 'La proibizione delle Opere di Campanella,' in *Processi*, p. 318; the letter is in Amabile, *Congiura*, I, p. 61

[32] *Syntagma*, I, 2, p. 36: 'nihil hac iactura deterritus.'

[33] Ibid., p. 38.

[34] The date suggested by Firpo, *Processi*, pp. 62, oscillates between two alternatives: the end of 1592 and the beginning of 1593. But Firpo appears to have preferred the latter.

disagreeable inquest into charges of sodomy perpetrated against the General of the Order.[35] Designated the 'second trial' (in which he was absolved), the true nature of the episode is quite uncertain. Of the incident we have only one report from Campanella himself, who alluded to it in two passages in letters written years later (in 1607) with expressions that strike one not so much for their understandable reticence as for the embarrassment and the weakness of the arguments that he used in his own defense. In the first passage – where he remembers being accused 'of having offended (*quod deturpassem*) the most reverend Father General in the convent at Padua, where I had been for hardly three days' – he limited himself to pointing out that, not having a room of his own, he was sleeping with a companion and had been wrongly accused, with others, of an act perpetrated at night only on the basis of the unfounded suspicions of envious fools.[36] In the second letter, the arguments brought in his defense turned out to be even more baffling (poor eyesight!) and not entirely coherent. It is not easy to understand why the fact of not sleeping alone ought to have implied responsibility also on the part of the others sharing the room: 'it was said that it was something done at night, which for me would be impossible because I do not see very well; also, I did not have my own room and was instead billeted with others. You ought to question those who were staying with me, because if I sinned against the prelate, then they sinned too. But the aim of the injustice was not to search for the crime, but rather to find me the offending party.'[37]

At Padua, Campanella met Galileo who, arriving from Florence, delivered to him a letter from the Grand Duke. This meeting too – like the virtual one with Telesio – took on a profound significance in his memory. He would remember it in the eloquent Latin letter that he would send to Galileo immediately after reading the *Sidereus nuncius*, at the beginning of 1611. Nor did he fail to remember the meeting in a commentary to the ode of Urban VIII titled *Adulatio perniciosa*, or again in the beautiful letter that accompanied the gift of the *Philosophia realis* to Ferdinand II.[38] The encounter with Galileo was very important, even if their paths would very soon diverge, only to converge again many years later. On the other hand, the idea of a meeting at

---

[35] The Father General, the already mentioned Ippolito Maria Beccaria, found himself in Padua between 4 and 18 January 1593; regarding Beccaria, see Amabile, *Congiura*, I, p. 23 and the entry by Carlo Ginzburg in *DBI*, VII (Rome, 1965), pp. 473–475.

[36] *Lettere*, p. 61: 'et noctu patratum scelus etiam mihi cum aliis ex sola aemulorum sciolorum ficta suspicione impositum est...'

[37] *Ateismo trionfato*, I, p. 10; *Lettere*, p. 107.

[38] *Lettere*, pp. 169, 389; Sante Pieralisi, *Urbano VIII e Campanella* (Rome, 1875), pp. 25–27. For the *Commentaria* on the poetry of Urban, see ch. 11, note 26.

Padua between Galileo, G. B. della Porta, Paolo Sarpi, and Campanella is to be discounted; such a meeting never took place. That meeting was conjured into existence on the basis of a summary redacted by a French librarian from a lost letter, a summary that seemed 'fabricated precisely so as to make one regret that loss all the more bitterly.'[39] The recent rediscovery of the letter, which completed the recovery of the three letters removed from the correspondence with Peiresc by the Florentine Count Guglielmo Libri, has proven that the librarian misunderstood the original. In that letter, dated 19 June 1636, Campanella again evoked the Telesian period of his youth in tones of affectionate nostalgia and offered extremely interesting information on the atomism of Galileo.[40] But on the subject of a supposed meeting at Padua, Campanella said only:

> And brother Paolo one knows *ab antiquo* to have been a follower of Democritus, because I was told as much by Giambattista della Porta – his friend when he was in Naples and with whom he had made many chemical experiments. And Signor Galileo spoke with him, when we were in Padua in 1593, when he distinguished himself from everyone else, and I – forced to leave (*forzato a partire*) – did not communicate with the aforementioned brother Paolo.[41]

While the French version does not hesitate to assert the existence of a meeting of the three scholars at Padua in 1593,[42] the letter informs us on the contrary that della Porta got to know Sarpi in Naples, and that Galileo and Sarpi met each other in Padua. It seems, moreover, that Campanella expressed his regret at not having had the chance – on account of the regrettable judicial events ('forced to leave!') – to meet the friar. On other occasions, Campanella would not hold back from virulent utterances against the friar, in so far as he was a supporter of Venice breaking politically from the Pope and because he was a bad teacher of the young on account of his atheistic doctrines, on a par with the Aristotelian Cremonini.[43]

---

[39] Luigi Firpo, 'Appunti campanelliani. XXV. Storia di un furto,' *GCFI*, 35 (1956), pp. 541–549: 544.

[40] See ch. 1, note 14.

[41] G. Ernst, E. Canone, 'Una lettera ritrovata: Campanella a Peiresc, 19 giugno 1636,' *Rivista di storia della Filosofia*, XLIX (1994), pp. 353–366: 363–364; also in *Lettere 2*, p. 116.

[42] Firpo, *Appunti campanelliani*. XXV, p. 545: 'Fra Paolo avoit aussi suivi ce système [atomism], comme il l'avoit appris de J. B. Porta, qui avoit vecu avec lui à Naples. Galilée, fra Paolo et Porta se trouvoient ensemble à Padoue en 1593 et Campanella les y avoit vus.'

[43] *Mon. Francia*, p. 554.

In the first months of his stay in Padua, Campanella enjoyed a period of great productivity and was able to compose a number of writings – all of which are, unfortunately, lost. Other than a *Rhetorica nova* and some occasional pieces, he also wrote an *Apologia pro Telesio*, primarily dealing with medical issues. In 1590, the Telesian Antonio Persio had edited for publication the shorter naturalist works of Telesio, among which was the *Quod animal universum ab unica animae substantia gubernatur* where the author argued for the corporeal nature and uniqueness of the animal *spiritus* located in the brain against the opinion of Galen who supported a tripartition of principles and incorporeal faculties that had their respective seats in the liver, the heart, and the brain (from where came the veins, the arteries, and the nerves, principles that remained distinct in the end so as to fulfill different nutritative, generative, emotive, intellective, and motive functions).[44] In 1593 the Veronese physician Andrea Chiocco published his own *Quaestiones naturales*, dedicating them to the college of physicians of the city.[45] Question XII was titled *De facultate irascibili et pulsifica pro Galeni sententia* and was addressed 'Ad Telesianum quendam virum doctissimum,' i.e. Antonio Persio. It was meant as a defense of Aristotle and Galen and as a confutation of Telesio, whom he accused moreover of wrapping his own doctrines up 'in so much Heraclitean obscurity'.[46] The centrality of animal *spiritus* and his identification with the soul came under particularly close examination. This attack on Telesian principles elicited the deepest bitterness and indignation in Persio, who had moved to Rome after years spent in Venice and Padua. He knew Chiocco well and had sought to dissuade him from taking up such a project. Campanella did not hesitate, once again, to defend Telesio. He composed the *Apologia*, which he sent to Rome to Persio and to the powerful Don Lelio Orsini, an old pupil and protector of Persio (from whom Campanella himself was hoping to receive protection).[47] The short work, delivered by Persio to Schoppe, has been lost. But one can read an effective summary of it in the ninth chapter of the second book of the *Senso delle cose*, where Campanella maintained, in the same manner as Telesio, the unity and the corporeal nature of animal spirit, the seat of which was in the brain, from where (through the extremely subtle nerve ducts) it

---

[44] Bernardino Telesio, *Varii de naturalibus rebus libelli* (Venice: ap. Felicem Valgrisium, 1590); modern edition by L. De Franco (Florence, 1981).

[45] Andrea Chiocco, *Quaestionum philosophicarum et medicarum libri tres* (Verona: ap. Hier. Discipulum, 1593).

[46] Ibid., p. 126. On the polemic, see Firpo, 'Appunti campanelliani. III. La perduta *Apologia pro Telesio*,' *GCFI*, 21 (1940), pp. 435–445; on Chiocco, see Idem, *Ricerche*, pp. 13–27.

[47] Lelio Orsini would be one of the noblemen involved in the conspiracy and he would die suddenly in 1603.

was diffused throughout the organism in order to fulfill all of its multiple vital, motive, and cognitive functions.[48] The defense of Telesian principles takes on a greater significance if one thinks that it was in this period that initiatives to condemn the works of Telesio were already taking shape, initiatives that would be realized with the banning of three works *donec expurgentur* ('until they are purged') in the Clementine Index of 1596 (namely, the *De rerum natura* and two smaller works, the *De somno* and indeed the *Quod animal universum*).[49] That ban would be remembered, many years later, by Campanella himself in an important biographical passage, where he evoked the arguments on which he had relied in his youth in order to defend his position on the sense of things before the judges of the Roman Inquisition:

> When the philosophy of Telesio was examined by the Holy Office towards 1592, this opinion on the sense of things was discussed. In fact at that time only three of his books were prohibited, *donec expurgentur*, as listed in the first Index of Clement VIII – that is to say, the works *De somno*, the *Quod universum animal* etc., and the *De rerum natura* – and Tiberio Carnelevari (physician, philosopher and fellow countryman) received from the Holy Office the propositions that were to be corrected in Telesio, among which this proposition was not to be found. Besides, in his other books (namely, *De mari, De iride, De usu respirationis, De his quae in aëre fiunt, De coloribus*) this opinion was to be found; and yet they are not banned.[50]

The Paduan period was also important on account of the formation of Campanella's political interests. Already in the letter to the Grand Duke dated 13 August, we encounter a fleeting indication of his understanding of how states are governed.[51] In the *Syntagma* he would later confirm having composed two works at Padua: the first, the *Monarchia de' Cristiani* – which would later

---

[48] *Senso delle cose*, II, 9, p. 47ff.

[49] See Luigi Firpo, 'Filosofia italiana e Controriforma. IV: La proibizione di Telesio,' *Rivista di Filosofia*, 42 (1951), pp. 30–47.

[50] *Defensio libri sui de Sensu rerum*, in *De sensu rerum* (Paris, 1637), p. 90: 'Cum examinaretur doctrina Telesii in S. Officio circa annum 1592, haec opinio de sensu rerum non venit in dubium. Nam tres tantum ipsius libri tunc prohibiti sunt, donec expurgentur, ut patet ex I indice sub Clemente VIII, videlicet liber de somno et liber Quod universum animal etc. et liber de rerum natura: et Tiberius Carnelevarius medicus et philosophus conterraneus accepit a S. Officio propositiones corrigendas in Telesio, in quibus haec non extat. Praeterea in aliis eius libris, videlicet de mari, de iride, de usu respirationis, de his quae in aëre fiunt, de coloribus, haec opinio habetur, nec vetiti sunt.' On the censorship of Telesio's works see now Saverio Ricci, *Inquisitori, censori, filosofi sulla scenario della Controriforma* (Rome, 2008), pp. 221–258, 377–389.

[51] *Lettere*, p. 7; a codex of the *Opere politiche*, conserved in Florence, Biblioteca Riccardiana, ms. 2340, which contains the early version of the *Monarchia di Spagna* and other political writings, is perhaps to be connected to the journey to Florence.

be cited quite frequently, but which has been lost – was concerned with demonstrating 'from a political point of view, the arts with which the Christian republic grew in the past and will grow in the future, those with which it usually declines, and those with which it is possible to reinvigorate it.' The second treatise, *Del governo della Chiesa*, was addressed to the Pontiff, suggesting to him 'the means by which he might establish one flock under one shepherd, not as a result of conflict with the opposition of the princes of all the world … but through ecclesiastical arms alone.' In this case also, the original version has been lost, although it was recomposed in an aphoristic format later in the *Discorsi universali sul governo ecclesiastico*.[52] Not to be excluded – indeed perhaps even likely (and understandable) – is the possibility that such texts were being used in an apologetic manner at such a difficult juncture in terms of legal proceedings, although this is not to say that they were the product of calculation or premeditated and sustained simulation. Indeed, these texts announce ongoing themes. They constitute a testimony that, right from the beginning, reflection on the relationship between religion and politics had been central in Campanella's thought. This relationship highlighted the necessity to rethink the forms and the modalities of a reconstruction of the Christian union that was threatened and fragmented by the forces of the Reformation, together with the necessity of redefining the relations between temporal and ecclesiastical power, within the perspective of a universal monarchy and the reconstitution of one flock under one shepherd.

The first nucleus of the *Discorsi ai principi d'Italia* probably also dates back to this same period. In that work, the appeal for unity is configured as an exhortation to the princes of the peninsula to turn themselves into supporters of a strict politics of alliance with the Pontiff, who (as a common father) could not but position himself as a guarantor of peace, defender of the rights of the weaker children when they are unjustly assailed, supporter of a union and of a defense against the enemies of the faith, who profit and take advantage of internal discords. Against those who maintained the advantages of division and a balance of power in Italy, Campanella claimed that in truth the weakness and the self-interests of the princes would only expose them 'to the maw of the great Turkish dragon.' He exhorted them not to oppose the Christian union, but rather to favor it by every means, in that it was advantageous also from a political point of view. It was futile to hanker after the splendors, by now extinguished, of the Roman Empire: 'there is no possibility of us recovering the empire, because the cycle of human affairs does not allow it.' Modern Rome wields a greater power, and a different kind of power, given that it is the seat of the Pope and the center of Christianity. This is a power 'more

---

[52] *Syntagma*, I, 2, pp. 38ff.

certain and august' that had taken the place of that ancient power based on military glory, as is said in a sonnet in which Christian Rome is celebrated. In this poem, Rome has been transformed from the 'Queen' of the world into its 'Mother,' who defends and gathers together the virtuous and the 'Christian armies' generously.[53] The *Discorsi* would later be reworked, with a greater emphasis on the prophetic role of Spain, to which the task had been given of reunifying the Christian flock. The princes are asked not to oppose, but rather to support the universalist project of the Spanish Empire, which was manifestly 'founded in the hidden providence of God ... for the purpose of uniting the entire world under one law.' They ought to do so, because regardless of the passions that move men, God's divine providence uses even errors and passions in order to realize his own plans.'[54]

These early thoughts of his youth would appear again in *Discorsi ai principi* in Campanella's French period. Even if the prophetic investiture of Spain would be dropped, the later *Discorsi* are dedicated to the reaffirmation of how the Christian princes might achieve advantageous and unbreakable alliances and full agreement with the papacy. Because the papacy is not the 'princedom of any family or nation in particular,' it does not aim at the expansion of personal power. Instead, the papacy has the character of universality and is oriented towards 'all the virtuous in all the world,' favoring the diffusion of understanding, while tyrannical princes – according to a tenacious conviction – 'want and work towards the ignorance of their vassals, so that they would not aspire to a condition of dignity achieved through merit,' reducing them to the condition of docile 'buffalos' so as to be able to dominate them without conflict.[55]

The Paduan period is full of encounters and experiences, some of them disconcerting, such as those pertaining to exorcisms or interviews with persons possessed by demons.[56] In fact, during his stay there, a particular episode tragically unfolded and provoked quite an uproar – namely, the brutal killing of the German astrologer Valentin Nabod. Having foreseen imminent danger in the stars, Nabod had closed himself up at home, sealing the doors and windows, pretending to have left. But he was killed by robbers who had broken into the house, precisely because they believed that there would be no one there. It was a tragic event and one on which, as an astrologer, Campanella had to reflect upon given that it seemed to extinguish the possibility of avoiding an event that had been established by fate.[57] From the judicial point of view, the stay at Padua

---

[53] *Discorsi ai principi d'Italia*, p. 93; *Poesie*, p. 597.

[54] *Discorsi ai principi d'Italia*, p. 119.

[55] Germana Ernst, 'Ancora sugli ultimi scritti politici di Campanella. I. Gli inediti *Discorsi ai principi* in favore del Papato,' *B&C*, 5 (1999), pp. 131–153.

[56] See ch. 1, note 5.

[57] The episode is recalled in the *De siderali fato vitando*, in *Opuscoli astrologici*, pp. 27–30, 127.

is full of events that would have a powerful influence on the years ahead. If the 'second trial' was, as it seems, a simple thing and devoid of consequences, the so-called 'third trial' would, in contrast, be very serious. At the beginning of 1594, Campanella was arrested, on the orders of the Paduan Inquisitor, together with two other persons, the physician Giovan Battista Clario from Udine and Ottavo Longo from Barletta, who would come to figure as the detainee accused of the most serious crimes.[58] The initial charges against Campanella – to which others would gradually be added – had to do with having contested *de fide* with a 'Judaizer' (that is to say, a converted Jew who had returned to the old faith), having composed a blasphemous sonnet (*canticum nefandum*) about Christ (that he would later say was Aretino's), and having possessed a prohibited book on geomancy. In the spring, the accused were subjected to torture, which was repeated during the summer. Given the seriousness of the situation, Clario, who boasted acquaintances among and protection from the Habsburgs, begged the Archduchess Maria, aunt of Emperor Rudolf II, to write a letter in their favor to the Pope, which arrived about half way through July.[59] But at the end of July there occurred an event that would trigger a judicial procedure that would last for years, and that has been specified only recently thanks to the discovery of new documents conserved in the archives of the former Holy Office.[60] Some friends of the prisoners would attempt to break into the prison of the Paduan Inquisition, so as to allow the three prisoners to escape. Among those friends were a certain Nicolò Fanti from Noventa and Francesco Brini of Tarvisio. Some time later, the name of the more disquieting and mysterious figure of the Mantuan Jew Isac Senighi would be added to this list in the documents. The attempt not only failed, but also worsened the situation dramatically. The external accomplices would suffer severe punishments and years of judicial investigation. The case was taken up by the Holy Office and on 11 October 1594 the three accused, who had been secretly extradited from Venice, were jailed in the prisons of the Roman Inquisition.

---

[58] See Firpo, *Processi*, p. 59ff.

[59] For Giovan Battista Clario, son of the court physician to the deceased Archduke of Stiria who would in turn become an imperial physician, see Firpo, *Ricerche*, p. 28ff, together with the entry, also by Firpo, in *DBI*, XXVI (Rome, 1982), pp. 138–141.

[60] Now Congregation for the Doctrine of the Faith. Firpo had already identified and tacitly used many decrees, including those published by [Enrico Carusi], 'Nuovi documenti sui processi di Tommaso Campanella,' *GCFI*, 8 (1927), pp. 321–59; see now Leen Spruit, 'I processi campanelliani tra Padova e Calabria: Documenti inediti dall'Archivio dell'Inquisizione Romana,' in *Congiura di Calabria*, pp. 233–53; Vittorio Frajese, *Profezia e Machiavellismo. Il giovane Campanella* (Rome, 2002); for the unsuccessful escape, see Giacomo Moro, 'Documenti veneti su Campanella e sul processo per la fallita evasione,' *B&C*, 15 (2009), pp. 463–487.

3. THE PALACE OF ATLAS

Dogmas and Politics

In October 1594, the suspects entered the prison of the Holy Office, where the famous philosopher Giordano Bruno and the Florentine heretic Francesco Pucci were already being held. Colantonio Stigliola, whom Campanella had already encountered in Naples, would also later be brought there. Drawing on the popular belief, according to which the 'timid and smiling' weasel experiences an irresistible and fatal attraction for the toad, 'the monster that then devours it,' Campanella spoke in a beautiful sonnet, titled *Al carcere* ('To Prison'), of the inevitability of the encounter of free spirits in such a terrible place, which he compares to the cavern of Polyphemus, the labyrinth at Crete, the palace of Atlas. These were spirits who had abandoned the 'stagnant pond' of trite conventional knowledge, in order to launch themselves boldly upon 'the ocean of the truth.'[1] We know nothing of possible conversations with Bruno, even though it is not completely absurd to hypothesize that – beyond, obviously, the explicit references to the Nolan, chiefly regarding cosmological issues – some of the echoes (subterranean and hidden, to be sure) of Bruno that lurk in some parts of Campanella's work could be the result of direct communication.[2]

In the case of Pucci, such direct communication certainly did take place. In a passage of the *Responsiones* that came after the *Epistola antilutherana*, Campanella would make explicit reference to the three months of conversations regarding Lutheran dogma held in the prison of the Holy Office with the heretic Francesco Filidino.[3] Pucci exercised a long-lasting influence on Campanella, both with respect to specific doctrinal points (such as the role of the

---

[1] *Poesie*, p. 254; for the weasel and the toad, see *Senso delle cose*, I, 8, p. 20.

[2] Cf. Michel-Pierre Lerner, 'Campanella lecteur de Bruno?,' in *La filosofia di Giordano Bruno. Problemi ermeneutici e storiografici (Letture bruniane III)*, ed. E. Canone (Florence, 2003), pp. 387–415.

[3] *Responsiones ad obiectiones Tobiae Adami… super epistola antilutherana*, in *Quod reminiscentur*, I, p. 144: 'ego loquutus sum cum Francisco Filidino haeretico, qui 28 annis servivit Luthero et Calvino eorumque libros memoria tenebat'; a variant of the ms. Lat. 1079 of the Bibl. Mazarine in Paris adds: 'et per tres menses cum

sacraments, instituted so as to extend and not restrict the path to salvation, the extension of salvation to children who died without being baptized, and the universally redemptive work of Christ) and also with regard to the expectations of an imminent and radical renewal – the 'awaited, new redemption.'[4] Later, after Pucci had been decapitated at the Tor di Nona on 5 July 1597 and his body burned on the pyre in Campo dei Fiori, Campanella would dedicate a moving sonnet to him that praised the loftiness and the nobility of his thought. In the splendid opening ('Soul, having now left your bleak prison'), he addressed Pucci as a soul that, releasing itself from the multiple prisons that had constrained it (the terrestrial prison, as well as those of the Holy Office and of the body itself), made its way back to its celestial home.[5]

Campanella was held in a cell with Giovan Battista Clario, in whose subsequently written *Dialoghi* we find traces of conversations with his cellmate. In the course of 1595, he wrote the *Compendium de rerum natura* that in 1617 – under the title of *Prodromus philosophiae instaurandae* – would inaugurate the series of Frankfurt publications edited by Tobias Adami. He also wrote shorter literary works and political discourses, including probably the one regarding the Low Countries that would later become the twenty-seventh chapter of the *Monarchia di Spagna*. New charges of upholding Democritean doctrines and of being the author of the *De tribus impostoribus* were added. This infamous, mysterious pamphlet had dared to argue that the founders of the three monotheistical religions were impostors – but, according to Campanella, he could not have been its author since it had been published thirty years before he was born.[6]

Tortured again at the end of April 1595, Campanella was condemned to recant a 'most serious charge of heresy' (*de vehementi haeresis suspicione*).

---

eo in S. Offitio conversatus sum.' On the relationship between Pucci-Campanella, see Luigi Firpo, 'Processo e morte di Francesco Pucci,' *Rivista di Filosofia*, 40 (1949), pp. 371–405; Germana Ernst, '"Sicut amator insaniens." Su Pucci e Campanella,' in Lech Szczucki (ed.), *Faustus Socinus and his Heritage* (Cracow, 2005), pp. 91–112.

[4] *Poesie*, pp. 476–477: 'Anima, ch'or lasciasti il carcer tetro...'; cf. notes 5 and 17. In recent years, new studies and the rediscovery of important unpublished texts in the Archive of the former Holy Office have contributed to the shedding of greater light on Pucci; see, in particular, Paolo Carta, *Nunziature ed eresia nel Cinquecento. Nuovi documenti sul processo e la condanna di Francesco Pucci (1592–1597)* (Padua, 1999); A. Enzo Baldini, 'Tre inediti di Francesco Pucci al Cardinal Nepote e a Gregorio XIV alla vigilia del suo "rientro" a Roma,' *Rinascimento*, 39 (2000), pp. 157–223; Francesco Pucci, *De praedestinatione*, ed. M. Biagioni (Florence, 2000).

[5] Titled 'Sonetto fatto sopra un che morse nel Santo Offizio in Roma' ('Sonnet concerning a man who died in the Holy Office in Rome'; *Poesie*, pp. 476-477), it is not among those included in the *Scelta* (see ch. 7.1).

[6] Regarding Campanella's references to the mysterious blasphemous work, cf. Germana Ernst, 'Campanella e il *De tribus impostoribus*,' *Nouvelles de la République des lettres*, 1986/2, pp. 144–170 (and then in *Religione*, pp. 105–133); Ead. 'L'enigma del *De tribus impostoribus*. Note di lettura,' in M. Marangio, L. Rizzo, A. Spedicati, and L. Sturlese (eds.), *Filosofia e storiografia. Studi in onore di Giovanni Papuli*,

According to Firpo, the recantation took place on 16 May in the Dominican church of Santa Maria sopra Minerva in a public and solemn fashion. That date, however, has recently been moved to 30 October of the same year, on the basis of evidence taken from an official note attached to a letter that Campanella would send from Stilo on 11 November 1598 to Cardinal Santori.[7] In the second half of 1595, Campanella was assigned to the Dominican convent of Santa Sabina on the Aventine hill as his obligatory residence, *loco carceris*. It was there that he wrote the *Dialogo politico contro Luterani, Calvinisti e altri eretici*, which at the end of the year he would dedicate and send to Michele Bonelli,[8] the Cardinal Protector of the Dominican order who had asked him to write the work, to whom Campanella would express his repentance.[9]

The *Dialogo*, a harsh reply to reformed doctrines, is set in the Naples of the day and has three interlocutors. The protagonist, who acts as the author's mouthpiece, is the Telesian scholar Giacomo di Gaeta, who right from the opening declares that as a philosopher he wants to confront the problem of sects 'that run against mother nature and the good customs of the republic.'[10]

---

3 vols. (Galatina, 2008), I, *Dall'Antichità al Rinascimento*, pp. 127–148. The critical edition of the Latin text, with a German translation by Johann Christian Edelmann (1761), is in Anonymous [Johann Joachim Müller], *De Imposturis Religionum (De Tribus Impostoribus). Von den Betrügereyen der Religionen*, ed. W. Schröder (Stuttgart-Bad Cannstatt, 1999); the Latin text, with an Italian translation by L. Alfinito, is in Anonimo, *I tre impostori*, ed. G. Ernst (Calabritto, Av., 2006).

[7] The note says, '30 octobris 1595 decretum quod abiuret de vehementi, [Conventu] sui ordinis Romae [pro] ... loco carceris.' Cf. Leen Spruit, 'I processi campanelliani tra Padova e Calabria,' in *Congiura di Calabria*, p. 237; Ugo Baldini and Leen Spruit, p. 185 (see ch. 4, note 2); Leen Spruit, 'A proposito dell'abiura di Campanella nel 1595,' *B&C*, 12 (2006), pp. 191–194.

[8] A passage of the *Dialogo politico* appears to allude to the fact that Campanella was an eyewitness to a shocking act of blasphemy on the part of an Englishman; Giacomo, the author's mouthpiece, claims that 'vidi in Roma un inglese gittar a terra l'Eucaristia per morire per gloria stoltamente.' The event took place on 15 June 1595 and the condemned was burned at the stake on 20 June. A contemporary account of the episode and of the condemnation of the offender is found in Germana Ernst, '"Quasi totius orbis theatro." Il supplizio di un inglese, Roma 20 Giugno 1595,' *B&C*, 7 (2001), pp. 517–534; Ead. 'Postilla sull'abiura di Campanella e sul rogo dell'inglese,' *B&C*, 12 (2006), pp. 195–199.

[9] The only edition of the *Dialogo politico* is highly unreliable, based as it is on an inferior manuscript; here I have corrected the text with ms. Ital. 106, of the Paris BNF; the dedicatory letter to Cardinal Bonelli is in Luigi Firpo, 'Appunti campanelliani. XVII. Due lettere inedite,' *GCFI*, XXIX (1959), pp. 80–81, and then in *Lettere 2*, pp. 21–22.

[10] The Telesian Giacomo (or Iacopo) di Gaeta, member of the Academy of Cosenza, was the author of the *Ragionamento chiamato l'Academico overo della Bellezza* (Naples, 1591); modern edition by Anna Cerbo (Naples, 1996); see ch. 2, note 10.

The *Dialogo*'s protagonist responds to solicitations from the second inter-locutor, Marquis Gerolamo del Tufo, who is invested with public and politi-cal responsibilities and does not hide his most acute worries concerning the diffusion of such sects as he moves on to ask for clarifications and counsel. The third character is the Neapolitan priest and scholar Giulio Cortese, who contributes to the debate with Biblical and poetic quotations. The work was written in vernacular, which was the language of political writers, as Giacomo indicates when Giulio deploys a refined citation of Latin verse from Terence. It was also consciously written using everyday language, together with very concrete and common images. As is emphasized several times, the interests and the practical advantages that motivate the supporters of the reformed doctrines derive from the 'heat of the cauldron' that had replaced the warmth of charity. The author did not hesitate to turn a vision recorded in Jeremiah back against Luther, who is identified as the pot that boils in the northern parts, and from which originates all evil.[11]

Beyond Pucci, Campanella could also have had information on reformed doctrines from conversations he had had with foreign students during his stay in Padua.[12] In the dialogue he recalled conversations with English students, who recounted to him how the old people of their country regretted the loss of the secret confession of sins, and deplored the serious consequences of its aboli-tion.[13] In the text, the author confronted the most hotly disputed points of the polemic with the reformers, discussing the origin and the content of their doc-trines. In the final part, the author put himself to the test on controversial points such as indulgences, purgatory, sacraments, and the celibacy of the clergy. But the heart of the work is the discussion regarding the compatibility of reformed doctrines with political association. Articulating one of the strong and persist-ent principles of his thought, Campanella asserted that in order to have an organized and stable political governance it is essential to have a unity of souls, on which depends the unity of bodies and of goods – a unity that is inseparable from the unity of a shared religion, which finds in the Pope its point of cohe-sion.

The reformers rejected this unity as they attempted to establish a 'partisan' religion that was useful to their own political interests ('with the excuse of maintaining their liberty of conscience, they maintained their political liberty').

---

[11] See Jer 1, 13.

[12] See notes 3 and 17.

[13] *Dialogo politico*, p. 134: 'Intesi di più in Padova da Inglesi stessi che in Inghilterra molto si lamentano gli anziani di aver levato via la confessione secreta....' Regarding Englishmen in Padua, cf. Jonathan Woolfson, *Padua and the Tudors: English Students in Italy, 1485–1603* (Cambridge, 1998).

With the view of undermining the unity of the Catholic Church, the reformers had not hesitated to spread new religious beliefs by taking advantage of the credulity and the volatility of ordinary people. In order to achieve his own ends, Luther – in an unscrupulous and highly dangerous political calculation – had attacked religious unity, uprooting it from the conscience of princes and subjects, thus turning princes into tyrants and ordinary people into rebels. On this account, his position came to be 'absolutely antithetical to civil order and destructive of it.' Drawing the 'foolish multitude' into disobedience of political leaders, the reformed doctrine unleashed conflicts and factions to deleterious effect, both politically and at a personal level. With regard to this diminishing of assurance and sound points of reference at the personal level, Campanella vividly described the scene of a dying man, whose family members had each called a minister of their own faith to his deathbed. The poor sick man – 'unsteady in the medicine of the soul' – could not even make use of the medicines of the body and 'died angry and uncertain.'[14]

During this discussion on the unity of the faith, Campanella considered the doctrine of predestination. Inaugurating an ongoing reflection that would span the entirety of his thought, Campanella intended to denounce the politically harmful consequences of a doctrine, that – denying the free will of man, so as to accentuate the exclusivity of divine initiative and as a result devaluing the merits and demerits of works for the purpose of salvation – ended up being, in his opinion, incompatible with an orderly political community. If God decides the destinies of men before their birth, such that they are born already judged and are not to be judged on the basis of the actions that they later undertake, then such men – believing in the irrelevance of every good or bad action (which would not change their already established fate in the slightest) – cannot but behave in a licentious manner. They are prey to instability and are drawn towards every innovation that might procure some advantage for them.

In an even more serious way, the 'counterfeit' God represented by the reformers is a deceitful and unjust God, who asserts that he wants to save everyone but in fact has already chosen those who are predestined. This is a God who exhorts men to do good without giving them the freedom to be able to do it and does not extend his grace to anyone beyond those few he has already decided to save. This is a God who plays the 'malicious joke' of calling men to the good, without giving them the possibility of achieving it and who 'enjoys putting them in a trap in order to make them fall, saying to them that they might help themselves whereas in fact they cannot – that they might fly without having given them wings.' In short, this is a tyrannical God, who acts according to his own whim and not according to justice:

---

[14] *Dialogo politico*, p. 138.

they created a tyrant God, who had determined that some would go to paradise, and many to hell, and that the former could not hurt themselves and that the latter could not save themselves, because God operates through them for his own enjoyment – good for some, bad for others – without attention to their own merits or demerits.[15]

When Gerolamo is not able to hold back a shout of dismay ('This kind of Christianity terrorizes me so much!'), Giacomo intervenes quickly to reassure him: 'the law of God, when it is well understood, is the law of consolation and joy.' To the unacceptable image of the Lutheran God is opposed the image, entirely different, of a God who is a father to all and loves all of his children equally, not creating anyone so as to damn them: 'God wants to save everyone … and … came to die for everyone, and … does not hate ab initio those whom he ab initio created.' This is a God who with 'a grace bountiful enough for all includes all without exception,' giving to all the possibility of salvation. After the original sin and the loss of primitive righteousness, Christ became flesh for the salvation of all and not, as the Lutherans believe, only in order to confirm the salvation of those few chosen before the sin of Adam. It is up to each man to accept and to make good use of the grace that he receives. Damnation does not depend on a kind of 'effective disgrace,' already established among the innocent multitude before original sin. Instead, damnation depends on the obstinate rejection of divine assistance that is extended to all:

> Christ came to save everyone without distinction and to confer upon us the greatest goods, without which grace would not be more common than crime, without which a craftsman would not be more powerful than his ruined creation, and without which he would not be greater in power and goodness. Given that God is the God of all men, there is thus sufficient grace for all, extended without exception.[16]

In proclaiming the universal redemptive value of the death of Christ, Campanella closely echoed themes from Pucci's *De Christi efficacitate*.[17] Acquaintance with the text appears to be confirmed when Campanella takes up a precise comparison to the book of merchants, where a creditor becomes a debtor: he 'is said not to be a creditor, not because he was not a creditor in the beginning, but because later he incurred such debts that he ended up not being thus described,' an image that serves to explain the sense of a verse from the Book of Revelation that asserts that reprobates are not written in the book of life.

---

[15] Ibid., p. 100.

[16] Ibid., p. 104.

[17] *De Christi efficacitate* (Goudae: typ. Ioannis Zafei Hoenii, 1592); Italian translation *L'efficacia salvifica del Cristo*, ed. G. Isozio (Pisa, 1991).

The passage is important, because it can prove that the conversations with the Florentine heretic in the prison of the Holy Office took place in all probability right at the beginning of the incarceration.[18]

Even though Giacomo (that is, Campanella) defends himself by saying that he is not a theologian, in truth, he engages in close interpretations of scriptural passages (particularly from St. Paul's *Letter to the Romans*) in order to reconsider and reinterpret the relationship between faith and deeds. The passages invoked by the reformers in support of their doctrine did not condemn the deeds themselves but only the Jews' external and ceremonial deeds, which Campanella held to be ineffective with regard to salvation. This is done with a powerful call back to the 'living faith' that redeems non-Jews too. Thus, the true children of Abraham, worthy of acquiring their inheritance, are his true imitators – his spiritual, if not carnal, children. If what the reformers upheld were true (that is, if God, having induced men into sin, continued to induce them to do evil, so as to have a means of demonstrating his own justice), then this planned slaughter of his own begotten children would make him similar to Medea, who, 'consuming herself with rage and disdain, not knowing how to show it, became angry with her own children and killed them.' Except that the God of the Calvinists would be even worse, because 'Medea was almost out of her mind with anger and tore them to shreds, but God had considered this butchering of his own children for a long time, even *ab eterno*.'[19]

This image of a cruel and tyrannical God could not help but render political leaders tyrants in turn, because they would feel themselves licensed to imitate a God who acts according to his own taste and whim, and not according to mercy and justice. As ordinary language also testifies, even the memory of the authentic meaning of the concept of justice had been lost, from the moment that it was identified exclusively with a punitive conception of justice and not with a distributive one, which consists in good laws. In response to the exclamation of Geronimo ('what is the "justification" of Abraham Was he perhaps decapitated in public, because you had no other term?'), Giacomo replies by deploring such distortion of the meaning of justice:

> If that divine justice is neglected in which God rejuvenates and animates us divinely and renders us similar to him, good and sanctified, and operating in accordance with his wisdom, then one mistakes justice for hanging, quartering – namely, the kind of justice that I called punitive, which is arrived at in uncertain and accidental ways; and this century is certainly so corrupt that it knows no other kind of justice. But it was very convenient for Calvin

---

[18] Firpo dated the conversations to the early months of 1597. Enrico De Mas drew my attention to the passage in the *Dialogo politico*, for which I am grateful.

[19] *Dialogo politico*, p. 123.

and Luther to persuade people that God compels men to do evil so as to show his justice. Nowadays, every tyrant thinks that he is being just when he condemns many people to death, so much so that the people, especially in Naples, now accept that the meaning of the term 'to justify' (*giustificare*) is to kill or put someone to death, rather than to sanctify or divinely hearten.[20]

A number of crucial and lasting themes are already spelt out in this early work: the undeniable political importance of religion, insofar as it is the basic unifying bond ('whether true or false, religion has always mastered hearts'); the fact that 'everyone makes God in his own image, such that, being partisan and disloyal, Luther preaches a God of that kind' and attacks unity for political reasons. Unity turns out to be politically fundamental ('unity is more important than anything else, because without that one cannot govern'), and the guarantor of that unity cannot be anyone other than the Roman Pontiff, who 'unites the earth with Heaven, as a bridge joins the two banks of a river.' In these pages, Campanella wrote a very long and eloquent encomium of the Pontiff, emphasizing how his prerogatives and functions are completely independent of the possible weaknesses of particular individuals. If some Pontiffs erred, many were good and holy. Thus, when one sees 'the sun of the holy church eclipsed,' one ought to think that 'these are momentary clouds in front of the sun that do not destroy it, but for a time obscure it before departing quickly, for the seat of the holy church remains pure and eternal.'[21]

Philosophy and Poetry

In 1596, still in the convent of Santa Sabina, Campanella composed the Italian *Poetica*, which he dedicated and sent to Cinzio Aldobrandini, a powerful cardinal and nephew of Clement VIII, who had a reputation as a generous patron of scholars and was the protector of Tasso. Soon thereafter, Campanella would be dispossessed of his own work, which he would have the chance of seeing again only years later (in 1618, in the prison of the Castel Nuovo at Naples) and in a surprising form: a Spanish author, who remains to this day unknown, had translated the work into his own language, putting it about in his own name. Campanella tells us that he laughed at this awkward and easily revealed plagiarism: in a footnote the Spanish author, in fact, was forced to justify the continual citation of Italian authors. He laughed also because he judged that distant draft to be an 'unripe fruit' (*immaturum partum*), having already planned to rewrite a Latin *Poëtica*.[22] In truth, on other occasions he found himself bitter

---

[20] Ibid., pp. 126–127.

[21] Ibid., pp. 158–159.

[22] Cf. *Syntagma*, I, 2, p. 40; *Poëtica*, in *Scritti letterari*, p. 1216; perhaps the Spanish translation remained in manuscript.

and disdainful on account of disloyal attempts to appropriate his own writings, taking advantage of his position in jail. In the prefatory letter of the *Atheismus triumphatus* addressed to Schoppe, he warned him in sorrowful tones against appropriating works that he had entrusted to him. Such an appropriation would constitute the theft of 'children not of the body, but of the soul,' a crime therefore all the more heinous. And such thievery is precisely what Schoppe would later practice. Worse, he would use Campanella's texts extensively in the context of an aggressive polemic against the reformers.[23] Other authors too would not be ashamed to plagiarize with impunity from unpublished texts.[24] And in a beautiful letter addressed, at the end of 1614, to Ottavio Sammarco, who was intent on publishing as his own the *Aforismi politici*, Campanella warned him not to do something so base, and gave him a highly moralizing lecture.[25]

Beginning in the early Italian *Poetica*, Campanella articulated a number of principles that would remain central even in subsequent discussions. In the form of a strong polemic against a hedonistic and gratifying conception of poetry, these principles address the relationship of poetry to truth and philosophy, together with the ethical and social role of the poet.[26] The poet, charged with an educational mission, ought to be 'the instrument of the legislator and ought to help him to spur the world to living well.'[27] The marvellous linguistic instruments that he uses – which are capable of inducing extraordinary effects even on uncultivated souls, with a kind of powerful magic – and the tales which he can make use of in particular circumstances have to be deployed in all cases as vehicles of the truth and should aim to highlight virtue and castigate vice. The true poet is a prophet, for the prophet is not so much – or only – he who foresees future events, but also he who 'chides political leaders for their malignity and vileness, and the people for their ignorance, seditiousness, and bad habits.'[28] It is up to the prophet, thanks to poetry, 'to make the sciences flourish,' and to light 'the ardent love of virtue and reason.' He who, like the 'perfidious and

---

[23] *Lettere*, p. 111; there is some information of Schoppe's use of passages from Campanella in Mario D'Addio, *Il pensiero politico di Gaspare Scioppio e il machiavellismo del Seicento* (Milan, 1959), pp. 288–319.

[24] Rodolfo De Mattei, 'Materiali del Campanella nell'opera del Canonieri,' *Accademie e Biblioteche d'Italia*, 35 (1967), pp. 291–316; see ch. 6, note 6; on the use of material from Campanella by Mersenne, cf. Gianni Paganini, 'Mersenne plagiaire? Les doutes de Campanella dans la *Vérité des sciences*,' *XVIIe Siècle*, 57 (2005), pp. 747–767.

[25] *Lettere 2*, pp. 65–68; see ch. 9, note 40.

[26] Long held to be among the lost writings, the Italian *Poetica* was rediscovered and edited by Luigi Firpo (Rome: Accademia d'Italia, 1944); there is a second edition in *Scritti letterari*, pp. 317–430, which I have used.

[27] *Poetica*, p. 325.

[28] Ibid., p. 359, 357.

lying' Greeks, turns to false tales so as to mock religion, corrupt good customs and ridicule virtue, does not deserve to be called a poet and is only welcomed in a state that is 'tyrannical, where lies are bought and sold in order to make the people ignorant.'[29] False poets are the favorite instruments of tyrants, because it is thanks to them that people can be held in ignorance and slavery. Meanwhile the poet-prophet who teaches and educates on behalf of liberty is abhorred and persecuted by them. In this regard, Homer is depicted as the negative model representing the perfidious tales of the Greeks. He persuades and entices an uneducated and child-like populace like a charlatan and huckster, touting vices rather than educating the people as the poet-philosophers do:

> Homer ... beneath the beautiful words and delicate figures and graceful man-ner of story-telling, which is well-adapted to the debased populace, confounds impiety with piety, good with evil, virtue and vice, and ruins everything with-out a second thought, because he was a huckster. In order to take in the oafish plebs, in the manner of our own charlatans or "the blind man of Forlì," he would spin yarns in the piazzas that so tickled Greek vanity that they made a poem out of it. Thus, it is a childish and plebeian thing to think that a charlatan is a poet, placing him under the protection of the gods, as if he were inspired by God to tell his stories and to say that there is no one who really tells the truth, thereby denying the title of poet to Pythagoras and Empedocles.[30]

Along with Homer, Aristotle is severely criticized as a codifier of and herald for the Greek 'tales.' Conversely, the Bible – particularly the Psalms of David, wondrous on account of the nobility and variety of their contents (which Cam-panella had been attempting to paraphrase or translate since his youth)[31] – is taken as a positive model of excellence. Another model is Dante, in comparison to whom 'all others are poetasters and are like a gondola compared to a galleon with respect to grandeur of subject and for their great usefulness and the good taste that purified philosophical (and not pedantic) ears derive from him.' Cam-panella had always understood Dante to be educating the public – 'Dante had something of the Pythagorean about him, given that he always told tales for the benefit of the people'[32] – and thought he had not received the appreciation he was due precisely because he was an advocate for truth and virtue:

> In a good republic, one ought to love Dante, given that he is the great praiser of goodness and the great critic of evil, a great analyst of things political and

---

[29] Ibid., p. 320.

[30] Ibid., p. 352. Cristoforo Scanello, known as 'il Cieco da Forlì,' was a sixteenth-century chronicler and poet; see Adamo Pasini, *Vita e scritti di Cristoforo Scanello detto 'il Cieco di Forlì'* (Forlì, 1937).

[31] *Poesie*, pp. 449–450, 488, 676.

[32] *Poetica*, pp. 347, 428.

a great conjuror for his readers of time and place and the historical personage who is speaking. As a portraitist of all manner of conditions, he is industrious to the point of wonder and yet he is little understood and little appreciated by the common people who are enemies of virtue.[33]

As far as the moderns were concerned, Campanella showed himself to be very critical of Tasso. In a sonnet, while praising the correspondence between 'the beautiful vestment' and the 'exquisite, rarefied concepts' of Dante and Petrarch and especially the 'fire in their chests' that generated such virtue, he rebuked Tasso for the fact that his formally impeccable verses., failed to raise up hearts towards the 'worthy objects of the human mind.'[34] In the *Poetica* too, Campanella emphasized the contrast between the beauty of his words and the 'commonplace and stolen concepts,' between the elevatedness of the style and the coldness and artifice of the content, which he found to be derived more from Homer and the Greek tales than from the nobility and novelty of his subject matter.[35] In contrast, Ariosto is very good precisely on account of his felicitous capacity to stay close to what is natural and reproduce it. He turns out to be 'admirable in all the parts of his poems for the sublimity of the tales, for the personifying of the heroes, ... for the descriptions of beautiful countries, rivers, mountains, seas, storms and every other kind of thing, such that one seems to have everything in front of one, as he paints it singing sweetly.'[36] His poem runs the risk of something else, however; it risks losing itself in multiple tributaries, losing sight of the central singularity that is indispensable for conferring harmony and unity to the composition, a center that in fact is certainly present in the works of Virgil and Dante as they represent the theater of human life, even as they are complex and varied as far as characters and places are concerned.

In the *Poetica*, Campanella goes beyond the polemic against rules and pedantry and his attack on Aristotle and false Greek fables. One finds a number of interesting points, such as the precise references to the *Monarchia dei Cristiani* and the reflection (Stoic in origin) on the correspondences between social roles and virtue. These correspondences prefigure, or echo, the themes of some sonnets in the *Scelta*.[37] Above all, Campanella insists on the educational

---

[33] Ibid. p. 328. Numerous studies have been dedicated to the relationship between Dante and Campanella, beginning with Vincenzo Spampanato, *Il culto di Dante nel Campanella*, in *Sulla soglia del Seicento* (Città di Castello, 1926), pp. 128–160; see Anna Cerbo, *'Theologiza et laetare.' Saggi sulla poesia di Tommaso Campanella* (Naples, 1997), ch. 5 as well as the bibliography cited there; Ead., 'Dante Alighieri,' in *Enciclopedia*, vol. 1, coll. 230-240.

[34] *Poesie*, p. 464.

[35] *Poetica*, pp. 342, 337–338.

[36] Ibid. p. 378.

[37] Ibid. p. 331; *Poesie*, pp. 69–73.

role of the poet, as he recalls the Lucretian image of the bitter medicine offered in a chalice with sweet edges. The poet is also compared to the physician, who, without ever losing sight of his own duty, should never become like an obliging cook who, pandering to the taste and whim of his young patient rather than curing him, ends up making the illness worse.

Memories of Calabria emerge from the lines, as when the author evokes the figure of Giacomo di Gaeta once again and the contacts with the Academy of Cosenza, emphasizing how in the 'prize' of this Academy the figure of the old woman was more beautiful than that of the young Danae, because more effectively represented.[38] Fragments of the stay at Padua emerge too, with allusions to Sperone Speroni and to 'dances in Paduan villas.'[39]

After multiple supplications and requests, Campanella was permitted to move to the convent at Santa Maria sopra Minerva at the end of 1596. In Naples, however, a common criminal called Scipione Prestinace of Stilo feigned religious revelations so as to obtain a stay of execution and accused Campanella of being a heretic. As a result, Campanella was then once again imprisoned in the jails of the Holy Office. This is what Firpo identifies as the 'fourth' trial, the last one prior to the one that followed the Calabrian conspiracy of 1599.

At the end of October 1597, with the death of the last Duke, Alfonso II, who had no direct heirs, the question of the succession at Ferrara began. As the Pope was preparing a military expedition (which would end with the annexation of the city), Campanella was discussing the event with Cardinal Del Monte and others.[40] He interpreted it as a harbinger of the progressive constitution of an ecclesiastical unity. Campanella addressed a sonnet (thought by Amabile to be one of the 'worst to appear, with a utterly banal ending') to Cesare d'Este, cousin of the dead Duke, who was pressing his claims to the city. The Pope, who was not recognizing d'Este as the legitimate successor, was ready to excommunicate him and Campanella addressed Cesare with the exhortation not to oppose himself to the claims of the Pontiff and to abandon 'so foolish an arrogance.'[41] Restored to liberty at the end of the year, Campanella was consigned once again to his Dominican superiors, who ordered him to return immediately to Calabria.[42]

---

[38] *Poetica*, p. 401 (cf. ch. 2, note 1).

[39] Ibid. p. 409.

[40] Cf. *Dichiarazione,* p. 112.

[41] *Poesie*, p. 478; Amabile, *Congiura*, I, p. 88.

[42] An annotation added to the letter written from Stilo to Cardinal Santori reads as follows: '17 decembris 1597 cum cautione de se repraesentando si libri et scripta prohibeantur. Consignetur suis Superioribus qui illum retineant in aliquo loco sine scandalo. Prima sententia maneat in suo robore' (Baldini and Spruit, p. 185).

4. BACK TO NAPLES AND CALABRIA

Natural Philosophy

On the way back to his homeland, Campanella spent several months in Naples, where he resumed contact with his old friends, gave lectures, debated and showed the most intense interest in astral doctrines connected to prophecy.[1] According to a document that was recently found in the Archive of the Congregation for the Doctrine of the Faith (the former Holy Office), a renewed attempt on the part of Mario del Tufo to find a position for Campanella as a theologian attached to the Bishop of Minervino Murge dates to this period. On 15 April 1598 Lorenzo Mongiò, called Galatino, bishop of the estate of this powerful gentleman, sent a letter to the Vice-Prefect of the Inquisition, Cardinal Giulio Antonio Santori, in which, reminding him of the request already advanced in the past at the behest of del Tufo, he informed him of having been subject to recent, insistent pressure, in response to which he had been obliged to ask Cardinal Antonio Caetani to nominate Campanella as his theologian. The letter expressed the extreme embarrassment of the Bishop, afflicted as he was by contrasting sentiments: even if he found it very difficult to turn down del Tufo's request, he did not by the same token want to do anything that was not welcome to Rome. The prelate was indirectly suggesting that Campanella should not be appointed to the office for which he was being recommended, but he also cautiously implored Rome to relieve him of the responsibility of the negative decision, for the matter had already caused him enough annoyance: 'and rejecting it, for the love of God do not subject me to enmity with this lord; he has constantly been reproaching me for not having agreed to his previous request.' The Roman authorities would understand the situation perfectly and on 13 May decreed by way of response to the Bishop that he ought not to take brother Tommaso Campanella into his service as a

---

[1] In the earliest statements made on 10 September 1599, immediately after his arrest in Calabria, he would begin by admitting his own interest in prophecy, connecting it with the conversations held at Naples with Giulio Cortese, Colantonio Stigliola, and Giovanni Paolo Vernaleone: see ch. 5, note 26.

G. Ernst, *Tommaso Campanella,* International Archives of the History
of Ideas/Archives internationales d'histoire des idées 200,
DOI 10.1007/978-90-481-3126-6_4, © Springer Science + Business Media B.V. 2010

theologian.' In the letter there is a precise reference to Campanella's journey to Apulia ('the said friar having come here') that the editors of the letter trace back to April 1598.[2] A passage of Campanella's commentary on Urban VIII's poetry, written many years later, confirms that he had journeyed to Apulia together with the marquises del Tufo. He also describes the conversations he had had with the local inhabitants on tarantism.[3]

At Naples Campanella completed the *Epilogo magno*, the first five books of which were dedicated to an organic exposition of the principles of natural philosophy, while the sixth and last book dealt with ethics.[4] The *Epilogo* opened by affirming that, when the primary Being – omnipotent, omniscient, and benevolent – decided to create the universe (meaning the totality of those 'statues and images' representing his own infinite goods), He extended an 'almost infinite space' in which this statue could be placed. This happened at the beginning of time, which flows from eternity. Space was defined as 'the basis of being, where the beautiful work – that is, the universe – resides,' and as 'a substance and room and immobile and incorporeal capacity, adapted to receive any body.' Space is homogenous in all of its parts. 'High' and 'low,' 'behind' and 'in front,' 'right' and 'left' are human words that refer to situated bodies and if the universe were not to exist, we ought to imagine empty space. But in truth, space desires plenitude and attracts entities to itself, above all those less resistant and similar to it, for 'it enjoys so much to substantiate those entities, given that it does not ever want to be completely empty.' Void, however, does not exist naturally and

---

[2] Baldini and Spruit, pp. 183–184; see the appendix at the end of this chapter.

[3] Commentary to the ode by Urban VIII titled *Clementi Octavo P. M. levamen podagrae* in Gianfranco Formichetti, *I testi e la scrittura. Studi di letteratura italiana*, Roma, 1990, p. 63: '… si credimus accolis, quos saepe interrogavi, dum in Apulia animi gratia cum Tufis marchionibus commorarer.' ('If we had to believe the words of the villagers, whom I often questioned during my stay in Apulia with the marquises del Tufo'); see also Idem, *Tommaso Campanella, eretico e mago alla corte dei Papi* (Casale Monferrato, 1999), pp. 14–15.

[4] Enlarged, reorganized, and translated into Latin, the text would constitute, under the title of *Physiologia*, the first of the four parts of the *Philosophia realis*. The projected youthful treatise in twenty books, titled *De universitate rerum*, has been lost. Yet two compendia of natural philosophy have come down to us: the early *Compendium de rerum natura*, which would be published by Adami to inaugurate the Frankfurt editions (cf. above, p. 34); the later compendium was redacted into an aphoristic form at Naples towards 1618 for didactic purposes: cf. *Compendium physiologiae/Compendio di filosofia della natura*, unpublished Latin text ed. G. Ernst, transl. and notes by P. Ponzio (Milan, 1999). On natural philosophy, see Paolo Ponzio, *Tommaso Campanella. Filosofia della natura e teoria della scienza* (Bari, 2002).

can only be obtained in a violent and artificial manner – which is fully reflected in bodies that, each in its own way, 'abhor the vacuum that divides them, each one enjoying the contact it has with the other.'[5]

God places in space the matter that ought to be considered as a physical entity. This is in stark contrast to the conception (already criticized extensively in the *Philosophia sensibus demonstrata*) of Aristotle and Averroes, who define it as privation and as pure *ens rationis* ('mental being'). Such matter is 'a pure body, without shape, without action, which is – however – apt to distend itself, bend, divide itself and unite and take any figure or action or artifice just as wax takes the form of all things.'[6] In imagination matter is divisible to infinity, but in reality it is divisible into the most minute particles known as atoms 'that appear in the rays of the sun.' This is called the 'passive principle of the composition of things,' and matter is described as a body that is inert, indivisible, black and shadowy, 'because such shadowiness is as invisible to the open eye as to the closed one.'

Testifying to the delicate theological problems that could arise from new physical doctrines, Campanella, in a marginal note added to the text, explains the sense in which matter understood as body does not turn out to be incompatible with the doctrine of transubstantiation. Having noted that other theologians before him had also maintained similar principles, he specified that in transubstantiation what is transformed is the matter configured in the form of bread, not matter as such, which miraculously is not made to lose quantity. The intrinsic transformation of the 'native heat' that constitutes the bread does not contradict the fact that the extrinsic and accessory qualities of the bread might continue to be perceived.[7]

Into this 'corporeal, material quantity' God imbues heat and cold, two principles that are active and diffusive in themselves, 'two incorporeal artisans.' Yet these are principles that could not subsist except in bodies. From the contrast between the two – in virtue of which each would like to impose itself and occupy the greatest possible quantity of matter – derive the two bodies or elements of the universe: the heavens, formed from matter transformed by heat (which is therefore extremely hot, clear, tenuous, and mobile) and the earth (constituted by matter made immobile, opaque, and dense by the cold). The sun, seat of light and heat, surrounds the earth with motions and distances that modify it in ways adapted to generating all entities, without destroying it: 'never surrounding the earth by a single means, but trying by all

---

[5] *Epilogo magno*, pp. 188–189.
[6] Ibid. p. 191.
[7] Ibid. pp. 193–194.

the means of approach to attack it, it happens that by no means can it burn it, but instead gradually transforms it, and makes these median things that are called stones, waters, plants and animals.'

In another annotation in the margins, moreover, the author emphasized a highly significant point – namely, how providence may use the conflict of the two contrary principles to productive and preservative ends, 'without impos- ing a restraint from outside, but using instead a native necessity of moving in such a manner that they might make entities without them destroying each other, a remarkable thing to contemplate.'[8] In delineating the constitutive principles of his own natural philosophy, Campanella articulated arguments that are further developed in the *Metaphysica*, where he insisted on the con- nection between naturalness and necessity. He connected the 'nature' of the elements and the entities that derive from them with what they receive in 'birth, in which is sown the being that the things were capable of having, and the power and the art and the love to preserve that being.' Focusing on the remarkable effects and finality of the artificial motion of the sun, Campanella referred to what he would call 'Major Influences' (*Influenze Magne*) – that is to say, Necessity, Fate and Harmony – that are the media through which the designs of divine providence are realized in the universe. He did so in order to conclude that 'everywhere necessary things are done in accordance with the free will of God and those things are made by the elements with a kindly necessity, since that which is by necessity happens because it is for the best.'[9]

From the conflict between the first principles derives the constitution of all the secondary beings, which in their infinite multiplicity and variety realize the infinite degrees of the first idea of God, 'whence shine forth all the modes and beings and operations of the things that emanate from him.' Here and in other texts Campanella insisted on emphasizing the fact that God makes use of elements as his 'artisans' and unwitting instruments, which – although they tend only to amplify themselves, guided by the preservative and expansive principle embedded in them originally – in fact produce the infinite variety of entities that comprise the wondrous statue of the world and that represent the infinite modes of the first idea. Without intervening in a direct way in natural processes, God makes it so that natural principles, asserting themselves, might realize at the same time what he has planned for them.

In the light of both the primary opposition between solar heat and cold, ter- restrial matter and the principle of self-preservation that organizes and rules both individual entities and the universe as a whole, Campanella analyzed the various aspects and motions of the heavenly bodies. He reaffirmed their igneous

---

[8] Ibid., pp. 204–205.
[9] Ibid. p. 209.

nature, distancing himself from the Pythagorean conceptions discussed with Stigliola regarding the elementary composition of the stars.[10] With respect to the heavens, it is one, not subdivided into spheres, and it moves itself according to heat – that is to say, by virtue of its own intrinsic working, which preserves it and vivifies it, without the need to turn to angels or motive intelligences. Indeed, such working is 'the habit of things that preserves them in themselves and in their being,' and it is distinct from action and passion. The former – which is a 'diffusion of the semblance of the active in the passive,' exercising itself on something that is different from itself – is laborious, while the latter is realized with joy or with sorrow. Passion, which is the 'reception of the semblance of others,' can be natural (as when the earth, affected by the sun, becomes hot) or artificial (just as, in an illuminating comparison, the book that the author was writing is similar not to the pen with which he is writing – which is a simple 'instrumental agent' – but rather to the wisdom that he, Tommaso Campanella, the principal agent, has in his own mind). In the same way, the world 'is not similar to heat and cold, instrumental agents of God, but to the divine Idea.'[11]

That sensibility (understood as the ability to feel) had the function of preserving being and life was reaffirmed expressly in the fifth book, dedicated to animal organisms, at the origin of which there stands a particular grade of attenuation of celestial heat, the *spiritus*, that is capable of detaching itself from the portion of matter that makes of it a wrapping thanks to its subtlety and to its movement. Not being able to exit from the corpulence in which it finds itself enclosed, this *spiritus* organizes it and moulds it so as to guarantee its own life, preserving it from external menaces and procuring for itself the nutrition of which it has constant need:

> Every living body has need of nutrition, and every vivifying spirit forms bodies with organs adapted for that life; thus, from within such bodies spirit makes feet in order to forage for food and flee from enemies, the mouth and hands to procure such nutrition, and internal organs to cook it, a liver to distribute it to all the channels of each limb, and a heart for converting it into spirit, together with lungs to light the internal fire, bones to hold the body up, flesh to defend it, nerves and ligaments to hold it together and move it.[12]

All sensorial processes are directed to the same end of preservation, and the organs of sense are the parts of the body organized so as to permit the spirit

---

[10] Ibid. p. 201.
[11] Ibid. pp. 224, 226.
[12] Ibid. pp. 326–327.

to come into contact with the movements of the air, the vibrations, the heat, the fumes, and the light that comes from the exterior. All sensation is a 'touching' of the spirit, which comes to be modified slowly and which from these alterations can judge the qualities of external objects, and discover if such modifications cause pleasure or pain. Sensation does not arrive, thus, by way of 'information' – that is to say, by means of accepting external forms – but rather by 'transformation,' that is to say, by the alterations perceived by the spirit..[13]

Dwelling upon the activity of heat, from which derive sense and *spiritus*, Tobias Adami emphasizes its nobility and its centrality. Even if his use of Latin is rather taxing and somewhat contorted, it is hard not to recognise precise echoes of Campanella:

> Our heat is that vivid, celestial light of a most noble nature; most subtle and most pure, essential agent and cause of all motion of things, which the Creator has put into all matter as his instrument and blacksmith that gives life. It penetrates everywhere to execute its wonderous works, establishing itself in its seat in the sun, heart of the Earth, of which the divine Moses also speaks. Thus, this tireless craftsman, which is never reduced, mixes itself into all things. When it pulsates through all things touching our spirit, it is perceived as heat. When it makes contact with our eyes, it is light and color. When it reaches the tongue, it produces taste and moves all the other senses of our body, such that owing to it the matters of our internal spirit may be known.[14]

Natural Ethics

The sixth book of the *Epilogo* is dedicated to ethics, and its contents echo the ninth book of Telesio's *De rerum natura* closely. In Campanella, as in Telesio, the great law that connects and renders diverse natural entities common is that of the preservation of one's own being. Every human action is directed at 'acquisition of the good that preserves' and 'flight from the evil that damages.' But since man is placed in a universe that is constituted by opposing forces, in which evil and good are tied to one another, and since 'the spirit desires and hates more or less than it ought to, or in a way that works to its own detriment,' it is necessary to find a rule 'of how much, how, and to what it ought

---

[13] Ibid., p. 367.

[14] *Ad philosophos Germaniae*, in *Opera Latina*, I, p. 22; Latin text and Italian translation in Germana Ernst, 'Figure del sapere umano e splendore della sapienza divina. La *Praefatio ad philosophos Germaniae* di Tobias Adami,' *B&C*, 9 (2004), pp. 119–147.

to be drawn – and this rule is called virtue.'[15] Virtue, therefore, is a 'wisdom regulating every affection and action' that imposes the right measure on the affections of the spirit. The spirit, pushed by the spurs of pleasure and pain, can fall into error 'because it laments, rejoices, loves, and hates more or less than it ought to,' but virtue – in light of the traces of divine wisdom that shine forth from nature – redirects every passion in the right measure towards the preservation of itself.[16]

The accentuation of the importance of the original purity of the *spiritus* also has its origins in Telesio's philosophy. Taking up again the Telesian comparison to gold, Campanella asserted that

> The virtue that renders good – that is, pure – that which possesses it and that preserves in it its pure being is the purity of its genus, placed at birth, preserved in education, and extended in exercise. Thus, human virtue is the purity of the human spirit, which knows itself and grows in use, just as in disuse it becomes obscured.[17]

In *The City of the Sun* too, Campanella would insist on the close connection between natural 'complexion' and moral virtue. He derived from that the careful choice, based on precise astrological calculations, of the moment most suited to the conception of the offspring, on which depends the purity of the complexion and the spirit. Education could do much to reinforce and exercise virtue, but virtue – in order to take root and grow – needed a suitable terrain, which is an original and not modifiable datum, the lack of which produces men devoid of an authentic, intrinsic virtue in their being.[18] In the *Epilogo* the diverse virtues come successively to be listed according to the degrees and kinds of self-preservation – in themselves, in children, in fame and in society. The list opens with solicitude, thanks to which man (on account of his capacity to imitate the divine art embedded in nature) invents the arts that provide necessary goods to him. Then one moves on to liberality, the virtue that permits one to make effective use of the goods procured by solicitude, and then on to sobriety and chastity, which set out the correct rules for nutrition and generation, which is a 'sacred thing' while its act is 'a natural sacrament.'

The political and social virtues follow on from there. There is justice, to which belongs the equal distribution of tasks and roles, such that society emerges organized with the same wisdom and harmony as the parts of the human body. There then follows truth, without which 'one would lose human commerce,'

---

[15] *Epilogo magno*, p. 505.
[16] Ibid. p. 510.
[17] Ibid. pp. 512–513.
[18] *Città del Sole*, p. 21; cf. ch. 6, p. 99.

given that the liar is 'an extremely unhappy animal, because he destroys himself doing and saying that which he is not in spirit, and reducing being to non-being'. Another virtue is the noble quality of beneficence, which proceeds from similarity to God and, just as in him, 'prizes more the whole than the part, more that which is common than that which is particular' and effuses goodness in the form of generosity, just as God does who offers it to all, 'being better than all, and not for self-interest, but rather for the delight he has in his own goodness.' The opposing vice is maleficence, typical of an evil and vile spirit, 'who does evil to others and the greatest evils to the virtuous, because it does not trust the living if it has not destroyed the best.' This is something that is characteristic of 'tyrannical princes,' who 'murder philosophers and saints, chase them from the court, and take up with base people, because they feel themselves unfit to command those who are their betters, and abhor their presence.

The list of virtues goes on: gratitude, sister of beneficence (while the ungrateful 'would like to see the person who surpasses him in benefits dead, because he is incapable of returning favors to him and has a hatred of being obligated'); equality, opposed to arrogance; the 'beautiful virtue' of happiness that 'contents itself with present goods and future hopes' without being prompted by future evils and that derives from a 'lucid and pure spirit, not despairing on account of evils, but rather effusive and playful with its own light'; tranquility, which willingly forgives, and kindliness, which enjoys the goods of others without hoping for anything in return; emulation which encourages imitation of the best and, finally, generosity, called also sublimity or magnanimity, a heroic virtue that regulates the divine desire for excellence in man.

The *Dialoghi* (Venice, 1608) of Giovan Battista Clario sheds light on the early ethics of Campanella. Fifteen or so years earlier, as we have seen, Clario had been close friends with Campanella at Padua and he had been involved in the 'third' trial.[19] The first three dialogues, titled *Della consolazione* ('On Consolation'), *Delle avversita'* ('On Adversities'), *Delle ingiurie* ('On Harm'), take up arguments that are found in the pages of Campanella. The place, suggestive and terrible, where the two interlocutors – Panfilo, the author himself, and Armenio, who represents Campanella – exchange reflections and fears is a cell of the Roman Inquisition in which they are both imprisoned. The central theme of the conversations is a meditation on the behavior of the wise man who is suffering from misfortune. The young Panfilo – who admits having been up to that point favored by fortune and having lived a happy life, devoid of any difficulty whatsoever – does not know how to give himself peace. He feels himself unjustly accused and asks for comfort from his companion, who calmly explains to him, above all, how the wise man is not altered by

---

[19] Regarding Clario, see ch. 2, note 59.

misfortune. Difficulties, in fact, are an exercise for the generous and strong spirit. Just as the waters of rivers and rain, mixing themselves with those of the sea, are not able to alter its taste (but, just the opposite, are forced to take on its nature), so 'the impetus of adversity, fighting against the spirits of the wise, not only lacks the power to change them, but in fact comes itself to be transformed by their nature.' Adversity, according to Armenio, is in point of fact an opportunity to transform a delicate spirit into a strong one, 'like the coral that, exposed to the air, becomes hard.' It is in this way that merit has the chance to reveal itself. The grain does not come out of the ear if it is not beaten and the saffron plant has to be trodden upon in order to produce its most beautiful flower. To Panfilo, who suffers from and refutes the dramatic conflict between appetite and reason, the friend replies that the metempsychosis imagined by Pythagoras and Plato is a projection of the continual risk on the part of man of being transformed into a beast, if he does not control himself and guide the sensible part of himself with reason. He reminds him that it is only virtue that renders life blessed and that often wise men are persecuted and put to death. In any case, the wise man is sovereign over himself and no external evil has the power to hurt him. For this reason, he should not seek revenge for the injuries he receives, which remain something extrinsic and do not have the power to offend his inner nature:

> When a young boy tears out his mother's hair, hits her and deafens her with his cries, she is not angered and does not consider herself wronged by him; just so, considering who has injured you – or better who you think has injured you – you ought not to judge yourself wronged by him.[20]

In the years following, the *Ethica*, reworked and translated into Latin, would become the second part of the quadripartite volume of the *Philosophia realis*. The table of virtues would be enriched with new entries and their description would be more detailed. Later, in the Paris edition, the work would be accompanied by three dense *Quaestiones*, concerned with the chief good, free will, and the virtues. If the basic system remained the youthful and Telesian one, some additions and modifications turned out to be quite significant: the tension between divine *mens* and corporeal *spiritus* became more present and precise, several Stoic themes were accentuated (themes that, already present in Telesio and in the young Campanella, were coming to acquire a place ever more relevant and useful as a point of connection between the naturalism of the new philosophy and the positions of the Latin and Greek fathers – above all Ambrose, Lactantius, and John Chrysostom). The virtues that came to be

---

[20] *Dialoghi* (Venice: G. B. Ciotti, 1609), pp. 5, 20, 80.

added tended to underscore the convergence and harmony between religion
and nature. Not by chance the list opened with *sanctitas* (holiness), which –
positing God as end of all the virtues and the horizon within which they
are collected – 'hallows and makes holy' (*sancit et sanctificat*), that is purifies
all intermediate ends directing them to God himself, from whom every thing
derives and to whom every thing returns. Every aspect of nature testifies to the
presence of divine goodness, such that even to the man who lives in a solitary
and isolated place it would suffice to look within himself or at natural entities
in order to recognize divinity 'as in an open book'; thus, the holy man ought
to move through the world 'as if in the house of God.' After that came *pro-
bitas*, which one can also call *bonitas* or *rectitudo*, a virtue that regulates love
towards oneself and others, coordinating the preservation of the individual
and the whole.[21]

A wondrous virtue, which the ancients had not taken into consideration
and on which in contrast Campanella focused, was the virtue that he called
protestatio – namely, the recognition, by means of exterior signs, of the goodness and the value of something with regard to its end. That virtue was divided
into various kinds: simple praise; honour, which is worthy of every man in the
correct and useful exercise of his profession, while the limb that is damaging to the social body merits disdain and merits being shunned; adoration,
with which one celebrates the excellence of an eminent nature that as such is
revered even in representations of it in so far as it is successfully conveyed.
Campanella recalled having seen someone who honored and kissed the ruins
of Rome, evidence of the virtue of that civilization. Worthy of praise is he
who excels for wisdom and moral virtue, and above all God and the divine
men who resist evil and generously spread good. *Protestatio* manifests itself
also in fame and glory, with respect to which Campanella indicated that only
a superficial examination would judge Alexander and Caesar heroes, because
in truth the most difficult war is the one that one fights internally against vice
and passion. Contraries of such attestation are horror, disdain, derision, the
worst form of which is that belonging to the man who persecutes holy men
and philosophers, accusing them of being ignoramuses, wretches, fanatics and
rebels. In doing so, they would be allowing sophists, hypocrites and tyrants to
rise to power, or else remain there without being challenged.[22]

Other virtues, which seem to follow Christian ones closely (such as modesty,
which consists in modes of dressing, speaking, and behaving so as not to offend
or scandalize others), in fact had a wider expression and a different depth, such
as *verecundia*, or demureness, which is a kind of castigation that the sinner

---

[21] *Ethica*, II, p. 813ff.
[22] Ibid., p. 888ff.

inflicts upon himself, experiencing shame at his own errors and at everything that renders him vile and base. The contrary vices are cheek and impudence, which are not only characteristic of prostitutes, but even of sovereigns who are not ashamed to execute pointless slaughters or to torment the human race simply to satisfy their slightest whims. Pushed to the extreme, modesty can induce suicide, as in the case of Lucretia (who was not able to overcome rape) and other characters who killed themselves because of shame for crimes and violations they have suffered. But he who suffers is not guilty, Campanella observed. The greatness of the human spirit is such that, even if the body is submitted to violence, the victim is greater than he who tortures, than the executioner, than he who disdains, than the master. Or take the case of humility, another virtue noted only by Christians, which is contrasted to arrogance, based in love of oneself, and that is a kind of compass for all the other virtues (*magnes omnium virtutum*) and is of all the virtues the most wise, because it places man beneath God – 'and here to serve is to rule' (*et hoc servire regnare est*). Because it has no presumption to know, it is able to learn the degree to which it has become conscious of its ignorance. Humility succeeds, precisely because it adopts an attitude of continual research. He who, conversely, believes himself to be wise and holy cannot progress on the road that leads to God, as he who believes himself to be satiated cannot partake of more food.[23]

In the more mature version of the *Ethica* too, the list of the virtues ends – as in the *Epilogo magno* – with sublimity. If already in the early work these are very beautiful pages (as they are in Telesio too), in the later draft they would become among the most intense and evocative pages in all of Campanella's writings, pages in which natural values are united with divine ones so as to constitute a vibrant manifesto for the 'dignity of man' (*dignitas hominis*). Sublimity is the heroic virtue that regulates the desire for excellence that is at the heart of the human being, at the heart of his straining towards the infinite and his aspiration to make of himself an image of divinity. The limitless avidity for praise and the hatred for every kind of servitude are so strong that even the devil yields to invoking divine mercy for fear of humiliating himself. Even if men know that they are mortal, pushed by that divine image that is within them, they started believing themselves to be immortal and started presenting themselves as divinities. With the basic importance of *puritas* (purity) of spirit reaffirmed in these pages (so that *mens* may manifest its own divine splendor plainly), Campanella sketched a portrait of the magnanimity that is an ideal program of life and the whole thing is shot through with touching autobiographical elements. Conscious that the true nobility is interior, Campanella did not concern himself with whether external honors would be withheld, nor would he avenge

---

[23] Ibid., pp. 909ff; 914ff.

himself for offenses received, well aware of the fact that insult could not touch his own essence. He would return evil with good, so as to set down a law and an example that others might imitate and so as to overcome wild spirits and render them human. Campanella would want to know all the arts and all the sciences, he would amend the doctrines of the ancients confronting them with the divine book of nature and he would study with attention the doctrines of the moderns. His heroes would be those like Columbus and Galileo who had dared to explore unknown terrain, discoverers of new worlds both terrestrial and celestial – or Origen, who had the boldness to push himself beyond the confines and the certainties of revelation. If one notation alluded to a program of life pathetically contrary to the reality of the facts ('if it will be possible for him, he will travel throughout the world, so as to experience everything'), in other passages autobiographical confession is more open and transparent. The magnanimous person would like to be judge and legislator for all humanity, so as to root out the shamefulness of false doctrines and false cults, and so as to put an end to tyranny. He would do everything possible for his homeland, lamenting its misfortunes and its condition of servitude, and he would seek to leave that homeland better than he had found it. Convinced that God is present even in misfortune, he would not concern himself with sufferings and with imprisonment, holding himself to be stronger and more worthy in that condition of imprisonment than in enjoying liberty, because the persecution of virtue (that is hated and feared by impure and false political leaders) could not but render it clearer and more manifest.

To sublimity are opposed, on the one hand, cowardice or pusillanimity and, on the other hand, arrogance. If the first is timid and faithless, the second is the root of every vice, in so far as it is a kind of misdirected love of excellence. Arrogance upsets the proper relationship between man and God and, making us turn our backs on the chief good, it closes us up in ourselves, such that we end up believing ourselves worthy of every kind of honor and we are ashamed to depend on God. The arrogant man will desire honors out of a vain ostentation and in dishonors he will lose all respect for himself. On the other hand, the magnanimous man, if he is put to death for the defence of reason and of justice, will reveal himself to be a true prince by nature, oppressed by false pretenders. Today, Peter and Paul have overcome Nero, and while Socrates lives and is worthy of praise his persecutors are detested by all:

> In fact, he – in his life and in his death – set down a law in sacred words that will remain forever, such that every one will want to be as he was. His persecutors, however, are so odious and detestable that no one wishes to be similar to them.[24]

---

[24] Ibid., p. 925ff; 935; *Epilogo magno*, p. 567.

Machiavellism and Universal Monarchy

One of Campanella's most significant political works is the *Monarchia di Spagna*, which has presented (and continues to present) difficulties with regard to date, philology, and interpretation. Campanella asserted almost constantly that he had composed this 'secret book' (in which he indicated to the Catholic sovereign the means by which to pursue a universal monarchy) at Stilo, in 1598 – or at least before the conspiracy – at the behest of the Spanish jurisconsult Martos Gorostiola.[25] Campanella did not forget to emphasize how the work (which favored Spain), having been written before his imprisonment, constituted a demonstration of his innocence and of the unfoundedness of the accusations of rebellion: 'I was building the majesty of Spain and of the Church when I was incarcerated as a disruptor of precisely those things ...'[26] Firpo, taking the unusual display of the date to be more suspicious than persuasive, believed that the work was written in the second half of 1600 and was opportunistically backdated by the author for the purpose of exonerating himself.[27] But since it does not appear to me that there are sufficiently strong reasons leading us to distrust the date indicated by the author (a date that is also confirmed in texts written considerably later than the dramatic events of the trials), I maintain that the date is to be accepted – bearing in mind two things.[28] For one thing, the first nucleus of the work goes back to a clearly earlier period. Testifying to the age of the text is the identification – amidst the extremely intricate maze of manuscripts – of a considerably shorter version of the work, which appears to be a first redaction composed in Campanella's youth.[29] For another thing, it is beyond doubt that from the earliest part of the imprisonment (and then in the course of the following years), Campanella added to his own text what he thought useful or necessary, both in order to improve it and in order to make use of it in the most appropriate manner. But the understandable decision to emphasize his own pro-Spanish loyalty and to use it for apologetic purposes does

---

[25] The 'don Alonso' to whom the work is dedicated in the Prooemium ought to be identified as the Spaniard Alonso Martos Gorostiola. Regent of the Vicaria and active at Naples in the last decades of the sixteenth century, he died in 1603. Gorostiola was friendly with the young Campanella from his first Neapolitan period; cf. ch. 2, note 18.

[26] *Lettere*, p. 28.

[27] Firpo, *Ricerche*, pp. 189–203. Amabile favored a first composition prior to the conspiracy that was lost, followed by a rewriting of the work during the first part of the incarceration. I have addressed the question in 'Note e riflessioni sulla *Monarchia di Spagna* di Tommaso Campanella,' in *La storia della filosofia come sapere critico. Studi offerti a Mario Dal Pra* (Milan, 1984), pp. 221–239; cf. also Ernst, *Religione,* p. 35ff.

[28] *Mon. Francia*, p. 492.

[29] *Monarchia di Spagna. Prima versione giovanile*, ed. G. Ernst (Naples, 1989).

not imply a feverish – and frankly improbable – drafting *ex novo* of so complex a work as the *Monarchia* in the first, extremely difficult months of his incarceration.

With respect to the philological issues arising from the text, only recently has the genuine Italian text appeared, cleansed of the interpolations taken in most cases from the *Ragion di Stato* of Giovanni Botero, which are present in the overwhelming majority of the manuscripts and in all the published texts.[30] The insertion of extraneous passages into Campanella's text appears to be the result of an unscrupulous action (certainly not attributable to the author) of which he was in all probability completely ignorant. In any case, it is beyond doubt that this is an intervention that is neither casual nor involuntary. The passages, at times opportunely recast, have been inserted with care and skill, so as not to alter the flow of the text, passing themselves off as digressions or amplifications. The question of who might have been able to carry out this work (probably for editorial purposes) has not yet found a reliable answer.[31]

If the philological issues surrounding the *Monarchia di Spagna* are complex, no less difficult are the issues of interpretation. From the end of the seventeenth century (in which the work enjoyed a notable diffusion above all thanks to the repeated Latin printings by Elsevier), the treatise did not fail to elicit both perplexity and the most harsh judgments. Some parts were viewed with particular suspicion. These included above all the explicit urgings addressed to the king asking that he establish the closest possible alliance with the Pontiff and that he eliminate all religious discord at its root, for the purpose of reconstituting that unity of faith which alone could have founded and guaranteed the unity of the dominion. The unscrupulousness of some suggestions aimed at dividing and weakening the enemies of Spain for the purpose of making it easier for the Catholic sovereign to realize a universal monarchy were also emphasized. The chapter on the Low Countries generated real indignation especially in Protestant lands. It was a chapter that, given the extreme actuality of the argument, took on a life of its own and was printed in Latin translation (and from that was translated into Flemish)

---

[30]The interpolations – present both in the seventeenth-century translations (German, Latin, English) and in the Italian text included in the *Opere*, ed. A. D'Ancona (Turin, 1854), vol. II, pp. 85–229 – have been indicated and documented by Rodolfo De Mattei, 'La *Monarchia di Spagna* di Campanella e la *Ragion di Stato* di Botero,'Rendiconti della R. Accademia Nazionale dei Lincei,' Classe di Scienze Mor., Stor. e Filol.,' s. VI, vol. III, 1927, pp. 432–485; reprinted in *La politica di Campanella* (Rome, 1928).

[31]It is possible that Schoppe had a hand in it – Schoppe, who was in close contact with the Roman circles concerned with Campanella's texts and who contributed actively to their diffusion.

independently of the text of which it was part.[32] In the furore of the polemic, the author was presented as a new, more insidious Machiavelli whose subtle stratagems it was good to know in order to oppose the best defences to them. In this way, Campanella was soon being presented as a master of the arts of dissimulation, who, while condemning the perfidy of the Florentine Secretary with his words, with his actions took from him maxims disguised in a more devious fashion. The influential notion synthesized vividly from these judgments of a Campanella who was at the same time 'a harsh critic and a subtle master of Machiavelli's maxims' goes back to Hermann Conring.[33]

It is beyond doubt that the encounter with Machiavelli constitutes one of the most important aspects of Campanella's thought. That encounter took place on the terrain of the relationship between religion and politics – which is one of the central nodes of his work. Campanella's criticism of Machiavelli is organized, above all, around two connected points. On the one hand, Campanella stressed what appeared to him to be the philosophical limits of the Florentine Secretary's thought, which carried over into an intrinsic weakness in his construction of politics. On the other hand, Campanella developed and inserted into a Catholic and Counter-Reformation context an element that was already present primarily in Machiavelli's *Discorsi sopra la prima Deca di Tito Livio* – that is, the attention to religion as the most powerful of the bonds holding the human community together. Right from the exordium to the *Monarchia*, with the articulation of the doctrine of the three causes that govern over political events, the author denounced the insufficiency of a historical vision limited to the consideration of human affairs only. Campanella

---

[32] Inserted in the collection *Speculum consiliorum Hispanicorum* (Leiden, 1617), the *Discursus de Belgio sub Hispanicam potestatem redigendo* or *De Belgio subiugando*, in a Latin translation that is not by Campanella, presents a text without interpolations. Regarding the relationships among the chapter of the *Monarchia*, the Latin translation of the *Discursus*, and a later Italian *Discorso sui Paesi Bassi*, see Luigi Firpo, 'Appunti campanelliani. XXII. Un'opera che Campanella non scrisse: il *Discorso sui Paesi Bassi*,' *GCFI*, 31 (1952), pp. 331–343.

[33] Hermann Conring, 'Introductio' to the Latin translation of N. Machiavelli's *Il Principe*, in *Opera* (Braunschweig, 1730), II, p. 979: 'Machiavelli dogmatum ... acerrimus pariter reprehensor et fucatus doctor'; see also Idem, *De civili prudentia*, ibid., III, p. 41. For recent contributions to the relationship with Machiavelli (beyond the volume by Frajese, ch. 2, note 60), see John M. Headley, 'On the Rearming of Heaven: the Machiavellism of T. Campanella,' *Journal of the History of Ideas*, 49 (1988), pp. 387–404; Germana Ernst, 'La mauvaise raison d'Etat: Campanella contre Machiavel et les Politiques,' in Y.-Ch. Zarka (ed.), *Raison et Déraison d'Etat. Théoriciens et Théories de la Raison d'Etat aux XVIe et XVIIe siècles* (Paris, 1994), pp. 121–149; Pierre Caye, 'Campanella critique de Machiavel. La politique: de la non-philosophie à la métaphysique,' *B&C*, 8 (2002), p. 333–351; Luca Addante, 'Campanella e Machiavelli: Indagine su un caso di dissimulazione,' *Studi storici*, 45 (2004), pp. 727–750.

articulated the necessity of going beyond the too restricted horizon of Machiavellian politics: 'Three common causes come together in the conquest and
maintenance of every great power – namely, God, prudence, and opportunity – which, united together, one calls fate, which is the coinciding of all the
causes acting by virtue of the first.'[34]

Thus, God is the first cause that guards and governs the others and is always
present in all historical events – even if in hidden or less evident forms. This
means that the able and shrewd politician has to try hard to integrate empirical causes with general ones, connecting human events to the laws of fate. To
that end, recourse to the 'highest sciences' of prophecy and astrology becomes
indispensable. These are sciences that allow the inserting of particular events
into a universal background. With respect to prophecy, the Bible (as a sacred
text) encompasses and prefigures the entirety of profane history. The wise interpretation of Scripture – an interpretation capable of identifying apt analogies
and correspondences – enables one to read historical events in the light of the
'archetypal' events of the Bible. In order to comprehend the arc of the evolution
of a specific political formation, it is necessary to identify the Biblical correlate
to which it refers, and from here trace back the essential steps of its transformation in the past and in the future, because 'when the auspices of fate are
followed everything prospers, and when one goes against fate one encounters
difficulty.' For this reason, Spain must identify the 'auspices of fate' under which
it might carry forward the great design of a world monarchy to happy completion. Appealing to apposite scriptural texts, Campanella concluded that the
Spanish, 'on account of fate, cannot have dominion except as liberators of the
church from the hands of the Babylonians, that is of the Turks and the heretics.'
He concluded also that the Catholic King would have to be inspired by the
model of Cyrus, invested by God with a mission as liberator of the church from
the infidels and as the congregator of peoples under a single faith.[35]

The reference to God as first and supreme cause of human history demonstrates above all the necessity of taking into account the totality into which
human events are inserted, so as to identify the specific role assigned by the
divine plan to each nation, and so as to act out of respect and in conformity
with such an assignment. In the second place, it underscores how religion is the
most potent instrument for unity, in that it constitutes an essential bond holding the political community together. Machiavelli understood this by studying
the Roman republic, but then went on to condemn the Christian religion as a
contributor to weakness, dispute, and division. Campanella did not hesitate to
affirm in this text (as he had already asserted in the *Dialogo politico contro*

---

[34] *Mon. Spagna*, p. 18.
[35] Ibid., ch. 6.

Luterani and would later reaffirm in other texts) that, independently of its truth value, religion establishes itself as the first and most powerful bond pulling the body politic together on account of the fact that it masters and connects the spirits of men (on which depend all the other bonds between human beings). Thus, 'religion – whether it be true or false – has always won out when people believed in it, because it binds the spirits of men together, on which depend bodies and swords and tongues, which are the instruments of empire.'[36]

Besides these general coordinates, which, although fundamental, constitute the hardest and most difficult aspect of the *Monarchia*, the text possesses some more lively parts, in which the dominant theme of unity is articulated in fresh ways and adorned with images and suggestions that derive from natural philosophy. Political association too, just like natural association, is a living organism: thus, the primary duty of political action is to favor the most efficacious connection between the various members. The particular virtue of this activity is prudence, which pertains to the duty of increasing natural bonds. In general, the duty of elaborating an entire series of unifying techniques is directed at consolidating the bonds of the parts with the whole, integrating the different to the similar, and attenuating the most violent contrasts in a way that works towards the ideal functioning and the prosperity of the entire organism. Campanella insisted on differentiating prudence from Machiavellian cunning, described by the moderns as 'reason of state,'[37] which is destined to failure because it is a technique dedicated to the affirmation of egotistical individuality. This is amply demonstrated in the tragic end of Cesare Borgia, 'student of the impious Machiavelli,' and in the likewise tragic ends of the various Neros and Ezzelinos, whose successes have revealed themselves to be deceptive and ephemeral: 'and although they might use a great deal of cunning to suppress the people, I say that in the end such cunning will ruin them'. They are compelled to live the bitter life of tyrants, tormented by continual suspicions and fears, disquieted by the consciousness of not being loved, 'which is death and not life for those who rule.'[38]

A wise politician is he who, having as his aim the solidarity and the well-being of the totality, is able to promote opportune bonds at three different levels. Above all, he must be able to unite the spirits of men through the impulse given to the letters and sciences, and especially the bonds deriving from the preaching of the best religion, which is the unity of the members and the soul that vivifies the organism. In the second place, he must be able to promote the

---

[36] Ibid., p. 44.

[37] On the comparison between prudence and cunning, see *Aforismi politici*, pp. 122–123; see also ch. 6.2, p. 93.

[38] *Mon. Spagna*, p. 42.

bonds of the body, and here Campanella's attention is focused in two directions. On the one side, he stressed the necessity of military reform. Considering with interest the Turkish military schools, he proposed the institution of analogous 'seminaries' in which illegitimate children and the children of the poor could be raised and trained in the use of arms, not knowing any father other than the King. On the other side, Campanella insisted on the appropriateness of increasing marriages, favoring the unions of people of diverse constitution and temperament – and of the Spanish with other peoples, so as to 'hispanize other nations and disperse seed, as trees do' and for the purpose of tempering the vices of Spanish blood, 'which is hateful to almost all other nations, because it is fairly humble in serving yet haughty in dominating, boastful and cunning in small things and not in big things.' The third type of bond is that of the goods of fortune, and in this case the issue is increasing, internally, the economic well-being of peoples and, externally, increasing goods, commerce, and above all shipping – that genuine lymph-node which permits the domination of distant lands and the connection of separate parts of the empire. [39]

It is in light of these principles that Spanish bad governance was not spared criticism that was at times quite harsh. One of the worst evils – and least known – is an extremely bad administration of justice, especially on the part of magistrates at the lower level, who 'are ready to exaggerate crimes in order to aggrandize themselves in the eyes of their superiors and who do not hesitate to condemn the innocent, because they pronounce their verdicts not according to the law, but according to the promptings of reason of state and of personal avarices and ambitions. Destructive also, for the most part, are the barons: lazy, parasitic, and overabundant, they abandon themselves to an unbridled luxury, and in order to maintain that luxury 'they rob from a thousand hands,' depopulating their lands and 'ruining the people from whom every fee that comes to the King derives.' On that score, it is better to treasure men than gold, and the greatest treasure is a large number of subjects united by reciprocal love. Campanella affirmed the common supposition that the gold of the New World had ruined the old world. It had let loose avidity and interrupted the reciprocal love between people, rendering social inequalities – and the vices deriving from them – more glaring. Men, said Campanella (and he would repeat it in *The City of the Sun*), 'are either too rich, which makes them insolent, arrogant, and soft or too poor, which makes them schemers, thieves and murderers.' This corrodes justice, because if a poor man takes legal action against a rich man 'he cannot find justice, and then becomes an outlaw, or dies in jail, and the rich man oppresses whoever he pleases, because the judge is dependent on him, and judges are made by favor, or even more by money.' [40]

---

[39] See Jean-Louis Fournel, 'mare,' in *Enciclopedia*, vol. 2 (forthcoming).
[40] *Mon. Spagna*, pp. 160, 174.

The final part of the *Monarchia* deals more specifically with relations between Spain and other countries, which Campanella surveys one by one, so as to identify from time to time the points of strength or weakness among friendly nations and among hostile ones – such as France, England, and above all the Turkish Empire. He also surveys these countries, so as to provide opportune plans for consolidating the bonds that exist with the first and for weakening the second and making them less dangerous, in such a way that they cannot oppose the universalistic plan of the Spanish sovereign. The most famous of these chapters (and the most discussed) is the one concerned with the Low Countries, which offers a kind of cross-check of the validity of the analyses carried out and of the remedies proposed.[41] The author showed how, in following policies that he was counselling against, one would risk finding oneself in situations without means of escape. In this enterprise, Spain had wasted enormous amounts of gold and men without obtaining its objectives, because, instead of favoring union, attenuating and crushing diversity, it had exacerbated contrasts, fomenting hatred and opposition.

The point of departure here was an attempted physiognomic analysis of the peoples in question, peoples who – like northerners in general – were said to be of a fierce temperament and dominated by robust passions. The cold, in fact, made it so that 'native heat does not escape outwards with its subtle parts, whence northerners remain full of essence and blood, and the bodies – growing a fair bit – are full of spirits and are extremely strong.' This inclines them to a liberty that is both political and religious 'hence a broadly defined law was suited to them, because the passions of their spirits were more capable of unleashing them than the law was of restraining them, and confident in their own power they respect no superior authority.' It is not to be wondered at that they have in large part joined the Reformation, since on both the practical level (with the elimination of fasts and other prohibitions) and the doctrinal level (with the rejection of free will) it supported the vehemence of their instincts and emancipated them politically from subjection to the Pope. On this matter, Campanella reiterated that judgment he had already expressed in the *Dialogo*: 'With the excuse of maintaining their liberty of conscience, they maintained their political liberty.'

From the moment that between the fair-colored and sanguine Flemish people and the dark, melancholic Spaniards 'love could not take root (there being no unifying similarity),' the bonds on which they ought to have counted were those undeniable bonds of religion and politics. Spain's most serious error,

---

[41] Ibid., ch. 27; see Jean-Louis Fournel, 'Du bon usage historique de l'hérésie. La revolte des Flandres dans la pensée politique de Campanella,' in M. Blanco-Morel and M. F. Piéjus (eds.), *Les Flandres et la culture Espagnole et Italienne aux XVIe et XVIIe siècles* (Lille, 1998), pp. 121–138.

though, was that of not having immediately crushed such heretical doctrines, the diffusion of which had then favored and supported political rebellion. Campanella did not hesitate to declare that the most rapid and effective solution would have been the suppression of Luther. If that had not taken place it was only because, once again, reason of state had revealed itself to be miopic and limited. Indeed, Charles V, deluding himself that he would be able to make use of Luther as a pawn in his political game (by dressing Luther up as a scarecrow for the Pope), made a mistake in his calculations, succeeding only in weakening Christianity and his own Empire: 'with the Pope enervated, all of Christianity was weakened. And after the heresy, all the peoples rebelled in the name of living in a freedom of conscience, as the peoples of Charles himself did in Germany and Flanders.'

In a situation that was compromised from the beginning, Spain did nothing but heap error upon error, exercising – in a counterproductive manner – a harshly repressive politics with respect to those populations inclined by nature to liberty. The continual wars, then, with their cruelty, did nothing but worsen the situation, provoking ever more fierce resistance – both moral and military – from the rebels, such that Campanella was convinced that 'today Spain does more harm fighting them than letting them be.' At that point, there was nothing to do but oppose the obtuse and violent machinations of Spain, interventions that were based on the 'subtle' arts, and go back to the wise interpretations of the 'learned' mythological fables of Antaeus, Cadmus, and Jason, which contain precious teachings. Campanella made an entire series of suggestions (some of which were rather unscrupulous), suggestions that echo the much deplored Machiavellianism, directed at dividing and weakening the rebels and at destroying military resistance around their leaders, drawing energy and resources from them in directions other than resistance and uniform hatred against Spain.

The two concluding chapters are dedicated to the New World and to shipping, the most 'wonderful' aspects of the Spanish monarchy, the extraordinary expansion of which in distant and unknown lands constituted one of the most evident signs of its prophetic mission and of the fact that Spain was guided by the forces of fate. In the *Monarchia* (as in the *Discorso sui diritti del Re Cattolico sopra il Nuovo Emisfero* (*Treatise on the rights of the Catholic King over the New Hemisphere*), the basis for the legitimacy of the conquest of the New World on the part of the Catholic Sovereign is identified with his prophetic role as a mystical Cyrus chosen by God for the purpose of reunifying the peoples of the earth in a single flock. Yet that did not prevent Campanella from severely criticizing the violent and cruel methods that had made the conquest and domination of those lands possible in the final pages of this text. Campanella deplored the irrationality of the preaching and the extermination of populations, who constituted a treasure much more precious than that of metals such as gold or silver. In time, such criticisms would become ever sharper, turning into a hard closing argument against those who had preferred the sinister roles of 'executioners and instruments of the anger of God' to the providential role of congregating the Christian flocks.[42]

Appendix

Letter of Lorenzo Galatino, Bishop of Minervino,
to Cardinal Giulio Antonio Santori
(Minervino, 15 April 1598)[43]

678r Illustrissimo et Reverendissimo Monsignor mio padrone Colendissimo

il Padrone di questa città il Signor Mario del Tufo, perché io cercai a Vostra Signoria Illustrissima quel Padre Dominicano Frate Thomaso Campanella detto, quando fui per partirmi da costì, essendo venuto il detto Padre qui, hora mi ha pregato, che io di novo lo dimandi al Signor Antonio Gaitano per mio Theologho, et io per vivere quieto questi pochi dì altri, ho scritto già, et lo pregho mi lo cerchi in mio nome. Ma dall'altra parte prego Vostra Signoria Illustrissima per amor di Dio, che resti contenta di provedere secondo Dio, et secondo lo spirito Santo la inspirarà, perché non pretendo altro io, che quanto è secondo Dio, et secondo il volere di questa Sacra Congregatione de Illustrissimi Signori Cardinali in torno a ciò, et in tutt'il resto, et negandolo, non mi faccino per amor de Dio pigliar' inimicitia con questo signore, perché per non haverlilo portato da allhora, sempre mi ha traversato, di modo, che mi elegerò più presto ritornare in Convento che vivere così: perché come gli scrissi il peso è insupportabile. Ne avedera rispondermi di questo, ma bastarà dire al servitore del Signor Abbate [Netio], che mi scriva, che sì. Et tanto mi basterà. Aciò le lettere non vengino in loro mani. Li bascio le vesti, et li prego vita, et contento.
Da Minervino li 15 di Aprile del 98.

Fra Lorenzo Galatino Vescovo di Minervino

685v Di Minervino
Di Monsignor Vescovo
De' 15 di Aprile 1598
Ricevuta a' VII di Maggio

13 Maji 1598. Scribatur Episcopo Minervini ne accipiat ad eius servitia pro theologo fratrem Thomam Campanellam.

---

[42] Cf. ch. 12, p. 252.

[43] ACDF, SO, Stanza storica, LL. 3. b, ff. 678r, 685v (autograph); Baldini and Spruit, pp. 183–184.

Essendo stato costretto ad istanza del padrone di quella città, dimandar per suo Theologo fra Tomaso Campanella, per mezzo del Signor Antonio Caetano; ha voluto per quest'altra via significar alle Signorie Vostre Illustrissime che questa dimanda la fa per forza e per gratificar quel Signore, e starvi in pace; ma dall'altro canto desiderarebbe che non se gli concedesse.

Di questa risolutione non si cura che se gli risponda, et cetera.

5. THE CONSPIRACY

The Utopia of Liberty

In the second half of July 1598, Campanella set out for Calabria. At the end of the month he reached Nicastro, where he had the opportunity of seeing once again some old friends – the brothers Ponzio and Giovan Battista da Pizzoni. Immediately, he became involved in the complex jurisdictional conflicts between ecclesiastical and state authorities. In the course of several months of relative tranquillity at Stilo, he was able to complete some works that were later lost (fifty *Articoli* against the doctrines of Luis de Molina, a tragedy about Mary Stuart, representing her as a martyr for Catholicism, and a short work entitled *De episcopo*). He was also able to work on the *Monarchia di Spagna* once again.[1] On 11 November he sent a short letter to Cardinal Giulio Antonio Santori. He asked that at Christmas the remaining period of punishment be remitted, in view of the six years of 'trials' that he had endured. He declared himself ready to obey, although he was very 'tired.'[2] But in the first months of 1599 a tumultuous and difficult period began. It would continue to intensify in the spring and summer, and concluded with the catastrophe of the accusation of conspiracy, the tragic consequences of which would mark the rest of Campanella's life.

On 10 August, approximately one year after his arrival in Calabria and precisely a month before the day designated for the beginning of the planned insurrection, two citizens from Catanzaro (Fabio di Lauro and Giovan Battista Biblia) set about disassociating themselves from the conspiracy about which they had been informed by Dionisio Ponzio. They signed a document in front of the fiscal advocate Don Luise Xarafa de Castillo affirming that

> brother Tommaso Campanella of Stilo and of the Dominican Order, a person who is held throughout the world to be a leader in the sciences, together with Dionisio Ponzio and in collusion with many lords, lay and ecclesiastical,

---

[1] Firpo, *Bibliografia*, pp. 182–184.

[2] The letter is in Baldini and Spruit, p. 185. On Santori, see Saverio Ricci, *Il sommo inquisitore. Giulio Antonio Santori tra autobiografia e storia (1532–1602)* (Rome, 2002).

both with the Pope and the Turk, have attempted and are daily attempting to raise a rebellion and deceive the people in order to turn them against the King our lord, denouncing him as the tyrant of the entire world. With persuasive words they spread the notion of the unacceptable wickedness of his ministers, who put human blood, justice, and everything up for auction, tyrannically stealing the labor of the poor with the many tributes and payments and murders that take place in the Kingdom of Naples.[3]

The leaders of the revolt, the accusation went on to say, maintained that the kingdom, feud of the Holy Church, was unjustly occupied by the King of Spain, and that the time had come that it please God to 'excise the filth of so many tyrannies and servitudes' through the work of his Vicar. In exchange for a modest tribute, that Vicar, 'empathizing with the disasters of the people, resolved to place them in the pristine liberty of a republic,' so that they might place themselves in God's service, whose help was assured by revelations and prophecies. The leaders of the revolt spread the opinion that, while those who governed ('not much of a government and one of mediocre talent') were blinded, the people were ready to fight and shed blood for God, the Holy Church, and liberty. Beyond practical advantage, they would win 'eternal fame for centuries to come.' Moreover, Di Lauro and Biblia revealed that a primary role in the plot was being played by Maurizio de Rinaldis, a young man of noble extraction, who had promised the support of two hundered armed men and who had close ties with the Turks and their commander Cicala, who had committed a fleet of sixty ships. A detailed list of the numerous adherents to the plot followed. On that list, there were many 'exiles and plebeian leaders,' feudal lords and bishops. But the weapon in which they put the most store was preaching and persuasion.

The picture represented by the accusation was not far from the truth. Until the middle of the nineteenth century, information about the conspiracy remained confused and vague. It fell to Luigi Amabile to present, with extraordinary passion and dedication, the most complete and minute reconstruction of the facts and persons connected to that event. His reconstruction appeared in three hefty volumes – the first two treating the narrative, the third consisting entirely of documents.[4] In this way, texts and materials became available to scholars that to this day constitute an inexhaustible goldmine and an essential point of departure and point of reference. The need for a thoroughly documented study of the conspiracy became apparent to Amabile

---

[3] Amabile, *Congiura*, I, pp. 226–228; III, doc. 7, pp. 15–17.

[4] In 1887, Amabile published his two-volume *Castelli* which was intended to complete Campanella's biography. The second volume included texts and short works, most of which had never been published before.

after dissatisfaction with hasty and uncertain judgments passed on the events in Calabria by scholars such as Michele Baldacchini, Alessandro D'Ancona, and Domenico Berti (whose biography of Campanella had just appeared).[5] In 1844, Count Vito Capialbi, a renowned Calabrian scholar, had put out two previously unpublished texts from Campanella in his own hand – the *Narrazione* and the *Informazione* – that had been redacted in 1620 at the prospect of a liberation that he thought was imminent.[6] Those writings, even though they were put together many years after the events, did not differ much from his initial defense. The author understandably played down and softened the events in which he had been a protagonist and insisted on inserting those events into a prophetic context. Some scholars (starting with Capialbi himself) invoked these texts in order to absolve Campanella of responsibility for the conspiracy.

Amabile was convinced on the contrary that there certainly had been a conspiracy, that it had been glorious, and that, therefore, it constituted neither a stain on the philosopher's reputation nor an infamy from which to excuse him, 'as if having attempted to liberate the country had been an ignominious action.' He gathered together and published a fairly abundant mass of documents, drawn from multiple sources, for the purpose of proving both the reality of the attempted insurrection and also the central role, as inspiration and organizer, played by Campanella. With praiseworthy scrupulousness he combed archives and libraries (both in Italy and further afield) so as to track down every last piece of useful information. He also had the good fortune of locating important private collections of documents relating to the heresy trials, which he was able to reorder and transcribe into six volumes that he donated to the Biblioteca Nazionale of Naples.[7]

From Amabile's narrative there emerged a portrait of the places and times that constituted the background of the event, which was characterized by

---

[5] Michele Baldacchini, *Vita e filosofia di T. Campanella* (Naples, 1840) with subsequent revised and augmented editions; on Alessandro D'Ancona, see the *Discorso della vita e delle dottrine di Tommaso Campanella*, a good 320 pages, added to the first of the two volumes of the collected *Opere di Tommaso Campanella* edited by him (Turin, 1854); Domenico Berti, 'Tommaso Campanella,' *Nuova Antologia di scienze, lettere ed arti*, s. II, vol. XL (1878), pp. 201–227, 605–616; vol. XLI, 1878, pp. 391–415.

[6] Vito Capialbi, *Documenti inediti circa la voluta ribellione di F. Tommaso Campanella raccolti ed annotati* (Naples, 1845).

[7] Many documents are drawn from the Archivio di Stato di Firenze, where the Strozzi papers conserve a precious if uneven collection of documents belonging to Jacopo Aldobrandini, nephew of Pope Clement VIII and Nuncio of Naples from 1592 to 1605. Other documents are drawn from the correspondence of residents and ambassadors (from Florence, Venice, and Constantinople) with their governments; those conserved in the Archives of Simancas, which include the correspondence between the court of Madrid and the Viceroy of Naples, are of particular interest.

conditions of grave disorder and widespread violence. The elements of greatest prominence in that portrait were the following: the heavy and continual jurisdictional conflicts between ecclesiastical and state powers, as a result of which bishops and state functionaries, jealous of their own prerogatives, confronted each other by inflicting punishments and excommunications; the conflict between the various factions of citizens, who bloodied the cities with a long sequence of crimes and vendettas; the resulting phenomenon of bandits and exiles, who often found protection in convents and churches, enjoying ecclesiastical immunity; the bad habits of the men of religion and the maladministration of the Spanish government, which Campanella did not tire of denouncing (a theme visible in the *Monarchia di Spagna* and ever more explicit in subsequent works); and above all an intolerable economic decline and an iniquitous systems of taxation, which caused exasperation in subjects who were put in dire circumstances.

In this atmosphere heavy with tensions and conflicts, anxieties of revenge and vendetta coagulated into a widespread aspiration for change. Campanella gave voice to and expressed suffering, resentment, and expectation when he proclaimed the coming of a period of profound change, a change predicted by a rich prophetic tradition, by unusual astral events, and by natural signs that in their aptness seemed to confirm that the time for change was not only coming, but was imminent and close at hand. In documents in which he defended himself, Campanella would later express regret that his message – which he intended to put forward as general and philosophical – had been misunderstood and misinterpreted in the light of narrow and personal interests. He would not hesitate to censure even Dionisio Ponzio (his best friend and closest collaborator) for having spoken in a thoughtless manner and for having grossly misunderstood the true nature of his words: 'you were speaking of things you did not understand.'[8]

Initial reports and subsequent depositions would concur in identifying Campanella as the true spirit of the conspiracy. Campanella's extraordinary intellectual gifts and his immense knowledge were emphasized: he was said to be an 'extremely famous scholar,' 'one of the chief men in all the sciences,' 'the most eminent scholar in the world,' 'extremely intelligent.' Emphasized also were his gifts of eloquence, with which he was able to persuade and seduce the people. He possessed 'arts capable of moving the spirits of men as he wished with natural reasonings and … the entire people followed him, and wherever he appeared in the countryside to preach he moved spirits so greatly that he was able to make statutes and laws for those people, who understood him and were ready to obey him.'[9] The accusation would be immediately corroborated:

---

[8] *Appendix ad amicum*, in *Art. proph.*, p. 295.
[9] Amabile, *Congiura*, III, doc. 244, pp. 130–131.

thanks to his knowledge of astrology and prophecy, he was convinced that – beginning in 1600 – great changes would come about, innumerable wars and revolutions overturning states, above all in the Kingdom of Naples and in Calabria. From this followed the exhortation to be ready and armed, so as to win liberty, and escape from subjection and from the tyranny of the King of Spain by transforming the province into a republic. The insurrection would have been sustained by the arms of outlaws and by the Turkish fleet, while Campanella – 'the most eminent man of the world, legislator and messiah' – would have promulgated 'new laws and returned every man to natural liberty.' In the spring and in the summer of 1599, meetings and discussions between friars, the preaching of imminent changes, and agreements with powerful local lords became more intense and feverish. At the same time, the organization of armed support became better defined, support guaranteed by Maurizio de Rinaldis and by pacts made by him with Scipione Cicala, the Turkish captain of Genoese extraction, who was responsible for raids on the Calabrian coast and who was to bring arms and weapons on his ships.[10]

When the detailed accusation came before the Count of Lemos, who had been invested as the new Viceroy of Naples little more than a month earlier, he hurried to notify the Spanish Ambassador at Rome and through him the Pope, who authorized him to transfer the friars to Naples, putting them in the hands of the Nuncio. Also worried at the 'extravagance' of a plot in which the Pope and the Turks were said to be involved, the Viceroy quickly decided to send two companies of Spanish soldiers to Calabria under the command of Carlo Spinelli with the pretext of protecting the coast from Turkish incursions. He vested Spinelli, who was distinguished both by his military valor in numerous campaigns and for his forethought and juridical competence, with full powers. But after these initial precautions, the secret was quickly revealed. Reaching Catanzaro at the end of August, Spinelli ordered the imprisonment of a member of the conspiracy who succeeded in escaping on account of the thoughtlessness of Alonso de Roxas, the governor of the region. Shortly thereafter, however, he would be found strangled in a vineyard and the episode revealed the true purpose of the expedition to the sharp disappointment of Spinelli. In this way, a vast operation began that took advantage of the close collaboration of local lords, who – after being promised

---

[10] On Scipione Cicala – who was born at Messina to a Genoese father in 1544, taken prisoner as a young boy by the Turks and raised as a Muslim, and went on to have a brilliant military career in the service of the Sultan – see the entry by Gino Benzoni in *DBI*, vol. XXV (Rome, 1981), pp. 320–340. Regarding the role that he played in the Calabrian conspiracy, see Amabile, *Congiura*, I, p. 134ff. On the relationship between the Turks and the City of the Sun, see Noel Malcolm, 'The Crescent and the City of the Sun: Islam and the Renaissance Utopia of Tommaso Campanella,' *Proceedings of the British Academy*, 125 (2004), pp. 41–67.

lavish rewards – were 'commissioned' (that is to say, authorized) to give chase to those under suspicion with bands of armed men. Suspects were subjected to interrogation on the spot by ad hoc tribunals, empowered by Spinelli himself, by a chancery secretary, and by the fiscal advocate Xarafa.

Immediately, the suspicion arose that the crime of rebellion and high treason was accompanied by the crime of heresy. As early as 14 August, brother Cornelio of Nizza[11] (against whom Campanella would later express the harshest judgments, accusing him of having despicably betrayed the friars and having brought them to ruin) wrote to the General of the Dominican Order and to the powerful Cardinal Inquisitor of Santa Severina, Giulio Antonio Santori, informing them of the vileness with which, as he had heard it, Campanella was stained. A parallel trial for heresy was initiated after a witness was forced into making a formal accusation. This was a trial that was even more ferocious – and without doubt more iniquitous – than the trial for rebellion. Alternating intimidation and terrible threats with flattery and promises of indulgences and reward, the trial went as far as extorting confessions and admissions from witnesses and suspects. In their denunciations of the blasphemy and heresies maintained by the two principal prisoners (Ponzio and Campanella), these confessions exhibited similarities that were suspiciously strong, almost as if the detainees had responded to a kind of preset questionnaire, as was common practice in witchcraft trials. The two main defendants, however, were never summoned to testify.

Campanella was arrested in the evening of 6 September. Warned by Ponzio of the danger but refusing to become an exile, he had taken refuge at Stignano with his confrere Domenico Petrolo. In tears, his father had said that he would prefer to see him 'dead rather than in exile.' Thus, both fled to Roccella Ionica, where for three days they lived hidden in a country cottage, with the hope of being able to find some embarkation, following promises from Antonio Mesuraca, who had welcomed them in the name of an old debt of gratitude. In a betrayal that would later be held against him in a sonnet, Mesuraca reported them to the Prince of Roccella instead, who hurried to send a company of armed men to capture the two of them. Having taken them into custody, he put them in the prison at Castelvetere, where some days later, Campanella made an important *Dichiarazione* on the events in Calabria to Xarafa, who in turn was accused of the worst infamies and cruelties in a series of sonnets.

In mid-September the appearance of Cicala with thirty ships off the Calabrian coast seemed to confirm the conspirators' plans. Unaware of the course of events, he dispatched two feluccas as a patrol and they released flares. Not

---

[11] On Brother Cornelio, see Firpo, *Ricerche*, pp. 33–36.

receiving any response, they had no option but to turn back. After the usual stopover in the ditch of San Giovanni, the fleet – which, it was said, was carrying many men, a hundred pieces of artillery, and a great quantity of spades, pickaxes, and forks' – abandoned the Italian seas to return home.

The number of arrests continued to grow in the course of an ever more ruthless man hunt. Desperate attempts to flee failed, such as that of Ponzio who was arrested on the coast of Apulia while he was trying to board ship.[12] The increasing number of prisoners meant that the tribunal had to be moved first to the Castle of Squillace and then to Gerace. On the journey from one locality to the other, Campanella responded to the Spanish leader of the soldiers escorting him in chains (who tormented him with the worst kind of death threats) with a philosophical reflection that death does not exist, since everything is transformation: 'Campanella also said to a company leader when he was being escorted from Squillace to Gerace that there was no such thing as death and that there was instead a mutation of one being into another …'[13]

Initial caution was then replaced by a fierce repression, with mass arrests and spectacular executions. At Catanzaro, two men thought to be among the leaders of the revolt were 'abused, tortured, strangled at the foot of the gallows, and then hung up by one foot, quartered two days later, their heads being posted in cages of iron above the city gates.'[14] At the end of October, the prisoners were forced to march in chains to places of embarkation. In a most beautiful passage of the *Theologia*, alluding to how many had wanted to take for themselves strips from the clothes ripped from Christ, Campanella would later remember that the soldiers cursed him as a heretic and rebel, and yet admired him in the confines of their own hearts and secretly asked for his blessing and for remedies to cleanse their evil deeds, and for many other things that they pretended to detest.[15] And when the torture of the *veglia* ('vigil') would later be inflicted upon him, even as many torturers would hate him, others in their hearts would experience admiration for the force of his spirit: 'Some of those present cursed me and intensified the pain, tugging on the ropes; others admired the strength of my spirit in their hearts.'[16]

On 8 November, four ships reached the gulf of Naples with a load of more than 150 prisoners and the horror of four men who had been hung dangling

---

[12] But three years later, he would break out prison in Naples, heading for Constantinople, where he would die a short time later in a brawl with a Janissary.

[13] Amabile, *Congiura*, III, doc. 319, p. 272; I, p. 327.

[14] Ibid., III, doc. 181, p. 93.

[15] *Vita Christi, Theologicorum liber XXI*, ed. R. Amerio (Rome, 1962), p. 118; Romano Amerio, *Il sistema teologico di Tommaso Campanella*, p. 229.

[16] See note 33.

from the bows of the ships. Entering the port another two would be 'quartered alive by four ships so as to strike fear into the people of that city, who gathered in almost infinite numbers after rumors of these spectacles began to circulate.'[17] Years later, Campanella would give an explanation of the meaning of this act, suggesting again a comparison with the life of Christ. If Christ was put to death between two thieves, in order to show that he was a common criminal, the execution of the four conspirators also had a demonstrative aspect and ought to have served to show to the King that 'there was a rebellion and that the ensuing judgments dared not absolve the leader whose supporters had been so harshly punished.'[18]

Heresy, Rebellion, and Prophecy

As soon as they became aware of the conspiracy, the residents hurried to inform the relevant authorities. On 8 September 1599, the Tuscan agent in Naples (the same Giulio Battaglino who in 1592 had already been consulted with regard to Campanella) let the Grand Duke know that it had become necessary to dispatch troops to Calabria, not so much and not only 'on account of a fear of Turkish ships' (as was at first thought) but 'so as to remedy a very grave situation.' It had been discovered that in Calabria, at Stilo, 'there was a conspiracy involving many people that ended in the armed uprising of that province as well as the dissolution of obedience to the King.' The hotbeds of the revolt had been attacked in various places and he predicted that 'this nascent tragedy ... will end in the punishment of many.' Among the known leaders, there was a Dominican, a certain Tommaso Campanella, who ought already to be known to the court as a 'bizarre brain.' Battaglino remembered well the dealings of the earlier years, when the Grand Duke was thinking of taking the young friar into his service and had asked him for information. Seven years later, that initial diffidence reemerged. The earlier negative impressions had been confirmed and he expressed the warmest praise for the Viceroy, who with his timely intervention 'discovered and remedied in a very opportune fashion a fire set by Turkish arms and heresy' that would rapidly have consumed the entire province. Battaglino urged the Grand Duke to send his own official congratulations for 'such an important service,' something that the Grand Duke did not fail to do. He had his secretary of state write a long letter in which he rejoiced warmly with the Viceroy for having 'rid this Kingdom and all of Italy from such a great disturbance.'[19]

---

[17] Amabile, *Congiura*, III, doc. 184, p. 94.

[18] Amerio, *Il sistema teologico di Tommaso Campanella*, p. 230.

[19] Amabile, *Congiura*, III, doc. 184, 94.

A report deriving from the earliest stages of the events – that Firpo described as 'journalistic reportage, written by a cultivated and well-informed person' on account of its immediacy and precision – described Campanella as a man 'of the most profound and universal learning in many fields of knowledge.' As usual, the report insinuated suspicions of a non-human origin for Campanella's doctrines (said to be 'infused with the work of the devil'). It described him as a man of 'restless spirit and no devotion,' who, disgruntled by the punishments inflicted upon him by the Holy Office, had thought to immortalize himself by introducing a new religion in order to satiate his own boundless ambitions.[20] He maintained that Calvin and Luther were merely grammarians, who had possessed neither the great spirit nor the high-minded thoughts to found new laws, whereas he intended 'to liberate the entire Kingdom from obedience, which he called his majesty's tyranny.' The new religion that he wanted to preach 'consisted entirely in a liberty of living in a republic, full of heresies, without knowing either God or church.'

A second, more hostile report described how 'a certain Tommaso Campanella' – a Dominican friar 'of great stature, pale face, black hair, and rare teeth, but commonly judged to be mad and ignorant' – had predicted the coming in 1600 of changes in state and kingdom 'necessitated by the constellations and the influence of the stars.' Swept up in his own 'delusions and fantasies, not without the persuasion of the devil, with whom he held himself extremely familiar,' he had preached the recovery 'of that ancient liberty ... that had been lost on account of the tyranny of powerful men and lords.' To Spinelli, who compared the heresies of which he was accused to those of heretics ancient and modern, Campanella confirmed having a low opinion of the reformers, whom he judged to be ignorant men who limited themselves to conjuring up glosses and to stretching the sense of the sacred texts. 'In truth, those of his kind had other things in mind: they wanted to establish new laws themselves and lay down rules by which one should live. He claimed that this was the business of great men, chief among them himself, for he had come into the world as a new Messiah for the good of mankind.' Emphasizing the effect of his speeches on those who listened ('in the first argumentation he would embarrass the brain; in the second souls were captivated'), the observer lingered on the pacts with the Turks, emphasizing affinities of dress and custom.[21] Already, the previous report had related that in the new city instead of hats – which 'denoted subjection and little life of the spirit in the head' – the wearing of 'well-fastened headgear' would have become common. The second report

---

[20] Luigi Firpo, 'Appunti campanelliani. XXXI. Tre relazioni contemporanee sulla congiura calabrese del 1599,' *GCFI*, 41 (1962), p. 386ff.

[21] Ibid., p. 395.

confirmed that 'a white vest down to the knee with long sleeves' was being worn 'but that underneath one could wear silk and brocade, while on the head a small hat with cloth wound around it was being worn.' And with Campanella maintaining that 'the sin of the flesh is not sin,' he was reputed to be bent on 'taking for himself eight or ten of the most prominent women of the province, first murdering their husbands and then creating a harem in the castle at Stilo.' To the men sent to capture him, he was supposed to have proclaimed with pride: 'you have captured a man, but that does not mean that what was supposed to happen will be prevented.' Already in custody, he warned that 'at least lords will learn to govern their vassals well, because of us, and they will not fall into excess as long as they see that the people resent them.'[22]

The trials in Calabria were followed by those in Naples, which were characterized by extremely complicated jurisdictional conflicts due to the fact that the accused included both laymen and members of the clergy. Many of them, moreover, had been charged with a double crime – high treason and heresy. The records of the trial for rebellion would relatively quickly be lost or destroyed. But the documentation of the trials for heresy turned out to be much richer. In fact, the accusations of heresy pose the most delicate problems, in that amidst the intrigue of the testimonies it becomes particularly difficult to distinguish truth from falsehood, equivocation from exaggeration. Even leaving aside the most vulgar and blasphemous gestures against the crucifix or the Host on the part of Dionisio Ponzio, the depositions refer from the outset to doctrines that amount to a rationalistic and unscrupulous critique of the supernatural and sacramental aspects of Christianity. According to such testimonies, for Campanella the sacraments 'were not set down by Christ' but were instead introduced for reasons of state, so as to induce fear and obedience in the people. In particular, the Eucharist is 'an absurdity and it is craziness to believe in it.' Demons do not exist, but are rather the products of mental illnesses and alterations in the body ('they are madnesses, sooty spirits or cold humors that wane'), just as heaven and hell do not exist either. Miracles are nothing but the 'imaginations' of those who believe in them. The crossing of the Red Sea took place thanks to a low tide, while the eclipse at the death of Christ was 'natural and not miraculous, and … particular rather than universal.' Campanella himself was said to believe that he was capable of true miracles: he was supposed to be convinced that 'he could not be wounded and that he could revive the dead and other extraordinary things.' Christ was

---

[22] Ibid., pp. 392, 397–98. The third report is taken from the unpublished *Istorie veneziane* of the Doge Nicolò Contarini (1553-1631); for the reactions to the conspiracy of the Venetian government, see Gino Benzoni, 'Campanella e Venezia: qualche appunto, qualche spunto,' in *Congiura di Calabria*, p. 43–60.

not the son of God and was not resurrected. His body was hidden and taken, as had happened with other legislators. Thus, 'Christ was stolen; he did not rise again, and … not letting their bodies be found was customary with legislators; the same had been done with Moses, Pythagoras, and others; and so it was done with Christ too.' He denied the virginity of Mary, said that Martha and Magdalen were the 'lovers' of Christ and that 'the venereal act was licit.' He pointed out in this example that just 'as a man may use an arm or a foot, so he is able to use his member.' According to him, the trinity was an 'illusion, depicting a body with three heads' and that the Antichrist foreseen by prophecy was the Roman Pope, whose authority was 'an usurped and tyrannical authority.' He maintained that God did not exist and 'he proved this by saying that it was unbelievable that some Christians might be saved and that the remainder would be damned because in comparison with the world the Christians are just a fingernail; that only some might be saved was not credible.' Those who put credence in all these tales were, in his opinion, awkward and ignorant asses, who could not understand that 'the Apostles told them these stories in order to inculcate the faith, not with reason but against reason.'[23]

When he became aware of such compromising depositions, Campanella would assert that the insistence on the heresies and their exaggeration was nothing but a clever expedient on the part of the brothers in order to be transferred to Rome and judged there by the tribunal of the Holy Office. With an affirmation that was at once disquieting and highly suggestive, he said that the heresies were modeled on a scheme of such heresies set out 'by one who was in the Holy Office at Rome.'[24] One cannot help but think of the encounter with Bruno in the jails of the Roman Holy Office. Even if it is difficult (except in the libertine and atheist theses reported and criticized in *Ateismo trionfato*) to trace the continuation of such evidently heterodox affirmations in the later works, some claims turned out to be recognizable and plausible.[25] They included the Machiavellian conception of religion as a political bond, the 'cold faith' and the absence of interior adherence to dogmas that he preached, the sexual licentiousness (which also echoed possible sympathies for Islamic polygamy), and the acceptance of sodomy, which would later be harshly condemned in *The City of the Sun*.

Regarding the accusation of rebellion, Campanella's defensive strategy found its strong-point in denying absolutely the crime of high treason and insisting instead on the prophetic character of his message. Right from the

---

[23] Amabile, *Congiura*, III, doc. 278, pp. 200–201; doc. 279, pp. 204–205.

[24] *Narrazione*, p. 301.

[25] See ch. 7, note 72; see also Vittorio Frajese, 'L'*Atheismus triumphatus* come romanzo filosofico di formazione,' *B&C*, 4 (1998), pp. 313–342.

beginning of the declaration that he made immediately after his arrest, he consistently stressed his foremost interest in prophecy:

> I, brother Tommaso Campanella ... make it manifest to anyone who will see this that I, having been in the Dominican religious order for fifteen years, was interested in diverse fields of science and prophecy in particular. On this account, I was fascinated with those things that give some indication of the future, according to what the Lord God has placed as signs of the future in the things of the world.[26]

The document went on to record how, in the preceding months, he had developed the conviction that in the entire world (and in the Kingdom of Naples in particular) great changes were at hand – changes that had been announced by multiple, concordant signs. The astrologers expected upheavals in the state, in light of an unusual sequence of eclipses and because the great conjunctions – that is to say, the encounters of Saturn and Jupiter – had returned after 800 years in signs of fire, beginning from Sagittarius, just like in the times of Christ and Charlemagne. Changes were announced also in the *Prognosticon de eversione Europae* by the physician and astrologer from Ferrara Antonio Arquato. The text was addressed to the King of Hungary Matthias Corvino in 1480 and was one of the most famous prophetic texts in the sixteenth century. With a disconcerting precision that made modern scholars speculate about a *post eventum* redaction, it seemed to anticipate some of the most unsettling events of the first decades of the century, from the arrival of a 'great heretic in the North' to the sack of Rome and the coming decline of the Turkish empire – of which it was said that in the reign of the fifteenth sovereign it would be divided into two realms, one of which would convert to Christianity. Saints and prophets – from Saint Catherine of Siena to Bridget of Sweden to Joachim of Fiore to Denis the Carthusian to Vincent Ferrer to Savonarola – were said to have hoped for a profound reform of the Church. A metallic sheet had been found recently with the prophecy of a certain Ubertino of Otranto, announcing great upheavals in the south of Italy. To these prophetic indications were added numerous natural signs that seemed to underscore the imminence of the crisis and a kind of fever of the world: comets, destructive earthquakes, rivers topping their banks, torrential downpours and floods, an invasion of grasshoppers, and visions in the sky – as in that of 'a black ladder above which there was a cypress.' To all of that was connected the restlessness of the people and the wide-spread expectations of change: 'I knew that everyone I talked

---

[26] *Dichiarazione*, p. 102.

to was ready for change and on the street every peasant was complaining: for this reason I became ever more convinced that this had to be.'[27]

In organizing his defensive materials in the following months, Campanella maintained the assertion that his own preaching in Calabria and the conversations he had with friends could not qualify as rebellion against Spain. He had not acted with malevolence towards the King. On the contrary, he had written in his favor, bestowing upon him the role of the gatherer of peoples and proclaiming that the Catholic sovereign 'would play the role of Cyrus ...: that with his sword he would in fact liberate the Church from the Babylon represented by the Turks and by the heretics, rebuilding Jerusalem – that is, Rome – and that he would institute the "perpetual sacrifice" all over the world.' Nor had he acted out of ambition. In fact it was clear that 'no one could decide to do things that are impossible, even if he desired them in the abstract.' How could he, a little unarmed friar, challenge the lord of two worlds? Not even a madman could think of drinking the sea or carrying a mountain on his shoulders. Furthermore, he had always abstained from positions of power and riches, preferring to live 'as an ordinary philosopher.' Neither resentment, nor lust for power therefore had been the motive for his action. Instead, he was moved by prophetic inspiration. The desire that the Kingdom of God come and that the earth be made according to his will (as is invoked in the *Our father*) was not yet realized. It would have its completion when 'Christ expels all the single princes, instituting a priestly monarchy.' The project in Calabria, however, was inserted in a precise prophetic context: Campanella did not intend 'to inaugurate a republic for his own advantage, but rather to institute for the Pope and for the King a seminary of men excellent in letters and arms, which the King and the Pontiff could use in matters of peace and war. He wanted to offer almost a preliminary example of the great universal republic one ought to work towards.' In doing this he had followed a divine inspiration, judging that he would have behaved wisely if he should have used the imminent and predicted calamities for a good end: 'yet everything that brother Tommaso said was a warning against an impending evil and not an attempt at rebellion; nor would he have instituted a republic except after the future transformation.'[28]

---

[27] Ibid., p. 108; on the signs, see also *Prima delineatio*, p. 133ff; *Poesie*, p. 496; *Art. proph.*, pp. 295–296. On the prophecy of Arquato, see Germana Ernst, 'Aspetti celesti e profezia politica. Sul *Prognosticon* di Arquato,' *B&C*, 11 (2005), pp. 635–646, and the bibliography indicated there.

[28] *Prima delineatio*, pp. 123ff.

Madness, Reason and Dissimulation

The first period of his Neapolitan incarceration was the most dramatic, and Campanella was conscious of the extremely high risk of being put to death. Rejecting every other defensive strategy, he turned to what seemed to him the only possibility of saving his life – namely, simulating madness. The law in fact forbade putting madmen to death. Given that madmen were incapable of repentance, their executioners would be responsible for the eternal damnation of their souls. Having found himself in a rather desperate situation, Campanella was ready to resort to any expedient. In a sonnet he recalled the great characters of antiquity – from Cato and Hannibal to Cleopatra – who had preferred death to a life that they considered worthless. With suicide rejected, however, he instead resorted to simulating madness, a measure used by other wise men (from David and Solon to Brutus) in order to escape the violence of tyrants.[29] He compared himself to Jonah, symbol and figure of the death and resurrection of Christ, who had accepted being engulfed in the stomach of a whale so that he might later escape to complete the divine command. Just so, Campanella chose to debase himself in prison (which later he would not hesitate to describe as 'worse than a thousand deaths'), in order to preserve, along with his life, the prophetic message of which he was the vessel.[30]

On Easter morning 1600, Campanella was found by his jailers face-down on a half-burnt mattress, uttering disconnected sentences in a cell filled with smoke. Thus began a simulation that would be maintained tenaciously for many months, even though the prisoner would be put under surveillance and surprised by nocturnal interrogations that were supposed to cast doubt on the pretence of madness. At the beginning of June in the following year, the juridical test of madness would be implemented when Campanella was subjected to the extreme torture of the *veglia*, an ordeal that lasted for thirty-six hours. The official written report of the torture cannot be read without horror at this violation and at all the physical suffering inflicted on the suspects. When the moment came to sign a declaration, a disfigured Dionisio Ponzio would have a pen placed in his mouth because he could not use his hands. In the long hours during which his body had been disjointed and broken (between the prayers, the pleas for help, the calls for basic physical needs to be met), Campanella uttered pregnant phrases – such as 'ten white horses' or '1600' – that recalled the plan for the coming of a new age. To those who asked him why he was so worried about his body and not his

---

[29] *Poesie*, n. 62, pp. 259–260; *Rhetorica*, p. 839.

[30] *Poesie*, n. 72, p. 291; n. 62, p. 260. On the relationship between Giona and Campanella, see Germana Ernst, '"Nascosto in ciclopea caverna." Natura e condizione umana in Campanella,' in *Il Neoplatonismo nel Rinascimento* (Rome, 1993), pp. 65–81 and then in Ead, *Il carcere, il politico, il profeta. Saggi su Tommaso Campanella* (Pisa-Rome), 2002, p. 11–34, esp. pp. 31–34.

soul, he replied with sublime simplicity: 'the soul is immortal.' Equally famous is the utterance that Firpo described as 'filled with plebeian vigor.' This was an utterance 'with which he confirmed his own pride at having survived the terrible ordeal' and that was reported by a jailer who was supporting Campanella as he was returning him to his cell: 'what, did they think I was a berk who wanted to talk?'[31] In a passage of the *Medicina*, he would later recall the prison doctor (*vir bonus* – 'a good man') with sober gratitude, for being able, against all hope, to make him well. Presented with a case of bruising 'deep ... and measureless,' he found a way to separate the healthy from the damaged flesh, rendering the damaged parts completely rotten so as to be able to remove them, all to the end of avoiding an infection and permitting the reconstitution of the flesh, and also so as to restore the two pounds Campanella had lost.[32]

Later, these biographical events would take on an exemplary significance. From the fact of having succeeded in not confessing, even as his body was subjected to extreme physical treatment, he drew the conclusion that the human will is not determined by astral influences, which must be much less violent than the tortures he had endured in prison. We find a passage to this effect already at the end of *The City of the Sun*, written immediately after these events. But even many years later Campanella would remember the event and its meaning in a very precise description:

> Even he who has been subjected to torture cannot be compelled to support evil, in thought or in actions ... I had experience of that when, for forty hours, I was strung up from behind with a rope, with my arms twisted and bound by other thin ropes that cut me to the bone. Sitting on a sharpened piece of wood, if I wanted to hold myself up with my arms I experienced an insufferable pain there – at the shoulders, in the chest, and on the neck – and if I lowered myself my buttocks were cut by the piece of wood. Out of the lacerated flesh from the neck of the bladder to the roots of the genitals a great quantity of blood poured out, until finally they gave up torturing me after forty hours, leaving me half dead. Some of those present abused me and intensified the pain, tugging at the ropes; others in their hearts admired the resistance of my spirit. From this experience I know that forfeiting or not forfeiting virtue depends on us. Indeed, I never gave in on anything, nor were they able to extort from me even a single word. Aristotle would have called me unhappy. But if I had followed his principles in order to avoid death, I would have been defeated – enslaved to fear and unworthy of life.[33]

---

[31] Firpo, *Processi*, pp. 265, 267: 'Che si pensavano che io era coglione, che voleva parlare?'

[32] *Medicina*, p. 590. For his entire life, Campanella would bear on his body the signs of the violence he had suffered, as testified to in the famous lines of the *Curiosites inouyes* by Jacques Gaffarel: see ch. 11, note 40.

[33] *Quaest. morales*, I, p. 8.

Beyond these meditations on the independence of virtue and the liberty of the will, the events that followed the Calabrian disaster led him to reflect on the role and fate of the prophet. When society is dominated by madness and the overturning of values, prophets – who are uncomfortable bearers of a truthful message – cannot but be persecuted and put to death. Such distortion of their message and persecution is the work of 'politicians,' who deride prophecy and brand the learned as rebels. They judge everything from their own point of view and project their own personal vision of the world onto others. Dominated by the reductive logic of power, they hold that every human initiative is driven by personal ambition for power. Fearful of losing the object of their desire, they become more prudent and suspicious than the most jealous of lovers: 'Indeed, jealousy of one's kingdom is stronger even than the jealousy one experiences for a woman when her lover fears she may be taken away from him by a passing fly.'[34]

This reflection on the conflict between politicians and prophets (and on all the implications and tensions that it carried with it) was central to Campanella's thought. In the first years of his detention, he wrote a Latin treatise divided into two parts, which is often alluded to but unfortunately lost.[35] The first analyzed the deep reasons underlying the inevitability of this conflict and the execution of prophets. But the second showed how prophets – despite and, indeed, precisely on account of the drama of their end and their apparent defeat – were reborn, after death, because of the loftiness of their message. While their persecutors were hated by all for all time, they were restored to a more enduring life. And that is what is said, with effective simplicity, in the final terzine of the sixteenth sonnet in the *Scelta*:

> He who knows that he is fit for serving
> Persecutes he who appears fit for ruling:
> Martyrdom is a sign of royal virtue.
>
> Such men rule even when they are dead and gone;
> You see tyrants and their laws perish,
> While Peter and Paul rule at Rome.[36]

---

[34] *Prima delineatio*, p. 163.

[35] Firpo, *Bibliografia*, n. 76, p. 187. On the theme of prophecy, see Ernst, *Il carcere, il politico, il profeta*, pp. 61–102; Ead., 'profezia,' in *Enciclopedia*, vol. 1, coll. 303-317; the collected volume *Tommaso Campanella e l'attesa del secolo aureo* (Florence, 1998); Lina Bolzoni, 'Prophétie litteraire et prophétie politique chez T. Campanella,' in *La prophétie comme arme de guerre des pouvoirs (XV–XVII siècles)*, ed. A. Redondo (Paris, 2000), pp. 251–263.

[36] *Poesie*, p. 71: 'Chi si conosce degno di servire,/persegue chi par degno da imperare:/di virtù regia è segnale il martire./ Questi regnan pur morti, a lungo andare: vedi i tiranni e lor leggi perire,/e Pietro e Paulo in Roma or comandare.'

Campanella returned to these themes several times – above all in his letters – to explain and clarify to his interlocutors the meaning of his experience. Among others, one passage in a beautiful Latin letter to the Pope and the Cardinals is highly significant. This was a letter in which he subtly laid bare the perversity of the mechanism by which prophets – chief among them Christ himself – are put to death by satraps and Pharisees, who are fearful of being unmasked and of losing their own privileges:

> And now these Machiavellians, according to whom religion is nothing but a deception made for the purpose of ruling, judge my own intentions on the basis of their own [*ex proprio animo coniectarunt de animo meo*] – and perhaps your own too – and they go about saying that I have said these things in order to set myself up in power. Yet is it perhaps not true that all the prophets and all the wise men – myself among them – have been hit with these same accusations at crucial junctures in history? The satraps and Pharisees (adulators who grow fat off their princes) rise up immediately. They see that sages are announcing the inauguration of a new age and are instilling belief on account of the integrity of their morals, and seeing also that their deceits will be revealed, and that the shadows in which they are shrouded for the purpose of doing evil things will be dispelled and that it will be they who lack the life-blood of lying and deceit. Given that such satraps and Pharisees are not able to say anything against the holy ways of these sages, they recourse to the accusation of rebellion and heresy and attack such men for what they have said simply because it does not accord with what they themselves say. Thus did they rebel against Jeremiah ... and against Isaiah and others; thus did they rebel against the apostles, as if the apostles were deceitful pseudo-prophets, seducers of the kingdom and lusting after it – and Christ is the exemplary figure for all of this.[37]

In an upside-down world in which violence and madness take the place of wisdom, simulation becomes an indispensible shield against persecutors. As Campanella explained in a letter, he feigned madness 'not in order to prolong my life, but for the public benefit to which I am consecrated.'[38] The necessity of dissimulation is expressed well in a famous sonnet, which revisited the parable according to which astrologers – foreseeing thanks to their expertise that a country would be driven crazy by malignant influences – decide to flee, so as to return after the event and 'then rule the injured peoples in a sound manner.'[39] Anton Francesco Doni, editor of the Italian translation of More's *Utopia* (the work of his friend Ortensio Lando), reported the parable in a lively fashion, when he

---

[37] *Lettere*, p. 67.

[38] Ibid., p. 79.

[39] See Lina Bolzoni, 'Le città utopiche del Cinquecento italiano: giochi di spazi e di saperi,' *L'Asino d'oro*, 4 (1993), pp. 64–81: 69ff.

told of how the learned emerge from their refuges triumphant and resolute 'like Easter candles' and come to be derided and swept away by dominant infantile madness. Doni did not refrain from a kind of satisfaction and a sense of bitter and liberating revenge against those who presumed to hold themselves back in safety so as then to profit from the situation and rule over a crazed people.[40] In Campanella, the parable had a different result. Right from its long and obscure title ('Senno senza forza de' savi delle genti antiche esser soggetto alla forza de' pazzi': 'Knowledge without the power of the wise men of ancient peoples is subject to the power of madmen'), the sonnet alludes to the tragic destiny of unarmed prophets, to the inevitable defeat of 'wisdom' unsupported by power in its desperate fight against brute force – and, of course, one is not dealing with 'ancient peoples,' but with quite recent events. When the wise return to give their good counsel, they are punched and kicked. If they want to avoid a worse end, they are forced to stay quiet and simulate, because the greatest madman occupies the throne:

> Such that, forced to do so the wise became used
> To living as dullards, in order to cheat death,
> Because the greatest madman sat on the throne,
>
> They lived, their wisdom shut up behind locked doors,
> Applauding in public with their words and their deeds
> The mad and twisted whims of others.[41]

In the most dramatic moment of his life, Campanella was forced to recourse to the simulation of madness. This is one of the stratagems used by the wise man in order to save himself from tyrannical violence, as Cardano had already pointed out in a beautiful passage of the *De sapientia*:

> The simulation of madness has proved to be of great use to those who are forced to live under irrational and brutal tyrants – just like Brutus, who seeing his relatives murdered by Tarquin, was able (thanks to the simulation of madness) not only to escape the violence of the tyrant, but also to expel him from the kingdom. Thus, simulated madness is equivalent to a double wisdom and in all of human wisdom there is nothing to be found that is greater than the opportune simulation of madness.[42]

---

[40] Anton Francesco Doni, *I Mondi e gli Inferni*, ed. P. Pellizzari (Turin, 1994), pp. 158–161.

[41] *Poesie*, pp. 63-64: 'Talché, sforzati i savi a viver come/gli stolti usavan, per schifar la morte,/ché 'l più gran pazzo avea le regie some,/vissero sol col senno a chiuse porte,/ in pubblico applaudendo in fatti e nome/all'altrui voglie forsennate e torte.'

[42] Girolamo Cardano, *De sapientia*, III, in *Opera omnia*, cura C. Sponii, 10 vols. (Lugduni: I.A. Huguetan & M.A. Ravaud, 1663), I, p. 556; see now the edition of *De sapientia* by M. Bracali (Florence, 2008), p. 207. For Bruto see Livius, I, 56, 7; there is praise for the simulation of madness in Nicolò Machiavelli too, *Discorsi sopra la prima Deca di Tito Livio*, III, 2.

6. PROPHECY, POLITICS AND UTOPIA

Articuli Prophetales

The bare bones of the apologetic document *Secunda delineatio defensionum* would be developed further as the *Articuli prophetales*, a title which had already been used as a sub-title for the original work.[1] The structure of the text lists works by saints and prophets, scholars, philosophers, astrologers, and Sibyls in order to prove the legitimacy of the expectations of the coming of a new golden age, with the following corollaries: the future Christian republic would be saved by a single King and Priest, holder of both spiritual and temporal power; that rulers would take on the role of defenders and ministers of the single monarch; and that the Catholic sovereign is to be identified with the mystical Cyrus, to whom fell the highest task of reunifying the Christian flock.

In order to clarify his own thinking on the 'first resurrection' and on the kingdom of the saints, Campanella specified that three positions could be distinguished. The first position – that of the millenarian heretics – maintained that after the defeat of Gog and Magog a paradise would establish itself on earth. It is from this opinion (condemned by theologians and prophets) that Muhammad derived his conception of a carnal paradise. The second position, rejected by most theologians, although not officially condemned by the Church, was the one maintained by the 'very meek' Fathers of the Church of the first centuries (such as Papias, Irenaeus, Lactantius, Justin Martyr), according to whom holy men alone will rise again before the resurrection of everyone and they will rule with Christ for 1,000 years. But Campanella maintained a third position: the first resurrection was to be identified with the reform and renewal of the Church and in the golden age saints would rise again – not bodily but in spirit and in repute. This reform began in the time of Constantine and would be completed after the defeat of the Antichrist. In that age of peace and justice, ignorance, tribulation, hunger, war, disease, and

---

[1] *Secunda delineatio*, pp. 173–213.

G. Ernst, *Tommaso Campanella,* International Archives of the History of Ideas/Archives internationales d'histoire des idées 200, DOI 10.1007/978-90-481-3126-6_6, © Springer Science+Business Media B.V. 2010

the gross sins that now reign would all be extinguished. In this republic Christ would rule with the Apostles, not visibly but in an invisible way, thanks to the observance of their doctrines. In the fourth chapter of the *Articuli* the author offers a *Clavis mirabilis* that permitted the unveiling of divine prophecies that were latent in Holy Scripture. He explained the legitimacy of interpretation *per figuras* and identified all the possible analogies between sacred history and human history. Following the *Clavis*, there came its concrete application, in which the author performed a re-reading of the entire history of the Church, establishing elaborate correspondences between the days of creation, the millennia of the world, the ages of the synagogue and those of the church, and at last the angels, seals, trumpets, and phials of the Apocalypse.

In the *Articuli*, considerable space was reserved for astronomy and its results. Campanella believed Copernicus to be 'extremely wise,' 'preferable to everyone,' and took Sibyl from the *Progymnasmata* of Tycho Brahe the prophecy of the Tiburtine Sibyl, which had assumed a particular significance after the appearance of a new star in 1572. Against Aristotle, who held the heavens to be unchangeable and the motions of the stars to be perpetual, new phenomena in the heavens demonstrated that the *machina mundi* did not remain immobile and immutable, but rather moved in space and underwent change. Campanella attempted to reinterpret the great events of history in the light of such changes, so as to be capable of making reasonable conjectures about the future. The final chapter of the *Articuli* (which would later be identified as the *Prognosticum astrologicum* sent to Galileo to which Campanella alluded in a letter of 1611) was dedicated to this 'unusual astrology' of the cosmos. This unusual variant integrated traditional astrology (based on the great conjunctions, eclipses, and comets) with the interpretation of other astronomical facts, from the precession of the equinoxes to the displacement of the apogees and the progressive constriction of the solar obliquity.[2] More worthy of emphasis was the fact that the variations of the velocity of the stars turned out to be irregular. The heavenly bodies moved 'now more quickly, now more slowly *ad nutum Dei* ('according to God's will'). If we ask ourselves why the anomaly was quicker in the times of Muhammad and Saint Gregory, while now it is slower, we do not find any reason other than divine will: 'the heavens do not move according to our measures (which until now have always remained deceptive and erroneous), but rather according to the measure of divine providence.' If calculations of the life-span of the universe (on which chronologists, astronomers, and theologians have exhausted themselves) turned out to be discordant and did not offer certainty, if it is true that the end of times for the world is unknown just as the day of our death is unknown to us, then – so Campanella affirmed – it was necessary to remain always vigilant. He was convinced that the end was nigh and that all the signs that would announce it

---

[2] See the introduction to the *Art. proph.*, pp. XXXVIIff.

had appeared, including those 'of the sun, moon, and stars,' as prophesied in the Gospel according to Luke.

The fourteenth chapter of the *Articuli* is dedicated to the Antichrist, a subject that in those years had acquired a pressing actuality on account of the polemics with the reformers, who identified the Antichrist with the Pope. In these pages, Campanella occupied himself with an exacting hermeneutical interpretation of passages from the Book of Revelation and the prophet Daniel, so as to specify who the precursors of the Antichrist had been in history and in the various kingdoms, and so as to formulate relevant conjectures on the coming of the last, more terrible figure. The central figure in this discussion was Muhammad, who is to be identified with the beast with seven heads and ten horns referred to in Book of Revelation. From his seed would originate the 'little horn' (*cornu parvum*), the last Antichrist who would recapitulate in his person all the evils and the persecutions suffered by Christianity in the past. The last and most renowned of the precursors of the Antichrist was Luther, whose doctrines presented (and not by chance for Campanella) notable affinities with Islamic beliefs: they both sharply circumscribed human liberty and proposed a tyrannical God, who commands us to do good but pushes us irresistibly to do evil. This is a God made in their image and similitude – 'impious, deceitful, tyrannical, cruel, fraudulent, and jealous.'[3]

Another amply treated point dealt with the desolation of Rome, a punishment that would probably be inflicted by the Turks, to whom fell the role of *flagellum Dei* ('scourge of God'). Some very harsh pages are dedicated to this thematic. These are pages that present an extremely dark picture of Christianity, giving the *Articuli* some rather gloomy, threatening tones. The authority most cited in order to confirm the catastrophe of Rome is St. Bridget of Sweden, 'the most illustrious of the Sibyls,' whose *Revelationes* were an important step in his own intellectual and spiritual autobiography, as Campanella himself indicated. In chapter eight, passages from the Swedish saint are recalled concerning the reunification of peoples in a single faith and the appearance of a universal reformer (whom Campanella suggested ought to be identified with the angelic Pope predicted by Joachim of Fiore). Chapters nine and ten included passages that threatened the most extreme punishments for Christians who had strayed from the evangelical message, but above all for the clergy and for the Pope, who, on account of cupidity for riches and ambitions for power, had reduced the Church into a crumbling edifice, close to a ruinous collapse, in a field where only discord and weeds grow, ready to be rooted out by a powerful ploughman.

Amidst this forest of texts and authors, Campanella paid special attention to his Dominican brothers, convinced that his own order (identified with the

---

[3] *Art. proph.*, pp. 202–203.

third quadriga of the vision of Zachariah and the white horse of the Apocalypse that appears victorious at the opening of the first seal) was to play
a prominent role in the anticipated reform of the Church. He manifested a
particular attachment to Catherine of Siena and cited Raymond of Capua,
St. Vincent Ferrer, and friar Rusticiano with pride. In the *Articuli*, we also
find a reference to Savonarola. In truth, Campanella (in a somewhat reticent
fashion) preferred to abstain from judgment on the person of Savonarola and
his undertaking (*sive bonus, sive malus*, 'whether good or bad'). But he did
not fail to cite the *Oracolo della renovatione della Chiesa*, which the faithful
disciple Luca Bettini had recovered from Savonarola's sermons and prepared
for the press. But the text was, in turn, put on the Index in 1558. Against the
background of such caution, which understandably resulted from the risks
involved in praising a condemned and controversial figure of the likes of
Savonarola, one can perhaps also detect fear of a dangerous conflation. Campanella insisted on distinguishing prophecy from political initiative in his
defensive declarations. He was extremely careful to repel every suspicion
of having wanted to exercise political power personally. The same accusation
had been leveled at Savonarola, and shone through in the famous judgment
of Machiavelli regarding unarmed prophets. In the eighteenth chapter of the
Atheismus triumphatus (aimed at demonstrating how the teachings of Machiavelli might in truth prove themselves to be ineffectual and unsuccessful),
Campanella rejected the derision heaped upon prophets by the Florentine
Secretary: they move on a completely different level from that of politicians,
since they speak on God's power (*Dei iussu*) and not on the human cause
for domination (*dominandi causa*). The politician is not able to understand
the prophet. Applying to him his own criteria and perspectives, the politician judges him to be someone easily defeated. In truth, the contrary is the
case and it is politics that is in need of prophecy, which must be integrated
and the absence of which condemns politics to failure and disappointment.
Entrenched behind the suspension of judgment, Campanella could do no
more than express a deep admiration for the touching commentaries on the
Psalms written by the Dominican friar on the eve of his tragic end: 'Shortly
before his death he showed great penitence and sanctity, writing emotively
of the consolation of death in a commentary to Psalms 31 and 50. A counterfeit Machiavellian would not have been able to read let alone write
such words inspired as they were by fervor of spirit and by a kind of lived
experience.'[4] In a few, intense lines of the *Syntagma*, Campanella expressed a
frank recognition of the extraordinary gifts of Savonarola, whose power as a
preacher ought to be contrasted to the vacuous facility of Cornelio Musso and

---

[4] *Ath. triumph.*, p. 235.

the other moderns who 'flower but do not bear fruit.' The judgment on the incisiveness of Savonarola's style became a judgment on the exceptionality of the person: 'even if on many points he fell into error, Savonarola was a great preacher: he inflamed the spirits of his listeners, forced the seeds of virtue to bear fruit, actively rid the soul of futile thoughts, and finally exposed vice and gutted them.[5]

Political Bonds

Two brief but extremely intense pieces date back to the earliest period in prison: the *Aforismi politici* and the *Città del Sole*. Together they represent the two poles of Campanella's political thought – the one 'realistic,' shot through with echoes of Machiavelli, and the other prophetic and utopian.

For the dryness of its style and the acuity of its contents, the *Aforismi* is one of the most successful of Campanella's political tracts. In all probability, it was composed at the end of 1601. Given to Schoppe in 1607, the text was not published as expected but circulated in a number of different manuscripts, which were read at once, used and also conspicuously plagiarized.[6] Later translated into Latin, extended and reorganized, the work would come to constitute the third part of the *Philosophia realis* under the title *De politica*.[7] It would have an exceptional reader in Hugo Grotius, who glossed the text with acute, even if often critical and prickly, observations.[8] In a text that was seen as his only treatment of political science 'going beyond every particular contingency, intent on locating general principles,' Campanella adopted a terse and edgy mode of expression. He analyzed questions concerning the constitution and organization of every kind of political community, formulating rules and counsels regarding their acquisition, preservation, decline, and death. The text makes precise use of *exempla* drawn from history both ancient and modern. Above all, however, it draws on the principles of Campanella's own philosophy – thereby rendering even the treatment of traditional themes strikingly original.[9]

The aphorisms follow on from each other in a concise and cumulative rhythm. They begin with the assertion that the 'naturalness' (as opposed to

---

[5] *Syntagma*, IV, 3, p. 98.

[6] See Rodolfo De Mattei, 'Materiali campanelliani nella *Philosophia regia* di G. A. Brancalasso,' *GCFI*, 26 (1947), pp. 373–393; see ch. 3, notes 23, 24.

[7] There is now a modern edition with an Italian translation of the *De politica* by A. Cesaro (Naples, 2001).

[8] The *Observata* of Grotius can be found in *Aforismi pol.*, p. 229ff.

[9] Luigi Firpo, introduction to the *Aforismi pol.*, p. 10.

the 'violence') of a dominion over a community presupposes that this community is itself natural in the sense that whosoever brings them together does so 'for the mutual natural good'. Natural communities exist on several levels: the most immediate level of man and woman, then that of families, those of cities, of kingdoms and finally 'of all men in the human species.' Campanella reaffirmed that 'dominion and community is more natural where the good is more common to all; that dominion is more violent where such commonality is absent.' The articulation of one of the central and recurrent principles of Campanella's thought follows – namely, that of the three kinds of bonds that bind the members of a community together (the goods of the soul, the goods of the body, and the goods of fortune, or riches). The healthiest bond is the first. The goods of the soul are obtained and conserved by 'rational religion, which is the soul of politics and which derives from natural law.' It has the capacity even to unite nations that are extremely different and distant. Virtue determines the degree of 'naturalness' in the person who commands: 'he rules by nature who is first in virtue. He who lacks virtue by nature serves. Where one does the contrary, there is violent dominion.' In turn, virtue in politics is connected to force of spirit, or body, or both. An exemplary case of the predominance of the former is Ulysses; for the second, Ajax; for the two combined, Caesar. Communities are classified according to dominion, defined as 'the highest power of the republic,' which is nothing other than 'the power of mercy, that is power over life and death,' held by one alone, by many, or by all (or in a mixed form). The author discussed diverse types of government (and their positive and negative forms), together with the internal and external causes of their transformation.

In the aphorisms that followed, Campanella announced themes that would later be taken up and developed further, asserting that 'only non-sophistical, genuinely philosophical – not hermitic, but civil – wisdom rules well and naturally.' 'Wisdom' has the function of integrating and also of inverting the 'natural' relations of dominion – for example, between male and female, the strong and the weak. Thus, underlining the diversity of those natural attitudes in different persons, Campanella identified the fundamental characteristic of the best republic as the correspondence between natural inclinations and social roles – which signifies the greater value of reason over chaos: 'the best republic is the one in which each is elected to perform that duty for which he was born, so that in this way reason may reign. That republic is worst in which each individual performs duties contrary to those for which he was born, so that chaos reigns.' In the following aphorism, which deplores the allocation of duties and honors according to incorrect criteria, the point is rendered more precisely:

> Where from early childhood duties are allocated according to natural aptitude by wise and unperturbed public experts, there the republic becomes most flourishing. But where people enter offices by chance – that is, they

become king because they are the sons of the king, they are officials because they are the sons of the nobility, or because they are relations or friends of the ruling class, or because they are rich and buy their way into power, and not because they are good and wise – there the republic is always ruined.[10]

The realization of this correspondence (which is vital for the state) requires the law, which is described as 'the consensus of the reason that is common to all, written and promulgated for the common good and conforming to eternal reason.' The eternal law is the law of nature, which 'is a rule and reason implanted in us and in the world; it is the art of God.' Human laws, which have contingent aspects directed at resolving particular problems and addressing particular needs, ought to follow natural law. It is that connection with eternal law that confers the quality of justice and equity on civil law. If political law can in some cases contravene the letter of the eternal law (but not its deeper sense), then the reason of state of modernity is instead a kind of counterfeiting and distortion of equity: 'Reason of state is a name dreamt up by tyrants on the model of *epichea* or equity. It appeared to them that in order to conserve the state they might transgress any law, and do the same in order to acquire a state. But the difference is that while equity looks to the public good, the reason of state considers the private good of the ruler.'[11]

The best laws are always 'few and brief.' They have to adjust themselves not simply to the common good but also to the customs and characteristics of the people, taking into account the diversity of climates and temperaments. For northern peoples ('fierce by nature' and intolerant of any restriction) liberal laws will be suitable, while for southern peoples, 'on account of the fact they are physically weak and cunning, only principalities that command by the rod and with severe laws are appropriate.' Guardians of the laws will be, according to a precise order that is not to be altered, the honor of those who observe it, the love of the useful that goes to those who observe it, and the fear of punishment of those who transgress the law. One of the primary ends at which the law must aim is that of establishing an 'equality, beneficial to the republic' and to eliminate 'destructive inequality.' As would be reaffirmed later in the *The City of the Sun*, 'people who are too poor are rapacious, scheming, and perfidious,' while 'people who are too rich are arrogant and dissolute.' Likewise, 'people who are too ignorant are ruinous,' while 'people who are too shrewd are extremely unreliable.' From here derives the extremely lofty role of the legislator, to whom it falls to coordinate all the sciences and arts of the republic and to know 'the customs of the country and the good and

---

[10] *Aforismi pol.*, 28 and 29, p. 99.

[11] Ibid., 35, p. 102; see Germana Ernst, 'ragion di Stato,' in *Enciclopedia*, vol. 1, coll. 317–329.

bad fortunes that ordinarily come to that country from the stars, or from the earth, or from its neighbors.' But the true secret of the legislator – defined as he 'who founds a state under new religious and legal auspices, arms and rites' – is that of being the messenger of God, like Moses, or presenting oneself in that way, as Minos, Muhammad, Jupiter, Osiris and other highly astute politicians did. These were politicians who 'pretended to be sent by God in order to gain credit, because the legislator must be very highly praised, extremely wise, divine, religious, and superhuman.' The wisest human legislator will take the human body as a model of the republic:

> As its soul, the republic has wisdom and religion. As its body, it has the senate and the council and all those who may take office. As external goods, it has soldiers, mercenaries and auxiliaries, if they do not partake in government or possess some office. As the spirit that connects the soul and the body, it has the law. For its eyes, the republic has the wise investigators of the sciences. For its ears, it has merchants and spies. For its tongue, it has preachers and ambassadors. For its hands, it has soldiers; for feet, artists and farmers. As sustenance for the goods of body and soul, it has the goods of fortune – that is servants, provisions, and moneys.[12]

Articulating one of the other fundamental motifs of his thought, Campanella affirmed that there are three instruments for 'acquiring, preserving, and governing' states: language, arms, and wealth. He also lingered for a time to analyze the duration and stability, strength and weakness of political formations in relationship to the impact of such factors. Taking up themes that were already present in the *Monarchia di Spagna*, the author emphasized the fittingness of mixing peoples, 'planting them like trees so as to make them stronger, and destroying old stock and dying plants.' He delineated a doctrine of three causes, that govern every political formation in modes and proportions that are different and more or less evident: God, prudence, and chance. From the insufficiency of human prudence derives the necessity, which extends to every political formation, to establish a communicative relationship with divinity, through oracles and prophets. From here came the importance of the role of priests, whose characteristics – of wisdom, force, and mercy – are made prominent in aphorism eighty. The soul of politics is thus religion. Religions and sects, like republics, 'have their own cycles.' When they arrive at atheism, denying the immortality of the soul or divine providence, then is 'born the final evil inflicted on the people and the end of the wrath of God.' This is followed 'necessarily by reform or change,' as many examples will confirm, and as the most recent examples of the Reformation will also illustrate. On the basis of such principles one is able to affirm the power of the Papacy – 'the

---

[12] Ibid., n. 58, p. 109.

armed Christian priesthood' – which is necessary for Christian princes. The Pope is 'the just arbiter of war and peace, and intervenes with arms on the part of he who has right on his side, and forces he who is in the wrong to concede, and unites them both against the enemies of Christianity.' In contrast, no single 'Christian king has ever been able to maintain a monarchy over all of Christendom by himself, because the Pope is above him and arranges and lays waste to his plans.' Having condemned every apostasy and heresy, Campanella foresaw that with all the cycles of all the changes completed, 'one will come to the first natural, divine reign, the rule of a King and a Priest in one.' He foresaw that one would reach 'a prime, innocent, natural state' through prophecy and by means of 'the cycle of things.'

Campanella insisted on distancing himself from the principles of the reason of state. Aphorism ninety-six is dedicated to a precise comparison between prudence and cunning, so as to underscore how the first (which follows with divine wisdom) aims at the well-being of the collective, while the second (daughter of egoistic individuality) concerns itself solely with the benefit of he who holds power:

> Prudence is the mark of a true king, to whom – after God – the kingdom belongs, and prudence is the opposite of cunning, which is the mark of the tyrant. Prudence agrees with God, that is with the primary intelligence, whereas cunning agrees with one's own will. Prudence is magnanimous, while cunning is arrogant and vile. Prudence exalts the great, the wise, and the strong. But cunning casts them down and kills them in order to rule without healthy dispute. Prudence invests in the minds of men and large numbers, whereas cunning invests in money and strong walls, diminishing its vassals ... Prudence studies in the religion of nature, while cunning is immersed in a superstitious religiosity that oppresses the minds of men so as to rule over them in a contemptible manner. Prudence takes the customs of a people and the nature of a climate into account, as well as the variations that have existed in the past and continue to exist in the present throughout the world in comparison to that which holds steady amidst so many varying things. Cunning, on the other hand, considers only that which is important in its back garden and only that which is important to its own household and time ... Prudence concentrates on steering; cunning, on the rowers ... Prudence passes laws that are for the good of all, while cunning passes laws that are good for itself alone ... Prudence deceives people for their own good and once discovered it is loved all the more. Cunning deceives people only in order to benefit itself and when it is discovered it becomes hateful.[13]

---

[13] Ibid., pp. 122–123. For studies of the relationship between Campanella and Machiavelli, see ch. 4, note 75.

Notwithstanding the polemics and attempts to distinguish his own thoughts, there are undoubtedly echoes of Machiavelli in the *Aphorisms* as in the *Monarchia di Spagna*, the unscrupulousness of which is justified insofar as these texts are inserted into and justified within a Christian and religious context. Recall, for example, the counsel to extinguish the nobility and the royal line (as the Turks do), so as to render succession more secure; or recall the advice of not inflicting punishments in person, except for those desired by all 'as in extinguishing usurers and rapacious officials'; likewise, recall the counsel of exposing governors and ministers who have exasperated and extorted their subjects to the wrath of the people, as Cesare Borgia did. As Machiavelli noted, Borgia ordered the quartering and displaying in the main square of Cesena of his own lieutenant Ramiro de Lorqua, so as to vent upon him the populace's hatred;[14] or again, recall the radicalness and speed of the suggested measures in the occupation of subjugated countries:

> He who acquires a new kingdom ought to inflict the following evils on his subjects – that is, cast down their leaders, change the laws, raise their fortresses to the ground, extinguish and exile the royal family. All these things ought to be carried out on the day of victory itself, by the hand and in the name of the victorious soldiers and captains. Rewards are to be handed out one at a time, not all together, gradually after victory, by one's own hand and in one's own name.[15]

In the final part of the *Aforismi*, Campanella dwells at some length on an analysis of all the possible causes of change and the decline of kingdoms and republics. It surveys the diverse problems that can present themselves, with precise references to episodes from ancient and modern history, and suggests opportune remedies from time to time. Among the principal causes of change was the appearance of new prophets ('where prophecy inclines, so inclines the state'), contests between aristocratic and popular classes, problems connected to the army or to an excess of taxes and tributes, and many others. Also sketched is the danger constituted by a possible 'conspiracy of strong and wise men':

> As a remedy, wise and strong men ought to be separated under the pretence of honoring them with high office in diverse regions. Their loyalty must be secured by means of rewards, they should not be extinguished but co-opted into the government, because ruin is more certain when the worthless and the ignorant are taken into government and given distinction. Just so, it is

---

[14] The episode, recalled frequently by Campanella, is taken from ch. 7 of Machiavelli's *Principe*.

[15] *Aforismi pol.*, n. 100, p. 124.

more dangerous when virtue hides itself, fearing the tyrant, because when the opportunity comes such virtue will arm itself against the prince, as Brutus and other wise men did. One must always put courage in the limelight, for the hidden fire does more harm.[16]

The Body Politic: The City of the Sun

Some three years after the fateful events of Calabria, it took Campanella six months to recover from the damage done to his health by the tortures he had suffered, and he was now in a state of mind of renewed hope after having managed to save his life by overcoming such terrible ordeals. He immediately started writing his most famous work, the short poetical dialogue which he called *The City of the Sun (Città del Sole)*.

As has been acutely said, the work presented itself as both the program for a failed insurrection and its philosophical idealization.[17] In giving it to the press in 1623 (when it appeared, in Latin, as an appendix to the *Politica*), Tobias Adami – struck by its purity and luminosity – defined it as a precious stone and identified the superiority of this ideal community with respect to the models proposed by Plato in antiquity and by Thomas More in recent times insofar as it had been inspired by the great model of nature. In fact, the references to nature, understood as an expression of an intrinsic divine art, and the critique of society, as it then existed (unhappy and unjust precisely because it was distant from that natural model, or because it did not imitate it in the right way), are the keys to a more simple and more persuasive reading of Campanella's utopia. In other political works, Campanella analyzed (often in a completely disenchanted manner) the harsh reality of his time and suggested remedies for correcting and holding in check the worst ills. In *The City of the Sun*, he adopted a different point of view. On a blank slate he sketched a map at once simple and detailed of a city that did not exist – 'a philosophical idea of a republic' and 'a poetical dialogue' – so as to suggest the criteria and the norms of a possible community in which men might live a more just and harmonious life. Aristotle himself, while emphasizing the differences between poetry and history, had pointed out that while history relates the particular as it happened, poetry deals with the universal and with what might happen.[18]

The city would be more united and happy the more it was a 'political body.' In proposing a new model of knowledge (based on direct investigation of

---

[16] Ibid., 129, pp. 134–135.

[17] Norberto Bobbio, introduction to his own edition of the *Città del Sole* (Turin, 1941), pp. 31–34. There is a bibliography of the various editions of the work in Margherita Palumbo, *La* Città del Sole. *Bibliografia delle edizioni. 1623–2002* (Pisa-Rome, 2004).

[18] Aristotle, *Poëtica*, IX, 1451b.

nature and not only on the books of philosophers), Campanella often recalled the image of the 'book of nature.' When he dealt with political association he made use of another great naturalistic image – that of the 'body,' apt to communicate a multiplicity of significations. The 'republic' is a living organism that ought to aim at preserving and improving its own health (including its physical health). Like all organisms, it is made up of multiple members that are differentiated by duty and function. Yet they are all working towards the well-being of the whole, a well-being that was the condition and horizon of the well-being of the individual parts.

Protected and defended by seven circles of walls, in which the dwelling places are incorporated, the city is located in a place with an ideal climate that is favorable to its physical well-being on the slopes of a hill so that the air is lighter and more pure. One of the most important aspects of this community is the conception and distribution of work. Once again, Campanella explicitly criticized Aristotle, who excluded artisans, peasants, and anyone who worked at manual labor from both the class of citizens who enjoyed full rights and also the highest levels of virtue. In the *Syntagma*, Campanella urged 'diligent consultation with painters, dyers, blacksmiths, jewelers, goldsmiths, peasants, soldiers, artillerymen, weavers, distillers, and other artisans,' so that in their workshops and in their activities there would exist 'a philosophy more real and true than in the schools of philosophy.'[19] For the Solarians, no activity is vile or base and everyone has equal dignity. In fact, those from whom greater labors are required (such as the blacksmith and the builder) are more praiseworthy. Everyone learns every trade and then each one practices that for which he shows the greatest aptitude. Even those who have physical disabilities contribute according to their capabilities. The Solarians have no slaves. They can fulfill their own needs, and no service is held to be undignified: 'no one holds it a dishonor to serve in the dining hall, in the kitchen or elsewhere; instead they call it learning, and they say that just so it is an honor to walk on one's feet and equally an honor to see with one's eyes.' They find laziness alone despicable, coming thereby to privilege the dignity of work and to overturn an absurd notion of nobility, bound up with inactivity and vice. Thus, 'he is held to be the greatest noble, who learns the most trades, or does them better. For this reason, the Solarians mock us for calling artisans ignoble and for describing as noble those who learn no skill, are lazy, and hold so many servants in a sloth and lasciviousness that ruins the republic.'[20]

Owing to the equal division of labor, it is sufficient that each person dedicates him or herself to work activities for four hours a day. But it is imperative

---

[19] *Syntagma*, II, 5, p. 78.
[20] *Città del Sole*, pp. 23, 13.

that everyone work, because the laziness of some would have repercussions for the exploitation and labor of others. This imperative follows from the most resentful observation in the dialogue, in which the outside world with all its injustice and suffering erupts violently into the serene atmosphere of the City of the Sun:

> There are three hundred thousand souls in Naples; yet barely fifty thousand of them are working; and these fifty thousand struggle with a quantity of work that is enough to kill them. The others become prey to idleness, avarice, lasciviousness and usury, and corrupt people by holding them in servitude and poverty.[21]

With regard to possessions and property, the Solarians own nothing. Everything is communal – from the meals to the houses, from the learning of the sciences to the exercising of political functions, from honors to entertainment, from women to children. There is an official who is charged with the distribution of all things and who makes sure that this happens in accordance with justice, but no one is permitted to appropriate anything. According to the Solarians, the possession of a house and of a family cannot but reinforce the 'love of self,' with all the sad consequences that this generates: 'they say that all property derives from making a house apart and taking children and wives for oneself, whence comes the love of self, which – so as to raise a child to riches and titles, and leave an heir to wealth – makes everyone either a public bird of prey (if, being strong, he has no fear) or avaricious and scheming and hypocritical (if he is weak).' They have chosen community, 'living philosophically together,' also because they are aware of the negative repercussions, both moral and social, of an unequal distribution of wealth: 'they also say that great poverty makes men vile, cunning, thieves, scheming, outlaws, liars, false witnesses; and that riches make men insolent, arrogant, ignorant, treacherous, disillusioned, and presumptuous about things they do not understand. Yet the community there makes everyone both rich and poor: rich, because they have and possess everything; poor, because they do not become attached to serving things, but instead let things serve them.'[22]

One of the most spectacular and imaginative features of *The City of the Sun*, which immediately strikes its readers, is the description of the painted walls. The seven walls are not only circles for enclosing and protecting the city. They are also the wings of an extraordinary theater and the pages of an illustrated encyclopedia of knowledge. Among the promises listed in his

---

[21] Ibid., pp. 23–24.
[22] Ibid., p. 25.

letters, Campanella made a commitment to build 'a city admirable to the King, healthy and impregnable, which would impart all the sciences historically just by looking at it.'[23] The external walls of the buildings are decorated with images of all the arts and sciences.

Starting with the wall supporting the columns of the temple and all the way down the various circuits of walls (in a manner parallel to the order of the planets from Mercury to Saturn), we encounter the representation of the heavens and of the stars, of mathematical figures, of every country of the earth 'with its rites, customs, and laws.' After that we come across all the wonders and secrets of the mineral, vegetable, and animal worlds and eventually reach men: on the internal wall of the sixth circle are represented 'all the mechanical arts and their inventors.' Campanella expressed the greatest interest in every ingenious discovery and in the city he provided many examples of his curious devices – from vessels capable of sailing without wind to carts with sails to stirrups that permit one to guide horses using only one's feet, thereby leaving the hands free. On the external wall of the same circle are represented 'all the inventors of laws and sciences and arms.' And it is here that the Genoese sailor of Columbus – who is one of the interlocutors of the dialogue, together with the Hospitaller [24] – recognizes Christ and the twelve apostles, in 'a place of high esteem' (alongside Moses, Osiris, Jupiter, Mercury, and Muhammad).

Knowledge is not closed up in books kept in separate spaces like libraries. Instead, it is displayed before the eyes of all. Visualization favors a more rapid reception of things and so the Solarians would learn in one year what among us is learnt in the course of ten or fifteen years. Visualization renders learning easier and more effective, in that it is connected to the art of memory, which insists on the evocative and emotive force of images. From a very tender age, children experience this theater of knowledge with appropriate guidance and according to a suitable rhythm and itinerary, and they learn with joy, as if playing, without effort or pain. The Metaphysician, the political and spiritual leader, ought to be the wisest of all. To the possible objection of the incompatibility between politics and philosophy ('he who attends to the sciences cannot know how to govern'), the Solarians reply that it is always better to entrust oneself to a wise man who, even if not an expert, will not be malicious, unlike 'you who suffer the ignorant, thinking that they are well-suited because they are born lords or are elected by powerful factions.' But

---

[23] *Lettere*, p. 28.

[24] A knight of the Order of St. John of Jerusalem, also known as the Order of Malta. On the character of Hospitaller, see Jean-Paul De Lucca, 'Prophetic Representation and Political Allegorisation: the Hospitaller in Campanella's *The City of the Sun*,' *B&C*, 15 (2009), pp. 387–405.

the real response emphasizes the different conception of knowledge held by the Solarians, who do not hold that 'he is wise who knows most grammar and logic from Aristotle (or any other author), in which case one only needs a servile memory, whence man makes himself inert, because he does not contemplate things but rather books, and abases his soul in those dead things.' The Metaphysician is 'swift of mind in all things.' He knows 'all the histories of the peoples and rites and sacrifices and republics and inventors of laws and arts.' He knows all the mechanical arts and all the sciences. And above all it is important that he be a 'metaphysician and theologian, who knows well the source and proof of all the arts and sciences, together with the similarities and differences of things.'[25]

Beyond the sharing of possessions and the painted walls, another aspect distinguishes the City of the Sun. It is a problematic and disconcerting point, one that Campanella himself presented as 'difficult and arduous' – namely, the sharing of women. The solution adopted by the Solarians addressed a specific problem: reproduction. Echoing the Pythagorean teachings of Ocellus of Lucania, Campanella said that the Solarians 'laugh at those of us who concern ourselves with the breeding of dogs and horses while neglecting our own.'[26] Reproduction is a basic problem for the city, and as such 'it is regulated religiously for the public and not the private good.' The reproductive act carries with it a great responsibility on the part of he who reproduces, and if that responsibility is exercised in an incorrect way it can give rise to a long chain of sufferings. Moreover, there is a tight connection between natural 'complexion' (which is primordial and not modifiable) and moral virtue, which in order to take root and prosper requires suitable terrain: 'they say that the purity of the complexion, out of which virtues develop, cannot be acquired by art and that only with difficulty can moral virtue take root without a natural disposition. They also say that men of an evil nature act well out of fear of the law and, in the absence of that, they destroy the republic both openly and secretly.'[27] For that reason, reproduction will have to respect precise norms, and should neither be entrusted to chance, nor to individual feelings. Indeed, the Solarians distinguish between love and the exercising of sexuality. The attraction between men and women (which is founded on friendship and respect more than 'ardent concupiscence') is expressed honorably and with a considerable gentleness that is very distant from sexuality. If 'a man falls in love with a woman, it is licit for them to speak to each other, to write poems, and to exchange jokes and floral arrangements.' In the evening, after dinner,

---

[25] *Città del Sole*, p. 13.

[26] See ibid., p. 10; *Quaestio quarta politica*, art. 3, note 10, in *Città del Sole* (1996) p. 155.

[27] *Città del Sole*, p. 21.

when 'hymns of love, wisdom, and of every other virtue are being sung,' 'each man takes the woman that he loves the most, and they dance under the beautiful cloisters.'[28] Reproductive sexuality has to respect an entire series of conditions, concerning above all the arrangement of 'judicious mating' with respect to physical and moral endowments and with respect to the choice of the right time (set by astrology, which in the City of the Sun plays a fundamental role, in that it is a kind of cosmic watch that indicates the best times for putting human events in agreement with the requisite celestial configurations).[29] Some of the most curious stipulations concern philosophers and priests, who are not permitted to reproduce 'if they do not fulfill a number of other conditions for many days.' Aristotle had already observed that the children of great men are often of limited value, and Campanella explained that wise men have weak animal spirits. Given that they are always engrossed in contemplation, during the sexual act they hold back the finest and most noble spirits of the brain, releasing only those lowest spirits: 'on account of the large amount of speculation, they are weak in animal spirits and they do not release the valuable spirits of the head, because they are always thinking about something, and because of this they make unfortunate progeny.'[30] In the City of the Sun, mating happens in a rarefied and cold atmosphere, in a context of precisely calculated astral positions: the union is not the expression of a personal relationship, and it is completely devoid of affective or passionate drives other than those of the social responsibility involved in generation and love for the collective.

Beyond the role of reproducers, women have an important function in the City of the Sun. Freed from the burden of raising and educating children individually, they engage in the same practical activities as the men – avoiding only the most tiring. They learn the speculative sciences and they can dedicate themselves to the arts, such as painting or music. Nor did Campanella exclude women from an auxiliary and defensive military role. Recalling the example of the ancient Amazons and of modern warrior-maidens defending the African empire of Monopotapa, he rejected the criticisms of Aristotle and of his Telesian friend Giacomo di Gaeta, who held that the use of arms was unnatural for women and incompatible with their natural role as mothers. The beauty of the Solarian women is an expression of the energy and health that derive from appropriate physical exercise. It is on this account that the inhabitants are banned from wearing clothes and shoes that render them clumsy, and they punish the use of make-up severely. On other occasions too, Campanella did not fail to deplore the use of female make-up, with which women

---

[28] Ibid., pp. 23, 45.
[29] Ibid., pp. 20, 22.
[30] Ibid., pp. 20–21.

are forced to mask the paleness that comes from a lazy and unhealthy lifestyle that is damaging to one's health and therefore to future off-spring.[31]

The Solarian religion (which recognizes fundamental Christian principles such as the immortality of the soul and divine providence) is a natural religion that sets up a kind of osmosis between the heavens and the stars. The temple is open and not closed in with walls; in a poem Campanella promised that 'I will make a temple out of the sky, with the stars as an altar.' In the prose commentary that accompanied the poem, he explained that 'God ought to be adored *in spiritu et veritate* (in spirit and in truth), and not under roofs of mud that lightning bolts and even the nests of birds put to shame.'[32]

On the inner surface of the cupola of the temple, the stars are represented with their correspondences to terrestrial entities. There is only one altar, in the form of the sun, and on it are placed, side by side, the two globes of the heavens and the earth. Prayers are addressed to the sky. The function of the twenty-four priests that live in cells located in the highest part of the temple (which is also a kind of astronomical observatory) is that 'of watching the stars and noting all their movements with astrolabes and the effects that they produce.' They 'stipulate the times for reproduction and the days for sowing and harvesting, and they serve as mediators between God and men.'[33]

Notwithstanding the undoubted affinities between the Calabrian initiative of 1599 and the subsequent utopia, unscrupulous heterodox doctrines are completely absent in the pages of *The City of the Sun*. Instead, a chaste naturalism dominates Campanella's dialogue, which possesses no polemical or aggressive tone. Even if in the course of years the text would be subjected to a process of attenuation, there was nothing from the first version that was not later taken up again and explained by the author. Already in these pages Campanella had embarked upon the road that he would continue to travel, communicating the intuition that he would later develop and perfect: between nature and religion there is no conflict or antagonism, but instead continuity and harmony. Nature is not presented as a weapon with which to unmask religious imposture. Religion

---

[31] See ch. 10, p. 183. See *Città del Sole* (1996), note 46, p. 58; note 73, p. 64; *Quaestio quarta politica*, art. 3, note 5, ibid., p. 149. On the persistence of more traditional attitudes towards women, see Lina Bolzoni, 'Tommaso Campanella e le donne: fascino e negazione della differenza,' *Annali d'Italianistica*, 7 (1989), pp. 193–216; on the role of women in Campanella, see also Margherita Isnardi Parente, 'Tommaso Campanella e la *Repubblica* di Platone,' *Archivio Storico per la Calabria e la Lucania*, 46 (1999), pp. 93–111; Jean-Louis Fournel, 'Le contrôle des mariages et des naissance dans la pensée politique de Campanella,' *B&C*, 7 (2001), pp. 209–220; Germana Ernst, 'donna,' in *Enciclopedia*, vol. 2 (forthcoming).

[32] *Poesie*, p. 327.

[33] *Città del Sole*, p. 44.

is a divine art and a divine reason, and it is bound up in every last fiber of nature. The more delicate problem has to do with the relationship between Christianity and natural religion. In this regard too, Campanella did not hesitate to affirm that there exists no tension. Christianity, the expression of a divine rationality, cannot but coincide with natural religion. The addition of dogmas and sacraments does not aim at destroying nature, but rather at perfecting it. And this is without doubt one of the most subtle, difficult, and elusive passages in Campanella's thought. This depiction of Christianity as the highest and most complete expression of rationality and of natural religion is, more than the affirmation of an existing reality, an implicit exhortation and an indication of the road to be taken, of the task to be realized.

The Solarians live according to the pure law of nature, prior to revelation. The result of such a condition is that they would have no difficulty in completing the passage to Christianity: 'when they come to know the living truth of Christianity, proven with miracles, they will consent to it, because that truth is most sweet.'[34] If between natural religion and Christianity there is no hiatus or break (and there ought not to be, because there is no reason for it), the consensus of the 'very sweet' Solarians contains a warning to Christians. It exhorts them to agree with this serene faith in nature, which offers itself spontaneously to the perfecting influence of revelation, and to become aware that the unifying power of Christianity resides precisely in pursuing a reconciliation and harmony with nature. Christianity offers itself as a vehicle of natural and rational values: 'if these people, who follow only the law of nature, are so close to Christianity, that nothing is to be added to natural law except the sacraments, I take from this relationship the argument that the true law is the Christian law and that, once its abuses are removed, it will be mistress of the world.'[35]

Campanella discussed various aspects of his political theory in four *quaestiones* that appeared in the Paris edition of his *Philosophia realis*. In the fourth question, titled *De optima republica*, he addressed the problems and objections that had been raised against the proposed model for an ideal city. The first of the three articles deals with general problems such as that of the very possibility of discussing a city that had never been seen and that probably would never be seen, so as to reassert the legitimacy of sketching an ideal model independently of its practical realizability. It also deals with more specific objections, regarding the place and climate of the city, or the isolation and the excessive austerity of the life of its inhabitants. The other two articles deal with two of the dialogue's more controversial points: the sharing of possessions and women. Regarding the first issue, Campanella made use of patristic

---

[34] Ibid., p. 25.
[35] Ibid., p. 54.

and scholastic sources to argue (against theologians of the time such as the Spanish Dominican Domingo de Soto) for the superiority and importance of sharing possessions. Such sharing took its foundation from the original right of nature, while division and private ownership had historical origins and took shape as a concession and a lesser evil arising from human law. Regarding the other controversial and harder to defend aspect of the dialogue (namely, the sharing of women), Campanella, in order to avoid misunderstandings, reaffirmed that it concerned the norms that regulate reproduction, which was one of the basic issues in the city and ought as such to be 'observed strictly for the public good, and not the private.' Aiming at good reproduction that avoids the damages and the sufferings (for individuals and for the city) that derive from unfortunate offspring, such unions have nothing in common with unregulated and promiscuous unions, or with the practices of certain heretical sects, modern or ancient. The sharing of women, understood correctly, is also, like the sharing of possessions, completely in tune with the law of nature, in the light of which the only criterion for the licitness of sexuality is reproduction. Sexuality becomes illicit only when it becomes prohibited, for pragmatic reasons, by prescriptions of positive law.[36]

Questions have often been raised about the origin of the work's title and several possible sources have been highlighted. Beyond the verse from Isaiah 19.18 – 'there will be five cities in Egypt … and one of these will be called the city of the sun' – the image of the sun is very present in the sixteenth century, in various authors and contexts. Authors well known to Campanella had spoken about it – such as Marsilio Ficino, who, in the context of resurgent interest in Platonism and Hermeticism, exalted the sun as the most appropriate image of the good and of divine goodness, because its extremely pure light penetrated everything, giving life and movement to all things.[37] Likewise, travel accounts and descriptions of distant lands that spoke of astral cults in Africa and in the New World had emphasized the image of the sun. Girolamo Benzoni spoke of how Atabalipa, the last king of Peru, responded to a speech of the Dominican Vincenzo de Valverde that exhorted him to submit and convert. He said that 'regarding the subject of religion … he would never leave his own religion, because if they believed in Christ (who had died on the cross), he believed in the sun, which had never died.'[38] Likewise, the scholar Girolamo Ruscelli, while speaking of the emblem of Philip II of Spain, warmly praised the sun that was represented on it:

---

[36] *Quaestio quarta politica*, in *Città del Sole* (1996) p. 145ff.

[37] *Liber de Sole*, in Marsilii Ficini *Opera* (Basel, 1576), I, p. 966; Italian translation in Marsilio Ficino, *Scritti sull'astrologia*, ed. O. Pompeo Faracovi (Milan, 1999), pp. 187–188.

[38] Girolamo Benzoni, *La istoria del mondo nuovo* (Venice, 1565), p. 121.

It opens the pores of the earth, nourishes bodies, renews plants, reinvigorates grass, instills natural understanding in men, moderates and tempers the other planets. Whence it is not without reason that the philosophers, theologians, and poets came to refer to the sun now as the eye of the world, now as the king of nature, now as the beauty of the day, now as the measure of time, now as light, ornament, and heart of the heavens, now as father, fount, and bestower of the sciences, of the virtues, and of divine glories.[39]

Without doubt Campanella was well aware of these and other echoes. But it is the Solarians themselves who remind us that the sun is the effigy of God, whom 'they served ... under the sign of the sun, which is the sign and the face of God, from whom comes light and heat and everything else.' The Solarians say that 'God displayed his own beauty in the heavens and in the sun, as his trophy and image.' The elegy that concludes the *Scelta* of Campanella's poems is titled *Al Sole (To the Sun)*. The author is conscious of the emotive contrast between the return to life (in spring, of waters, plants, and animals, which thanks to the sun throw off their wintry sleep), and his own painful situation, which made him envy the reawakening of vipers and worms. Yet, he could not help writing a hymn full of admiration to the star that is the face of God and the emblem of his own philosophy:

> You are a living temple, a statue and revered face
> Of the true God, the supreme pomp and torch.
> Father of nature and blessed ruler of the stars,
> Life, soul, and sense of all secondary things,
> Under your auspices an admirable school
> I erected for the Supreme Intellect through my philosophy.[40]

---

[39] Girolamo Ruscelli, *Le imprese illustri* (Venice, 1584), p. 191.

[40] *Poesie*, n. 89, vv. 39–44, p. 455: 'Tempio vivo sei, statua e venerabile volto,/del verace Dio pompa e suprema face./Padre di natura e degli astri rege beato,/vita, anima e senso d'ogni seconda cosa;/sotto gli auspici di cui, ammirabile scola/al Primo Senno filosofando fei.'

7. IN THE CAVE OF POLYPHEMUS

The Poesie

In the very first lines of the *Syntagma*, Campanella recalled his own precocious and natural aptitude for poetic expression. As an adult, this aptitude took on a certain poignancy and sharpness, and came to be directed towards the expression of difficult philosophical matters. The poetic production that has come down to us was transmitted primarily in two collections. The first included the poems of his youth, completed prior to 1601. The second consisted of compositions put together and published under the title *Scelta di alcune poesie filosofiche*. The poems of Campanella's youth survived in the so-called "Ponzio Codex," located by Amabile in the nineteenth century.[1] They include eighty-two poems, mostly sonnets, of which only fourteen would be included in the *Scelta*. The codex is named after Ponzio because it conserves the poems that Campanella's friend and fellow prisoner Pietro Ponzio collected, until the codex was confiscated in the prison of the Castel Nuovo in August of 1601, after a violent argument between the inmates. All that Campanella himself tells us is that many of those compositions were written in the earliest days of the imprisonment, for the purpose of instilling courage in his fellow detainees and friends and so as to help them resist the terrors of torture. Transposing episodes and characters from the events in Calabria into verse, Campanella expressed his certainty about being on the side of reason and justice. He refers to the conspirators as noble and chosen spirits, united in their determination to fight against the violence and ignorance of tyranny in the name of liberty and truth and united in disdaining – with the aid of the 'ardor' of reason – the most atrocious tortures and persecutions.[2] The poems exalt friends and companions, such as the three brothers Ponzio (Dionisio in particular for the courage with which he confronted and derided 'so horrible a torment/that undid his entire body/ limb by limb'), the loyal Pietro Presterà, and Domenico Petrolo, for not having hesitated to simulate terrible things so

---

[1] The collection of poetry was published for the first time in Amabile, *Congiura*, III, doc. 436–517, pp. 549–581.

[2] *Poesie*, p. 519.

G. Ernst, *Tommaso Campanella,* International Archives of the History of Ideas/Archives internationales d'histoire des idées 200, DOI 10.1007/978-90-481-3126-6_7, © Springer Science + Business Media B.V. 2010

as to help him and to save his life.[3] At first, Maurizio de Rinaldis is exalted as a 'generous man' on account of the courage he showed in resisting torture: 'for six nights and six days he prevails/torments old and new he disdains'; he endured '… suffering for 300 hours/unusual torments with a magnanimous heart, alone and naked.' In a later palinodic madrigal, he came to be detested and labeled 'extremely vile' and 'devoid of virtue,' because of the confession that he rendered at the point of death so as to cleanse his own conscience.[4]

In contrast to the heroic figures of the conspirators, who fight and suffer for high ideals, negative figures are harshly condemned – figures such as Antonio Mesuraca. Having promised to help Campanella, Mesuraca instead betrayed and denounced him, delivering him tightly bound to his master's men ('why, in binding me, do your associates turn on me ferociously?').[5] But above all others loomed the fiscal lawyer Luise Xarava, for whom the harshest epithets – 'impious monster,' 'without a human mind,' 'lying snake' – were not spared, because he had combined violence with the most subtle arts of intrigue and deceit.[6] When writing about himself, Campanella speaks of a prophet and interpreter of signs, a champion of a just cause and not a rebel: 'He who reprimands degenerate representatives/Conspires neither against God nor against King.' He did not hesitate to protest against God, who 'appeared to be sleeping,' consenting that 'his white champion, be oppressed with false testimonies,/that represent his devotion as evil.'[7] In other verses, inspired by the Psalm 129 *Saepe expugnaverunt me* ('Much have they oppressed me'), Campanella felt himself to be under God's protection against the persecutions that had afflicted him since childhood, and he pronounced himself sure of the approaching defeat and punishment of the tyrants:

> The day is coming, on which haughty heads
> Together with subservient necks and lying tongues
> Will make a meal for tigers, bears, and panthers.[8]

The Ponzio Codex also includes early poems that predate the conspiracy.[9] One sequence addresses political themes, such as the role of Christian Rome and the universal monarchy of Spain. Other verses are addressed to noble female figures. Other poems – not inelegant if somewhat conventional – are of an amorous nature. The most original and realistic sonnet alludes to an erotic relationship imagined despite the painful physical separation of the lovers ('Me standing behind bars, she outside').[10] The strongest and most evocative poem (titled

---

[3] Ibid., p. 519.

[4] Ibid., pp. 490, 492, 494.

[5] Ibid., p. 504.

[6] Ibid., p. 498ff.

[7] Ibid., pp. 528, 500.

[8] Ibid., p. 488: 'Vicino è 'l dì, che le cervici altiere/e i colli torti e le lingue bugiarde/farà pasto di tigri, orsi e pantere.'

[9] See ch. 3, notes 5, 34, 41.

Sdegno amoroso) is presented as a definitive break from the amorous condition and from its deceits. Betrayed in the sincerity and depth of his own feelings, the amorous heat of his heart hardens into the chill of hate and into a cold marble. The break from 'amorous intricacy' is translated into a proud commitment to self-sufficiency – 'I draw sustenance from myself' (*me di me nutrico*).[11]

The most important nucleus of Campanella's poetic activity, however, is constituted by the eighty-nine pieces that were published in 1622 in a work titled *Scelta di alcune poesie filosofiche di Settimontano Squilla, cavate da' suo' libri detti La Cantica, con l'Esposizione.* The text was prefaced by a dedication from Tobias Adami that is signed 'Paris, in the year 1621.' It was sent to three German friends – Wilhelm von Wense, Christoph Besold, Valentin Andreae – with the certainty that they would enjoy this 'gift small in appearance, but truly great in its reality,' on account of the 'sublime conceits' conveyed in the poems. Only six exemplars are known still to exist and of those two are in Italy, both at Naples. Not only rare, the edition is obscure in several respects.[12] The author hides behind a pseudonym that alludes to his own surname and to the seven "mountains" of his head. The edition is also devoid of typographic information and only recently was it confirmed that it was published in Germany at Köhten, in Saxony, under the auspices of Prince Ludwig von Anhalt-Köhten.[13]

---

[10] *Poesie*, p. 564.

[11] Ibid., pp. 568–571.

[12] Regarding the known copies, see Francesco Giancotti, 'Note e Tavole sul Testo,' in *Poesie*, pp. C–CIV; Id., 'Postille a una nuova edizione delle *Poesie* di Campanella. 1–3,' *B&C*, 4, 1998, pp. 423–426. The Neapolitan exemplars are held in the Biblioteca Croce and the Biblioteca Oratoriana dei Padri Girolamini. This second copy – on which, see L. Amabile, *Il codice delle lettere del Campanella ... e il libro delle Poesie dello Squilla della Biblioteca dei PP. Girolamini in Napoli* (Naples, 1881) – is of the highest importance, because it contains autograph corrections by Campanella, which have been for the most part lost following the havoc wrought by an inept restoration justly deplored by Firpo; see 'Storia della poesia campanelliana,' p. XI, in the anastatic edition of the *Scelta* published by him (Naples, 1980).

[13] See Arnaldo Di Benedetto, 'Da Campanella a Manzoni: Due Note. I. Sul luogo di stampa della *Scelta d'alcune poesie filosofiche* di Settimontano Squilla,' *Giornale Storico della Letteratura Italiana*, 112 (1995), pp. 421–425; 'Notizie campanelliane: Sul luogo di stampa della *Scelta d'alcune poesie filosofiche*,' *B&C*, 3 (1997), pp. 154–158. Even before the *Scelta* was sent to press, Johann Valentin Andreae had translated and published six sonnets in German in 1619 (see Italo M. Battafarano, 'Attorno ai sonetti di Campanella tradotti da J. V. Andreae,' *Annali dell'Istituto Universitario Orientale di Napoli*, Sezione Germanica, XX, 1977, pp. 7–45). In 1802, Johann Gottlieb Herder would translate and publish twenty-seven of the poems (then in *Sämmtliche Werke*, ed. B. Suphan, vol. III, Berlin, 1881, pp. 332–354). But only in 1834 would Gaspare Orelli, professor of philology at Zurich, succeed, after years of fruitless research, in tracking down a copy of the extremely rare old edition in Wolfenbüttel and in editing a modern (if imprecise) version of the *Scelta*, which A. D'Ancona inserted into the edition of the *Opere* that he put together.

The collection of eighty-nine poems, selected and arranged with careful and sophisticated attention, presents itself as a complete cycle of great originality, an example, extremely rare in the Italian poetic tradition, of philosophical and metaphysical poetry. The author achieves results of an exceptional value and vigor that has increasingly been acknowledged by an attentive scholarly tradition that has gradually liberated itself from limited judgments about the presumed incompatibility between philosophy and the supposed 'brusqueness' of Campanella's poetic expression.[14] The assertion in the *Syntagma* that Adami chose the contents from a larger corpus of poems *iuxta ingenium suum* ('according to his liking') is rather perplexing and should not be taken literally.[15] There is reason to believe that the choice of poems was the product of collaboration between Campanella and Adami to select and organise the most philosophically important poems. The poems are, in many cases, extremely difficult on account of their profundity and speculative sublimity. In view of the publication, Campanella added a helpful exposition in prose, so as to render the comprehension of his own poems easier.

One of the things that is at first sight rather surprising (but that can in fact provide a key to the reading of the complex spiritual experience of the author) is the fact that the most intense compositions stem from the period of the hardest isolation – namely, the years of the tragic seclusion in the dungeon of Castel Sant'Elmo (1604–1607). This was a period in which the prisoner was forced to live in conditions of absolute privation, in a damp, unhealthy, gloomy cell, feeding on food that was 'measly and dirty.' This was a situation that made writing extremely difficult and at times impossible. Over and above presenting the most philosophically important themes of his thought in a remarkable way, the *Scelta* is shot through with intense autobiographical motifs, which trace the dramatic stages of the intellectual and spiritual journey of the author, who is represented as an exemplar. It depicts radical inner upheaval, from the proud declaration of his own ideas and the fracturing of certainties, to the moments of crisis and doubt, followed by the humble acceptance of the inscrutable (but always wise) plans of divine providence.[16]

---

[14] For the vast bibliography on the poems, see the fine list in the *Poesie*, pp. CLI–CLV.

[15] *Syntagma*, p. 42.

[16] See ch. 8, pp. 154–155.

In a dense, corporeal but also refined idiom, the *Scelta* attempts to translate the most important themes of Campanella's thought into a poetic language. Cultivated terms are mixed together with more popular expressions and images. The aim is to arrive at an effective correspondence between words and things. A programmatic sonnet, functioning as an introduction, announces the intentions of the author. In the name of a true philosophy, he intends to call 'the raving world, in revolt against itself' back to divine and natural values. The *Scelta* opens out into a planned sequence of sonnets and canzones. Cast in madrigals, the canzones are charged with addressing the most complex metaphysical themes. In conformity with the principles of the *Poetica*, the 'prophetic' role of the poet, bearer of a message of truth is underlined. The work addresses the investigation of the world of nature, which – as the 'book in which the Eternal Intelligence/wrote its ideas' (n. 6) – is represented as the original model to which the opinions of men refer in order to be judged. For this reason, we have the exaltation of Telesio, who emancipates a philosophy understood as a direct reading of the infinite book of nature from the yoke of Aristotle's philosophy, which is said to be based on nothing more than words and opinions that have lost all connection with nature (n. 68). The reference to nature serves also to denounce the injustice and irrationality of an upside-down social world, the contortions and sorrows of which have their origin in the fact that the roles of the social comedy are assigned according to chance and fortune, rather than by reason and in conformity with natural attitudes. A harmful and painful break is set up between being and appearing when human skill imitates badly the divine art that is intrinsic in nature. Thus, false kings come to be prized, such as Nero, who 'was a king in appearance on account of chance,' while wise men such as Socrates – a king 'in truth and by nature' – are put to death. In a society where the inversion of values rules, the prophet cannot but be persecuted by those in power, because he is an inconvenient witness and a messenger of virtues and truths that have been suppressed and replaced by hypocrisy, sophistry, and tyranny. Moreover, the prophet is rejected by the plebs, which possesses a strength of which it is unaware (the plebs 'is a diverse and massive beast/that ignores its own strength'). The masses are held in a condition of unconsciousness and ignorance by the 'spell' cast by sophists, a bad magic that induces torpor and corrupts their ability to perceive reality clearly: 'They cast a spell, that swells their senses' and in this way they hold subjects chained in a kind of perverse complicity with those who are in power and exploit them. From here derives the painful astonishment of the wise man who is persecuted and killed (n. 33), precisely because he attempts to awaken the masses from this abasement and to render them conscious of their own power ('everything between heaven and earth belongs to them').[17] Reduced to silence and forced into dissimulation, in order to save his own life and to preserve his message against tyrannical violence (n. 13), the prophet appears to be condemned to an inevitable defeat. But this defeat is only apparent, in that the prophet's message outlives him. Campanella is moreover persuaded of the necessary arrival of a 'golden and happy age,' anticipated by a dense prophetic tradition. This is an age that – with the abolition of private property and of the evils that begin in blind 'love of self' – heralds the instauration of a form of living together that is based on the values of a common love.

From a more general point of view, this human 'comedy' is placed in the context of a 'universal comedy.' This is one of the most complex themes in Campanella's work. It joins difficult metaphysical nodes together, such as the necessity of tension and discord (in order to achieve a 'felicitous harmony' at the level of the whole), the relation between the first divine Idea and the infinite modes of its manifestations, and above all the problem of evil, which turns out to be connected to the necessary limitation and distinction of single parts, the suffering of which is to be considered in the context of the universal life of the whole – 'but the part that groans smiles at the whole' (n. 3, v. 102). If every evil and destruction is the expression and the condition of the unfolding of the infinite forms of being, then the suffering of the individual parts is connected to and derives its meaning from the universal comedy: 'In the end, this is a universal comedy,/and he who philosophizing unites himself with God/ and sees with him that every ugliness and evil/is a beautiful mask, that man smiles and rejoices.'[18]

The moment of the crisis, which constitutes a watershed between the earlier period of his youth and the later more mature period, is conveyed with particular intensity by the four canzones titled *Dispregio della morte*, which recall Hermetic and Platonic motifs. The author turns to his own soul, so as to comfort it and exhort it not to be affected by desperation and fear of death. The tyrant can be cruel only to the body, which is the soul's 'prison by birth.'

---

[17] Regarding this famous sonnet entitled 'Della plebe,' see G. Ernst, 'Sapiente e popolo in Campanella. Rileggendo il sonetto "Della plebe",' in *Bene navigavi. Studi in onore di Franco Bianco*, ed. M. Failla (Macerata, 2006), pp. 283–294. For a fuller version, see G. Ernst, '"Il popolo è una bestia varia e grossa." Passioni, retorica, e politica in Tommaso Campanella,' in *Renaissance Learning and Letters*, ed. D. Knox and N. Ordine (forthcoming). For an English version of some of the compositions in the *Scelta*, see *The Sonnets of Michael Angelo Buonarroti and Tommaso Campanella*, translated by John Addington Symonds (London, 1878); a recent reprinting of that translation (complete with the Italian text and Campanella's own prose exposition) can be found in T. Campanella, *Sonnets*, ed. S. Draghici (Washington DC, 1999).

[18] *Scelta*, n. 29, madr. 10 in *Poesie*, p. 144: 'Alfin questa è comedia universale;/e chi filosofando a Dio s'unisce/vede con lui ch'ogni bruttezza e male/maschere belle son, ride e gioisce.'

The evils and the trials that the soul suffers cannot but liberate it and resurrect it from its corporeal 'tomb.' Invited to consider the human condition in relation to the entire cosmos, the mind is presented with the image of an immense space, 'completely saturated in serene light,' in which are gathered the luminous celestial bodies, where the blessed spirits live 'in happy liberty.' Only the earth is obscure – the earth, which is an 'exile and sentence' for fallen spirits. At the center, 'the most rebellious' are punished 'in eternal night/under the greatest weight.' Souls that are sent to the surface, a place of both sorrow and joy, shadow and light, for the purpose of struggling for their release are closed up within their bodies as if those bodies – which are derived from the earth (which itself is a common prison) – constitute individual prisons.[19] Nature and terrestrial entities – constituted by the encounter between cold and heat, which forgets the heavens so as to wear a 'terrestrial veil' and produce all entities – set the scene for a comedy that is represented 'for the amusement of higher spirits' and in which man plays the central role. Souls are sent into bodies 'so as to set the scene with greater prettiness.' This serves to satisfy the doubt regarding the sufferings of the good and the triumphs of the evil 'that contorts every mind.' To the good, God has assigned 'the difficult part of the play,/so as to draw them to greater good from filthy tombs' (n. 77, madr. 6).

In this respect, the body – even as it is praised on account of the wondrous anatomy of its parts – becomes the 'tenebrous weight' that tends to hold back and impede the flight of the soul. Aware of not depending on the elemental world and claiming its own liberty and autonomy, the soul addresses the body with epithets that resonate those of a Hermetic dialogue:

> You, living death, nest of ignorance,
> Moving tomb and vestment
> Of sin and torment,
> Weight of concern and labyrinth of errors,
> You pull me down with charms and fears,
> Such that I do not aim at the heavens, my true home,
> And the good that rises above all others:
> Whence, in love with its beauty and overcome,
> I disdain and desert you, an extinguished ember.[20]

In its dialogue with the body, in its view of the cosmos, in its own aspiration towards and capacity for the infinite, the soul clarifies for itself its own

---

[19] *Poesie*, p. 338.

[20] Ibid., pp. 363–364: 'Tu, morte viva, nido d'ignoranza,/ portatile sepolcro e vestimento/di colpa e di tormento,/peso d'affanni e di error laberinto,/mi tiri in giù con vezzi e con spavento,/perch'io non miri in Ciel mia propria stanza,/e 'l ben ch'ogn'altro avanza:/onde, di sua beltà invaghito e vinto,/non sprezzi e lasci te, carbone estinto.'

role and its own divine nature. In the fourth canzone, the author upholds the immortality of the soul – a point on which he evidently had nourished some doubts – on the basis of an anomalous proof. In fact, the author makes reference to his own direct experiences of demonic evocation, thanks to which he had reached a 'higher philosophy,' by overcoming error and doubt. If the devils had deceived him, inducing him into false beliefs, they had also rendered certain the existence of abstract spirits, on account of which the existence of good angels and of a future life are also rendered certain. This was a future life in which men would be reassembled in ranks of good spirits and bad, in accordance with their actions in life. The commentary to the fourth madrigal emphasizes that the author 'knew from experience that there was indeed another age after death; the many visions and demons manifested to the exterior senses tormented him and sought to deceive him, feigning to be angels. And then he wrote this canzone and it is dedicated entirely to the true religion.'[21] The anxieties of the soul frightened by the thought of death seem to be soothed by the certainty of its celestial life and by understanding that wisdom and happiness consist in adhering to the will of the eternal Intelligence. 'But he who in his own mind cultivates the great Wisdom/wanting and not wanting in accordance with that great Wisdom/dulls every pain and rejoices in Him.'

The four canzones are followed by that famous poem addressed to Berillo – namely, Basilio Berillari of Pavia, unofficial dungeon confessor and consoler of Campanella. The poem, as is announced even in the title, presents itself as a confession or disowning of the author's own errors and a declaration of penitence. The author is no longer astonished by the 'atrocious martyrdom' to which he is subjected. The consciousness of errors and sins no longer allows him to presumptuously identify himself with Christ and his suffering, which had led him to believe that his reverses were the result of the message of truth and justice – of which he felt himself the spokesman. In the most important madrigal he disowns his own personal prophetic investiture, founded on an arrogant hope that his own actions were righteous, given that it seemed so to his human reason, without bothering to verify it or to wait for divine assent:

I believed that I held God in my hand,
Not following God,
But following instead the acute reason of my own intellect,
Which led to my own downfall and the death of so many.
Although wise and pious, the human mind
Becomes blind and profane,

---

[21] See madrigals four and five of the *Canzone quarta* in *Poesie*, n. 79, pp. 369–370. For the lines cited below, see madrigal 1, p. 367: 'Ma smorza ogni doglia/chi nella mente sua il gran Senno cole,/seco vuole e disvòle,/ di lui se stesso in se stesso beando.'

If it thinks to improve the lot of men
Unless you manifest yourself to its senses, you the true God,
And you deign to dispatch it and arm it,
As your messenger
Of miracles and proofs and testimonies.[22]

Important too is that 'wondrous sonnet' titled *Della providenza* that follows shortly after, in which it is affirmed that the order and the beauty of every part (even the smallest) in the 'artifice of the world' proves that everything is the work of 'an infinite and excellent Intelligence.' The evil deeds and deviations of men and animals generate the suspicion that on account of negligence or tiredness God does not care about the world, or that he delegates his governance to a lesser god. But the final triplet reaffirms the unity of God, who will put an end to all evil, rending manifest his own reason, which remains for the moment hidden:

But there is only one God, by whom will be ended
So much confusion, and the hidden reason
Why so many sinned will be made manifest.[23]

After the declaration and the overcoming of the crisis, the *Scelta* concludes with an explosion of four poems in which all creatures (which all are 'beautiful, good, and happy') are invited to celebrate he who has endowed being ('you, all things, I invite to celebrate/ he who has made us – what we are /since we were – nothing'). Every aspect of life and love for life is exalted and the poems sketch the image of a cosmos shot through and coursing – in a manner that is very close to that of the *Senso delle cose* – with animated and positive energies. The first hymn exalts the power and the role of man. Though born crying, naked, and defenseless, man is later able – as the 'image of God' – to imitate divine art and creativity, becoming 'a second god, miraculous creation of the first' and the author of wondrous inventions such as writing, the watch, and fire. As the poem relates, 'in his den he makes it day when it is night; /Oh broken laws – /Oh broken laws! That is a mere worm/ King, epilogue, harmony, – end of everything' and he is capable of establishing laws – 'he proposes laws, as a god.'[24]

---

[22] Ibid., p. 382: 'Io mi credevo Dio tener in mano,/ non seguitando Dio,/ ma l'argute ragion del senno mio,/ che a me ed a tanti ministrâr la morte./ Benché sagace e pio, l'ingegno umano/ divien cieco e profano, se pensa migliorar la comun sorte,/ pria che mostrarti a' sensi suoi, Dio vero, e mandarlo ed armarlo non ti degni,/ come tuo messaggiero,/ di miracolo e pruove e contrassegni.'

[23] Ibid., p. 404: 'Ma un solo è Dio, da cui sarà finito/ tanto scompiglio, e la ragion nascosa/aperta, onde peccò cotanta gente.'

[24] Ibid., p. 409: 'Fa alla sua tana – giorno quando è notte:/ oh, leggi rotte!/ Oh, leggi rotte! ch'un sol verme sia/ re, epilogo, armonia, – fin d'ogni cosa'; p. 408: 'Ei legge pone, come un dio.'

Three 'elegies composed in a Latin manner' were added in an appendix to the *Scelta*. These are the only three examples that have come down to us of this innovative attempt to reproduce the schemes of hexameter and pentameter in the vulgar tongue.[25] The first is titled *Al senno latino* and it possesses a novelty of language and of meter that aims at exhorting a general renewal; 'For the new age a new instrument, a new language was reborn:/a new generation can fashion a new singing'. After that, there is a paraphrase of Psalm 111 – *Beatus vir qui timet* ('Blessed is the man who fears [God]'). Finally, as a worthy conclusion to the entire *Scelta*, there is the splendid elegy *Al Sole*. The poem celebrates the springtime reawakening of life 'in everything, secret, languid, dead, and lazy' thanks to the vigor of the sun; thus, 'the frozen rivers melt into water/pure, that, being released, is happy and irrigates the earth./ The badgers and dormice awake from a long sleep;/ you give spirit and motion to the lowest worm'. All of this induces in the prisoner a reflection on the painful contrast between this renewal and his own situation of exclusion and suffering: 'why is it that I, more than everyone, tremble in darkness and in cold?,' for 'I live, am not dead, green and not dry I find myself/ although for you I am buried like a cadaver.' This is a situation so much more painful in that, forced to envy all manner of 'pallid serpents,' he has celebrated the sun in the higher world, as a 'living temple' and 'statue and venerable visage' of God – a star that confers 'life, soul, and sense' to everything and that has been chosen by Campanella as a symbol and sign of his new philosophy precisely on account of such characteristics. But in these final poems the contemplation of and the love for life that returns to show itself and to flow forth seem to prevail, with a certain melancholic composure, in the shout and protest that in the end are mitigated and returned to the 'serene light' of the sun.[26]

Sense, Spiritus *and Natural Magic*

One of the most beautiful and original of Campanella's writings is the *Del senso delle cose e della magia*. After the confiscation at Bologna and the dispatching of the early Latin version to Rome, an Italian text was composed in four books towards 1604 in the prison of Sant'Elmo.[27] Translated into Latin,

---

[25] An attempt that would be appreciated by Giosuè Carducci, who would reproduce the three elegies in his collection *La poesia barbara nei secoli XV e XVI* (Bologna, 1881), pp. 401–407.

[26] *Poesie*, p. 452ff.; see ch. 6, p. 104.

[27] The work was handed over to G. Schoppe in 1607, so that he might organize its publication. But at the end of the following year the German scholar, having encountered difficulties with the editor Giovan Battista Ciotti regarding a Venetian edition, advised the author to translate it into Latin and to attempt to publish it in Germany – something that Campanella did in the course of 1609.

the *De sensu rerum et magia* was published in 1620 in a series of works edited by Tobias Adami.[28] The work received a good deal of attention across Europe and generated discussion after it received some contrasting judgments.[29] The Italian text was edited for the first time only in 1925 by Antonio Bruers. The anatomically explicit prose of the unpublished work had elicited the severe judgment of Amabile ('the Italian style there turns out to be rather rough; some of the words denoting the sexual organs and reproductive acts could not be repeated; and one would have to say that the author was feeling the influence of imprisonment in the tower and in Sant'Elmo'[30]). In truth, in that work we find ourselves in the presence of an absolute expressive masterpiece. In a language of extraordinary power, Campanella extols his vision of a universal animation, the 'great chain of the highest universal concord.'[31]

The text discusses in great detail the notions of *sensus* and *spiritus*, and all their implications at an epistemological and philosophical level. The text exhibits a wise orchestration of themes, which, once announced, are then taken up and developed at different levels of elaboration, as if in a succession of waves. The polemic against Aristotle is precise and constant; he is accused of incoherence and abstraction, while philosophers such as Anaxagoras, Pythagoras, and Hermes Trismegistus are considered favorably. Even if atomist doctrines are criticized (because they cannot explain the purposeful and vitalistic organization of all natural entities), one can nevertheless comprehend the late reference of 1635 that we find in a letter to Peiresc to 'the Epicurean Lucretius, by me much studied and esteemed.'[32]

Right from the exordium, the author announced the explicative principle of the entire work: 'no entity can give to others that which it does not possess itself.' Since it is confirmed in a completely clear manner that animals are endowed with sensibility, it follows that one ought to affirm that 'the elements, which are their causes, sense.' All natural beings, without exception, are produced by the encounter between cold and heat and by the action on terrestrial matter of solar heat, which modifies it according to various modalities and in accordance with the divine design that has preestablished the way in which agent causes are instruments that 'imprint in matter the various models of

---

[28] The work would be reprinted at Paris, in 1636 and 1637, preceded by a dedication to Cardinal Richelieu and accompanied by a *Defensio*, in which the author demonstrated how his doctrine was fully in line with the doctrines of the Church Fathers and the Scholastics.

[29] See for example Michel-Pierre Lerner, '"Campanellae deliramenta in Tartarum releganda": une condamnation méconnue du *De sensu rerum et magia* en 1629,' *B&C*, 2 (1996), pp. 215–236.

[30] Amabile, *Congiura*, II, p. 370.

[31] *Senso delle cose*, p. 23.

[32] *Lettere*, p. 324.

the first idea.'[33] The positions of Lucretius and the atomists are criticized. For them, sense is born in things that are insensate and men, who laugh and cry, are descended from elements that do not laugh and do not cry. Campanella claimed instead that 'laughter and crying do exist in the elements, although they are not there in the same mode as they are in men.'[34] Still polemicizing against the atomists, Campanella denied that from the chance clash of inert particles (which are passive and devoid of quality) virtues could derive that are active and incorporeal – such as heat, light, and cold. Taking up again the example of Lucretius, Campanella affirmed that the letters of the alphabet, even if they were rearranged innumerable times, would never arrange themselves in such a way that they composed, by chance, the book that he was writing in a deliberate fashion.[35] If one admits that a sword or a book is brought into being deliberately and for a particular end, how much more absurd is it to attribute to chance, rather than to divine skill, much more marvelous compositions like the eye, the heart, a plant, or the entire world.

When Campanella then went on to specify what one ought to understand by 'sense,' he defined it as 'passion' in the first place. We sense when we undergo an alteration, and immediately that being acted upon divides into two kinds – being either pleasing or displeasing, according to what would be described as utility or harm from the point of view of preservation: 'those things delight that conserve the symmetry of our sensing and in those organs so adapted, whence it is that a mild warmth (which is a warmth similar to our own) delights; those things that destroy displease, such as hot iron; so it is with all objects – if they conserve us, then they please, but if they destroy us, then they displease.'[36] Sense thus turns out to be connected to preservation and destruction. Campanella specified, against Aristotle, that undergoing can also be corruptive, and not only perfective. Moreover, as he had already asserted in the *Epilogo magno*, that which is sentient does not take into itself the form of the thing felt, for that would imply a destruction of its own form. Instead, in the sensing the spirit undergoes a partial change, in virtue of which it is capable of evaluating the entire nature of the sensed object. Sense, thus, is not only passion (things can be undergone that are not sensed, as when during sleep one is bitten by an insect), but rather the *perception* of passion – always insofar as it is connected with a capacity to distinguish the useful from the

---

[33] *Senso delle cose*, pp. 3–4.

[34] Ibid., p. 7.

[35] Ibid., p. 8.

[36] Ibid., p. 11. On the concept of sense, see Massimo L. Bianchi, 'senso (sensus),' in *Enciclopedia*, vol. 1, coll. 351–364.

destructive. If these first elements and the entities to which they give rise do not sense, then all the world would be an indistinct chaos. The connection between self-preservation and a sensing that is sufficient to realize it is the chain that links the diverse levels of reality – and the explicative principle of those diverse levels. It turns out that every entity participates in life and sense, albeit to different extents and in distinct ways.

A confirmation of the pervasiveness of sense is to be found in the fact that every entity abhors a vacuum, which is perceived as a threat to the integrity both of individual beings and of the whole: things 'enjoy reciprocal contact' and for the common good lay down particular repugnances. As in the human body, the individual parts love their own union; just so, the great animal of the world abhors division and vacuum:

> It is necessary, therefore, to assert that the world is a complete sensate animal, and that all the parts enjoy the common life. In us the arm does not want to be separated from the humerus, nor the humerus from the shoulder-blade, nor the head from the neck, nor the legs from the thighs – instead, all hate division. Just so, the whole world abhors being divided, as happens to it when a vacuum intercedes between particular bodies.'[37]

To the repugnance for the void is connected the conception of a space that is 'born to be located,' and attracts bodies with 'appetizing sense' to itself. Campanella recalled that some Arab philosophers (the allusion is to Avicebron, the Jewish philosopher believed by the Western world to be Arab) had identified space with God, on account of the characteristics that seemed to make it resemble divinity: 'it sustains everything and is contrary to nothing and receives everything benignly; nothing ever dies in it or on account of it and only particular bodies die with respect to other particular bodies. Space is extremely large, not as a material quantity, but as an incorporeal quantity; and it is held to be infinite beyond the universe, a lover, and benefactor of everything.'[38] Campanella said that space was 'the basis of every created thing and that it precedes all beings; if it does not precede time itself, then it precedes at least the origin of nature,' while God – infinite, without corporeal dimension and antecedent to the entities created by him – has greater 'sovereign magnitude.' Campanella then specified that things fill space and obstruct the void, not only because those things enjoy mutual contact and act in the name of preservation, but also because, being similar to God, they are endowed with intrinsic expansive and dilative energy:

---

[37] Ibid., p. 24.
[38] Ibid., p. 26.

Since we experience in them the love of dilating themselves, multiplying themselves, and living a spacious existence, it is to be found that – for the purpose of ruling and dilating themselves in space – all things multiply, grow, and diffuse themselves in the territory of the enemy, chasing out all others and longing to be the only one so that they might conserve themselves, render themselves eternal and deify themselves – since all things imitate God who is eternal and they yearn to render themselves similar to him, given that he is their cause.[39]

One of the complex themes discussed in the second book of the *Senso delle cose* is the centrality and primacy of the hot and subtle animal *spiritus*, analyzed in the entire rich gamut of its vital, passionate, and cognitive functions and in terms of the relationship it establishes between men and immaterial and divine *mens*. Made up of extremely attenuated matter that is purified by solar heat, imprisoned in matter, and incapable of emanating as it would wish, spirit is the hot and vital breath that moulds and organizes the organism in the manner most adapted to its own needs: 'the soul thus will be hot spirit, subtle, generated in the humor, inside a gross matter, whence, not being able to emanate, it shapes and forms that matter to the point that they are able to live together.' The body is presented as a wondrous animated machine and all the organs turn out to be constituted for and coordinated towards the end of providing for the reconstitution of spirit, which strives to escape and consumes itself continually, through the search for and the assimilation of foods rendered similar.

Spirit thus made the mouth so as to imbibe [such foods], the teeth to mash them and ready them for passage to those parts where there is a lack, and the stomach for cooking, veins to transport it [the spirit], the liver to improve and distribute it, the arteries to vivify it, the lungs to ventilate it, the heart to attenuate it, the head to house it as the sovereign, bone to structure the machine, ligaments to raise that machine up as well as lower it, nerves to diffuse the spirits and move the machine as necessary (in the manner of a system of cables), feet to carry itself to food and towards friendly beings (as well as flee the unfriendly), and flesh to clothe its mass.[40]

The sentient soul or *anima* – from which the word 'animal' derives – is thus identified with the 'hot spirit ready to take on every passion easily and to sense and to move the body.' It is thanks to heat that 'the eggs of the hen, placed under a hot dung or in hot sand (as they used to do in Egypt) come to life just as when the mother covers it with her heat; similarly, when placed

---

[39] Ibid., p. 27.
[40] Ibid., pp. 38–39.

close to a fire, the egg of the silkworm in Calabria awakens and develops.'[41] The hot soul of animals is born therefore from the heat that attenuates matter and that can give rise in a direct manner to small animals and insects: 'and we see frogs produced in water that is thick, viscous, lying in the hot dust of summer, suddenly made crust and [sensitive] subtlety; and often I have seen horsehair in hot rain water come to life and become extremely small serpents …; moreover, in tepid waters you even see the thread and lining of flax turn into animal insects'; from this, it can be concluded that 'it is therefore true that everything is full of soul, since it contains heat.'[42]

Beyond describing it as a principle of generation and movement, Campanella insisted on underscoring the unity of corporeal spirit, which – hot, made up of an extremely subtle matter, mobile, pliable – becomes capable of discharging multiple functions in diverse organs variously disposed and conformed. As he had already explained in the *Apologia pro Telesio*, he rejected the distinctions of Galen regarding diverse temperament and abstract faculties: spirit is one and has its seat in the brain, whence, running through extremely subtle nerve ducts, it performs its duties.[43] Through the sense organs it comes into contact with external reality, and from the modifications that it undergoes all its passions and understandings take their origin. Every sensation is a form of 'touching' of the spirit that enters into relation – in the various sense organs – with the exhalations, motions, and light that derive from external objects. Beyond taste (which is the 'most intrinsic touch' and derives from direct contact with the substance), smell too is made from touch, 'because the smell is a subtle substance that emanates from everything, given that all those things are hot and full of pores, made by heat emanating victorious into the heavens' and is perceived by the spirit of the nose. Hearing also is a kind of touching, because the ear is organized in such a way that spirit can notice motions coming from the outside, and some sounds are particularly enjoyable to the spirit, because 'the spirit has a mobile nature and enjoys being invited to motion, an operation that ventilates it, purges it, diffuses and augments it, according to its own symmetry.' If some sounds appear to be dissonant to individuals, 'all the voices of the world are a music for the entire world.' Sight 'is the contact of light tinted by the things that are illuminated.'[44] If every sensation is touch and if diversity depends on the different size and subtlety of the matter, it follows that everything senses, even if in different degrees and modes, and that one ought to suppose that

---

[41] Ibid., pp. 39–40.
[42] Ibid., p. 41.
[43] For a summary of the lost work, see ibid., p. 47ff.
[44] Ibid. p. 60.

The hardest things, such as stones, feel little, because they are not liable to be acted upon much, and have a sense that is similar to the bones of an animal; and that plants have a greater degree of sense, similar to that possessed by flesh; and that some liquids (such as the sanguinary kind), and the stomach and the air sense extremely easily, as does the spirit of the animal. Moreover, they sense not only when struck from close at hand and with a great deal of force, but also from far away on account of the possibility [the ability to feel or undergo] that is communicated to them and that moves them and on account of the affection for light that is placed within them and for the tinting of every figure. It is, thus, necessary to think of heat and light as the most sentient things in the world, and that the entire world senses in greater or lesser degrees.[45]

Perception varies according to the proportions and conformations of individual things: 'but in the world there is neither smell nor stench, neither sweetness nor bitterness, neither music nor cacophony, unless it be relative to various, particular things; yet considered from the perspective of the entire world everything is music, sweetness, sweet smell.'

The sentient soul, because it is corporeal, fine, and 'passes from sense to sense' is not 'affixed to a particular organ, but remains like the many soldiers in a ship or people in a house or men in a city who perform their different duties in various forges, workshops, squares, and rooms.'[46] It is not necessary to postulate differentiated and specific faculties for different operations, which are all functions of the same sentient soul. In fact, the soul is able to conserve the modifications and impressions that it receives, and to reawaken them and reuse them whenever similar situations present themselves. From this derives memory, in virtue of which when 'we remember something painful and nauseating or happy that we have sensed, that happiness or nausea or sorrow renews itself in us,' even if with diminished intensity, 'because the object is not present and remains only as a scar' and 'there are as many memories as there are similarities.' Imagination too is connected with memory and sensation: 'imagining something, all the things similar to it are awakened and all the passions similar to it are renewed in extremely subtle spirit.' In turn, speech is related to imagination: one discusses 'things unknown by means of those known to sense.' Discourse is a sensing of the similar, a passing and a moving (*discurrere*) from similar to similar. As many kinds of similitude as there are (of essence, quality,

---

[45] Ibid., p. 61.
[46] Ibid., pp. 73–74.

quantity, and so forth), there are an equal number of modes of speech and argumentation. Understanding and the universal too are connected to the sensate spirit: understanding collects similitudes stripped of particulars and, on account of being 'the sense of something absent,' such understanding is a distant and confused sense whereas sense proper is 'understanding from close at hand.'[47]

The dimension of sense also permits comparison between the level of animals and that of human beings, such that affinities and differences between them may be noted. Campanella takes delight in underscoring the extraordinary capacities of animals: equipped with sense organs that are superior to human ones, they know how to perform wondrous and ingenious deeds; they adopt forms of collective organization; they know how to use arts such as medicine or the arts of war; and, beyond that, they are endowed with forms of reasoning, language, natural prophecy and even, as in the case of elephants, with religiosity. But such analogies ought not to obfuscate or put in doubt the distinctiveness and specificity of human beings. Man is not only furnished with a *spiritus* that is considerably more refined and pure than that possessed by animals; it is also able to move with agility between more capacious brain cells, which allows him to elaborate extremely complex argumentative chains.

The genuine (and radical) distinctiveness of man consists in the fact that he is endowed not simply with that *spiritus* which connects him to all other natural beings but also with a *mens* that has a divine origin and that constitutes and gives shape to his specific dimension. The proofs in favor of this *mens* (and as a consequence in favor of the excellence and the divinity of man) are many. Fundamentally, they stem from the principle articulated at the beginning of the book, according to which 'no effect can elevate itself beyond its cause.' Man does not exhaust all his capacities within the natural world: 'man does not stop at the nature of elements and of the sun and the earth, but understands, desires, and works far above them – such that he does not depend on them, but depends on a much higher cause that is called God.' Man's capacity to extend himself with thought and desire towards the infinite demonstrates that he is not only a child of the sun and of the earth, but is also the child of an infinite cause. Thus, 'when man cogitates, he thinks beyond the sun and then higher still, and then beyond the heavens, and then beyond an infinite number of worlds.' If Aristotle held that 'it is a vain imagination to think so high,' Campanella agrees 'with Trismegistus for whom it is a non-

---

[47] Ibid., p. 81.

sense to think so low.'[48] The connection of man with the supernatural world is confirmed by his capacity to go beyond the immediate limits of natural self-preservation. The philosopher and the religious man are able to disdain corporeal goods, honors, and pleasures for the purpose of attending to higher goods and ends. Moreover, man can take hold of superior forms of prophecy and ecstasy that are not explainable with reference to physiological or medical theories. Above all, man is free in his willing, able to resist external pressures, and able both to value and to evaluate the objects of his choosing. Such objects are usually mixtures of the good and the bad and he is able to choose the greater good, even if it is not linked to an immediate advantage or utility.

The third book surveys the different degrees of sense with which each entity is endowed, beginning with the heavens and the stars, which are composed of an extremely pure spirit and have 'an exquisite power of sensing.' Against the Aristotelian doctrine that has heat derive from friction, Campanella did not tire of reaffirming the celestial nature of all heat, which is reawakened by blows to the stones in which it was imprisoned. It is the same heat that burns and destroys when it is potent, and that generates beings when it is mild. Precisely because it is hot, the entirety of the heavens senses and celestial motions are not the product of separate drives, but are rather the operations of heat. The heavens are one, the spheres do not exist, and faster or slower stellar motions derive from diverse quantities of heat conferred by the sun in accordance with distance or proximity.

A beautiful page is dedicated to light, which is endowed with 'the most acute sense' and is diffused everywhere 'in order to multiply itself, generate, and amplify itself with great delight,' with a pleasure that is similar to the pleasure that plants experience 'in thriving, growing, flowering, bearing fruit, and spreading' and similar to the pleasure experienced by human beings during sex, a pleasure that accompanies the sensation of the spreading of its own being. Shining 'through other bodies and each atom of air with infinite angles and pyramids,' light attempts to enter even in the darkest caves and grottos: 'but in transparent bodies, such as water and crystals, it starts longing for, enhancing itself and penetrating things that are similar and then savors and unites and sets ablaze the things that are not white, because they are dissimilar to it.'

The air senses, because it is 'the shared soul that helps all things and through which all things communicate.' In the air the movements and passions of the spirit are conserved as 'scars.' 'Coarse vapors' in the bowels of the earth also sense. These are vapors that 'break out and escape' with great force and 'seem like distressed animals struggling to free themselves.' Fire too

---

[48] Ibid., p. 90.

senses, for, when it is enclosed in the earth, it 'expands powerfully, breaks free, and destroys everything that could cause its own death.'[49] Water senses, for within it grow fish and plants; and the earth senses, the earth which Pythagoras compared to a 'large animal' – 'its skin and pelts are the grass and trees, its stones the bones, its animals are like lice for us.'[50] Plants sense and they are those 'immobile animals' that Campanella looked upon with a particular affection. They have 'mouths, nerves, veins, hides, bones, tissue, cloths, horns,' and in summer on account of the excessive heat 'they are drab, dull, with foliage lowered like sickly animals; yet with the arrival of some rain or when they are able to drink they raise themselves up straight; lifting themselves up, they come to life, become beautiful, and show a manifest sentiment of happiness and restoration. They produce flowers and fruit, and 'so as to preserve their seeds they close them up in bone and then in pulp; with their leaves, they protect those seeds from heat and from cold; and with their thorns, they protect them from animals whenever they can.'[51] Even minerals sense (if dimly). Minerals feed and convert in themselves the liquids of the earth; in time, they come to construct mountain ranges, 'like living bone.' Darkness–the symbol of matter and of cold–also senses; even the shadow of our body, when 'drawing close to another shadow, extends itself in the manner of a pyramid so as to unite itself with that other shadow as quickly as possible.'[52]

The fourth book, which would also circulate independently, was dedicated to natural magic.[53] While taking note of the most curious hidden properties of minerals, plants, and animals, Giambattista della Porta (limiting himself to dealing with the spectacle of the natural world) had asserted that it was impossible to offer a rational explanation for the relationships of sympathy and antipathy that exist among natural entities. Campanella attempted to re-read and to re-interpret this exuberant tradition in the light of his doctrine of the sense of things. Having recalled that the ancients defined as magicians 'those who investigate the occult ways of God and nature (God's artifact) and who then, applying those occult ways to human use, are capable of wondrous acts,' Campanella could only deplore the condition of abasement and decadence into which this noble doctrine had fallen. In modern times, the name of "magician" was given to 'superstitious friends of demons'; 'tired of investigating things, such people had looked to demons for shortcuts to do that which they could not do or could not pretend to do.' The very learned attempt by

---

[49] Ibid., pp. 131, 97, 136, 135, 132.
[50] Ibid., p. 133.
[51] Ibid., pp. 159, 98.
[52] Ibid., pp. 97, 133.
[53] See Guido Giglioni, 'magia naturale,' in *Enciclopedia*, vol. 1, coll. 265–277.

Porta to restore this doctrine was praiseworthy, but insufficient – in that it was limited to speaking of the magician only 'historically,' in a descriptive and empirical way, 'without entering into the business of causes.' Magic, as Pliny remembered, is constituted by religion, which 'serves to purge the spirit and to make it ready to understand and to make it a friend of the first cause to instill faith, honor and reverence in the spirits of those to whom it was applied.' Magic was also constituted by medicine, 'by way of understanding the powers of plants, stones, and metals and the sympathy and antipathy among them and towards us,' and by astrology, 'so that one might know the time that was appropriate for action.' This is a wisdom that is 'speculative and practical at the same time, because it applies understanding to works that are useful to human kind.' It is divided into several kinds: supernatural or divine, natural, deceitful and diabolical. Divine magic consists in friendship and faith in God, considered as 'good, holy, and just, as something that can and wants to do us good.' If the soul 'cannot extend itself to know the infinite,' it can nevertheless believe in God as the cause of all things and render itself unanimous with him and achieve in that way a new faith that 'is, one might say, not only historical,' but is a faith that 'has so much power that it changes created things into that which we desire.' There is a crucial distinction between a 'historical' faith (which is external and cold) and a 'living' faith, which calls for purity of heart and intrinsic adherence to divinity, in such a way as to 'will and nill in accordance with him, and in a manner greater than vulgar lovers do with the things that they love.' This living faith is one that transforms 'man into God and makes him divine.' It can offer us a key to interpreting the transition from Campanella's earlier positions to those that came after the crisis of the years in Sant'Elmo. This transition consisted precisely in a movement from a cold and completely exterior faith to an intrinsic faith that is fed by divine love and that transforms 'the lover into the object that he loves.'[54]

A very lively page describes the most delightful deceits of tricksters and charlatans and the abilities of tightrope walkers, revealing them to be 'useless fictions.' His interest was entirely concentrated on natural magic. On the one hand, such magic was connected with the arts and the sciences. At first and above all to ordinary people ('as long as the art was not understood'), all discoveries or wondrous inventions seemed to be the result of magic. But 'later such "magic" would be common science.' On the other hand, natural magic retained its particular sphere of rarer and more esoteric knowledge and Campanella attempted to re-read it in the light of his doctrines of sense, spirit, and the passions. The magician is he who, knowing the specific quality of sense that belongs to every being, is able to use it in a useful way and is able to induce particular

---

[54] *Senso delle cose*, pp. 168–169.

alterations in mobile and fine spirits that are ready to undergo and receive any impression. The basic passions are those of sorrow and joy, love and hate, and hope and fear. And 'he who knows how to engender all these effects in man, with herbs, actions, and other opportune things one may call a magician.'[55] That man will know how to increase vital powers, by suggesting those foods, drinks, climates, sounds, and herbal and animal remedies that are useful and that fortify vital energies and by discouraging all those that have anything to do with putrefaction and death. He will know the secrets of bringing death and life, in that he knows everything that is either useful to the spirit or damaging (or lethal) to it. He will know the secrets of reproduction and the secrets of diseases. He will know how to raise up passions for the purpose of achieving particular ends, both in people and in particular organs. Campanella presents examples of these things that are very curious. One such curious example is the remedy suggested for avoiding an excessive hardening of the liver, which involves generating the kind of 'dry blood' and 'paucity of spirits and powdery material' that bring ageing and death. So as to keep a liver 'as soft as the livers of babies,' it is good to feed on 'milk and soft things without excrement.' It is also advisable 'to fasten a vase of water up high and to let some drops of water come down through canals now and again onto the liver, which is an excellent magical remedy, because the liver fears and retracts, thereby softening; and the emanating heat no longer dries it out.' If one suffers from a swelling of the spleen, then one should place another spleen that has been dried with smoke on it; this will induce a cure – and not by some work of the devil, but rather because 'the emotion of the patient generates fear in his own spleen, which then retracts itself, squeezes, and vomits the humor, because it is sympathizing with the other spleen, which is similar to itself.'[56]

The lingering of sense in latent and dormant forms in beings and in the air, which are then awakened on particular occasions, renders explicable events that appear to be prodigious, such as the bleeding of a cadaver (in which there remains an 'obtuse sense') in the presence of the killer. As Campanella explained, 'men who have been murdered, spew forth blood in the presence of the murderer and they boil almost out of anger or out of fear, sensing, on account of the intervening air, the presence of the odious enemy; and this is the sign used for discovering the killer.'[57] The continued existence of affects and of sensation is connected to the efficacy of the weapon salve, thanks to which one can cure a wound even at a distance if one treats the weapon that inflicted the wound, as if the spirit closed up in the wound might acquire faith

---

[55] Ibid., p. 177.
[56] Ibid., pp. 183, 188.
[57] Ibid., p. 184.

when it senses the cure through the air, and might experience 'something like a rejoicing in vengeance.'[58] Campanella also dealt with the explanation of a famous example that is mentioned in every book on magic. In the example, a drum made out of sheepskin fell to pieces upon hearing the striking of a drum made out of wolfskin, on account of the reawakening in it of an ancient fear. In a kind of analogy, a fierce Bohemian captain ordered the construction after his death of a drum made out of his own skin so as to terrorize his enemies.[59]

It is also in the light of the doctrine of sense that it is possible to explain the true metamorphoses that take place in persons bitten by rabid dogs or in peasants of Puglia attacked by tarantulas.[60] The former, after forty days, 'faint and shout' and bite; they cannot look upon water, for fear of seeing their own image reflected; in the end, they bark and 'die rabid and miserable, thinking themselves to be dogs.' Regarding the tarantula example, Campanella gave a precise description, which suggests that he had seen the phenomenon for himself.[61] Those who have been bitten become weak and 'stupid.' They dance and jump to the sound of various instruments, before collapsing, exhausted. In both cases, the acrid spirits and humors that are introduced by the bite induce an alteration in the temperament and the imagination of these poor souls, in whose organism the spirit of the animal that has attacked them gains the upper hand. In this way, they forget who they were. In the case of tarantulas, the infected vapors are forcibly expelled by the dancing and the sweating it induces. But usually the symptoms last as long as the cause that has produced them and only the death of the spider that has bitten them will lead to a complete remission of the illness. The connection between universal and particular causes is confirmed also in the peculiar case of a nose graft, completed at the medical school of Tropea, in a man who, having lost his nose as the result of an injury, reconstructed it from the meat of the arm of a slave, to whom he promised liberty in exchange. The new nose took root and grew, but, when the slave died, it began to putrefy – proof of the fact that the life it received from the new organism in which it was inserted had not annulled its original and root connection with the life of the slave. Thus, they are 'stupid who deny the duration of a mortal life and the sense and consensus of the entire world.'[62]

The general rules of magic are concerned with empowering vital and preservative qualities by all relevant natural means. Music and sounds, which act upon the spirit, also have a great effect. The intonations and words that – as

---

[58] Ibid., p. 188.
[59] Ibid., pp. 186–187.
[60] See ibid., l. IV, ch. 10, p. 189ff.
[61] See ch. 4.1.
[62] Ibid., p. 197.

in the case of the poet and the orator – generate passions also have a great effect, but they can also be changed into superstitious ceremonies and practices, into which the devil himself can intrude. The final chapters linger on the relationship between magic and astrology, the understanding of which is indispensible for acting in accordance with the unfolding of events and in choosing the right moment and the most favorable astral situations. The work ends with an *Epilogo del senso dell'universo*, a lyrical celebration of the world as a divine moving image, in which life ends and begins in an uninterrupted vicissitude:

> the world, thus, is all sense and life and soul and body, statue of the Highest, made with power, wisdom, and love for his glory. Nothing is to be lamented. In him so many die and so many live in order to serve his great life. Bread dies in us and is transformed into mass, and then this mass dies and is transformed into blood, and then the blood dies and is made into flesh, nerve, bone, spirit, seed – such that various deaths and births, various pleasures and pains are suffered; but they serve a purpose for our lives, and we do not lament them on that account, but rather celebrate the process. Thus, all things are a source of rejoicing for the world; all things serve and everything is made for the whole; and the whole is made for the glory of God.[63]

Religion and Nature

The *Ateismo trionfato* was written in 1606–1607. It constituted a watershed in Campanella's thought and testifies to overcoming his deep spiritual and intellectual crisis. Among the promises that the prisoner dedicated himself to realizing, we find a commitment to writing 'a volume against politicians and Machiavellians, who are the scourge of this century and the scourge of that monarchy [the universal monarchy]; this would be a volume that would show reason of state to be founded on the basis of love of self and that would demonstrate to them with new and effective arguments how deceived they are in the matter of the doctrine of the soul and in thinking that religion is an art of government.'[64]

The polemic against reason of state and the Machiavellian conception of religion as a human and political invention and as a useful *figmentum* (a clever expedient), developed by a cunning clerisy and by political leaders in order to gain and maintain power, was connected to the important task of undertaking a full rational inquiry that would survey and evaluate all religious beliefs and philosophical doctrines in order to show how religion is, on the contrary, a *virtus*

---

[63] Ibid., p. 235.
[64] Letter to Cardinal Odoardo Farnese, 30 August 1606, in *Lettere*, p. 26.

naturalis (natural virtue) inherent in man. The subsequent period of research would be dedicated to verifying the relationship between natural religion and Christianity, for the purpose of concluding that there was no contrast but rather a deep and original concord between Christian law and natural law. After all, Christ had not nullified or abolished natural law; he had simply added moral precepts and ceremonies to it that completed and perfected it.

Writing to Paul V, Campanella asserted that – having examined faith 'through the philosophies of the Pythagoreans, Stoics, Epicureans, Peripatetics, Platonists, Telesians, and through the philosophy of all other sects both ancient and modern, as well as through the laws of ancient peoples and those of the Jews, Turks, Persians, Moors, Chinese, the inhabitants of Cathay, the Japanese, Brahmins, Peruvians, Mexicans, Abyssinians, and Tartars' – he had come to the conclusion that 'the pure law of nature is the law of Christ, to which only the sacraments have been added in order to help nature to work better by the grace of he who had given those sacraments (which are also natural and credible symbols).'[65]

Campanella did not conceal his suspicion of having perhaps been pushed too far by his rational effort, or of having perhaps committed errors, as might happen to anyone when taking up an art: 'I concede that I have been too eager to examine the Christian law, and I may have erred as happens with every craftsman in his art, like the tailor who ruins a great deal of fabric before he knows well how to make clothes, or the doctor who kills many patients before he becomes skillful.'[66] But pointing to the honesty of his research and the sincerity of the attempt to demonstrate the coincidence of first reason and Christianity, he declared to the Pontiff his own ability and intention to persuade others of such truths: 'the world over, I will never encounter a sectarian I could not convince of the falsity of his faith; at once, I reduce it to the natural law of first Reason, and … arguing on the basis of the moral and ceremonial precepts of Christ, I show with vivid divine magic that those precepts are in accord with the law of nature.' Campanella concluded by revealing that, 'as I have convinced myself, so I convince others.'[67]

At the beginning of the summer of 1607, the *Ateismo trionfato* had been finished and on 1 June 1607 it was dedicated to Kaspar Schoppe, who had arrived at Naples in the spring in order to establish contact with the prisoner. Campanella made a gift of it to him with a gesture of profound gratitude towards the visitor, whom he saw as an angel sent by the Lord in a deeply desperate situation. In the following weeks, the author made reference to the volume in a famous letter to Monsignor Querenghi dated 8 July 1607. In that

---

[65] Ibid., p. 15.
[66] Ibid., p. 16.
[67] Ibid., p. 55.

letter, he emphasized the particularity of his own philosophy, which did not rely on 'human schools' and on books but instead 'learned in the school of nature and in the school of art' and informed the prelate that he would find an overview of his thought in the recent book dedicated to Schoppe.[68]

Written in Italian, the work was later translated by the author into Latin. It was then published in that translation in Rome (1631) and in Paris (1636) and, until recently, it constituted the only known version of the text. But, thanks to an amazing rediscovery, I had the great satisfaction of locating the original version of the text, written in Campanella's hand, and was able to publish a critical edition of it in 2004.[69] In the original version, the text was called *Recognoscimento della vera religione*, but it was Schoppe himself who suggested to the author that he change the title (which emphasized more the direction in which the research was heading than a truth already possessed) to the more peremptory one by which the work is usually known. In the original version, the work was preceded by a dedicatory letter to the author's German friend (which later in the Latin edition would be replaced with a more sober *Praefatio*), in which he gave an emotional evocation of the dramatic events of his life. References to trials of his youth, culminating in the Neapolitan trial following the conspiracy, and the terrible torture, are combined with a strong contrast between light and dark, between an age of darkness dominated by reason of state and, on the other hand, the prospect of ascending to the light so as to permit the distinguishing of truth from error and thereby restoring man to a new dignity: 'the age is dark, and it does not know where the heavens are; the stars are obscured by fog, the lights extinguished, the sun is in shadow, the moon covered in blood,' he lamented. Again, 'every sect boasts of miracles, prophecies, testimonies, martyrs, and arguments so as to prove that it is authorized by God: we are in the dark and we all appear to be the same color, philosophers and sophists, saints and hypocrites, princes and tyrants, religion and superstition.' The work was given to Schoppe as a torch with the following instruction: 'tighten it into the hearts of men; perhaps from brushwood they will turn into animals, and from animals into humans.'[70]

The first chapter serves an introductory function and proposes to map the diversity of possible attitudes concerning religion. At first, Campanella focuses on those who are the most numerous, for whom the acceptance of native

---

[68] Ibid., pp. 134–135.

[69] *L'ateismo trionfato*, 2 vols. (Pisa, 2004); the first volume contains the critical edition of the work and annotations; the second contains an anastatic reproduction of the ms Barb. lat. 4458 of the Biblioteca Apostolica Vaticana, repository of the autograph version.

[70] *Ateismo trionfato*, I, pp. 3–5.

religion coincides with an uncritical adherence and a passive acquiescence that is undisturbed by doubt. He then speaks of those in whom such adherence is conditioned by the passions, among which are to be numbered the enjoyment of personal advantages or fear of persecution. There follows the group of those frail types who do not deny religion and are not bad people and who behave badly only because they are misled by the bad example set by the majority. In any case, prostitutes and publicans are certainly preferable to sophists and hypocrites, who are all intent on simulating 'a knowledge and kindness that they do not possess.' But there are two figures that dominate the scene and they are represented both as authentic protagonists and also as antagonists – namely, politicians and philosophers. The first, deniers of God and of his providence, uphold the political origin of every religion: 'they do not believe in any law, and they hold that law is an art of living discovered by astute people.' For them sin does not exist, and 'can only be established by the law for the preservation of the community, and so that ordinary people obey.' Miracles, when they are not to be attributed to chance, are produced by 'illusions of the ignorant' or by the 'cunning of the intelligent.' Such doctrines, founded in love of self, are extremely difficult to uproot and constitute the bane of every age, in that their supporters reject every counter-argument, holed up in the arrogant certainty of possessing the truth. They are too sure that 'seeking another truth is for impoverished people, who do not know how to live, or of astute people so as to create a new religion as a foundation for the state.' On the other side, there are the philosophers, who believe that there is only one law – a law that is true and certain, natural and common to all. Skeptical with regard to supernatural dogmas, they live in a virtuous way that conforms to nature. Without doing harm to anyone, 'they serve the first cause with good will and perform works that are at once honest and beneficial to the human race'; they do not desire honors or riches, but 'they are happy with little, and derive their joy from contemplation, and feel better than a king, pope or monarch.'[71]

The second chapter, which is one of the most controversial parts in the entire work, takes us into the heart of the problem. This chapter presents a long list of arguments against religion in general, and Christianity in particular. As has been indicated, it takes the form of an 'extremely full list of libertine propositions' and 'an organic expression of the anti-Christian doctrines of the period.'[72] Those objections are then presented in so crude a light and in a sequence so littered with interrogatives that it elicited perplexity and unease both before and after the book was published – not just in the Catholic

---

[71] Ibid., pp. 17–18.

[72] Giorgio Spini, *Ricerca dei libertini. La teoria dell'impostura delle religioni nel Seicento italiano* (1950[1]), new edition (Florence, 1983), pp. 85–86.

camp, but among Protestants too. With the interlocutors described and the objections listed (to which responses are given in the central and concluding chapters of the work), the other chapters of the first part – the most limpid – are dedicated to proving the naturalness of religion, which is intrinsic to every aspect of nature, which is in turn the expression of divine art. From the central point that God exists as Reason and Wisdom diffused throughout all the aspects of reality derive the following corollaries: the radiating of the 'trace' of the Trinity in every natural being; the reasonableness of the Incarnation; the acting of Providence in the world (which is a theater and statue of divinity rather than a dark labyrinth of suffering); the non-existence of death and the relativity of evil, which is connected with non-being and which is therefore something that is necessary for the distinction of things; the profound solidarity of man with nature, even if at the same time his intrinsic divinity and eminence renders man capable of elevating himself to a higher world. From here the text moves on to the difficult problem of the immortality of the soul, a certainty that is attained following paths that are different from those taken by the Aristotelian tradition. Campanella insisted instead on the particularity of man as the only being capable of going beyond his own natural limits and acquiring a consciousness of his own relationship to the infinite.

In the ninth chapter, it is reaffirmed, against all skeptical attitudes, that the existence of multiple false religions is not a sufficient reason to conclude that every religion is radically false. Just as the inexpertness of many physicians does not prove the falsity of medicine in general, so the fact that many wines are adulterated does not prove that there are none that are pure. If it is true that there are differences among the various positive religions (in their rituals and in their supernatural beliefs), it is also true that 'it is natural for man to incline towards justice and to live in religion' and that therefore one can grasp with 'discourse' and experience with 'sense' that religion is *de iure naturae* (in accordance with natural law). A strong confirmation of religion's naturalness appears in the fact that it is the indispensible foundation and connective tissue of every political community, which without religion could not subsist and would dissolve.[73]

The tenth chapter is, then, concerned with proving that between natural religion and Christianity there cannot be anything other than a profound and basic agreement, given that nature is the expression of the divine Word, which is the principle of every rational value and of every virtue, since Christ – who is that same Reason made flesh – did not nullify and abolish natural law but rather added moral precepts and ceremonies to it that completed and perfected it. With an audacity that would not fail to raise the ire of censors (the same audacity that would appear to raise the specter of Pelagius because

---

[73] *Ateismo trionfato*, I, pp. 92–93.

it exalted natural and rational values extended to all humanity), Campanella affirmed the unity and universality of a single law, in which all men were participants insofar as they were rational, from the moment that Christ is eternal wisdom and first reason:

> We say that Christ is eternal wisdom and first reason, and that everything that is against reason is against Christ, and that all those living in accordance with reason are Christians. Therefore, all nations, recognizing Christ as first reason, cannot take other laws, ... because every law is reason or a rule for reason; thus, every law constitutes the splendor of the light of Jesus (that is to say, the Redeemer), because reason or wisdom is that which governs and saves all things.[74]

The criterion by which to evaluate the goodness of a law is thus its conformity with rational values. Such conformity implies, on the one hand, that those who live according to reason are in fact Christians implicitly, and therefore participants in the economy of salvation, even if they are ignorant of the revelation. On the other hand, such conformity implies that the condition of explicit Christians does not in itself offer guarantees and does not obviate the duty of living in accordance with rational principles: 'Thus, all nations are implicitly Christian, because they all profess to live rationally, and insofar as nations depart from that rationality they are not Christian, and thus we explicit Christians are not Christian in those acts in which we distance ourselves from reason.'[75]

The incarnation of Christ took place in order to confirm and restore (after the original sin) the law of nature, which applies to all humanity, not so as to exclude, separate, or make enemies of the different faiths: 'And Christ was made flesh in order to make us see the universal natural law more clearly through deeds and doctrine. It is a great wonder that, willingly or not, men are subject to Christ regardless of whether he is known or not. Thus, the diversity of laws is no argument, given that positive laws are specifications and applications of that same first natural law, and their variety does not make them for us either unreasonable or unchristian.'[76] Christianity is not a particular sect among other sects. Instead it sets itself up as an expression of the 'same law of nature, pure and innocent' that is integrated and perfected by supernatural beliefs, dogmas, and ceremonial elements – elements that, in turn, are not alien to rationality and naturalness.[77] Therefore, the Christian religion, both for the simplicity and universality of its

---

[74]Ibid., p. 100.
[75] Ibid., pp. 100–101.
[76] Ibid.
[77] Ibid.

moral message and because its ceremonial apparatus is not contrary to nature, is more closely conformed to nature, and it is therefore the most universalizable. The concluding chapters, finally, confront particular aspects of Christianity, regarding rather delicate points such as the Eucharist, miracles, prophecy, specifying the 'signs' and marks that distinguish true Christian belief and confirm its excellence in comparison with other beliefs. In those final chapters, the polemic is deepened against the doctrines of Machiavelli and the supporters of reason of state, who deny the 'naturalness' of religion in order to emphasize its political character.

For Campanella, however, being persuaded of the excellence of Christianity did not entail excluding other beliefs or erecting walls around the citadel of truth. On the contrary, Christian rationality opens up the possibility of a universal confluence of every creed in an ecumenical consensus. While holding fast to the principle of Christian superiority, it remains true that every faith that is conformed to reason contains some share of the truth; irrational faiths, on the other hand, are abuses and 'contorted rules.' From here, Campanella's attention turned to every form of religiosity, wherever and however it is manifested. He revealed himself to be more intrigued than scandalized when he underlined the analogy between the Christian sacraments and the rough ceremonies of the American Indians, who possessed primitive forms of confession and the Eucharist, even if exterior pressures then forced him into contrite condemnation of the deceits of the devil, *simia Dei* (imitator of God.)[78] In another passage, recalling an episode in which unarmed Anabaptists succeeded in resisting the soldiers of an imperial army, he was not able to hide the most vivid emotion, revealing how the force of faith was irresistible wherever it manifested itself:

> When the Emperor ordered the killing of the Anabaptists, they all knelt down in the countryside waiting for death. When the soldiers arrived they became stricken with shame, and did not want to lay a hand on them, and they let them live; and the Emperor concurred. See how powerful is the law of Christ in anyone who observes it.[79]

---

[78] *Ateismo trionfato*, I, p. 169; see *Ath. triumph.*, p. 175: 'De Americanis cum admiratione audivi, quod confessione peccatorum utebantur: plebs principibus, principes regi, rex Soli confitebantur: Sol autem deo, ut putabant; et panem quasi eucharistiae manducabant, formantes idolum ex pasta, et distribuentes et communicantes in illo, quem vocabant nomine Dei sui, sicuti nos Iesuchristi. Profecto isti ritus si fuissent cum cognitione veri Dei, et eius instinctu vel lege a Deo instituta, nequaquam irrationabiles essent, sed palam est esse commenta diaboli, simiae Dei.'

[79] *Ateismo trionfato*, I, p. 105 (*Ath. triumph.*, p. 113); Campanella would refer to the persecutions brought down on the community by Jakob Hutter based in Moravia and chased out of there by Emperor Ferdinand II in 1622: see Roland Crahay, 'Une référence de Campanella: l'utopie pratiquée des Anabaptistes,' in *Le discours utopique* (Paris, 1978), pp. 179–192: 182ff.

Campanella spoke also of the suggested analogy between Christian and pagan miracles – such as that of the Vestal Virgin who, in order to demonstrate her own purity, transported the water of the Tiber to the temple in a sieve. Instead of simply disregarding or naturalizing the prodigy, he took it as a demonstration of how divine presence works in every place in every time. Highlighting similarities between prodigious events did not have a skeptical or naturalizing aim (as in libertine interpretations); instead, it was directed at emphasizing the spatial-temporal continuity of divine presence. The real targets of this polemic were those who believed that the personal possession of truth is a motive for separating themselves from others who are held to be living in error. For Campanella, these are people who are more worried about indicating boundaries and raising up obstacles than imagining a common project or a shared adherence to a single school of the First Wisdom. In a fine passage of the *Syntagma*, Campanella offered us a persuasive key for interpreting his positions. In a sober *laudatio* of Justin (one of the 'authors' of the *Atheismus*), he said that he 'demonstrated that religion, which others hold to be planted only in their own garden, is in fact sown in the entire human species.'[80]

In the course of the almost thirty years that passed between the composition of the *Ateismo* (1607) and the definitive edition that came out in Paris (1636), the work encountered endless problems and obstacles, due to the diffidence and the suspicions of the ecclesiastical authorities.[81] The *Ateismo* was not published by Schoppe (as Campanella had originally hoped); nor was it among the texts published in Frankfurt between 1617 and 1623 under the auspices of Tobias Adami. After the failure of these attempts, the author would consider publishing it in Italy. In the spring of 1621, he sent it to the Holy Office in order to obtain the necessary approval. At first, the opinion of Cardinal Bellarmine, who was charged with overseeing all such approvals, appeared to be favorable. But subsequently the judgment – arrived at by three different commissioners – was negative. The censors maintained that 'it is not appropriate that the said Father Campanella write and publish his works.'[82] Campanella hurriedly composed a passionate defense of religion as *virtus naturalis* and sent it to Rome – but to no avail.[83] When he reached Rome, the *Ateismo* was subjected to a full trial, begun in the middle of November 1627 and concluded in March 1628. The propositions submitted to the judgment of

---

[80] *Syntagma*, p. 110.

[81] See Luigi Firpo, 'Appunti campanelliani. XXI. Le censure all'*Atheismus triumphatus*,' *GCFI*, 30 (1951), pp. 509–524. See also Ernst, *Religione*, p. 73ff and the texts cited in the following notes.

[82] Enrico Carusi, *Nuovi documenti sui processi di Tommaso Campanella*, *GCFI*, 8 (1927), doc. 72, p. 351.

[83] See Germana Ernst, 'Il ritrovato *Apologeticum* di Campanella al Bellarmino in difesa della religione naturale,' *Rivista di storia della filosofia*, 157 (1992), pp. 565–586.

the inquisitorial commission elicited in the censors a profound, indefinable unease. They concluded that it was hard to say whether it was by ingenuousness or malice ('either he is very ignorant or he is very malicious') that the author appeared ambiguous and evasive – 'he is as slippery as an eel.' The philosophical assertions were said to be absurd, foolish, fatuous, fantastical, and scandalous, while, at a theological level, the accusation that circulated ever more insistently was the accusation of Pelagianism. The discussion began with propositions drawn from the tenth chapter and the censors were unanimous in specifying the radical error of the book: the author was said to have confounded nature and grace, raising the first up too much and binding the second within parameters that were too restrictive: 'it exalts nature and abases grace, and reduces everything to nature.'[84]

On 23 March 1628, the Pontiff decided to release the book, which in the summer was returned to the author, so that he might make the necessary corrections – or so that, if necessary, he might rewrite it from scratch.[85] Campanella did not welcome this last discomforting invitation. Without becoming despondent, he undertook the punctilious work of revision tenaciously and the volume was published at Rome at the end of 1630. The author was scarcely able to rejoice in that success before the work was pulled from circulation, blocked by fifteen late-arriving queries of an unknown censor – objections that Campanella would refer to bitterly as 'post-censoring.'[86] Under fire in particular was the crude list of objections against religion and Christianity in the second chapter. The fifth query argued that while the 'arguments' against the Christian religion were 'extremely strong and rather pressing,' the replies from the appendix added to the chapter were 'too short and inadequate.' Despite defending himself strenuously, Campanella was forced to flank the objections with 'brief responses' that anticipated the contents of those parts of the text where such objections were answered more fully, 'so that the reader would not waver under the blows and would have close at hand an immediate antidote.'[87] In spring 1631, the work was put back in circulation. But once again the success was short-lived. A few months later, the new anti-astrological sensitivity of Pope Urban VIII was triggered by a passage in the text asserting that the positions of the stars were favorable to the reform of the Church.

---

[84] The texts of the debate are contained in Germana Ernst, 'Cristianesimo e religione naturale. Le censure all'*Atheismus triumphatus* di Tommaso Campanella,' *Nouvelles de la République des Lettres*, 1989, 1–2, pp. 137–200. On the issue of Campanella's suspected Pelagianism, see the last chapter of the recent monograph by Jean Delumeau, *Le mystère Campanella* (Paris, 2008), p. 499ff.

[85] Carusi, *Nuovi documenti*, doc. 94, p. 358.

[86] 'Risposte alle censure dell'*Ateismo triunfato*,' in *Opuscoli inediti*, pp. 9–54.

[87] *Ath. triumph.*, p. 8b.

So as not to appear stubborn, the author declared himself ready to suppress the criticized passage, but when Niccolò Riccardi, Master of the Sacred Palace, advanced new requests for modifications and suppressions, Campanella, exasperated and conscious of the fact that these were mere pretexts, refused to yield to further interventions and the book was confiscated. After his flight to France, Campanella would not fail to express his own bitterness that a text so fundamental for the fight against atheists would remain 'boarded up.' His requests for a revocation of the sequestration fell on deaf ears and he eventually took the decision to reprint it. The *Atheismus* was published, along with other writings, at the beginning of 1636 in a volume dedicated to Louis XIII. For the Papal Nuncio in Paris there was nothing to do but communicate to Rome his disappointment 'at not having been able to prevent the publication of the book ... titled *Atheismus triumphatus*.'[88]

---

[88] Carusi, *Nuovi documenti*, doc. 100, p. 359. On the censorship of Campanella works, see Saverio Ricci, *Davanti al Santo Uffizio. Filosofi sotto processo* (Viterbo, 2009).

8. CHRISTIAN UNITY

Campanella and Venice

The first of Campanella's letters to have come down to us from the period
of his imprisonment in Naples is addressed to Pope Paul V (13 August 1606).
Description of the painful conditions is combined in these pages with an
account of a recent meeting with the Nuncio. Campanella recognized his own
error and was certain that he could 'defend Christianity against the entire
world,' and become thereby 'an eyewitness of its truths' as well as 'extremely
sound in matters of faith.' Several days later, Campanella added a postscript
to the letter, in which he affirmed having become aware of the 'news regarding
Venice' and rushed to give opinions and advice. In the next letter to the Pope,
Campanella specified having found out from a barber and some soldiers at
the castle that the Venetians had been excommunicated.[1] Assuring the Pope
that he had many things to say on this extremely grave matter, Campanella
emphasized the necessity of waging a campaign that was not grammatical but
rather spiritual. He predicted a sure defeat for the Most Serene Republic if it
intended to follow the paths of reason of state in order to liberate itself from
the authority of the papacy. The event gave Campanella the chance to recall
the diabolical evocations practiced three years earlier together with attendant prophecies, some of which pertained to the sure ruin of Venice were it
to revolt.[2] It is in this context that the shorter works consigned to Schoppe
had their origin – works that Schoppe would felicitously title *Antiveneti*. It
was above all as a result of this work, found to be full of insults and injuries towards the Republic, that the German scholar would be arrested and

---

[1] *Lettere*, pp. 19–20.
[2] Letter to Paul V, September 1606, ibid., p. 38ff.

G. Ernst, *Tommaso Campanella*, International Archives of the History
of Ideas/Archives internationales d'histoire des idées 200,
DOI 10.1007/978-90-481-3126-6_8, © Springer Science + Business Media B.V. 2010

imprisoned in the course of his stay at Venice en route to Germany.[3] The work is divided into three parts, and Campanella made use of diverse arguments – political, prophetic, astrological – in order to dissuade the Most Serene Republic from what he took to be its ruinous attempts at religious schism and political separation.

Venice constituted a constant point of reference for Campanella's political thought, appearing as it did once again at the center of the final political writings, during his French period. In the course of his residence at Padua, Campanella had the chance to know and to come to value the institutions of the Republic. In one of his political sonnets, Venice is praised on account of the wisdom and judiciousness of its government ('time-piece of princes and a wise school'), and for the fact that it had made itself the sole bearer of the onerous burden of liberty ('bearing the weight of liberty, alone').[4] In the *Antiveneti* this praise was transformed into a bitter reproach. Campanella inserted a harsh palinodic sonnet into the text, in which Venice, which had earlier been identified with the providential ark of Noah, became the ship of the infernal boatman Charon.[5]

In the third part of the *Antiveneti* (which was probably the first to be conceived and written), the author presented astrological and prophetical arguments, in order to demonstrate how the times were not favorable to republics in general. From 1603 the major planets, Jupiter and Saturn, had returned to combine in the signs of fire, as in the times of Christ and Charlemagne. Such a celestial aspect was favorable to vast empires, such as the universal and Catholic monarchy of Spain. In the pages titled 'secret key,' Campanella identified Venice's biblical analogues as Egypt and Tyre.

In the first part, titled *Ragionamenti in spirito* and consisting of nine *Lamenti profetali*, the harsh reproaches against Venice all turn on the image of rape. The declared intention of the author is to construct a 'mystical parable' and to refer to biblical models. But one ought also to say that the insistent and artificial recourse to negative sexual metaphors is evidence of conventional, counter-reformation idiosyncrasies. Venice is the virgin 'never raped by a tyrant, or by a prince, or by a lover, or by a husband.' Wishing to free herself from the guardianship of her father, she risks losing all liberty and dignity. Venice is the

---

[3] For a vivid and precise reconstruction of Schoppe's misadventure in Venice, see Luigi Firpo, 'Non Paolo Sarpi, ma Tommaso Campanella,' *Giornale storico della letteratura italiana*, 158 (1981), pp. 254–274, esp. 268ff. Perhaps as a result of this mishap, after mentioning the work in an index soon after the events (see *Lettere 2*, nn. 10–13, pp. 36–37), Campanella would subsequently make minimal and reticent references to the work.

[4] *Poesie*, p. 205.

[5] Ibid., p. 608; *Antiveneti*, pp. 38–39.

'glorious lady' whose brutal and shameful love affairs would degrade her and take from her, along with the flower of her virginity, every trace of youth and beauty ('you will make yourself old, emaciated, wrinkled'). Venice is the 'little nun of Christ' who wants to leave the convent so as to prostitute herself 'in a brothel with the other whores.' Paying for the temptation of this false 'promiscuous freedom,' she would make herself the victim of every ruffian – and of Muhammad, 'a powerful lover.'[6] The person responsible for this situation would be Machiavelli: the generous winged lion of San Marco is transformed into a dragon with the wings of a bat, which has in its clutches not the Gospel but rather the books of the Florentine Secretary – who is called 'a scandal, a disaster, poison and fire of this age.' In another passage (in an etymology that is completely fantastical), Machiavelli is he who defiles tombs (*'macchia gli avelli'*) – that is, the necromancer who calls the derisive spirit of Lucian out from hell, together with those more sinister spirits of Tiberius and the great priest Caiphas, so that they might teach disdain for God and religion, ready to simulate and deceive the people, and to replace justice with personal utility.[7]

It is, however, in the second part of the *Antiveneti* that the most disconcerting pages are located. These are pages in which religion is presented as the indispensible support that guarantees the obedience of subjects and wards off sedition. These are entirely unscrupulous pages in which Campanella considered things from the point of view of pure political advantage. He criticized those who hold power and make errors in their calculations by undervaluing the undeniable advantages of religion. Casting the myth of Venice in a fairly crude light, he revealed that it is precisely religion that compensates for the violence and the injustice of the oligarchic regime. At a more general level, he described religion as the secret of political obedience and social stability:

> Now, when princes make blunders and their peoples become discontented or are solicited by bandits, religious men are the reason why they do not rebel and why they remain obedient. And this is a result of preaching or on account of the secret confessions in which they are advised to live well – thus, religion detaches them from their depraved wills, comforts them with the thought of Paradise, and terrorizes them with the prospect of Hell.[8]

The author affirmed in no uncertain terms that religion performs precisely the function of controlling the claims of the people. In other passages, he would attribute such claims to political leaders of a Machiavellian stripe and those who argue that religion has the capacity to turn the entirely human appetite for the goods of the earth towards the kingdom of the heavens.

---

[6] *Antiveneti*, pp. 9–10, 20, 22.

[7] Ibid., pp. 49, 66.

[8] Ibid., p. 103.

Religion is a way of returning to obedience the unhappy 'scoundrels' who would otherwise 'look with a callous eye' at the noblemen who sleep 'fat-bellied in their villas or in their boats.' The conflict of Venice with religious men is thus myopic and suicidal, because it is precisely religious men who safeguard power from the protests and requests of those classes that are excluded from the well-being and privileges enjoyed by the dominant classes: 'But you Venetians now say that you do not believe in priests; and they, desperate for paradise, will covet the villas and riches of this world, like you, and they will do everything so as to bring about change ...'[9] From this comes the political short-sightedness of a clash with religious men, whose role remains fundamental: 'do religious men, thus, appear to be useless to the state? But, even according to reason of state, they are the most useful people even if God did not exist.'[10] In these pages Campanella did not refrain from affirming the magical force of religion, which remains powerful even if it is false. As he put is, 'religion, whether true or false, has also a natural magical power that unites spirits and capabilities; he who disdains it becomes vile and abominable for his vassals and soldiers.' But in a way that is even more unscrupulous and in tones that are very crude, Campanella showed how the coupling of piety and obedience was indispensable, and he insisted on the power of religion, including the true one, to sustain even an unjust government.[11]

Many years later, in a political treatise where the 'fateful' role that had been allotted to the monarchy of Spain would be transferred to the French monarchy, Campanella reaffirmed the need to demonstrate to the Venetians 'the utility they would draw from aligning themselves with France and with the Church, together with the necessity of religion in their state and the necessity of the Papacy, as well as the grave dangers of atheism, spread among the new generations by thinkers such as Cremonini and Sarpi, who in the *Antiveneti* is referred to meanly as 'a turncoat theologian' and 'the devil's charlatan.'[12] The warning to the Venetians would have to aim at reaffirming the necessity of that political and religious bond, independently of the content or truth of that religion, thereby demonstrating that

> even if religion does not seem to them to be true, they ought not do disdain it, knowing that religion is the supreme remedy for maintaining a state and given that it binds souls together, a foundation on which communities and fortunes depend. And they know also that their citizens would kill the prince and the senate, if they were to begin to believe that religion is nothing more than an art of the state by means of which to rule over its peoples.

---

[9] Ibid., p. 84.
[10] Ibid., p. 104.
[11] Ibid., pp. 109–110.
[12] Ibid., pp. 36, 37.

They would never be obedient, remaining always discontented, because they would have neither material success in this world nor hope of reward in the next. There is no greater bestiality in the prince that ruins him more quickly than revealing himself to be impious.[13]

The Papal Primacy: The Monarchia Messiae

During his sojourn at Padua, Campanella had already written a *Monarchia dei Cristiani*, which is unfortunately lost and to which had been attached a treatise titled *Del governo della Chiesa* that Campanella had addressed to the Pontiff in order to suggest to him the best means by which to constitute a single flock under a single pastor.[14] This is one of the most persistent and pervasive themes in Campanella's work, but the treatment of the problem of the Christian monarchy is also among the most difficult to comprehend. The *Monarchia del Messia* is to be understood as a manifesto that constructs a theorization of Christian monarchy. It finds its real point of reference and indispensable foundation in the absolute primacy of the Pope and in the incorporation of supreme spiritual and temporal power in his person.[15]

The solemn opening chapter lays out the fundamental coordinates of Campanella's theocratic thought, setting down foundations and rules for all human states and dominions (both good and bad) and for universal monarchy. The preliminary and primary distinction is that of the two modes of dominion: that dominion which is absolute (which properly speaking belongs exclusively to God, as creator of every being) and that which pertains to human states – which cannot be but relative and bound to particular conditions. In fact, man is not the absolute master of anything, and so much less of other men, because 'he cannot in his own way or by his own caprice make use of anything' if not in conformity with the rule laid down by the creator. Man can therefore make use of something within certain reasonable conditions, that is according to eternal reason, whether natural or written down, but he can never take the material possessions or the lives of others when it suits him and without cause, because originally he received everything from God.[16] If in animals the foundation of

---

[13] *Mon. Francia*, p. 554. These are themes that would reappear in the treatise *Avvertimenti a Venezia* of 1636 (see ch.12, note 26), in which Campanella reaffirmed the political destructiveness of the doctrine of predestination and polemicized against the Reformers as well as Spanish Dominicans such as Domingo Bañez and Diego Alvarez.

[14] See ch. 2.3, note 52.

[15] In his edition of the previously unpublished Italian text, Vittorio Frajese connects the composition of the *Monarchia del Messia* tightly to that of the *Antiveneti*, and he interprets the work in the light of a specific polemic with Antonio Marsilio, author of one of the numerous works discussing the interdict.

[16] *Mon. Messia*, pp. 47–48; *Mon. Messiae* (2002), pp. 54, 56.

dominion is corporeal force or a natural mark, in men (who are not born 'with crowns on their heads'[17]) it is wisdom and love that are the signs denoting the naturalness of a dominion. On that account, tyranny is defined as 'lordship without natural foundation,' and impiety cannot constitute the foundation of a natural and legitimate authority, in that impiety is 'distance and separation from God, the source of all foundations for authority.' From these considerations follows the distinction – also expressed effectively in a number of sonnets – of those who are princes 'by nature' (and possess legitimate and natural gifts and foundations) from those who are princes only 'on account of fortune,' which means by chance or lot or fate. Wisdom is thus the strongest natural foundation, and 'he is most truly a king by nature, when obeying him brings happiness, [and] is a tyrant or an idiot, when [obeying him] brings unhappiness.'[18]

But since wisdom can degenerate into sophistry and since sovereigns are not always wise, God has provided that states be ruled by law, 'which is the wisdom of the whole.' Such wisdom is divided into two kinds: eternal (which is the wisdom 'with which God guides all his creatures to particular ends') and natural (which is participation in the first). 'Thus, no law obliges the republic unless – by means of the divine law, whether natural or written – it be explicative of the eternal law.' The law thus has the function of integrating and balancing the components of the dominion. Tyranny is founded on force, cunning and love of self, loving others not on account of God, but on account of utility and glory. But from the moment that 'the true authority is founded on valor of spirit and on love of the public,' law intervenes in order to make up for 'the lack of force and wisdom.' Law intervenes so that 'authority only benefits he who loves God perfectly, who loves the people as the children of God, and who rules for the benefit of others – dedicating his life to them.'[19]

Remembering, as in other texts, that there are three means by which to acquire 'true or violent dominion' – by conquering spirits ('as the wise do with virtue'), by conquering bodies, or by means of the goods of fortune – Campanella emphasized how the last two are fragile and ephemeral when deprived of the first foundation. The wise men, for their part, can lose their lives, but – echoing motifs that would extend throughout his work after the conspiracy – he emphasized that 'even in death, they command the living.' Since prophets are 'masters by nature' (in that they are bearers of truth and virtue), they are vilified, persecuted, and put to death by spurious princes and princes thrown up by fortune. But their death is merely an apparent defeat.

---

[17] See *Poesie*, p. 73: 'Non nasce l'uom con la corona in testa,/ come il re delle bestie…'
[18] Ibid., pp. 49–51; *Mon. Messiae* (2002), pp. 60, 62.
[19] *Mon. Messiae* (2002), pp. 52, 58, 70.

In fact, death is 'a sign of true authority,' and they continue to rule even after death, humiliating their persecutors.[20]

As a result, government by a single master is preferable, in that this guarantees and reinforces unity. It is a good thing if he be chosen by election, after the death of the incumbent prince. It is also better if he be chosen from any nation whatsoever (and not only from his own), that he be 'experienced' and expert in the ways of government, and that he be unmarried and not 'distracted' by personal or family interests. But the most relevant and auspicious characteristic is that he also be a priest, as a 'sign of the strength of spirit, and of wisdom, and a sign of divine love for God.' Spiritual and temporal power should be united in his person, lest he become a sycophant to temporal princes, so that he has the power to punish bestial transgressors of the law, and lest he fall victim to heretics 'and other false scholars.'

In that context, a reprise of organic metaphors (beyond establishing correspondences between roles and body parts) highlights forcefully the unity conferred by religion (which is identified with the soul) and the unity in relations between soul, spirit, and head:

> Religion is the soul of the republic, because it is found in all the parts of the republic, ... and this soul joins those parts with each other and with God in a wondrous bond; it makes that unity extremely strong and most lovable. [Its] spirit is the particular law of princes, and these spirits move through the nerves of the body politic and have each part execute its office properly; they are commanded by the soul to respond to every sign and, when they obey its orders, they do not err, whereas when they disobey they fall into error and condemn the whole to death. The sacred high prince is the head, in which resides the soul and from which the spirits, the nerves, veins and arteries take their origin – as the most learned Telesio has it, even though Aristotle says that they come from the heart and even though Galen derives them from the heart, the liver, and from the head ... The princes and captains are the hands; the soldiers, the claws and feet. Peasants are the liver. The secular prince is the heart, while the plebs are the bowels, stomach, and flesh that complete the body. Bones are the foundations of the republic, which is the country itself by which it is supported; the learned are the sentiments, servants are the spleen, veins, bladder, and other conduits of filth.[21]

Moreover, since God constituted the first man as a father, a governor, or a guide for those who were similar to him, it follows that he who wants to exercise such a role in an appropriate way ought to be wiser than all his subordinates. In this way, he might rule over them and confer virtue on them, be more

---

[20] Ibid., p. 53; *Mon. Messiae* (2002), pp. 70, 72.
[21] Ibid., pp. 54–55; *Mon. Messiae* (2002), pp. 76–78.

powerful than them (in order to hold them back from vice), and be a greater lover of their well-being than his own. As Plato had already said, it is not the billy-goat that is able to command all other goats, but rather the shepherd who comes from a superior species. It therefore follows that man can command naturally only insofar as he is a divine man – that is to say, authorized by God, the one, true master, receiving his title and foundation from his own authority. Following the examples of Adam (who was father, king, and priest) and of Hermes Trismegistus (who united in himself philosophical, regal, and priestly gifts), the convergence of temporal and spiritual authority in the same person is excellent and auspicious: indeed, the people obey more willingly those they believe come from God – his laws are more venerated and observed both in public and in the hearts of the people.

The original unity of temporal and spiritual authority, derived from the unity of God, implies that, following the multiplicity of sects introduced by the devil and fomented by ambition and by ignorance (which are the causes of schisms and heresies), the human race returns to a single priestly law, in which the entire race can come together, beyond divisions and particularities. The age in which a single priest-king would rule is identified by Campanella as the golden age in which the evils that afflict men (such as war) will cease because there is no longer any reason for them to exist. Men would search after glory not 'through war, which is against nature among men, but through philosophy and heroic works undertaken for the benefit of all humanity.' In this golden age many evils would disappear: hunger and scarcity, because the sterility of the countryside and the lack of food could be corrected and remedied by the abundance of produce from other countries; plagues (derived from the corruption of the air or water) would not claim any more victims, because migrations of people in healthy countries unaffected by contagion would be possible; all the sciences would finally know a wondrous flourishing, on account of greater exchange and communication – for 'what the one does not know, the other does' – thereby bringing with it great advantages to humanity.[22] Division and separation between men are always works of the devil, who, jealous of the good of unity, induces in men 'a forgetfulness of the fact that we are all children of one father, Adam' together with 'an obliviousness to fraternity':

> But the devil, jealous of this gift, wishes that all might remain within the borders of their countries, as worms in cheese, so as to make us ignorant, deceive us, and not inform each other of what we observe – lest we go around from one country to the next investigating the works of God, lest we get to know one another, lest we begin to understand. Instead, the devil

---

[22] Ibid., pp. 62–63; *Mon. Messiae* (2002), p. 94ff.

wants us to have different languages and religions, so that with understanding between us lost we travel from country to country only when making war and causing death, in continual fear, without charity towards God as our father and without charity among ourselves, who are his children.[23]

In response to the arguments used by Aristotle to deny the possibility of a universal government by a single person, Campanella argues that those arguments are without value and that the analogies Aristotle uses are not adequate. Indeed, Campanella argued that Aristotle did not take into account the fact that religion and not the prince is the soul of the republic – and religion 'one finds everywhere entirely and in every part entirely.' The pagan philosophy, ignorant of the wondrous uniting power of the true religion, knew only 'servile fear and the power of the non-sacred prince ... It did not know the wondrous power of religion and of the age regenerated by God united in one faith, but rather aimed at the corrupt man and schismatics of its time.' In turn, Domingo de Soto repeated 'stupidly' with Aristotle that 'it is contrary to nature and impossible for power over all the world to be concentrated in the hands of one single person.' The assertion is not surprising, given that 'it is customary among the Peripatetics to declare contrary to nature that which does not please Aristotle.'[24]

The primary purpose of the Incarnation was to restore nature to its primitive innocence. Christ had promulgated the precepts of a law that was proposed as a law abolishing every particularity and separation, one law common and universal in which all people could come together, because it was based on the most universal presuppositions, among which the love of God and neighbor.[25] The golden age thus appeared in the form of a union of all men under a single temporal and spiritual sovereign, so as to recover the original unity that Christ had come to restore. But so that this prospect could be realized, it was necessary for Christ to be considered a genuinely universal master and titleholder of the royal priesthood of Melchisedech (not the simply spiritual priesthood of Aaron) and that a double power, both temporal and spiritual, be transferred to his vicar on earth. Campanella was fully aware of the arguments fielded against this position, in both the Protestant and Catholic spheres, by theologians, canonists and philosophers alike – and he does not hold back

---

[23] Ibid., pp. 65, 62–63; *Mon. Messiae* (2002), pp. 108, 110.

[24] Ibid., p. 64; *Mon. Messiae* (2002), p. 108.

[25] Campanella's notion of *ius gentium* further shows the importance of a universally applicable law within the context of the ideal of political and religious unity; see Jean-Paul De Lucca, 'diritto dei popoli/diritto delle nazioni (*ius gentium*),' in *Enciclopedia*, vol. 2 (forthcoming).

from polemically addressing the doctrines of Dante's *Monarchia* regarding the necessary distinction and separation between imperial and papal powers. The greater part of the chapters of the *Monarchia Messiae* are dedicated to the minute analysis and confutation of whoever holds doctrines that are different from his own with regard to the origin and the capabilities of the power of the Pontiff, with regard to the manner of the convergence of the material and spiritual sword, and with respect to relationships with princes.

In a passage in a letter to Paul V (in which he rejected the subtle distinctions made by the sophistries of human logic with irritated impatience), Campanella asserts the absoluteness of the Pontiff's power in a decisive manner:

> Christ is first reason, wisdom, word of God the Father. Therefore all the things of the world, being guided by first reason, are subject to him in heaven and on earth ... Therefore if the pope is his vicar he will be head and shepherd of the entire church ... Therefore the vicar of the first reason and of the first wisdom is head and shepherd of all reasonable men – which is to say the entire human world.[26]

In identifying only the aspect of spiritual dominion and moral reform in Christ, one risks not knowing how to identify him with the Messiah, as in fact the Jews had failed to do. One risks declaring the rabbis right – that is, the rabbis who live waiting for the advent of the messianic kingdom. Whereas they imagine it to be something future, it is instead present and progressively unfolding under the dominion of the vicars and successors of Christ – as is proven by the correct interpretation of a dense series of passages from Psalms. And it is in light of these principles (and in the identification of Christian arms with those of the Messiah himself) that the legitimation of the conquest of the New World on the part of the Spanish sovereign is to be found. Campanella proposed to set out the *ius* of the king of Spain in that conquest in a *Discorso sulle ragioni del Re Cattolico sul Mondo Nuovo*, which was written in these same years and which, significantly, was added as the last chapter in the Latin edition of the *Monarchia Messiae*.[27] Independently of the rapacious and cruel means by which it had been realized (which would be mercilessly denounced and deplored in later writings), that *ius* belonged to the king only insofar as he was performing the biblical role of Cyrus and establishing himself as the congregator of the Christian flock and the prophetic monarchy of the Messiah. So as to reinforce his position, Campanella did not hesitate to criticize the positions of some of his illustrious Dominican brothers – starting with

---

[26] *Lettere*, p. 48.
[27] *Mon. Messiae* (2002), pp. 424–459; see ch. 12.2, notes 30–31.

Cardinal Cajetan, who had not specified a single motive for just war in the conquest. In the famous *Relectiones indicae*, Francisco de Vitoria for his part had intrepidly demolished a series of reasons held to be legitimate. He denied the temporal authority of the Pope, and asserted that the occupation of the kingdoms together with the expropriation of the properties of the indigenous populations was not legitimated by their sins; and he denied that the Spanish could claim any right of occupation after disembarking on American soil. In his turn, Soto, even as he admitted the enormity of the sins and the violation of natural law committed by the inhabitants of the New World, denied that the Pope was a competent judge to punish even such atrocious crimes. The use of arms could not open the way for the conquest, but it could be tolerated only in a second moment, in the event that preachers, sent to spread the evangelical message, were maltreated. In Campanella's view, these positions "adulated" princes, in that they did nothing but suggest to them excuses attempting to justify the war. For his part, he reaffirmed the fullness of the right of the Catholic sovereign considered as the executor of the divine plan for the reunification of the world in the name of the Pontiff.

Structures of Ecclesiastical Government

The early *Monarchia dei Cristiani* was accompanied by a treatise titled *Sul governo della Chiesa*. Sent to Cinzio Albobrandini, Cardinal San Giorgio (nephew of Pope Clement VIII), this writing was also lost in its larger original form. Later it was rewritten in an aphoristic and more synthetic form as the *Discorsi universali del governo ecclesiastico*, which right at the outset is presented as a 'secret treatise for the Pope' on the paths to follow and the methods to adopt in order to gather a single flock under a single pastor, without provoking the remonstrances of secular princes. Taking up once again the theme of the golden age, Campanella affirmed that such an age would be possible when the 'most perfect law' of Jesus would rule over all the earth before the universal judgment. What he meant was that, once the worldly princedoms are vacated, the vicar of Christ alone would rule, accompanied by princes in the capacity of vassals and children.

The *Discorsi* intended to emphasize the differences between the two types of government (the ecclesiastical and the secular) at various levels and in various respects, both in the acquisition and in the preservation of power. In the first, the bond instituted by religion is dominant. As Campanella did not tire of repeating, religion guaranteed the greatest possible compactness and duration for a state on account of the manner in which it bound the spirits of men together – even between countries that were very distant. On account of the venerability induced by religion, the Papacy was invincible. It 'conserves itself

with love and veneration,' while 'the principality does so with fear and punishment.' In the former, it is better to have rich, great, powerful, and learned
vassals,' in that 'it is a living body, vivified by religion, in which the soul is everywhere entirely and in every part entirely.' Contrarily, for the 'secular state
vassals who are powerful and wise in their own right are harmful, because it is
a dead body and cannot control its great limbs; it is only vivified by religion,
soul of the Papacy; and here are concealed great secrets.'[28] Language is the
primary instrument of ecclesiastical government: from here derives the necessity of sending legations to all political and religious leaders, as the author
had done in the *Reminiscentur*, for the purpose of inviting them to a general
council to discuss with them the true faith, demonstrating that 'Christ is not
a sectarian (as are the leaders of other nations) but is instead the Wisdom of
God, the Word and Reason of God ...; thus, all men – being rational in accordance with the first reason of Christ – are implicitly Christians, and yet they
ought to recognize God in the Christian religion explicitly.'[29] Campanella then
insisted on the necessity of favoring collaboration among the wise. They are
to be rewarded and appreciated and not persecuted or humiliated, because
the 'hidden fire burns one's hands unobserved.' The sciences and philosophy
would be reformed in the light of nature and in the light of the thought of the
Fathers, so as to extirpate the discords of peoples and to cut out the scandal
of the doctrines of Aristotle and Machiavelli, which are contrary to Christian
principles. Ecclesiastic schools would open even for laymen (and in this the
Jesuits ought to be imitated), and useful sciences such as medicine, pharmacy,
and legal assistance would be offered free of cost.

One of the chapters that attracts the most attention is the eleventh. It deals
with rather delicate problems of the day and is also tightly connected to the
biography of the author himself in that it deals with issues such as heretics,
the Holy Office, and prohibited books. The sixth aphorism holds that 'all the
new heretics ought to be affectionately called to Rome, where they should
be made to abjure as mistaken people and not as heretics, unless they are not
excessively pertinacious.' The next aphorism emphasizes with acuity that 'to
the extent that the Office of the Inquisition is more benign with the learned
and more severe with the ignorant, heretics fail to take root.' And the eighth
aphorism reaffirms that 'one ought not to make any learned man of great
spirit abjure if he himself does not confess to heresy, and abjuring *de vehementi*
ought to be avoided.'[30] But the aphorism of greatest interest is the eighteenth,

---

[28] *Discorsi universali*, p. 473; the content of the *Discorsi* are reproduced verbatim
in the *De regno Dei*, with which the Paris edition of the *Philosophia realis* closes.
[29] *Discorsi universali*, p. 476.
[30] Ibid., p. 493.

which is advanced as a vibrant appeal against the prohibition of 'high and new doctrines' and the suffocating of the *libertas philosophandi*. This kind of repression severely harmed Christianity, which ought instead to present itself as the harbinger of the inexhaustible rationality of the Word:

> One ought not to prohibit books containing new and high doctrines, if one does not give a time and place for the author to defend himself (and likewise for those who follow his doctrine); and, in the absence of that, one ought to accept attorneys and lawyers, because to prohibit such representation raises the suspicion that the law of Christ is actually like the law of Muhammad and other sectarians, who fear being exposed. Actually, in this manner one extends to prohibited books a certain kind of reputation, and it gives the author an occasion for apostasy. If the authors are good, this actually damages the republic, and it is a scandal for the Catholic church – for it takes away the freedom to philosophize. And this is what modern writers want, who are in fact merely copyists and not writers, *nil altum sapientes* (who can reach no higher wisdom); it is an insult to Eternal Wisdom (as Saint Leo says) to think that every truth has been discovered and that it is necessary to shut the mouths of new philosophers.

If there ought not to be any indulgence for books 'of deceit' nor for those of 'lying and lascivious poets,' it is necessary nonetheless to adopt an attitude of maximal caution before unwarranted prohibitions – for 'the more one prohibits, the greater the number of heretics.'

Of great interest also is the twenty-first chapter, which consists of a short work that Campanella had drafted on the occasion of the conclave of 1623, in which Urban VIII had been elected. These are exemplary pages, seeking to prove that reason of state dominates in the heart of Christianity itself and that 'political reason' (according to which 'everyone seeks to elect as Pope he who was his own slave, so as then to be able to command him and make him act according to his wish') turns out to be disastrous, as usual. So as to exhort the cardinals to elect a Pope after taking only his real merits and virtues into account, Campanella showed how a terrible connection is established between those who are elected to the Papacy and those who have favored their election as a result of political calculations (with the hope of deriving from them a personal advantage). The inversion of the relationship between servant and master, rather than generating gratitude on the part of the beneficiary, unleashes in him an impressive spiral of hate. He who from below has reached the pinnacle of power wants to enjoy his new freedom fully and does not tolerate feeling himself chained to anyone. If before ascending to the pontifical seat he was hiding his true sentiments with a servile guise (out of fear of not achieving his aim, for 'every fear induces some servitude'), once he has become Pope he throws down the mask. The manner in which he will turn

against the disturbing evidence of his old baseness is described in a lividly Tac-
itean passage, shot through with an obsessive crescendo of implacable hate:

> Being then elevated and made Pope with your support, he hates you not
> only intrinsically, but also extrinsically. He will persecute you because he
> thinks that you will hope to command him as you did previously, when he
> was your servant. Being your master, he will disdain you and hate you as a
> person who not only wanted to be his superior while he was in a subordinate
> position (which is in itself hateful), but as someone who wants to remain
> his superior even in the period of his clear superiority, almost as if you do
> not recognize the situation for what it is – something that is extremely odi-
> ous... Thus, the benefices that you expect him to bestow upon you he will
> want to give to others who are naturally similar and debtors and not to you
> out of an obligation – whence it appears to him that he remains your slave
> still, and he hates you ... because the benefices that you want from him he
> knows derive from an obligation and obligation is a bond that is contrary
> to native liberty. For this reason, he hates this bond considerably, believing
> himself to be superior and in such a state of liberty that he not longer has
> superiors or equals on the earth and is no longer to be constrained. He will
> wish that it had never been possible to tie him up. Thus, he will be ungrate-
> ful to you at the slightest, trumped up opportunity; he will persecute you
> and hate you, not wanting ever to have you in his sight, just as one would
> not want to lay eyes upon a collector of taxes, levies or debts.[31]

A final interesting glimpse of an ecclesiastical monarchy is offered by two
Discorsi della libertà e della felice suggezione allo Stato ecclesiastico, which
followed the Latin text of the *Monarchia Messiae* that was published at Iesi
in 1633. As Firpo observed, the two dexterous shorter works have the singular distinction of being, apart from the *Scelta* of the poems, 'the only piece
published by Campanella in Italian during his lifetime.'[32] Their composition
dates back to the last period of his incarceration in Castel Nuovo and is
to be put in the context of the polemics originating in the question of the
devolution of the Duchy of Urbino to the pontifical state. The annexation
appeared inevitable in June 1623, following the sudden death of the young
heir Federico Ubaldo, found dead in his bed, destroyed by a disordered life.
The annexation became even more likely with the accession to the pontifical seat, shortly thereafter, of the energetic Urban VIII, who worked ever
more insistently on the old Duke Francesco Maria II Della Rovere – with
the result that the annexation took place with the invitation of representa-

---

[31] Ibid., pp. 512–513.

[32] *Mon. Messiae*, p. 6; the critical edition of the two *Discorsi* in the anastatic reprinting of the *Mon. Messiae*, ed. L. Firpo (Turin: Bottega d'Erasmo, 1960), pp. 19–42.

tives of the Pontiff to the city in 1625, even before the death of the Duke. The episode had elicited protests and caused some bad blood, with some harsh criticism being made of the terrible administration of the pontifical state. In a short work of 1627, Campanella would recall having taken part in a dispute on such questions, so as to criticize the opinion (widespread among the people) that 'the ecclesiastical government is very bad' and so as to fight against the sarcastic expression 'priestly justice.' Against detractors of the papal government, Campanella committed himself to show in these fast-moving pages (which have a certain intrepidness) how in truth the Pontiff constitutes a greater guarantee of justice and liberty in comparison to secular princes, who rule for their own personal advantage alone, without any ethical restraint and without any real respect or interest in the well-being of their subjects.

In the first discourse (which is the more developed one), Campanella maintained that the Pope guarantees a liberty greater than that of any other monarchy or republic, in that he is able to free men from the most ruinous forms of slavery. He is able to free men from the slavery of sin above all else, thanks to the Papacy's more just and rigorous tribunals, which permit the punishment and repression of public sins as well as hidden and secret ones. It is undeniable that even at Rome 'there are sins and hatreds,' but they are not so 'blatant as elsewhere.' Moreover, the Papacy is more effective in countering the great scourges that afflict humanity – such as the crimes of war, famine, and plague. According to Campanella, at Rome one can wander around at night 'with gold in one's hand,' while elsewhere 'he who walks in the city after the Ave Maria is murdered.' Thanks to the severity of the punishments in the holy city, there are fewer homicides in a year than there are elsewhere in a month. Human life is more secure and women more protected; moreover, women 'cannot be killed or beaten by their husbands without great punishment.' The people are not oppressed by usury, nor sent by force into war, nor suppressed by the caprices of their leaders. Justice and power are in the hands of old men expert in government and the laws, 'not in the hands of young and ignorant princelings, who know neither how to serve nor how to command those who do know.' In any case, it is 'better to sin by simulation than by audacity.' Usually, the Pope does not wage wars of conquest and tributes are used for the benefit of his subjects, while in other states all resources – all grains, wine, iron, wood, the blood itself of the subjects – are used for the purpose of 'venting the passions of the prince.' Regarding hunger, people are better nourished at Rome, where it is also true that a greater amount of money circulates than elsewhere due to the affluence of foreigners. Regarding the dangers of pestilence, remedies from the arts and sciences are sought. At Rome, one enjoys a greater degree of liberty in comparison to the slavery present in other governments, mainly because the sciences are cultivated and everyone has access to them, thanks to schools that are open to poor and rich alike – and the most 'virtuous' (i.e. gifted) can reach the highest offices. Slavery is the daughter of ignorance and for this reason tyrants hold their peoples down 'in ignorance and unarmed and in servile games so as to dominate them more effectively and so as to lead them by the nose having turned them into a herd of buffalo.' Campanella maintained that 'the nerve center of this power is wisdom, as elsewhere it is ignorance.' To he who objects to the prohibition of books, he replied that the only books to be prohibited are those filled with 'falsities and sophistical and heretical arts' deriving from a vain curiosity and not from the true sciences that proceed from studiousness. Even as they have a natural foundation, the papal prohibition on doctrines such as astrology and chiromancy derives from the fact that dangerous doctrines are prohibited, not only false ones. It is the duty of the good pastor 'to take away poisonous grass and pastures from the mouths of the sheep in their care.'

In the second short discourse, the author reaffirmed that while lay princes use their subjects in order to realize ambitious personal projects, holding them in ignorance 'in order to be able to lead them by the nose like buffalo,' the Pope 'does not spill the blood or waste the possessions of the people in order to acquire distant territories.' He governs his own subjects with greater wisdom and virtue. In response to protests of nobles who lament the excessive severity of the laws (which inflict capital punishment and confiscate the goods of he who kills someone, such that 'noble families disintegrate and are not able ever to indulge their desires'), Campanella warns them recalling that 'defacing a sacred temple such as man is a very grave sin and merits the greatest penalty' and that desiring to 'indulge in evil' is characteristic of the 'arrogant, and not of people who are innocent.'

Christianity as Universal Religion

The great quadripartite treatise that takes its title from Psalm 21.28 (*Reminiscentur et convertentur ad Dominum universi fines terrae*) and was edited for the first time by Romano Amerio between 1939 and 1960 was one of the works closest to Campanella's heart. Indeed, he claimed he had almost been forced to write it by God. It is structured as a series of eloquent speeches directed to princes, to republics, to all the diverse sects and faiths of those four 'nations' of the world – the Christian nation, the Gentiles, the Jews, and the Muslims. Having laid down the weapons of war (which are proper to beasts) and the weapons of grammar (which are proper to sophists), they are all called to a universal ideal assembly to discuss the true faith and are called upon to recognize 'the true religion' by means of spiritual arms alone, in accordance with a divine and not merely human logic. As the author recalled in the dedication to Paul V written towards the end of 1617 from Castel Sant'Elmo (the work would later also be dedicated to two successive Popes, Gregory XV and Urban VIII), the initial inspiration for the piece went back many years earlier to an exhortation from the Pope that Campanella make a better use in the future than he had in the past of the talents that had been given to him by God. These were words that had elicited 'pious desires' in Campanella's heart and melted his soul at the thought that the Papal majesty had deigned to warn 'such a small buried worm' (*tantillum vermiculum sepultum*).[33] From here derived the desire to contribute to a radical reform of the sciences, in the light of nature, and to write in a way that would prepare the arrival of Christ as the supreme reason. Campanella wrote the text of the *Reminiscentur* with his hopes of liberty having vanished and having been sent back into his former cruel prison (*in prioribus angustiis*). Directed towards the conversion of all nations, it was presented as the 'epitome, colophon, and end' of his studies.[34]

The treatise began with the affirmation that nothing is more natural than the return of everything to its own beginning. The innate love of self-preservation and of living forever generates in everything the irresistible desire to be reunited with its own totality: the parts of the earth go towards the earth, from which they are detached; all waters run towards the sea, from which they are separated when they are deposited on mountaintops by hidden and mysterious means, 'from the subterranean veins of the earth almost as if through alembics and sponges.' Likewise, so as to reach the celestial fire the sparks imprisoned in the deepest subterranean cavities erupt with a violence able to demolish mountains and whatever else might stand in their way. Driven by such instincts of preservation all creatures, conscious of their own insufficiency, tend to return to their Creator – the ocean and origin of being. But souls do not know God and things divine in a distinct fashion, because their secret aspiration for the heavens is impeded by the passions of the body in which they live. If souls desire to nourish themselves on divine notions, bodies instead feed on 'the flesh of the plants and the animals of the earth.' Many waters, separated from the sea, seem to lose their flavor as well as the path by which they might return; many fires hide themselves in stone, in wood, in metal, from which they are reawakened only with repeated striking and rubbing – but the sparks fly at once towards the sky.[35]

Recollection is the *renovatio* (renewal) of past sensation or understanding reawakened by something similar to those things known previously: and 'there

---

[33] *Reminiscentur*, I, p. 3.
[34] Ibid.
[35] Ibid., pp. 7–8.

are as many memories as there are similitudes.' It is asked whether the soul, divine in origin, retains the mark of God. Some maintain that it is a tabula rasa. But from the moment that it is not produced by the elements, but rather by God, from him derive 'the seeds of the sciences and the seeds of virtue, on the basis of which the soul can become extremely wise, powerful, and loving.' This is true even if at the beginning, while completely enmeshed in the fabric of the body, it seems not to love anything except the body itself. The waters of the sea remember the direction of the sea, even when they are separated from it. The heat of the sun, when it is introduced to the earth, continues to tend by instinct towards the heavens. That is why it wants to render the earth subtle, to burn it and drag it up with itself towards the sun. In this way, the soul knows God through an 'innate seminal tendency,' and not on account of an extrinsic (*illata*) knowledge that distances it not only from God but also from itself (to the point of not knowing itself and coming to recognize itself only with effort after a long journey).

The history of the relationship between God and the human race is modeled on this schema. From an initial love and reverence for God (who is understood as a benevolent and beneficent father), men are lost into an oblivion of the Creator as they transfer to men and to things the worship due only to him. But after successive visitations, God recalled humanity to its common origins and to the necessary return to unity. Thus, 'the people of the earth, reawakened by the preaching of the truth as the sparks of fire closed up in a stone and almost buried in dormancy will remember their own nature thanks to the striking of the stone and of the iron; with the stone of the hardened heart and of idolatry abandoned, they will turn to God and begin again to raise themselves up towards heavenly things.'[36] Numerous signs indicated that the time of such a universal remembering and return was near: celestial novelties (which do not happen by chance and are instead a universal divine language), discovery of the New World, indications of the arrival of the Antichrist, and the aspiration in all humanity that 'the will of God' be done 'on earth as it is in heaven.'

After the announcement of the book's theme and scheme, important autobiographical sections follow in which Campanella turns to God so as to confess his own youthful disorientation and reconstruct the most significant steps of his own spiritual journey. It is above all to these pages that scholarly discussion of the question of 'conversion' refer. With chiaroscuro touches and in an allusive fashion, Campanella confessed having neglected precisely this *reversio* to God in the years of his youth. With the abandonment of the shield of his protection and the sword of his word, he was consigned to an unknown

---

[36] Ibid., p. 10.

enemy of his own accord, believing him a friend. Without even knowing how, he was convinced that there is nothing better than serving the most impure desires and pleasures. From here derived the justice of divine punishment, which was enacted with a precise overturning of every aspect of his life:

> While I wandered in the perversity of my sense, you mired me in an abyss of unhappiness. Not only did you denude me of temptations and pleasures of the body, you also filled me with torments. You added prisons to my prison, so that I might learn not to love such a prison. You tortured me cruelly and repeatedly – nineteen years in the deepest pit with spiders, salamanders, scorpions, a cell of shades and in the shadow of death, enchained in poverty and in irons. I had not obeyed my fathers and superiors, because it seemed to me almost appropriate to raise myself above them. Thus did I become a slave to the hangman and executioner. Disdaining the cells of the saints, I lived in the cell of devils…. I held your temple in contempt, and I desired almost to cast it down and destroy it…. Until now, it was not permitted for me to see it and I could not even look upon the sun and the moon and all the temples of the sky. On this account, I envy mosquitoes, flies, animals (even the smallest among them) their ability to do this.[37]

The play of contrasts, wittingly laced with references to Psalms, proceeded with a reference to his own wisdom and his own doctrine. He who had read everything and written about everything presumed to reform the sciences without first having reformed his own heart. For this reason, God had seen fit to humiliate his pride and his presumption, depriving him of every opportunity to exercise his mind. He had made him show his learning before 'dragons and ostriches, to whom discussions of the most elevated matters were of no interest, and who thought that whoever is not interested in dice and cards and vanities and other stupidities is a madman.' Deprived of books and everything, he had learned to grasp – almost 'to touch with the hands of the intellect' – the plausibility of the most holy Trinity, the signs of which shone forth from all things: 'from this point on my soul recognized itself, and the body and its chains, and with which wings one flies up to you; remembering the fullness of your beauty, reawakened from the splendors that shine from the matter of things, my soul yearned for union with divine things, so far away, and so close to us.' Campanella, the derider who had devastated with scandal and vanity the vineyard of the church of Christ, wanted to offer himself as a parable and example, so that others might not despair of divine mercy.[38]

Within the context of this psychological and intellectual condition, Campanella included eloquent appeals directed at political and religious leaders,

---

[37] Ibid., pp. 23–24.
[38] Ibid., pp. 24–25.

so that, after overcoming conflicts and self-interests, they might once again locate bonds of fraternity in the acknowledgement of a single God. The appeals of the first book are directed to several recipients: the Pope and to the Cardinals; to God, praying for pity for the human race which like a baby that knows neither father nor mother and lives abandoned in the woods among the beasts; to angels and also to demons, so that they might abandon their vain arrogance; to all Christians, so that they might be true; to monks, so that they might emerge from their cloisters under the standard of the cross so as to join battle armed with the logic of Christ; and above all to his Dominican brothers, the 'dogs of the Lord,' exhorting them not to keep quiet when they ought to raise their voices. Appeals to the emperor and to the sovereigns of Europe, both Catholic and non-Catholic, follow and after that an appeal to the German nation, to which is appended an address on the beliefs of the Lutherans and the reformers from testimony of the debate with Adami.[39]

The second book (perhaps the first to be written) is given over to the sects of the Gentiles. In using information acquired from his reading of books and the reports of travelers and missionaries, Campanella showed a great curiosity for the rites, customs, and beliefs of a great diversity of peoples. Those narratives seemed to confirm the fundamental and original unity of humanity, which was expressed in the affinities between their ceremonies and rites, on the one hand, and Christian ones, on the other – even if those ceremonies and rites are subsequently condemned as forgeries and diabolical suggestions. The appeals are directed to sovereigns and priests in distant kingdoms: in Japan, China, India, Narsinga, Pegu, Burma, Siam, to the great Khan of Cathay and to Monopotapa, the sovereign of a vast African realm who is also mentioned in the *Città del Sole*.[40] All the interlocutors are invited to abandon the cults of lesser beings, of animals and men, and to give up cruel and unbecoming rituals, so as to come together in universal rationality and Christian naturalness and so as to recognize a single, infinite God who shines forth in all things and who cares for every being. This God is the greatest being and the supreme cause, the God from whom comes all virtue, who is every nature, and who 'makes everything in everything.'

The third and fourth books (which were published by Amerio as *Per la conversione degli Ebrei* and *Legazioni ai Momettani*) are directed to the other two great monotheistic religions, whose accusations against Christianity are reported so that they might be confuted and so that the grave limits

---

[39]The *Epistola antilutherana*, the *Responsiones*, and the *Responsiones secundae ad obiectiones*, added at the conclusion of the first book of the *Reminiscentur*, pp. 107–194.

[40] *Città del Sole*, p. 56.

of their beliefs might be made clear along with the arguments that ought to persuade them to join Christianity, which is taken to be more universal in that it conforms to a greater degree to reason and to nature.[41] Common to the two religions is a derisiveness towards the mysteries and dogmas of Christianity, which they hold to be impossible and unreasonable, among which the divine Trinity, the incarnation of Christ (whose divinity was denied, so as to make him a heretic and an impostor, and who supposedly completed his miracles thanks to magical discoveries), the Eucharist, and the virginity of Mary. Replying to those accusations, Campanella invited the Jews to give up the obstinacy that rendered them certain of being the only repositories of the truth, not recognizing in Christ the Messiah and the instauration of the temporal kingdom. Above all, he beseeched them to abandon the delusions of the Talmud, on the basis of which they looked for God 'where there is no God, except for an imaginary one,' for a truth where there are only lies, for virtue where there is only vice.[42] The rabbis are accused of presumptuousness, in that they believe themselves to be wiser than God, and in that they pretend to substitute the Talmud for Scripture, each one opining in his own head without sense of God or Pope, without miracles and prophecies. Even more serious is the fact that they present an image of God that does not correspond to the God of Moses or David: it is a God who is not capable of all things, who is ignorant of many things, a God who prays, as if he were admitting that there was someone superior to him, a corporeal God in that he wears garments of cloth, a God who is lazy and inept, who learns to act in the world in the course of many successive attempts and who in order to exercise himself destroys those who do not satisfy him.

The fourth part is made up of five addresses directed to the diverse sects of the Muslims – to the great Turk, the Shi'a of Persia, the Arabs, the Sheriff of Fez and Morocco, the Tartars and the Great Mongol. Amerio considered it the weakest part of the *Reminiscentur*, due to the scarcity and questionable reliability of the information and sources used by Campanella, and because he lacked knowledge of Arabic, and also for the controversial method adopted, which often resorted to a tone that was 'derisive and disdainful.' The polemic is in fact rather sharp at many points, but the text does not lack arguments that are of interest. As in the preceding book, the author commits himself to replying to the most frequent accusations against Christians, which have to do above all with the Trinity and the Eucharist. To assert that Christians worship three gods and devour their own god is evidence of possessing a crude intel-

---

[41] *Per la conversione degli Ebrei* (Florence, 1955); *Legazioni ai Maomettani* (Florence, 1960).

[42] *Per la conversione degli Ebrei*, p. 91.

lect, one that is capable of understanding neither the unity and distinction of the persons of the Trinity nor the powerfully uniting function of the Eucharist, which does not consist in assimilating in ourselves the body of Christ as a food, but rather in decanting ourselves into him, as the beloved into the beloved. Conducting a detailed and minute analysis of the various assertions made in the Qur'an, Campanella insisted on pointing out that if taken literally some assertions are fabulous and impossible. In contrast, only the Sh'ia of Persia wisely agree with an allegorical and metaphoric interpretation. Turning his attention to the Turks in particular, he deplored their carnal understanding of everything. The cosmological doctrines of the Qur'an are completely fantastical, while new geographical and celestial discoveries – made possible thanks to the wondrous discovery of the telescope and thanks to the work of 'our friend' (*amicus noster*) Galileo – shattered the Qur'an's fictitious heavens and seas of hyacinth, gold, and emerald. Accentuating aspects of sensuality shared with animals (who not by chance are held to be worthy of beatitude), they propose a morality that is not human but rather extremely vile and bestial. It is the same morality that dominates the Islamic conception of paradise, which is tinged with carnality. In more than one passage, Campanella noted and strongly deplored the practices, tainted with an unbridled sexual license, of the priests of North Africa who are called Marabouts.[43] The prohibition against science, together with the defense of the faith with arms (rather than with reason), accentuate the tyrannical and violent aspects of the Muslim sovereigns. That Muslim rulers should be tyrannical and violent ceases to surprise from the moment that – and this is the most insistent and fundamental accusation – they become imitators of a God who (just like the God imagined by the Reformers) is quite similar to the god Maozim – that is to say, the god of force and not goodness or wisdom. The Christian God, who has bestowed liberty on men (and thus the possibility of meriting salvation), is not a weak god, but rather a prudent one, good and extremely powerful, in that he adapts himself to exigency and human limitations. Muslim princes, imitators of a god of power, are tyrants and wolves, not pastors of the people.[44] The cessation of wars that tear to pieces the human race, the union of peoples, the inauguration of a golden age in which everything is common and men come together 'in a single faith, a single hope, a single truth' (just as God himself is but one) – all these things can be realized concretely only if one presupposes universal belief in a God who is not partial or flawed, a God who genuinely draws within him those prerequisites of universality, rationality, and conformity to nature that are apt to herald the reunification of peoples.

---

[43] *Legazioni ai Maomettani*, pp. 143, 157 (on the Marabouts, see also ch. 10, p. 182).
[44] Ibid., p. 166.

9. NEW HEAVENS

Science and Faith: The Apologia pro Galileo

On 13 January 1611, immediately after having read the *Sidereus nuncius*, Campanella wrote an elaborate Latin letter to Galileo, the first of nine letters to his famous contemporary that have survived. The letter expressed both astonishment and admiration for his celestial discoveries, but added a number of doubts, perplexities, and suggestions as well.[1] In these pages – which years later the author would have the pleasure of seeing published following Galileo's *Dialogo*,[2] – are reflected emotions elicited by the extraordinary celestial messenger and by the novelty revealed by Galileo in the heavens thanks to the 'wondrous instrument' discovered by him. The emotion is a mixture of enthusiasm and perplexity, praise and reservation. Right from his first encounter with Galileo in his youth at Padua (which is evoked once again here), Campanella would express constant sentiments of friendship and esteem for him. In later years too, he would be in epistolary contact with him, participating in discussions on his doctrines.[3] In 1614 he wrote four articles, now lost, lamenting the scientist's adhesion to atomism:

> The manner in which you wrote last summer pains me greatly, you who have applied yourself to the study of floating bodies and have discovered everything there to be atoms, nothing other than relations between such things, etc. You have affirmed many propositions that you cannot prove and hold to be true as well as many others that you cannot uphold so easily, such that you have spurred your enemies in order to deny all those wondrous things that Your Lordship has gifted to us. I wrote four articles in response to that *Discorso* …

---

[1] *Lettere*, pp. 163–169.

[2] In a postscript to the letter to Galileo of 1 May 1632 (*Lettere*, p. 236), one reads: 'I would have liked it had you published the first letter I sent you on this matter.'

[3] See Michel-Pierre Lerner, 'La science Galiléenne selon Campanella,' *B&C*, 1 (1995), pp. 121–156.

G. Ernst, *Tommaso Campanella,* International Archives of the History of Ideas/Archives internationales d'histoire des idées 200, DOI 10.1007/978-90-481-3126-6_9, © Springer Science + Business Media B.V. 2010

so that Your Lordship might arm his pen with a perfect mathematics and leave this talk of atoms for later etc.[4]

The spirited dialogue, which was not without disagreements, would find its high-point in the drafting of the *Apologia pro Galileo*.[5] The treatise (which enjoyed a considerable circulation in the seventeenth century and helped to connect the names of Galileo and Campanella, his 'defender') had been composed in the first months of 1616, in an extremely delicate moment in the debate on the doctrines of Copernicus, which had been openly supported by Galileo after the *Sidereus nuncius*. The inquiry, opened the previous year, into the relationships between the new astronomy and Scripture concluded with the opinion of the inquisitorial commission of 24 February 1616, which declared the principles of the immobility of the sun and the motion of the earth 'stupid and absurd, philosophically speaking.' From the point of view of faith, the first opinion was deemed formally heretical; the second, erroneous or worse. In this way, the decree of the Index on 5 March was reached, in virtue of which the *De revolutionibus* of Copernicus would be suspended from the *donec corrigatur* clause, and those texts that explicitly maintained the compatibility between the heliocentric position and Scripture were prohibited. This prohibition extended to the beautiful letter of the Carmelite Paolo Antonio Foscarini written in 1615.[6] The *Apologia* is situated in that context, and it took shape as an attempt to intervene in the debate in order to avoid a condemnation that is portrayed as both wrong and ruinous. Years later, Campanella would affirm having known that his text could not be taken into consideration, given that it arrived in Rome too late after the verdict had already been delivered.[7] Sent to Adami, the *Apologia* was published in Frankfurt in

---

[4] *Lettere*, pp. 176–177. The question of floating objects and of conceptions of "heavy" and "light" generally, addressed in the light of the doctrines of the ancients (Empedocles, Democritus, Plato) and in the light of the modern philosophy of magnetism, is discussed in *Quaest. phys.*, XXXII, pp. 304–324; *Metaphysica*, part I, pp. 221–228; on that issue, see Francesco Paolo de Ceglia, 'Campanella versus Galileo. Una risposta metafisica alla *Quaestio de Natantibus*,' *Annali della Facoltà di Lettere e Filosofia dell'Università di Bari*, 40 (1997), pp. 241–267.

[5] *Apologia pro Galileo/Apologie pour Galilée*, text, translation, and notes by Michel-Pierre Lerner (Paris: Les Belles Lettres, 2001), from which I cite; there is an Italian translation (Pisa, 2004) and an English translation – *A Defence of Galileo*, translated with an introduction and notes by Richard J. Blackwell (Notre Dame, 1994).

[6] The letter has been republished in an appendix to the edition of the *Apologia pro Galileo* edited by P. Ponzio (Milan, 1997; Milan, 2002²). Regarding the placing of Copernicus on the Index in 1616, see Michel-Pierre Lerner, 'Copernic suspendu et corrigé sur deux decrets de la Congrégation Romaine de l'Index (1616–1620),' *Galilaeana. Journal of Galilean Studies*, 1 (2004), pp. 21–89.

[7] *Quaest. phys.*, X, 4, p. 106.

1622. In that edition, there was a foreword by the editor (who, after a meeting with Galileo, had declared himself very much in favor of the new astronomy) and a dedicatory letter from the author addressed to the Cardinal Bonifacio Caetani, who had been charged with carrying out the emendation of Copernicus's text.

The *Apologia* was an act of great courage and intellectual honesty not just because Campanella took up the delicate question even as he was still in prison but also because he was not defending his own doctrines. As he would later remind Galileo, his had been the only voice to speak out in his defence: 'and recall that my text alone was published in your defence, and not the texts of others.'[8] His image of a living book of nature is in fact fairly different from Galileo's notion of a book written in the language of mathematics. Further, he had reservations with regard to the doctrine of Copernicus (which was not easily reconciled with the physics of Telesio), and above all with regard to the motion of the earth, seat of the principle of cold, a principle that renders beings heavy and immobile. Campanella wrote in defense of Galileo's *libertas philosophandi* and more generally in defense of the freedom of opinion of the Christian scientist, whose first right and duty is to read the book of nature. He brought into focus with great lucidity the core of the problem, which is identified as the marriage of Aristotelianism and theology and the undue dogmatic value conferred upon Aristotle's philosophy. Like every human doctrine, Aristotelianism ought instead to be corrected on the basis of comparison with the book of nature and, when it no longer corresponds to experience, it is to be abandoned, without fearing that such a shift would have negative repercussions on theology.

The text, which adopted the structure of a *quaestio*, was divided into five chapters. The central chapter, fairly complex, furnished contents and coordinates for replying in a satisfactory way in the final chapters to the anti-Galilean objections listed in the first chapter and for vindicating those arguments in Galileo's favor as set out in the second chapter. The initial arguments against Galileo denounced in the first place the subversive character of his thinking. Destroying traditional doctrines that were in agreement with the principles of theology, it was feared that such new ideas risked putting theology itself in jeopardy. On this account, some feared that there was a discord between the letter of some scriptural passages and the presumed heretical implication of some of his assertions. Finally, generally speaking, his presumption of investigating things that extend beyond the limits of human reason was deemed troublesome. The arguments in favor of Galileo stressed that in the past renowned theologians had welcomed the Copernican position with favor. It was amazing that those authorities might be blind like moles, while contemporary theologians (who, what is more, are not even as famous) have more eyes than Argus.

---

[8] *Lettere*, p. 236.

Copernicus's doctrine had attracted interest and agreement also from well-regarded men of science and philosophy, and Campanella did not fail to make an extremely audacious reference to 'the Nolan [that is, Bruno] and others,' who had been condemned as heretics for other doctrines, but not insofar as they were supporters of a Copernican and Cusanian cosmology. Copernicus and Galileo, furthermore, renewed the ancient doctrines of Pythagoras, who was a disciple of Moses, and his followers. In that way, a buried and forgotten truth returned resplendent: 'sepulta veritas elucescit.'[9]

The central part of the work presented the three pillars on which one ought to found responses to such arguments. The first asserted the necessity that a judge in such matters be in possession of the zeal of God, to the end of investigating the truth with a mind free of every passion. At the same time, however, he had to be scientifically competent, so as to avoid errors that even holy and learned Church Fathers such as Lactanctius and Augustine had run into, when they denied the existence of the antipodes, something that was aggravated by having upheld false theses on the basis of appeals to Scripture.

The second pillar – articulated in turn in several points – specified from one side how Scripture was the bearer of a moral message, expressed in an everyday language (beyond being the bearer of supernatural and revealed truths) that mirrored common experience and was accessible to all as a result. On the other side, Campanella specified how man possessed adequate instruments with which to develop his interpretation of the book of nature ever further, and how it was precisely on account of his cognitive capacity that man might realize his own progressive deification. Thus, we ought to show gratitude, and not hostility, to Galileo, in that he allows us to improve and perfect our understanding of the work of God. It is in this part of the work that we encounter the more radical positions with regard to the inescapable bonds between Christianity and science, that are in a way intrinsic to Christianity itself and represent for it a constitutive characteristic, insofar as they are deployments of rationality and truth. Because it is not a partial sect but instead embraces the totality of the truth, Christianity has nothing to fear from its progressive unfolding. Indeed, he who forbids someone to be involved in the sciences prevents him from being truly Christian. Persecution of he who searches for the truth is a sign of weakness and fear on the part of someone living in error and in ignorance and someone who fears being found out. This is something that is characteristic of the Muslims, who ban the sciences in order to maintain puerile or fabulous beliefs and so as to defend their lies with the sword. When they do this, they act like the tyrant, who has an interest in rendering the people ignorant and base. Thus, those who attack Galileo seem to be moved more by jealousy and ignorance than by love for the truth. They do it out of the embarrassment of having to go back to their

---

[9] *Apologia*, p. 25.

school desks like children, they who consider themselves teachers. If Christians are called wise and rational by Christ, the Word and First Reason, he is truly Christian who makes himself a spokesman for and disseminator of rationality. Praying that he not be forced out, Campanella did not hesitate to profess that the favor accorded to the sciences ('approbatio scientiarum') had been the strongest bond keeping him within Christianity.[10]

The concluding assertion of the central part insisted on the theologian's duty to know the entire exegetical tradition, so as not to bind the interpretation of sacred texts to any particular philosophy in an exclusive way and instead render himself sensitive to a multiplicity of possible meanings and interpretations. Campanella himself would do just that when responding to arguments against Galileo. Beyond reaffirming the full compatibility between research and faith, he showed how on some specific points the doctrines of Pythagoras that had been relaunched by Galileo permitted a literal interpretation of some scriptural passages that was simpler and closer to the text than that proposed by other doctrines, and certainly much simpler and closer to the text than interpretations proposed by the philosophy of Aristotle. Far from being blameworthy, the fact that Galileo was anti-Aristotelian was a sign of merit. Pronouncing prohibitions and setting up obstacles to the reading of the book of nature was truly an absurd and impious project, especially when dealing with someone who 'speaks soberly, following the observation of evidence, and by conjectures,' instead of 'out of his own mind' (*de cerebro suo*) as Aristotle does.[11]

Of particular interest was the response to the eighth argument on the multiplicity of worlds that seemed to renew a Pythagorean vision of the cosmos and to bring to life again the doctrines of Philolaus on the elemental constitution of every star. As has already been recalled, in his youth Campanella had discussed this hypothesis with Colantonio Stigliola, according to whom it was irrational to support the notion that stars are only 'idle fire' (*ignis ociosus*) and not worlds similar to our own instead. Campanella had responded to Stigliola's arguments by maintaining that to him on the contrary it seemed irrational to multiply on other worlds the ignorance, unhappiness, deceit, and blasphemies of our own world and that he preferred to consider the stars devoid of such corruption and sorrow and to consider them home to angelic spirits instead.[12] But the discoveries of Galileo on the irregularity of the surfaces of the moon, the phases of Venus, and the 'small clouds' around the sun reopened the argument and made him doubt his former certainty – to the point that he did not even discount the possibility that the stars, instead of being the abode of

---

[10] Ibid., pp. 69–71.

[11] Ibid., p. 91.

[12] See ch. 2, note 9.

hallowed spirits, were populated with inhabitants, even if they might be different from us on account of the diversity of the environments in which they found themselves.[13] That did not, however, entail an adherence to the position of Democritus regarding the multiplicity of worlds strewn about randomly in an infinite space. Instead, it made him hold onto the possibility of a plurality of systems coordinated in a unitary whole. In a subsequent letter to Galileo, he would exhort him to discover 'the theaters and scenes in which the eternal intelligence represents such great games of wheels upon wheels.'[14]

In the *Apologia*, Campanella uses incisive and tightly-knit arguments while displaying an exceptionally remarkable hermeneutical skill – at times making it hard for the reader to follow without getting lost in the myriad of citations and references. He seeks to demonstrate how the union between theology and Aristotelian philosophy (which theologians held to be necessary and indispensable) is actually shaky, outdated and open to revision, while showing that this in itself did not put theology at risk. He intended to show, on the contrary, that precisely the opposite is true – namely, that theology would be damaged by a stubborn and blind adhesion to a physical system that did not agree with new data and was contradicted by new discoveries. The abandonment of Aristotelianism would not only not carry with it the collapse of theology, it would also permit the recovery of a correct conceptualization of science, something that could not but consist, precisely as it did in Galileo, in open-ended research and in a continual reading of the infinite book of nature, which is the expression of infinite truth and Christian rationality. From here came the invitation to Christianity to accept its calling to rationality with faith and courage.

In September of 1616, Pietro Giacomo Failla, a disciple of the prisoner, advised Galileo that Campanella had sent to Cardinal Caetani at Rome an 'apology, in defense of Your Lordship's manner of philosophizing, demonstrating that it is not 'against the unanimous agreement of the Church Fathers and the Sacred Scriptures and that he who prohibits this manner of philosophizing prohibits the Christian intellect from being Christian.'[15] On 3 November, Campanella himself confirmed to Galileo that he had sent to Rome 'a *Quaestio* in which it is proved theologically that the manner of philosophizing practiced by you is more compatible with divine Scripture than its opposite, or at least rather more than the Aristotelian manner of philosophizing.'[16]

---

[13] *Quaest. phys.*, p. 99.

[14] Letter dated 14 March 1614, in *Lettere*, p. 177.

[15] Galilei, *Opere*, XII, p. 277.

[16] *Lettere*, pp. 179–180. In the same letter, Campanella went on to lament that he had not had a reply from Galileo; in truth, some months later, there would be a reply, but Galileo's letter, send to Failla, had trouble reaching its addressee: see the letter of Fabio Colonna from Naples, dated 3 February 1617, in Galilei, *Opere*, XII, p. 305.

Many years later, in 1630, Campanella would meet Galileo in Rome. In a letter to Peiresc (June 1636) that has recently be rediscovered, the author hints at the contents of their discussions in Rome in order to confirm Galileo's adherence to atomism.[17] Between April of 1631 and October of 1632, Campanella would send another six letters to Galileo. The first two had a rather formal tone, in that Campanella felt himself unjustly neglected by his friend, who had shown and sent the manuscript (and later the printed edition of his *Dialogo*) to others and not to him: 'Your Lordship did me wrong showing it to so many others and not to me, I who am more your devotee than anyone else....' One year later, Campanella wrote again to the effect that 'Signor Galileo, truly illustrious, who illuminates our century in an uncommon fashion, it pains me that I receive your favors only rarely.... I am the one who most esteems your works and who judges them with a judgment more purified of every passion ....'[18] But in August of 1632, having received a copy of the work, Campanella communicated to Galileo his own admiration for the brilliant success of this 'philosophical comedy':

> I received Your Lordship's *Dialoghi*. Everyone plays his role perfectly – Simplicio, for instance, as the amusement of this philosophical comedy, who demonstrates simultaneously the stupidity of his sect and the inconsistency and stubbornness of his manner of speaking.... Assuredly, there is no need to envy Plato. Salviati is a great Socrates who helps in giving birth even more than giving birth himself and Sagredo is a free spirit who, without being polluted by the schools, judges everything with a great deal of wisdom.[19]

Yet only about two weeks later Campanella shared with his friend the first alarming news on the intensification of threats and dangers with regard to his work: 'to my great disgust, I have heard that irate theologians are uniting and moving to prohibit the *Dialoghi* of Your Lordship, and among them there is no one who knows mathematics and recondite things.' Campanella added that he was 'afraid of the violence of people with hardly any knowledge' and suggested to him that the Grand Duke ask Rome to nominate as his defenders the Abbot Benedetto Castelli and himself. The extraordinary thing is that Galileo accepted the proposal. Even if he did not share some of the scientific doctrines of Campanella, he without doubt ought to have appreciated Campanella's theological competence and sincere attachment. But the proposal was quickly rejected by Rome, as the Ambassador Francesco Niccolini informs us in a letter to Secretary Andrea Cioli. He writes that the request

---

[17] *Lettere 2*, p. 116: 'e dal discorrer c'ha fatto meco in Roma' ('from discussions that he had with me in Rome'); see ch. 1, note 14.

[18] Letters dated 26 April 1631 and 1 May 1632, in *Lettere*, pp. 232, 235–236.

[19] Ibid., p. 240.

advanced was impossible to grant because Campanella 'had written a pretty similar work that had been prohibited and because it was not permissible that a guilty man such as Campanella should defend him.'[20]

The situation worsened quickly, eliciting in Campanella the deepest bitterness together with a recognition of the necessity of a difficult resignation: 'I did what I could to be of use to you ... but it was not acknowledged.... Let us agree with divine will, and let us believe that if natural things are all made with art and infinite wisdom then the same is true of moral and political things, even if to us it seems like a reverse: and let us be children of obedience. When the blood cools, I will tell you more.' In the final letter, a sense of impotence and defeat emerged as a result of not being able to do anything more for his friend: 'may Your Lordship forgive the weakness born of long worries and slanders; know that men aim not at truth, but at delighting and excusing themselves by denouncing us.'[21]

Philosophy and Theology

Some years before the *Apologia*, Campanella had redacted another important *quaestio* that was in many respects similar and complementary to the *Apologia* – namely, the *De gentilismo non retinendo*. On account of its complex and radical confrontation with Aristotelian philosophy, combined with its treatment of the relationship between philosophy and theology, it would be reprinted in 1637 as the opening to the Paris edition of the *Philosophia realis* (after first being published the year before), with the title *Disputatio in prologum instauratarum scientiarum*. The text constituted an introduction to and foundation for Campanella's general project of an overall reform of the sciences.[22]

The work is not very large, but it is very dense, and we shall highlight some of its essential points. So as to respond to the question of whether it is permissible (and in some respects necessary) to found a new philosophy

---

[20] Galilei, *Opere*, XIV, p. 389. On Benedetto Castelli, see the entry by Augusto De Ferrari, in *DBI*, 21 (Rome, 1978), pp. 686–690.

[21] *Lettere*, pp. 242–245.

[22] The 1637 edition, used here, was preceded by that of 1636; that edition had a different title, by which the work is better known, *De gentilismo non retinendo*, in the volume which included the *Atheismus triumphatus* and other texts. The later edition constitutes a revised and amplified text in comparison with the earlier one, after the publication of which Campanella became aware of condemnation of the texts of Aristotle at Paris. See John M. Headley, 'Tommaso Campanella and Jean de Launoy: The Controversy over Aristotle and his Reception in the West,' *Renaissance Quarterly*, 43 (1990), pp. 529–550. A recent adjustment of the relationship between theological and scientific truth in Michel-Pierre Lerner, 'Vérité des philosophes et vérité des théologiens selon Tommaso Campanella o. p.,' *Freiburger Zeitschrift für Philosophie und Theologie*, 48 (2001), pp. 281–300.

and in order to repel the arguments that such a refounding of philosophy was unnecessary (in that we can already make use of the philosophy of the ancients and in particular the philosophy of Aristotle), Campanella appealed to the disposition of the eighth session of the Second Lateran Council as a point of reference. Accentuating the fact that no truth can be contradictory to truth, the Council rejected any possibility of a schism between true theologians and true philosophers and exhorted a healing of the 'infected roots' of pagan doctrines and the founding of a new accord between philosophy and theology. Campanella agreed fully with the rejection of any notion of a double truth. Convinced that grace perfects and does not destroy nature, he maintained that illuminated by grace Christians could achieve results greater than those of the ancients – not only in theology but also on moral and natural questions. From here there derived the necessity of undertaking and carrying forward a general project of refounding the sciences, so as to emend them, improve them, and make them progress in the light of the two books of God – the one embedded in Nature, the other written in Scripture. As he reaffirmed on numerous occasions, this had been and would remain the project of his entire life.

The remarkable inventions of the moderns (from the art of printing to the discovery of new terrestrial and celestial worlds), together with the renovation of the sciences in all fields (from astronomy to the philosophy of nature), proved that it is necessary to correct the errors of the ancients and to go beyond the results achieved by them. Likewise, these things proved that the Christians (who took Christ, the wisdom of God, as their master) can and ought to work without begging from the sciences of antiquity. But in the schools it happened instead that the masters taught the doctrines of Aristotle and his commentators, which it turned out were profoundly different from the doctrines of Christianity. Students thus learned a mass of false doctrines: that the individual soul was mortal and only that soul which was universal and the same for all men was immortal; that the world is eternal and not created by God; that heaven and hell do not exist, nor as a consequence did the rewards and punishments of another life; and that God did not know and did not care for the inferior world of men. The doubts that are planted in the minds of those who learn in this way are reinforced by the cold confutations of those doctrines provided by their masters, which induces the suspicion that they are declared false only on account of fear of the Inquisition. He who then behaves in an immoral way or commits crimes hopes and desires in his heart that the doctrines of the ancients are true, so as not to have to settle accounts with God. The distorted will 'makes arguments appear true that are more in accordance with their passions.'[23] The most noxious upshot of this

---

[23] *Disputatio*, f. B ɪɪv.

way of thinking is Machiavellism, which is 'the root of all evil' and holds religion to be a mere political expedient utilized by princes on account of reason of state. Machiavellism is a doctrine that spreads like the plague, occupying the thrones of sovereigns and the leaders of the people. From here comes the so much more urgent necessity of ousting false doctrines and refounding true ones, in that 'it is impious to extinguish the light of our minds and to continue to utilize the smoking torch of the pagans.' Campanella exhorts Christians to light the lamp of the sciences 'in the light of the sun of divine wisdom.'

The strong call to correct the fallacious books of men in the light of the original book of nature is made as an exhortation to emancipate oneself from human authorities, so as to open oneself up to new doctrines and discoveries that derive from a correct reading of nature and are not to be rejected but rather evaluated with attention and welcomed. St. Jerome suffered at the hands of many bishops, who accused him of arrogance and criticized him heavily for having dared to make a new translation of the sacred texts. Columbus was held to be a heretic, because he proposed to find the antipodes that had been denied by St. Augustine and Lactantius. Likewise, the Bishop of Salzburg was condemned as a heretic by a national synod for having upheld this opinion, which today has been proved true. Experience had proved Columbus and the Bishop right and so many truths that had previously been hidden had now been made manifest: 'thus it is a heresy to assert that Aristotle has exhausted truth, and that we cannot philosophize beyond his limits; it is a heresy to prefer a heart immersed in the shadows to those illuminated by the Gospel.'[24]

On the basis of such presuppositions, Campanella affirmed forcefully that on some points it is necessary to reject the authority of Aristotle, while on other points he remains useful. Those doctrines that are evidently in conflict with Christian principles are rejected without reservation. These included positions on the eternity of the world or the denials of the immortality of the soul, providence, and the rewards and punishments of the afterlife. Also to be condemned is the denial of angels and demons, the possibility of prophetic dreams, and in general the radically naturalistic interpretation of prophecy explained in the light of medical doctrines (such as the notion that the Sibyls and the prophets were affected by melancholic humors and made their divinations in a kind of madness). As he would reaffirm in the *Apologia pro Galileo*, Campanella emphasized how there is no uniform adherence to Aristotelianism in the Christian tradition; he was happy to recall multiple discordant voices and the various adoptions of Plato, Socrates, and Pythagoras. Holy men such as Vincent Ferrer and Serafino of Fermo came to define the Peripatetic philosophy as the

---

[24] Ibid., f. B ɪvᴠ.

phial of the anger of God turned upon the waters of Christian wisdom, 'which became bitter like absinthe.' It is from such doctrines that the greater part of the theological and philosophical heresies took their origin, from the Monophysitists to the Arians, from the partisans of Gilbert de la Porrée to Amalric of Bène, to the rationalism of Abelard, who passed even the Scriptures and the Church Fathers through the sieve of Aristotle. As has already been noted, it is from here that the political doctrines considering religion as an *ars regnandi* and the laws as an imposture instituted by the cunning have their origin. As the Spanish theologian Melchior Cano had also noted, one of the most dangerous fruits of Aristotelianism is precisely Machiavellism, which is the 'root of sin and of the insolence of princes, of the sedition of the people, and of the audacity to give birth to heresies in order to gain power.'[25] In order to combat what seemed to him an undue involvement and authority of Aristotelian philosophy in the schools of Christianity, Campanella did not hesitate to recourse to the most disparate sources, including the eccentric Ortensio Lando's *Paradossi*. In the twenty-ninth chapter of that work (titled "That Aristotle was not only an ignorant man, but also the worst man of his time"), he undertook an unscrupulous desecration, both philosophical and ethical, of the philosopher.[26] Denouncing the philosophical errors and the immoral conduct of Aristotle, he deplored the fact that 'we madmen worship him like an idol,' putting faith in him 'like an oracle,' and he invited Christians to wake themselves from this dangerous dream, emphasizing the extremely grave risks of abandoning the sacred texts 'in order to attend to the dreams of this oaf':

> then Martin Luther turns up without this taste for Aristotle, without recourse to the formality of Scotus; armed only with the Holy Scriptures and his own understanding of them, he put to flight all those reverend Aristotelian theologians from Leipzig, Louvain, and Cologne – making them recognize how great an error it had been to leave the grain in order to eat the acorn.[27]

The delicate problem of the reasons for the acceptance of such doctrines in the schools, and for the marriage between Aristotelianism, Thomism, and Scholastic theology took shape in the context of this ample and radical riposte to Aristotelian doctrines, which is already delineated in the early works. In that regard, Campanella completed a drastic redimensioning of the primacy

---

[25] Ibid., f. C ɪɪ*r*.

[26] Campanella did not cite the author of the anonymous *Paradossi*, most probably for reasons of prudence with regard to an author who had been placed on the Index and who was highly suspect in the eyes of the ecclesiastical authorities.

[27] Ortensio Lando, *Paradossi*, anastatic reprint from the Lyon edition, 1543, ed. by E. Canone and G. Ernst (Pisa-Rome, 1999), p. 206; modern edition by A. Corsaro (Rome, 2000), p. 253f.

of Aristotle and intended to show how the decision to favor Aristotle resulted from a particular historical juncture. Thanks to the Arabs, the Aristotelian texts were the only ones to have survived in an age that had known the loss of the books of the ancients and the destruction of its libraries. Beginning in the age of Charlemagne, the schools reopened after the long silence that followed the invasions of the barbarians. With the texts of Plato lost, the only surviving texts were those of Aristotle, whose fortune was thus connected with a chance historical circumstance and was not a function of their intrinsic excellence. Moreover, the insertion of Aristotle into the curricula of the universities was not so peaceful and consensual as had been supposed. Campanella specified and was happy to list every condemnation of Aristotelian works on the part of the Sorbonne or on the part of the Pontiffs. Regarding Aquinas, Campanella appreciated the efforts that went into his commentary of Aristotle and the amendments and criticisms he made to his philosophy. But the attempt to find an accord between that philosophy and Christian theology was in certain respects so difficult that it brought upon him accusations of having misunderstood or deformed the genuine significance of the texts of the Greek philosopher. Aristotelian philosophy was thus introduced into the Christian world *casu diro* ('due to an unfortunate circumstance') as, in the age of Antiochus in the schools of Jerusalem, Greek philosophy had taken the place of the doctrine of Moses, redeemed later by the Maccabee brothers. Later still, it had become difficult to oust it on account of the convergence of many factors – among which habit, ignorance, and a Machiavellian impiety that had a vested interest in maintaining it. In any case, it was heretical and impious to assert that theology had its foundation and confirmation in that philosophy. One ought not to recourse to Aristotle either as an arbiter or as a judge. In general, one ought not to chain the interpretation of the sacred texts exclusively to any specific philosophy. Instead, one ought now and again to make use of those doctrines that were more in agreement with the divine books.

With regard to Aquinas, he was not a Peripatetic but instead a Christian philosopher who was in fundamental accord with the Church Fathers, who were themselves often hostile to the philosophy of Aristotle. On various occasions, Thomas did not hesitate to dissent from the texts upon which he was commenting, sharing fully the position that it is necessary and useful to take those aspects from every philosophy that are positive and that are in accord with Christian wisdom. In his attempt to draw a clear distinction between Aquinas and Aristotle, Campanella intended above all to maintain that the adoption of anti-Aristotelian positions did not necessarily imply pitting oneself against Thomas. So as to defend his own positions (which were at once informed by a decided anti-Aristotelianism that had been very clear from the years of his youth and by an acceptance of Thomism if it were correctly understood), Campanella spoke of the grave trial of his youth prior to that related to the conspiracy in an important autobiographical passage. In that trial, he had been called upon by the Holy Office to defend himself with respect to the anti-Aristotelian doctrines espoused in the books that had been withdrawn deviously at Bologna in the autumn of 1592. In particular, he was called upon to speak on the doctrine of the *Senso delle cose*. When he had spoken, the commissioners, having listened and evaluated his arguments and his explanations, not only did not reprove him in any way, but even praised him:

> The most learned fathers have not punished me, nor have their reproached me orally, nor have they ordered me to desist from confuting Aristotle, nor have they done so with arguments. On the contrary, the fathers, particularly, the Cardinals Santori, Bernerio, Sarnano, have praised me for having redeemed the fathers from the offenses of the pagans. I cannot understand why now others see things differently: let them go and see for themselves the records of the trial.[28]

Telesio, for his part, had not been condemned on account of being an anti-Aristotelian, but rather because some points of his thought turned out to be liable to deeper investigation. In any case, he had not been subject to a total ban of his work; only some treatises were forbidden *donec expurgentur*. With regard to the accusations against the *novatores*, Campanella believed it was necessary to make some opportune distinctions. Rejecting the coloring of that term with exclusively negative connotations, Campanella asserted forcefully that not every novelty in the state and in the church ought to be liable to condemnation: 'rather, all the new doctrines please and render admirable both the state and religion, and they make it so that subjects turn more willingly to their duties; from foreigners they elicit admiration and obedience.'[29] When he discovered the new world that had been denied by saints, Columbus not only did not abase them, but rather 'embellished and exalted governments and the Christian sciences,' just as Galileo had done in discovering new stars that previously had

---

[28] For this episode, the 1636 edition gives 1595, while the later edition gives 1698 (clearly erroneously). Here, as in the passage from the *Defensio* (see ch. 2, note 50), Campanella is referring to the conclusion of third trial. It is important to remember that Cardinal Sarnano died at the end of 1595. I quote here the Latin passage from the 1637 edition, putting in square brackets the passages omitted in the 1636 edition: 'Et quidem anno 1698 [*sic*] interrogatus ego a Patribus in S. Officio de opinionibus quas contra Aristotelem scripseram [in libris furto mihi sublatis datisque S. Officio ab impiis sciolis,] et praecipue de sensu rerum, [pro quo Apologiam feci postmodum] nec reprehensione vocali nec praecepto recedendi ab impugnando Aristotelem, nec rationibus Patres doctissimi me obiurgarunt, sed laudarunt, [praecipue cardinalis Sanctorius, et Bernerius, et Sarnanus], quod PP. SS. ab iniuria Gentilium vendicarem. Nescio cur nunc alii murmurant scioli? Videant processus in S. Officio et meas opiniones ibi examinatas.'

[29] *Disputatio*, f. E 1r.

been unknown. In the same way, one could not call the person who 'introduces truths that are not damaging to the old truths' (as founders of religions orders do) a *novator* in a negative sense. Innovators that are worthy of condemnation are those who 'come up with new things in order to destroy old well-established ones.' Heretics and the founders of sects constitute the most renowned examples of such bad innovation. But he who reforms the sciences in the light of the two divine books puts himself forward as a restorer (*instaurator*) of the sciences. He is to be praised in that, revealing the errors of the sectarians, he presents himself as a liberator of Christian minds from the tyranny of the pagans. On the contrary, they are lazy and vile who content themselves with putting into circulation a well-worn money in place of a genuine currency minted with gold. One is dealing here with inert men, lovers only of their own comfort and traitors to the state. These are men endowed with servile minds, who are ignoble and convinced that we must overtly and secretly make use of monetary currency (even to the point of falsifying it and coining it with new brass) to the detriment of the state. They reject the reformers who use ancient gold and they reject the best of the fathers. Their abuse is similar to that of the gentile philosophers who thought they had to uphold false gods against their own consciences.[30]

In response to the final question of the treatise (whether it be permissible to swear allegiance to the words of a philosopher), Campanella reaffirmed that the sole master is Christ, who is the wisdom of God. He reaffirmed that God alone is truthful, while every man has a limited and partial understanding, and argued that he who prefers a single thinker and disdains all the rest deprives the church of its defenders. Swearing allegiance to a single philosopher is a heresy, a perjury, an impiety in that one is closing the door to continual improvement. Thus, chaining minds to a single book is not useful for the republic, because it weakens it and deprives it of new discoveries. Every day the experience of new things enlarges and renews the sciences, on account of which it is necessary to favor a 'studium multiplex,' without which there would never have been such wondrous inventions.

Astrology

In the extremely bounteous corpus of Campanella's works, we also encounter a treatise containing six books called the *Astrologia*. This was an area that was the object of constant reflection on Campanella's part, after a period of youthful skepticism that he described in the *Senso delle cose*: 'I was very much against astrologers and wrote against them in my youth, but my studies made me conscious that astrologers say many true things.' In a famous letter to

---

[30] Ibid., f. E ɪᴠ.

Monsignor Querenghi, Campanella drew a comparison between himself and Pico, recalling that the Count of Mirandola 'found fault with the astrologers for not having aimed at experience, just as I found fault with them when I was nineteen years old; but afterwards I saw much wisdom lodged in the midst of their many idiocies.'[31] When he made reference to the skepticism of his youth, Campanella was alluding to the digression on astrology in the third dispute of the *Philosophia sensibus demonstrata* and to the criticism of those astrologers who 'thought that they could easily escape reason and to take refuge in occult powers, with which they can cover their errors and confound the minds of men.'[32] Later on, and perhaps due to the friendship with Giovan Vincenzo della Porta and other Neapolitan 'mathematicians,' Campanella acquired specific competences in astrology, demonstrating a great interest in individual horoscopes as well as in those celestial doctrines that connect astral events with terrestrial developments.

Prophetic and political themes were connected, and, as has been seen in the first declarations immediately after his arrest in the attempted conspiracy, he emphasized his own interest in 'those things that yield signs of the future,' and recalled the conversations that he had had at Naples with Nicolantonio Stigliola, Giulio Cortese, and Giovan Paolo Vernaleone.[33] Both the aspects of astrology – the individual and the general – are then recalled in connection with the final lines of *The City of the Sun*, where the author had emphasized that the astral beliefs of the Solarians did not conflict with the freedom of the will. As a confirmation of the continued existence of liberty even in the context of celestial influence, he evoked two things. On the one hand, he evoked the terrible torture he had recently suffered: if an extreme physical ordeal is not enough to dent the freedom of the will, so much the less could a much weaker and more distant conditioning that was operated by the stars do it, given that only he who follows more the senses than reason is really subject to the stars. On the other hand, he showed how in the recent past, persons such as Ignatius of Loyola, Martin Luther, and Hernàn Cortéz had been born under the influences of analogous astral arrangements. These were individuals who were in some way linked by the impulse for renewal, even if in terms of the diversity of their situations and contexts they were very distant one from another:

---

[31] *Senso delle cose*, p. 226; letter dated 8 July 1607 in *Lettere*, p. 134.
[32] See ch. 1.1.
[33] *Dichiarazione*, p. 102; see ch. 5.1.

One knows this – that they [the Solarians] subscribe to the liberty of the will. And they say that, if in forty hours of torment a man does not let slip that which he has resolved to keep to himself, much less can the stars, which exercise their influence from afar, force him to do it. Because in sense changes are made very subtly, he who follows sense more than reason is subject to the influence of the stars. Whence it is that the constellation that drew infectious vapors from the cadaver of Luther, also drew odorous fumes of virtue from our Jesuits who existed in his time, as well as from Hernàn Cortéz who spread Christianity into Mexico in the same age.[34]

An eloquent confirmation of his interest in worldly astrology, which was based on the new information provided in the system of Copernicus (who is referred to as '*sagacissimus*,' '*vir admirabilis*'), is prominent in the *Prognosticum*, which had been drafted on the occasion of the great conjunction of 24 December 1603. Starting from that date, and for the next 200 years, the conjunctions of the greater planets, Jupiter and Saturn, would be found in the signs of fire, beginning with Sagittarius. In the preceding 200 years they had been situated in the trine of the signs of water, dominated by Venus and by the moon. This was to have brought with it, among other things, the triumph of the Muslims and the dominion of female figures, facts that are recalled in *The City of the Sun*. The return of the conjunctions in the trine of fire (which was the same situation that had presided over the birth of Christ and the empire of Charlemagne) announced a profound political and religious upheaval. Campanella looked with great emotion upon the astral event, which was expected precisely on the day of the birth of Christ. He composed a number of prophetic sonnets as well as the *Prognosticum*, which would be added as a final chapter to the *Articuli prophetales*.[35] Among the changes he expected, Campanella foresaw great advances in the sciences, new discoveries and inventions, as a result of the particular positioning of Mercury. He would bring this to Galileo's attention in the closing of his great Latin letter written immediately after having read the *Sidereus nuncius*. In a subsequent letter of March 1614, announcing to Galileo the completion of the astrological treatise, Campanella rebuked his friend for the contradiction between his declared 'skepticism' (on the basis of which he rejected an astrological consultation for his own health problems, declaring that he did not believe in it) and the precise astrological allusions present in the dedicatory letter to Cosimo II contained in the *Sidereus nuncius*, where the excellent qualities of the Grand Duke were put in relation to the felicitous positioning of the 'very benign star of Jupiter' in his horoscope.[36]

---

[34] *Città del Sole*, pp. 58–59.

[35] The *Prognosticum* thus would not be numbered among the lost writings: see *Art. proph.*, pp. XXXVII–XL, 260–300.

[36] *Art. proph.*, p. 278; *Lettere*, p. 169.

Campanella emphasized that, if such references to the influence of planets were only affected and were the function of an encomiastic and courtly praise, devoid of any internal conviction, then they ought to be avoided, since 'it is not permissible for Your Lordship to use false opinions that are believed only by the vulgar.' He therefore went on to admonish him, bidding him not to disdain a doctrine that was without doubt 'full of fallacies' but that also contained 'extremely divine things' if the proper distinctions with regard to various levels of certainty regarding contents were taken into account.[37]

The six books of the *Astrologia* dealt with the foundational assumptions of astrological doctrine: from the enunciation of basic doctrinal principles to previsions of general events; from indications on climates and seasons to true and proper horoscopes, to which the fourth book was dedicated; from the calculation of the times of celestial events to the problem of 'elections' – that is to say, the evaluation of opportune moments for executing the most advantageous decisions.[38] Campanella's long acquaintance with the compilation and interpretation of nativities is evident in the text. In these pages we come across many references to famous personalities and to their horoscopes: Emperor Rudolf II, whose decline and whose end are related to the appearance in 1607 of a comet in the sign of Leo, his ascendant sign; Pope Paul V, whose extremely difficult birth is recalled and whose clash and reconciliation with Venice are reread in the light of celestial positionings; the Duke of Nocera, irascible, arrogant, martial on account of the positioning of Aldebaran, whose fleshy reddishness was so changeable on account of the moon that 'no painter was able to complete a faithful portrait of him'; Francesco Caracciolo, favored during his rise in society by an unusual concentration of planets that would also ironically bring about his sudden demise. In these pages, one also encounters Campanella's companions and friends: Dionisio Ponzio, who died a violent death far from his homeland; the faithful Tobias Adami, noted for his long voyages; or Giovanni Alfonso Borelli, who was loved like a son and who Campanella sought to protect from a dangerous positioning of Mars.[39]

In a magisterial reconstruction of the context in which the letter to Ottavio Sammarco of 1614 was situated, Giorgio Fulco demonstrated the tight web of contacts that connected Naples (the 'Siren jailer') to the illustrious prisoner,

---

[37] *Lettere*, p. 177. For the relationship to Galileo with regard to astrological issues, see Germana Ernst, 'Aspetti dell'astrologia e della profezia in Galileo e Campanella,' in *Novità celesti e crisi del sapere*, ed. P. Galluzzi (Florence, 1983), pp. 255–266 (then in *Religione*, pp. 237–254; an English transl. in *Culture and Cosmos*, 7 (2004), pp. 21–36).

[38] For the *De fato siderali vitando*, added at press as a seventh book, see ch. 11.2.

[39] *Astrologia*, pp. 1180, 1177, 1207, 1223, 1263–1264, 1270, 1277, 1336. I addressed these issues in 'Vocazione profetica e astrologia in Tommaso Campanella,' in *La città dei segreti. Magia, astrologia e cultura esoterica a Roma (XV–XVIII)*, ed. F. Troncarelli (Milan, 1985), pp. 136–155 (and subsequently in *Religione*, pp. 19–34).

who was the object of curiosity and admiration during visits from foreigners and famous persons. Sammarco, a young writer on political subjects, had written to Campanella requesting an astrological consultation for a friend. The prisoner replied, but in his response he did not hold back from chastising the interlocutor for supposedly grave offensiveness with respect to his person and above all with respect to his books.[40] The most complete example of Campanella's expertise in the interpretation of births is set before us in the horoscope compiled for the young Flemish Philibert Vernat, imprisoned at Naples by the extremely suspicious Viceroy, the Duke of Ossuna, who believed him to be a hired killer sent by Venice. Luigi Firpo described this horoscope as 'the complete ... practical demonstration of the theoretical teachings indicated in the *Astrologicorum*.'[41]

Campanella set himself the task of liberating astrology from the superstitions of the Arabs, so as to refound it as a natural and conjectural doctrine that would be compatible with Christian positions, a project that we see set out in the introductory pages of the text. In the first place, this was a matter of separating astrology from that mass of useless (*nugaces*) doctrines, towards which the human mind is also irresistibly attracted. If the human desire to know the future is in itself positive, in that it is one of the ways of indicating his own participation in divinity, it can also become an illusory and ruinous passion if it is not corrected and ruled by a superior reason and if man, forgetful of the Prime Cause, begins to prostrate himself before secondary and instrumental causes. Neither idolatrous nor demonic, astrology must always be attentive to correspondences between stars and nature, cautious in its methods of investigation (for only a few cases are genuinely 'demonstrative,' whereas most must be reasoned *probabiliter* or conjecturally), and aware that events depend on a multiplex concourse of causes. Astrology practiced in this mode is not unworthy of the name of 'science,' and only he who does not respect its natural limits falls into superstition and risks falling into diabolical deceit.

With regard to the most prickly problem (namely, the influence of the stars on the free choices of man), Campanella kept his distance from deterministic positions, reasserting the liberty of the human will in a passage that alludes to the tortures he had suffered: 'Man is so free that, if he does not so will it,

[40] See Giorgio Fulco, 'Il fascino del recluso e la Sirena carceriera: Campanella, Ottavio Sammarco e Napoli in una scheggia di carteggio (dic. 1614),' *B&C*, 2 (1996), pp. 33–56; the text of the letter can also be found in *Lettere 2*, pp. 65–68.

[41] Firpo, *Ricerche*, p. 151. For the text of the horoscope, see Luigi Firpo, 'Un inedito autografo campanelliano (*Calculus nativitatis Domini Philiberti Vernati*),' *Atti della R. Accademia delle Scienze di Torino*, vol. LXXIV, tomo II (1938–1939), pp. 286–305 (in truth, as Firpo himself would later indicate, the text is not autograph except in parts).

he cannot be beaten by any torment or death. How much less of a threat, then, are the stars that do not exert an influence that is so atrocious? Even if they burn the body they do not succeed in dominating the will.'[42] In truth, the question was complex and required an entire series of distinctions and specifications. Going back to Albert the Great and St. Thomas, Campanella affirmed that the will of man is subject to the stars – but not *directe* and only *per accidens*. The sky and the stars influence the body and the *spiritus*, which carries the affections thus received to the incorporeal soul infused by God and which can choose to consent or instead oppose itself to the solicitations of the passions. If, as in to a famous astrological aphorism, 'the wise man will dominate the stars,' it can also be said that the astrologer often hits the mark when making his predictions, because men, in most cases, indulge sensuous inclinations rather than making rational choices.

Celestial Signs

In the final months of 1618, unusual celestial phenomena appeared: the 'beam' of November (a celestial body with an elongated form, like a spear, a sword, or a pen) and above all a spectacular comet (with a tail that extended for more than 40°) that would remain visible for several weeks. The appearances would not fail to elicit the most lively emotions both among the learned and among ordinary people. As Virginio Cesarini wrote on 1 December from Rome, 'the celestial novelties to be seen in recent days in the heavens have awoken men, even those who are not curious; even the sleepiest and laziest people in the city of Rome have forced themselves to rise up from bed.' Cesarini himself, notwithstanding the precarious condition of his health, had not gone to bed during the previous night, despite the bitter cold, so as to observe the 'extremely clear heavens cleansed by a powerful northerly wind.'[43]

Since this concerned the appearance of major celestial phenomena after the invention of the telescope, there was a lively expectation that Galileo would make a pronouncement on the event, and he was asked by many to do so, both in Italy and from abroad. Francesco Stelluti wrote to Galileo on Christmas day from Acquasparta (where he was as a guest of Prince Federico Cesi) and informed him of the observations of the comet through the telescope and the discussions about it. As he related, 'the new celestial appearances of the beam and the comet have provided for the discussion and speculation of many, and particularly for he who is able to observe it minutely....'

---

[42] Regarding the torture, see ch. 5, pp. 80–81. Giordano Bruno had been burnt on the stake in 1600.

[43] Galilei, *Opere*, XII, p. 422.

He solicited the opinion of his interlocutor: 'but we expect with greater reason to hear something about it from Your Lordship, which would be extremely welcome to all.'[44] But Galileo, kept in bed by an attack of arthritis, could not complete any observations. Only the next year, after the publication of the *De tribus cometis* (a work published anonymously, but written by the Jesuit Orazio Grassi), would he be induced to take part in the dispute that would culminate in 1623 with the publication of the *Saggiatore*.[45]

Rather surprisingly, Campanella was among those who observed the comet. As he himself informs us, the conditions of his detention during this period were somewhat more lenient than they had been previously. He opened a letter from that time with the assertion that 'for three months I have found myself outside the lake of Jeremiah half free in the Castel Nuovo.' He was able to observe both the beam and the comet between 25 November and 2 December, and hurried to set down a discourse and send it to the Viceroy. The Duke of Ossuna,[46] who served as viceroy at the time, had taken an ambivalent attitude towards the prisoner but showed a certain propensity towards the possibility of giving him his much-desired freedom. At the same time, Campanella already and yet again foresaw set-backs and difficulties. As he wrote to the Duke of Mantua, '[the Viceroy] promises freedom and other graces, but these things are continually deferred.' Likewise, he wrote to Giovanni Fabri in Rome that 'this promise does not seem likely to be fulfilled.'[47] On 22 December, the piece was sent to the Pontiff in the form of an epistolary tract.

The first reflections are of a prophetic nature. The work displays conspicuous similarities to the *Articuli prophetales*, particularly in those chapters (the fifth, the sixth, and the seventh) that set out a prophetic interpretation of astronomical facts, examining the various doctrines concerning the age of the world and comparing the observations of the astronomical tradition of the past with those of most recent astronomers, so as to identify signs announcing the approach of the end of times. In the years that followed, Campanella would deepen his own more properly scientific opinion on the comet in the twenty-fourth *Quaestio* of the *Physiologia*. There, he would take up the theories of authors such as Tycho Brahe, Telesio, Santucci, and Galileo, for the

---

[44] Ibid., pp. 430–431.

[45] The treatise *De tribus cometis anni MDCVIII disputatio astronomica* (Latin text and Italian translation) was published by O. Besomi and M. O. Helbing in Galileo Galilei and Mario Guiducci, *Discorso sulle comete* (Rome-Padua, 2002); the same scholars are responsible for the recent edition of Galileo's *Saggiatore* (Rome-Padua, 2005).

[46] Pedro Tellez Giron y Guzmàn, third Duke of Ossuna (1574–1624), was Viceroy of Naples from 1616 to 1620; see Firpo, *Ricerche*, p. 48ff, and also 'Cinque sonetti inediti di Tommaso Campanella,' ed. G. Ernst, *B&C*, 1 (1995), pp. 13–14, 19–21.

[47] *Lettere 2*, pp. 70, 72.

purpose of evaluating the most discussed aspects of the question – namely, the nature of comets, their proper place, and their motion.[48] But even before such astronomical considerations, he reflected upon the prophecies of the Sibyls, which Tycho Brahe had also recalled, and came up with interpretations of the extraordinary appearance of the new star in 1572 and of the comet in 1577.[49]

Comets, 'great signs written in the book of the heavens with the fingers of God,' are the characters of a universal language that reveals itself to all men – for 'in every land and language they speak shining forth' – and the meaning of which ought to be deciphered. Campanella intended to assume himself the role of 'final sentry in this age of divine judgments.' Such extraordinary phenomena cannot derive from chance, and their explanation cannot be exhausted with an appeal to the fortuitous concourse, devoid of all finality and meaning, of material components such as vapors. To argue thus would be like saying (taking up again in a polemical manner an image from Lucretius) that the letters of the text that the author was composing 'are written by themselves the result of randomly spilt ink.' Many years later, in two letters to Gassendi, Campanella would not fail to reaffirm the insufficiency of an explanation of celestial phenomena that did not take divine wisdom into account.[50]

The appearance of comets is an opportunity to reflect on the approach of those signs 'in the sun, the moon, and the stars' of which the gospels and the fathers of the church such as Ambrose, John Chrysostom, and Gregory speak. If Aristotle had deduced the eternity of the world from the immovability of the celestial figures and from the regularity of astral motions, then new phenomena contradict in the most evident way such notions of the inalterability and the perpetuity of that order and of the world itself. The hinges of the *machina mundi*, held to be immobile, in fact moved: constellations were not fixed as had been held and the apogees of the planets were not fixed either. The obliqueness of the sun was tightening and the sun was inexorably getting closer to the earth, which would end up being burnt, rendering vain all the expedient mathematical calculations to which astronomers recoursed – Copernicus too – so as to render regular the anomalies of the motions and the displacements of the stars in space.

---

[48] *Quaest. phys.*, XXIV, pp. 219–240. In the summer of 1624, Campanella asked the physician Marco Aurelio Severino to procure for him the books that were necessary to bring to conclusion 'quella questione *De cometis*' (*Lettere*, p. 204; the *de secretis* that one reads in the Spampanato edition should be corrected in the *de cometis*; see Firpo, *Ricerche*, pp. 280–281); see Paolo Ponzio, 'La disputa sulle comete nelle *Quaestiones physiologicae* di Tommaso Campanella,' *B&C*, 2 (1996), pp. 197–213.

[49] See *Art. proph.*, pp. 75–79.

[50] *Discorso sulla cometa*, pp. 57–88; *Lettere*, pp. 236–39; see ch. 11, pp. 236–237.

Campanella did not intend to replace scientific explanations of celestial phenomena with prophetic explanations. Instead, he claimed forcefully that the natural explanation did not preclude or exclude prophetic interpretation and prophetic insight. He who denied such a dimension was preventing men from paying attention to celestial signs so that they might prepare for the coming of the Lord and not be surprised by him as 'by a thief in the night.' Putting himself forward as a spy on divine judgments, Campanella intended to denounce and unmask the silent conspiracy of all those – Aristotelians, astronomers, politicians – who agreed, even if from different points of view, in their desire to deny or deride the prophetic meaning of celestial signs. They persecute those who reveal such meaning, with the intention to deceive people, dissuade them from being vigilant and keep them in a deceptively restful sleep.

The appearance of the comet could not but give rise to astrological discussions. If Cesarini accentuated the immediate diffusion of 'stupid and popular explanations,'[51] Campanella concluded his own work with sober predictions, imbued with a caution that bordered on reticence. Reserving the right to return to the argument at a time when he had more complete and secure data, he limited himself to connecting the first comet to 'great journeys of preachers ... not without upheavals among the people' subject to the signs in which it had appeared; at the same time, in the sea could be verified 'the great smashing and wrecks of warships and war.' With regard to the second, it indicated 'great undertakings' in the islands of the south 'with arms and preaching.' He invited the Pope to put himself in charge of the process of the reunification of nations, a duty that pertained to him rather more than that of 'intervening in celestial matters or deciding against Copernicus.' The Edict of 1616 was recalled twice, in tones that seem to reveal a certain annoyance at an unwarranted intrusion even as on the outside they feign the required obsequiousness. At last, Campanella sought to calm down the Pope, who was evidently worried ('Your Holiness, do not be anxious ...') and whose horoscope Campanella knew well: in the *Astrologia* he had spent some time considering the moment of his extremely difficult birth.[52] In fact, the Pope would die two years later. His death would be followed, another two years after that (in the summer of 1623), by the death of his successor, Gregory XV – deaths that Campanella would not refrain from relating to the appearance of the two comets, which are always heralds of upheavals and disorders, wars and discord – such as the invasion of Bohemia, announcements of the crisis of the Spanish monarchy, deaths of Popes and sovereigns, 'and changes in all things.'[53]

---

[51] Galilei, *Opere*, XII, p. 422.
[52] *Discorso sulla cometa*, pp. 80–81; see *Astrologia*, p. 1177, 1207.
[53] *Quaest. phys.*, p. 237.

10. THE NEW ENCYCLOPEDIA OF KNOWLEDGE

Philosophia Realis

Having overcome the most difficult period of imprisonment (a period that surprisingly gave rise to remarkable texts such as the *Senso delle cose*, the *Poesie*, and the *Ateismo trionfato*), Campanella dedicated himself to the systematic refoundation of the sciences in the years that followed. As he would emphasize in a beautiful passage in the dedicatory letter addressed to Chancellor Pierre Séguier that precedes the *Philosophia realis*, even the long years in jail could be reread as elements in a providential design:

> Spending my life in the prisons of ungrateful masters, God, through whose wisdom all things are made and ordered, wanted that I be shut up for the time required to refound all of the sciences, a refounding that (always following his divine inspiration) I have conceived in my mind. This was a feat that I would not have been able to complete in a condition of ordinary happiness or without solitude. Deprived of the world of the body, I travelled through the world of the mind which is a great deal more vast and is therefore the infinitude of that Archetype that rules over every thing with the word of its virtue.[1]

After the frustrated expectations caused by Schoppe's reluctance to publish his works, Campanella's experience with Tobias Adami was much happier and more profitable. Adami had returned home after a long journey and would dedicate himself to publishing the works of his friend with alacrity. In view of such expectations, Campanella reworked his texts and translated them into Latin. The first of the four parts of the *Philosophia realis* is the *Physiologia*, which is a reworking of the *Epilogo magno* and to which the *Ethica* is added, after being rendered autonomous from natural philosophy. After that follows the *Politica*, developed and reorganized from the earlier *Aforismi*, to which he added as an appendix the *Civitas Solis*.

---

[1] *Lettere*, p. 379.

G. Ernst, *Tommaso Campanella*, International Archives of the History
of Ideas/Archives internationales d'histoire des idées 200,
DOI 10.1007/978-90-481-3126-6_10, © Springer Science + Business Media B.V. 2010

The volume closed with a section dedicated to *Oeconomica*, concerning running of the household and the family, which he considered a constitutive part of society. Society could, in turn, be organised like a family with the same ends of preserving the individual and the species (as elaborated in *The City of the Sun*). The text opens with interesting questions on whether other communities can be considered families, communities such as, for example, religious orders or the communities of the Brahmans, the Bhikkhus, and the modern African Amazons, or those of the priests of Muhammad, the Marabouts, who live in North Africa, 'in monasteries closed on every side by walls, in each of which a lord commands who has four wives and more than forty concubines, each of whom is closed in her own cell and has a multitude of children.'[2] Even as they had an important role to play in society, in Campanella's opinion religious communities could not be considered families. He had words of lively reproach for the Marabouts. Life dedicated to pleasure distanced them from contemplation and knowledge, such that they were extremely ignorant and superstitious. Their relationship to society was similar to that of 'a worm born in the limbs or in the stomach, which devours the body and is not useful but rather harmful to the whole because it invades it and extracts nourishment from it.'

Many suggestions made in this text echo principles articulated in *The City of the Sun* – rules on the suitability of location, of climate and air, on distance from noise (which, even if it sometimes serves to purify the air, distracts from contemplation). Emphasizing the nobility of agriculture, Campanella encouraged an attitude of respect towards 'mother' earth, which offers nourishment. He argued that it is necessary to avoid the violation and excavation of the earth that comes from greedy searching for metals, lest we make ourselves similar to the matricide Nero. All the arts and crafts are praised for their utility, while lazy and harmful gaming such as playing cards and dice was condemned. The author offered sensible advice on every aspect of the organization of the household and domestic economy – on the roles, the activities, and the functions of the persons who lived together in the family, from fathers to wives, children, and servants, as well as on the prudent administration of wealth owing to profitable investments (something that was to be achieved without involving oneself in usury). Campanella also recommended avoiding superfluous expenses, such as those for sumptuous weddings, banquets, and the purchase of livery; in general, he discouraged indulgence in all wasteful things that aim at pointless display.

With regard to marriage, monogamy was held to be more respectful for a woman. Moreover, monogamy led to stronger and tighter affective ties

---

[2] *Oeconomica*, p. 1039.

both between the marriage partners themselves and between the parents and children. Campanella came to this conclusion about monogamy even though he did not consider polygamy against nature. The wife, a companion to be loved and respected, ought to be an object of great respect within the family, given that she was a participant in and co-principle of generation. She was not merely a 'container in which the seed is deposited, which produces fruit by itself, without the participation of the container (something that works only for onions).' In turn, the wife has to love her husband; she must not give him any reason to be jealous, and she must stand by him even in adversity. That said, it is a deplorable excess to be buried alive alongside a dead spouse (as was customary among the Scythians) or to burn oneself on a pyre (as in the kingdom of Narsinga). The wife had to lead a wise and active life, without indulging in laziness, which notoriously produces the worst evils. The wife was to be irreproachable in her conduct and also in her person. From here came the condemnation of inappropriate clothes and shoes, and above all, as mentioned also in *The City of Sun*, the artifices of make-up. Applying ointments and colorations to the face was not so much diabolical (as the Fathers say, given that it was equivalent to 'corrupting the divine image'), as it was unhealthy. In fact, such beauty treatments lead to bad breath and headaches, while also inducing darkening, weakness, and painfulness in the teeth. They make women pallid and horrible like corpses, and so they are forced to apply make-up upon make-up, time and again. They make it so that the woman is no longer the same woman, something that is equivalent to the annihilation of self. Moreover, when they kiss their husbands they transfer the poison of the pigment, dirty their lips, and induce nausea. Beyond that, the thickness, weight, and height of their shoes make it such that the woman is no longer able to take physical exercise. If she wants to move, she requires the assistance of a servant on whom to lean, as if she were a paralytic. This image elicits disdain and disgust in whoever sees her as well as a kind of stupefaction – just as when we look upon something that is dead or ugly or sick.[3]

This style of life had very negative consequences for women themselves, for their children and for society as a whole. In contrast, 'Calabrian women, who are not afflicted by such raised shoes or beauty treatments or laziness, are tall of stature, agile, robust, vivacious in their movements, in their coloring, and in their voices.'

In the years that followed, these sections would be provided with a dense apparatus of *quaestiones*. Already announced by Tobias Adami in the 1623 Frankfurt edition of the *Philosophia realis*, these *quaestiones* would only appear in the monumental tome published at Paris. There were three questions in the

---

[3] Ibid., p. 1062.

Oeconomica: regarding the relationship between society and family, marriage, and the acquisition and preservation of riches. Highly impenetrable (and largely unexplored) are the *quaestiones* that were added to the first part. Surveying and discussing classical and contemporary authors, the sixty-one *Quaestiones physiologicae* took up a good 570 pages of the massive folio volume. It is in these pages that one finds references to, among others, Galileo, whose doctrines on sunspots, comets, the buoyancy of bodies, and the tides are discussed.[4]

The three *quaestiones* added to the *Ethica* are rich in suggestions, considering the chief good, free will, and the virtues. Likewise, the four *quaestiones* attached to the *Politica* are also very rich. In the question on free will, Campanella confronted the heart of the problem of human freedom, which is decisive for every moral doctrine: virtuous action (and the merit that follows from it) depends in fact on the possibility of a choice, which is independent of both the co-existence of a decree that has already been established and the presence of an external force. Human liberty constitutes one of the peculiar qualities that distinguish man from other living beings. Campanella holds this opinion against those who tend to exclude or curtail human freedom in significant ways – whether because they only want to accept the role of chance (like the atomists) or because they want to insist on the exclusiveness of divine initiative. For Campanella, he is free 'who moves himself at will and with intent, and who can desist from such acting by himself, not pressed into it by others: this person is called master of his actions, and this person is responsible regardless of whether he acts well or ill.'[5] Animals and servants act spontaneously, but not freely, in that they are moved by passionate solicitations from external objects, or from masters. They are not able to choose to stop something when they want to, but only when someone or something outside of them decides it. Man, on the other hand, initiates an action and desists from it through his own choice. He is free both before and after deliberation. He can resist the passions and even the most atrocious sufferings cannot change his will. As Campanella had argued elsewhere, if a man is able to set himself against the violent passions that assault him from outside, so much more will he be able to control those rather less intense passions that are impressed upon him by the stars and the heavens. He is overcome by the passions only when reason is destroyed by serious diseases, such as epilepsy or as in other kinds of madness. But in this case there is neither sin nor merit. Man is not responsible for the first carnal passions that he suffers. He

---

[4] See ch. 9, notes 3, 4, 48.

[5] Cf. *Quaest. mor.*, quaest. secunda *De libero arbitrio*, p. 27. On Campanella's conception of liberty, see Germana Ernst, 'Libertà dell'uomo e *vis Fati* in Campanella,' in *Humanistica. Per Cesare Vasoli*, ed. F. Meroi and E. Scapparone (Florence, 2004), pp. 207–229.

is responsible instead for his responses. Even as he experiences desire, he can resist amorous flattery and the songs of Sirens, as Ulysses did when he bound himself to the mast of reason. In contrast, an animal is disturbed from its food or from another passionate activity only by a stronger passion.

But the more interesting question is the first, entitled *De summo bono*, in which the author surveys the doctrines of the Aristotelians, Epicureans, and Stoics so as to confute their positions with his own, according to which the chief good is to be identified with the preservation of being.[6] The position most compatible with that doctrine was the Stoic one, which identified the good with virtue, the bad with vice, and held all other things to be indifferent. If virtue is the true good, then the virtuous man alone is happy, in that he is able to convert every evil into good while no external evil can cause him harm or alter his interior condition. Without doubt Socrates is happier 'dying for virtue than were his killers who were living in vice.' The Stoics were right when they asserted that the virtuous man is a king by right, because his spirit is regal and because he masters his own passions and rules in a rational and appropriate way.[7] By way of confirmation of the fact that no one, as Seneca and Chrysostom had asserted, can injure the virtuous man whose interior virtue cannot be tarnished by any external evil, Campanella evoked his own tragic experience of torture and asserted that even the most atrocious sufferings inflicted on the body are not able to nullify virtue or to force the virtuous man into an internal assent to evil, which he is always capable of rejecting.

Along with the great ethical traditions of the past, Campanella also presented and discussed the doctrines of the modern 'political writers' and the 'Machiavellians,' who identified the chief good with dominion and power. They affirm that all the actions of man are directed at ruling and there is nothing that he is not willing to do in order to obtain power. Thus, every prince violates religion and morals in the name of reason of state, in the hope that power will make up for all the evils and losses incurred, even those impugning virtue and reputation. When finally he comes to power (even if by means of fraud or violence), he becomes at once famous and glorious. He comes to be praised and not referred to as a violator of the common good or virtue. He is instead praised as courageous and magnanimous for have risked so much.[8]

Campanella did not tire of admitting that the practices of dominion of which Machiavelli spoke had not been invented by him and that such practices could be detected in times both ancient and modern. It is indeed true that

---

[6] *Quaest. mor.,* quaest. prima *De summo bono,* pp. 1–23.

[7] Ibid., pp. 6f, 20–21.

[8] The exposition of the doctrines of political leaders is there, pp. 2–3; the response, at pp. 8, 11–13.

many men are ready to do anything in order to exercise power and, above all, that they embrace with enthusiasm those doctrines that present themselves as justifications of their passions. But for Campanella it was certainly not enough to concede that happiness and the chief good can be indentified with the crimes or preoccupations of power. With regard to the positions of the 'politicians,' Campanella could not but repeat his own point of view: the value of power – just like that of glory, riches, or any other kind of external good – depends always on the use that is made of it, and virtue resides always within us. That happiness does not coincide with power is also demonstrated amply by the unhappiness of tyrants and Machiavelli's heroes, who most often 'meet a base and sudden end, with the loss of their kingdom.'[9] Tyrants and princes can appear happy only after a superficial and vulgar examination, one that limits itself to seeing only the external ornaments and ephemeral pleasures of power. The gaze of the philosopher, who penetrates into the interior of things, reveals that they are akin to 'whitened sepulchers' or 'an apple that looks very nice on the outside, but is all eaten up by worms on the inside.' In the first political question, going back to traditional elements that are somewhat moralistic yet not without efficacy, Campanella added further touches to the gloomy portrait of the tyrant dominated by the horrible monsters of vice and ambition that disfigure life and render man servile. The tyrant is represented as the protagonist in a tragic farce generated by the unbearable gap between appearance and reality, pulled apart by the conflict between the parts recited on the stage of the world, dressed in the royal mantle, and the consciousness of his own unworthiness, which is the harshest of punishments – a conscious-ness of being 'a dog dressed up in imperial purple.'[10]

Of the four questions added to the *Politica*, the first investigates the nature of power, the second and third confront various aspects of the politi-cal opinions of Aristotle (denouncing their contradictions and insufficien-cies), while the fourth – *De optima republica* – lingers on the problems and objections attendant to proposing an ideal city.[11] The first, the most com-plex, is titled *De dominio et regno* and it is divided into two articles. The first concerns the issue of whether dominating and ruling are to be identified with one another. The second deals with the subject of whether 'a man can

---

[9] Ibid., p. 11.

[10] *Quaest. pol.*, *quaest. prima De dominio et regno*, pp. 80, 83–84. On the relationship with the doctrines of Machiavelli, see ch. 4.3.

[11] A modern edition, with Italian translation, of the third political question in *Città del Sole* (1997), together with subsequent reprintings, pp. 112–137 (Italian trans. by L. Firpo); there is likewise a modern edition of the fourth question in *Città del Sole* (1996) and subsequent reprintings, pp. 96–173 (Italian trans. by G. Ernst). Regarding the fourth question, see ch. 6, pp. 102–103.

be the lord of other men on account of some right that is natural or divine, or whether every dominion is derived from violence or art.' It is in this context that once again the Machiavellians play a leading role. Against those who hold that every dominion of men over men is violent, the new politicians maintain that dominion is to be pursued as the chief good and that this is completely in line with nature. According to the politicians, war and violence are natural and all kingdoms in the world have been acquired and maintained with arms. It is for this reason that every legislator is careful to make the republic strong and dominant and careful to bestow the greatest honors on those who fight, erecting for them, posthumously, the most splendid memorials, as if all virtue consists in military valor. Nature seems to confirm the supremacy of the strongest. Indeed, clashes and conflicts among elements and animals are themselves natural. Heat battles against cold; the wolf sheep; the falcon preys on doves; the eagle dominates all birds and the lion is universally considered the king of beasts.[12] But Campanella emphatically rejected the arguments of the political writers, Aristotle, and all those who sought to justify the legitimacy of the dominion of the strongest or to sanction the inequality of men with an appeal to nature.[13] Campanella denied firmly that there was any distinction between the free and the enslaved and above all he rejected the pretext of justifying it on a natural basis. He affirmed that no one is a slave by nature, because all men are participants in reason and in Christ, who is first reason. He reaffirmed that the only true slavery is that of sin, on account of which only tyrants are true slaves, while the wise man and the virtuous man are free.

In light of such positions, Campanella vindicated once again the full and equal dignity as citizens of peasants or artisans. They are political animals in precisely the same sense as any nobleman. They contribute as does any other part of society, and constitute the 'body of the republic.' Aristotle's exclusion of these categories of men from virtue and blessedness is completely absurd: Jewish society was made up of shepherds and peasants; the Roman republic (whose most illustrious men even took their names from vegetables) held agriculture in the highest esteem. This also suggested that the moral virtues are to be found more often and more copiously in illiterate people or in people with simple spirits. So, it is necessary to distrust those who with excessive subtlety and sophistry seek to obfuscate the transparency of truth. Cato the Censor was right to be alarmed by the avidity with which the young people of Rome listened to the discourses of Carneades for and against justice. Among those young people were Caesar, Pompey, and Crassus – and Campanella could not

---

[12] *Quaest. pol.*, p. 72.
[13] Ibid., pp. 78–79.

help commenting that it would have been better for the republic if they had remained in the countryside and occupied themselves with vegetables.[14] To Aristotle's notion that from the natural excellence of some men and from the natural inferiority of others derived the natural right of some to command others, Campanella opposed the organic model set out in a famous passage from St. Paul's Letter to the Corinthians, according to which every member of the body plays a part of equal dignity, and all together contribute to the unity and to the good functioning of the entire organism.[15] On this account, it is not people who carry out duties that are commonly considered vile and distasteful who are unworthy of qualifying as citizens, but rather the parasites and all those who do not contribute to the common good. The latter deserve to be excluded from citizenship, since they live in laziness and dedicate themselves to pointless and harmful pleasures.

The Books on Medicine

Campanella's interest in medicine was both constant and important. This interest was already present in his first readings and works. It manifested itself in a number of treatises (which are unfortunately lost, for the most part) and which were later gathered and organized into the seven books of the *Medicinalium* edited by Jacques Gaffarel and published in Lyon in 1635.[16] In dedicating the volume to Prince Odoardo Farnese, Gaffarel called this a new and incomparable medicine. In a letter to the readers, he asked them not to be amazed if the author turned out to be a 'monk and theologian,' recalling the illustrious predecessors in that tradition and recalling that Ficino, physician and theologian, had tried to connect the study of the remedies and ailments of both mind and body.[17] And it is precisely Ficino who is one of the authors upon whom Campanella called most often in his work, a work in which, as in many others, the role of *spiritus* is central.

---

[14] Ibid., p. 97: 'si autem in rure de oleribus tractassent, melius reipublicae fuisset.'

[15] Ibid., p. 92 (see 1 Cor 12, 14–26).

[16] On l'*Apologia pro Telesio*, see ch. 2, pp. 27–28; there is a tract of the plague in *Lettere*, pp. 112–117; there is also another on ways of avoiding summer heat (ibid., pp. 124–130); lost, however, are short works on hernias, on how to extract mercury from internal organs, and on how to avoid excessive cold.

[17] Regarding medicine, see Michael Mönnich, *Tommaso Campanella: Sein Beitrag zur Medizin und Pharmacie in der Renaissance* (Stuttgart, 1990); Marie-Dominique Couzinet, 'Notes sur les *Medicinalia* de Tommaso Campanella,' *Nuncius*, 13 (1998), pp. 39–67; Guido Giglioni, 'La medicina di Tommaso Campanella tra metafisica e cultura popolare,' in *Laboratorio Campanella*, pp. 177–195; Id., 'Healing and Belief in Tommaso Campanella's Philosophy,' *Intellectual History Review*, 17 (2007), pp. 225–238.

In the exordium to the book, medicine is defined as 'a species of practical magic' (*quaedam magica praxis*), which works on man in so far as he is susceptible to disease in order to restore him to health. In order to achieve such an end, the good physician has to know man well in his totality and his particular parts, as well as in terms of the environment in which he lives. That human 'totality' is made up of four parts: the incorporeal *mens*; *spiritus*, luminous, hot, and mobile, made up of the most subtle matter; the humors and the solid parts. Regarding the humors, Campanella distanced himself from traditional medicine, increasing the number of them and ruling out supposed correspondences with the four elements. Furthermore, he emphasized the centrality and the preeminence of blood, of which the other elements are but waste (*excrementa*). They execute the function of aides (*comites auxiliarii*) and concern only the part in which they are contained, not the whole of the organism. Campanella paid particular attention to the *atra bilis* or melancholy. Here, as in other texts, he wanted to specify the correct relationship between this humor and prophecy. Constituted by a sediment of dark and heavy blood that is the residue of heat and cooking, black bile was collected in the spleen, just like in a vase that collects impurities. It functioned as a stimulus for hunger and, when necessary, for fear. In modest quantities, black bile could also be of use to contemplation, but certainly not on account of the fact that it was 'wise and prophetic and meditative' or because it was a direct cause of contemplative activity (as Aristotle and Galen had mistakenly maintained). That physiological explanation had no foundation: how could an insensate thing, Campanella asked himself, be the origin for wisdom?[18] It is, instead, true that the presence of this humor is a sign of an intense heat in the spirit, which renders it extremely subtle and thus particularly ready to receive the impressions of the passions. It is therefore the subtlety of the spirit (and not its sootiness) that renders it well adapted to prophecy. For when it is plentiful such sootiness tends to obscure and terrorize the spirit, interrupting its discourse and disturbing its notions.

Campanella insisted upon the importance of prevention and the necessity of adopting every possible remedy for conserving the innate heat of which life consists. Old age occurs precisely when the relationship of solidarity and exchange between spirit and body is altered, when the spirit produced by the organism is not able any more to be retained and utilized properly and tends to exhale away. Natural death, which happens without pain, takes place when the entire spirit expires, just as the fire from the candle flies away when the wax and oil have been consumed. The spirit abandons the organs that, having become dry and hard, are no longer able to elaborate and assimilate the new heat produced by food, just as the old walls of a house are no longer able to

---

[18] *Medicina*, p. 16: 'quomodo enim res stupida sapientiam pariat?'

assimilate fresh plaster. And the house, having become creaky and full of fissures, opens the way to the aggressions of its enemy – namely, the cold – and permits the escape of vital heat.

The remedies suggested emphasize the importance of the adequacy of food and drink, location and climate, the limpidness of water and the purity of air, which should be rarefied, luminous, temperate, and far from infected places. Campanella reaffirmed the importance of music, which excited the spirit to motion, its natural operation, which can induce various actions and states of mind, and can pacify madness and restore serenity to the turbulent motions of the spirit. Regarding sexual activity, the author, just like Ficino, affirmed that in very old people it is harmful, even if frequenting young men and young women and 'chastely lying down with them' (*casta cubatio*) is helpful in postponing old age: 'the joy of Venus (but pure, without sin) is much more useful than many medicines.'[19] Insisting on the importance of healthy physical exercise, Campanella deplored the excessive use of carriages on the part of Neapolitans, with the resulting risk of a weakening of sexual activity. Above all he denounced the grave effects of laziness on women.[20]

One question that fascinated Campanella was that of whether medicine might offer remedies that could delay old-age and restore youth.[21] Even if it is as extremely rare as the alchemical transformation of iron into gold, the possibility did not seem to him to be excluded in principle. Even if the best medicine against old age consisted in 'interior serenity with a victory over the passions' and in occupying oneself with happy things and philosophy and avoiding sadness (which is worse than poison), one of the secrets of youthfulness is that of keeping the liver soft. Campanella provided recipes for pharmaceuticals and ointments that were apt to favor a general renewal of the organ. Other profound alterations are possible in animals and men – some for the worse (as happens in the person who is bitten by a tarantula), others for the better (as happens in the person who, in order to be cured of syphilis, is subjected to a cure that works a complete transformation of his *temperies*). Therefore, the possibility of restoring one's youth ought not to be excluded.

In the central books of the work, Campanella set out remedies for curative medicine that are always displayed in the light of his own philosophical principles. He insisted on the importance, on the part of the good physician, of an attentive and all-encompassing diagnosis that is dedicated to identifying the seats and causes of disease and to interpreting their signs and symptoms

---

[19] *Medicina*, p. 56: 'Veneris laetitia, sed pura absque peccato, multis praevalet medicinis.'

[20] Ibid., pp. 63–64; see note 3 above.

[21] 'De retardando insigniter senio et de reiuvenescentia,' ibid., pp. 66–70.

correctly. Many pages are dedicated to the *pulsus*, the pulsations connected to the continual actions of compression and dilation to which the lungs, the heart, the arteries, and the brain are subjected. This is an action that constitutes the very rhythm of life and that is the vital action of the spirit, whose nature is continual motion. This is not an action of the organs, but rather their 'preservative being acted upon,' through which life is preserved and restored.[22]

The question of the hidden powers of herbs, animals, and stones is treated in the fifth book. Campanella explained those powers in the light not only of celestial influences, but also of the bonds of antipathy and sympathy present in the entirety of nature. In one passage, Campanella observed that he who fights does so not only because he has a body and armor, but because he recognizes an enemy and wants to kill him.[23] He reiterated the doctrines of Ficino and of the Platonists on the properties derived from the stars and he intended to gloss them in the light of his own principles. He insisted that everything acts on account of the properties that is has, and that the marvelous power of certain stones or herbs is not dependent on the stars or on demons only, but depends also on the enduring in things themselves of passions and sensibilities that have been communicated to them by a common sense. He appreciated the doctrine of *signaturae*, in virtue of which every herb, metal, and animal that presents some analogy with regard to figure or color or consistency with some part of the human body is without doubt of use to that part.[24] On this subject, Campanella recalled with appreciation the *Phytognomonica* of Giovan Battista della Porta. Holding the connections between terrestrial and astral beings (which are universal causes that act in the inferior world) to be undeniable, Campanella spent some time discussing the seven kinds of beings – animals, plants, stones, odors, tastes, ages, seasons, diseases – that are connected with the planets and their properties. He began with the two considered to be malicious (Saturn and Mars), and then passed on to the two considered beneficial (Jupiter and Venus). From there, he dealt with the Sun and the Moon and finally with Mercury. Regarding Saturn – to which is connected black bile, animals that are solitary, slow, or cold (such as badgers, dormice, mice, toads, and lice), sterile and dry plants, heavy metals and dark stones – he emphasized the ambivalence of its influences. Saturnine people can be both extremely wise, aware of secret and prophetic things, and 'stupid, rough, and impious.' Likewise, the solar man (precisely like the star to which he is orientated) is the expression of dignity and of true regality:

---

[22] Ibid., p. 142.

[23] Ibid., p. 244.

[24] On signatures, see Massimo L. Bianchi, *Signatura rerum. Segni, magia e conoscenza da Paracelso a Leibniz* (Rome, 1987).

he loves the whole more than the part, he is beneficent, generous, ambitious, and delights in all the sciences, loving to dedicate himself to great undertakings. But it is the moon that administers and executes all the celestial virtues. Inferior things depend on the moon to such a degree that it is not possible to operate correctly 'with regard to movement, sense, birth, growth' in anything without observing of the moon's aspects. This is so much more true in medicine, moreover, where proceeding without having first observed the position of the moon is like being blind and acting entirely by chance, in that it is the moon that governs the 'critical days,' the stages of a disease and the passions of the humors.[25]

The sixth book deals with the diseases of the *spiritus*, neglected or interpreted in an erroneous manner by traditional medicine. The seventh and last book is dedicated to an analytical treatment of fevers, interpreted in an original fashion not as diseases but as positive symptoms of the reaction of the body and the war that the organism is waging against the aggressions of disease.

Psychological suffering can be explained as a blundering or mistaken reaction to passions elicited by external objects. The avaricious man kills himself when he loses money; likewise, the person who is in love takes his own life if his desire is frustrated. The violence of certain passions can be fatal, just as a light that is too dazzling can cause blindness. One can die from the joy of seeing a son believed to be dead, and a strong fear can turn one white with shock. Remedies consist in detaching oneself from obsession, even if in a deceitful way. Even the illusory satisfaction of desires can assuage fears and lessen interior tensions. Above all, the important thing is to purify and purge the spirit affected by damaging passions, comforting it with appropriate foods and remedies, reconstituting it little by little. To this end, Ficinian remedies will be highly useful – such as looking upon or frequenting amenable places such as gardens filled with plants and flowers. It is extremely important to breathe fresh and pure air, which contributes to a reconstituting of the good qualities of the spirit. If it is not possible to live in contact with nature, it is advisable to recreate a domestic garden inside the house itself, with flowers, plants, and fountains.[26]

Campanella expressed a very negative opinion on black bile and pathological melancholy.[27] If some are melancholic by nature, others can become melancholic in the wake of particular circumstances, such as prolonged fasting,

---

[25] *Medicina*, p. 275.

[26] Ibid., p. 317.

[27] On the relationship between melancholy and prophecy in Campanella, see also Germana Ernst, '"Contra l'ombra di morte accesa lampa." Echi ficiniani in Campanella,' in *Forme del Neoplatonismo. Dall'eredità ficiniana ai Platonici di Cambridge,* ed. L. Simonutti (Florence, 2007), pp. 147–175.

insufficient sleep, excessive application to studying, living with anxiety, or deep pain at the loss of things or people they loved a great deal. In any case, the personality affected by melancholy lives in a condition of great suffering.[28] The interior light of the spirit – which by virtue of its nature enjoys the light of the sun, reinforcing and amplifying it – comes to be dimmed by murky, sooty vapors that stain the spirit in the same way that ink colors paper. From here comes a melancholic delirium that is characterized by constant sadness, fear, aversion to relations with human beings, a disturbed imagination, and a desire for death. In serious cases, when obscurity completely invades the spirit, remedies can be extremely difficult. If it is not possible to separate water from ink, how will it be possible to distill the spirit? In the event that the shadows invade the interior only in part, there is some hope, thanks to the possibility of consuming suitable food and drink and in general thanks to the possibility of turning to jovial, venereal, and solar remedies while avoiding everything saturnine. One can also make use of the therapeutic powers of music, which can settle the disordered motions of the spirit and purify blood that has been harmed and poisoned by bile.[29]

On the basis of this conception of black bile, Campanella criticized harshly what Aristotle affirmed in the *Problemata*. There, he had attributed poetic inspiration and the prophecies of the Sibyls to precisely this humor, instituting an analogy with the effects induced by wine that Campanella held to be superficial and false. For him, prophecy can be of several kinds. There are forms that are natural and shared with animals, who sense the coming of rains and storms or notice in the air the premonitions of events before they come to pass. Man can be endowed with particular dispositions that are apt to perceive in the air the causes of events that are in the process of forming. But natural divination does not exclude prophecy communicated by God to human minds, and indeed this form of prophecy is one of the signs that distinguish the human level from the animal one. Campanella rejected with disdain the affirmation that the presumed divine inspiration of the prophets and the Sibyls is to be ascribed to humoral imbalance and is reducible to causes and explanations that are entirely physiological. Again, Campanella held in greater esteem the positions of Ficino, who did not limit himself to connecting black bile and prophecy, but explained the modest proportions of melancholic humor that need to be present in the blood in order not to damage it. Ficino correctly took account of the spirit and its characteristics, something that had been ignored by Aristotle who attributed to wine and to black bile something that in fact ought to be attributed to the subtlety of spirit. He who has such subtle spirit can foresee the future in that he

---

[28] *Medicina*, p. 319.
[29] Ibid., p. 338.

perceives in the air the causes of future events that are already present, just as birds foresee the rain. Certainly, those who are affected by a melancholic humor cannot do this, for in the most serious cases such victims are sordid, stupid, and love graves, cry, and desire death; because, when it becomes gloomy, the spirit desires things similar to itself. Black bile is not useful to science except if the spirit, frightened by the darkness, pulls back into the interior to contemplate. Indeed, in the worst cases, there is the possibility of demonic possession. The melancholic person is the victim of the intervention of demons, who make use of this humor to torment he who has fallen into the shadows – and that person believes himself a wolf and becomes a game for the devil (*ludus daemonum*).[30] For poetic inspiration and distinguished works is required, on the contrary, a pure, lucid, tenuous spirit, in which sootiness is scarce or absent. This is a spirit that permits impartial judgment and a healthy memory that is thus capable of forgetting or letting rest those memories that are too painful due to their association with unberable emotions.

Like Ficino, Campanella knew well that Saturn could kill his own children, on account of an excessive dedication to studying. Too concentrated a spirit heats up and becomes embittered, giving rise to hardness, infesting vapors, and all the negative consequences of the passions, when they become exclusive and obsessive. Remedies against the harms done by saturninity would be those that we know: suspension of studies, mollification of anxieties and fears, inducing serenity and faith, satisfaction (even if illusory) of frustrated desires, abandoning occasions of excessive effort, the defusing of obsessions and fixations.[31] But the best things to do, above all, are breathing in the serene and open air, walking in green gardens full of flowers, listening to music, dedicating oneself to light and playful things, returning to all that which is venereal and jovial in nature, nourishing oneself with white, sweet, and soft foods – the opposites of black, bitter, and dry bile.

There are frequent autobiographical insertions in the *Medicina* that offer to the scholar interesting and curious information regarding Campanella's life.[32] He recalled a host of things: the remarkable eyewash with which della Porta treated him for inflamed eyes, causing great astonishment in those who were looking on because of the immediate beneficial effect; sciatic pains he suffered as a result of a long horse-ride combined with the luxurious kitchen at the Del Tufo palazzo; the terrible consequences of torture and the years spent in subterranean prisons; the pains due to a hernia from which he suffered when

---

[30] Ibid., p. 345.

[31] Ibid., p. 348.

[32] See the original contribution from Romano Amerio, 'Autobiografia medica di fra Tommaso Campanella,' *Archivio di Filosofia*, special issue *Campanella e Vico* (Rome, 1969), pp. 11–19.

he was almost fifty years old and from which he was cured after drinking iron filings in an egg every morning for a month and wearing an iron belt with a poultice for three months (although the hernia returned after the interruption of the cure); the curious observation, recalled in several passages, that lice did not take root in his person 'due to the nobility of his temperament' and the non-greasy quality of his sweat;[33] the buzzing and hissing in his ears, apparently caused by the dampness of his cell (even though in general he was naturally blessed with an extremely acute power of hearing). Those noises persisted for years; he heard them always as a hissing and blowing of the wind, as 'when it passes through narrow passages'; or they were like the sounds of reels on which is wound thread taken from the cocoons of silkworms that is being transferred onto larger reels. Attacks of 'canine hunger' are then recalled, attributed to the consumptiveness of his body after the fasting of Lent or when, in extreme poverty, he had been nourished by bread and adulterated wine only. He treated such hunger by eating vegetables cooked in milk and by sleeping on a straw mattress, so as to combat the wave of heat by which he felt himself consumed and almost dismembered – something 'not so very different from leaves as they are being burnt.'[34]

Arts and Sciences of Language

The collection of the five parts that constituted the *Philosophia rationalis* – that included the *Grammatica*, the *Dialectica*, the *Rhetorica*, the Latin *Poëtica* (fully reworked from the Italian version), and the *Historiographia* – would be published at Paris in the projected *Opera omnia*.[35] The *Dialectica* (not reprinted after the seventeenth-century edition) still remains to be studied, but we should at least comment on the exordium, where dialectic is defined as an 'art or rational instrument of the wise man with which to regulate the discourse of every science,' so that we can account for why dialectic is termed an *ars* and not a *scientia*:

> Science is of God and of the things made by God (such as the world, the animals, the elements that exist before the actions of the human intellect). Art, however, because it is made in the wake of human reason, is both external to soul (like clothing, an abode, or an astrolabe) and internal to it (such as a word, a syllogism, a fable). Therefore the object of every art is the being of reason, and its end is utility. The object of science on the other hand

---

[33] *Medicina*, pp. 125, 218, 223, 395, 422, 433, 517–518.

[34] Ibid., pp. 398–399, 433.

[35] On that work, see the contribution of Lina Bolzoni, 'La *Poetica* latina di Tommaso Campanella,' *Giornale storico della letteratura italiana*, 149 (1972), pp. 481–521.

is the being of the thing and its end is understanding. The being of reason is
constructed from art in a useful manner, both for teaching and for acting, as
the fable, the letter, the sword. That, however, which is useless or harmful,
... one ought to refer to as the being of irrationality and deceit – whether
it is active (as in the case of liars, nonsense, sophistry, and stories that do
not teach anything) or passive (as in the false proposition of a heretic that
God be body or that the sun does not shine with its own light). In fact, the
useful parable to teach is the being of reason, not that of deceit. Therefore
in a unwise manner the majority of the logicians hold that the Capricorn,
the chimera, and the false proposition that "man is an ass" are all beings
of reason. These are in fact beings of irrationality – active, passive, or both
combined .... Therefore logic is the art that deals with the beings of reason
and the beings of deceit, just as the physician deals with the healthy and the
sick.[36]

Grammar is defined as an 'instrumental art used for expression that is coherent, rational, and simple; as a consequence, it is used for writing and reading
all that which our spirit has perceived through all its means of knowing.'[37]
Campanella addressed the distinction between 'civil' and 'philosophical'
grammar in a beautiful passage, written against the pedants and rule-fetishists
and in defense of the permissibility of coining new words and inventing new
languages that are well-suited to the expression of new concepts:

> Civil grammar is an ability, not a science, because it is founded on authority
> and on the usage of famous writers .... Philosophical grammar, by contrast,
> is founded on reason and achieves the status of a science. In fact, it is the
> method of the intellect that investigates and it notes how much it has inves-
> tigated; among the things that are found in nature it establishes relation-
> ships and distinctions.... Grammarians condemn it ... and they harass us
> when we derive words from things instead of from authors.... What terrible
> thing do they not say when we have discovered something new that we can-
> not express in terms that were used by Cicero (which is a situation in which
> we mould new words)? ... Instead, the conceited want to impose laws on us,
> and thereby imprison science too.[38]

If, with respect to the *Poetica*, we can refer to what was said with regards to
the early Italian text,[39] we ought not to fail to comment here on the important
Rhetorica, listed as the fourth of the 'arts of talking.'[40] By way of definition,

---

[36] *Dialectica*, I, 1, in *Philosophia rationalis* (Paris: I. Dubray, 1638).

[37] *Grammatica*, in *Scritti letterari*, p. 435.

[38] Ibid., p. 439.

[39] See ch. 3, 2, bearing in mind that the Latin text, as usual, develops the material
more amply and organizes it more systematically.

[40] The initial core of the work dates to the period spent in Padua.

the author emphasized the differences between rhetoric and dialectic with reference to object, method, and purpose. If dialectic is concerned with the true and the false and makes use of rational demonstration, rhetoric has to do with good and evil and recourses to verbal persuasion, and does not work by means of logic. If the first 'has its seat in the schools and is orientated to philosophers,' with brief and incisive discourse, rhetoric is at home 'in the piazzas and temples and is orientated to the people,' making use of longer and more easily understood arguments, often using examples and proverbs. In a certain way, legislators, priests, prophets, and generals can all be considered orators. No society – whether made up of soldiers, bandits, or saints – can do without two doctrines, namely grammar, which is 'the tongue of the community,' and rhetoric, which speaks on behalf of that which is good for the community. When Campanella then defined rhetoric as the instrument 'by means of which to advocate that which is good for us and to dissuade us from that which is bad,' he was sure to make a number of specifications that distanced him from the doctrines of the 'pagans.' Not only and not so much a simple art of speaking well, rhetoric ought to be understood as an 'instrumental art dedicated to inducing us orally to the good and distancing us from evil.' Upholding this thesis, Campanella had to defend it both from philosophers such as Socrates and Plato (who condemned it as an embellished whore, set apart from the virginal beauty of science) and also from those who, on the contrary, permitted recourse to every kind of lie and deceit, admitting the possibility that rhetoric might be used to defend and justify scoundrels, tyrants, and those who had committed the worst crimes. For Campanella every true art is, as such, always the daughter of wisdom, on account of which the purpose of true rhetoric could not be anything other than persuasion towards the good, irrespective of whether it achieves its aims of not. If it happens that rhetoric leads us into evil, then it is no art, just as the physician who kills out of ignorance or malice is not employing the art of healing. Lying is never permissible. It is, however, true that in order to defend oneself from violence and from injustice, or to save one's own life, one may recourse to reticence or equivocation, making use of dissimulation – not so as to deceive or do evil, but as a stratagem, following thereby the example of numerous episodes from the Bible.

In order to persuade, therefore, rhetoric has truck with the passions and the affects. It is for this reason that it has certain similarities to magic, as Campanella had already maintained in the *Senso delle cose* (where he emphasized the magic power that words exert over the imagination of he who listens). It was thanks to the spoken word that Menenius Agrippa was able to pacify the Roman plebeians who were rebelling against the senate and it was thanks to speech that preachers had been able to convert innumerable peoples. Rhetoric acts on the passions in order to elicit 'love and hate, anger and fear, docility and amazement' in the most efficacious way. Yet orators do not persuade like physicians who achieve their results with medications, nor do they 'call upon devils to raise up those passions that move the fantasy with incantations; instead, rhetoric makes use of argumentations, movements, potent incitement, and a fascination with words that is almost magical.'[41]

All persuasive speech pertains to rhetoric, even that speech which is spontaneous and uncultivated. Even the apostles taught thanks to rhetoric, although it was a rhetoric very different from that of the schools, in that it was alive and divine – and a word from Solomon, Isaiah, or Paul was more convincing than the prolix discourses of the sophists, as the author said he had experienced for himself. Yet, it is true that the orator makes use, in a proper sense, of a 'refined technique rich in artifice.' The central and final chapters of the work dealt with every possible aspect of the art with vividness and argumentative richness. With regard to the prerequisites of the good orator, he has to be endowed with natural predispositions that are to be perfected with exercise, among which are ingeniousness, style, and voice (but 'if he stammers a little, sometimes this adds grace, as I have often been able to confirm'), vividness of expression, a strong memory, apt gesture (which is a 'second language of the body').[42] Above all, a kind of identification with the sentiments that are to be induced is important: 'he does not persuade who is not first himself persuaded. As the heated object heats and as the cold object cools on contact, just so he who is sad communicates to his auditors his own sadness, while he who hopes communicates his hope, and the angry man communicates anger; in this way the efficacy of this magic is great.'[43] If it is true that the soul is free and can always follow the orders of reason, it is also true that 'usually men are governed rather by the passions than by reason.' It is for this reason that the orator has success, 'communicating to his auditors his own sentiment with the impetus of discourse, since by nature men cry with he who is crying, laugh with he who is laughing, become irate with he who is irate, yawn with he who is yawning.'[44]

In reading these pages, it appears almost as if one is seeing from behind the scenes some 'secrets' of Campanella's oratorical talent, which impressed both Campanella's interlocutors and the public for its passion and vivacity. Or perhaps it is almost like catching sight of technical aspects of argumentation to which he himself would turn, as when he suggested listing arguments for and against in cases of doubtful questions. In making an example of the question

---

[41] *Rhetorica*, pp. 742–745.
[42] Ibid., p. 749.
[43] Ibid., p. 751.
[44] Ibid., p. 763.

of whether the conquest of the New World had been a good thing, arguments that raised doubts and perplexities about the enterprise followed those that justified it; thus, they give voice to a kind of inner debate. One has a similar feeling when Campanella advised that, in order to attract the good-will of the listeners, one ought to praise them as 'prudent, just, lovers of truth, saying that one is turning to them with confidence, hopeful of success. Then it will seem to them that they are unworthy of such praise if they do not act in that way.' This is not simply an acute observation, but a kind of insight that enables us to understand better why, for example, in the letters Campanella turned to illustrious persons and praised them for their merits, even when they were anything but benevolent towards him and certainly not worthy of the tributes he paid them. This is not a courtly adulation. Rather it is a philosophical praise given so as to transform a personality into what it should be.

In the brief text of the *Historiographia*, one also finds plenty of sharp judgments. Defined as 'the art of writing history well so as to establish the foundations of the sciences,' the author specified that history consists in a narrative discourse that is clear, truthful, and 'well adapted to providing the bases of the sciences.' On account of this function of 'first light,' it ought not to be hazy, because that would offend the eyes without being of any use to the view. Among the prerequisites required in the good historian, three are fundamental: that he be well informed on the basis of direct testimony or at least reliable testimony regarding the subject he narrates; that he possess a virile spirit, such that he is not induced to lie or alter the truth out of the impulse of the passions; that he be honest and motivated to tell the truth. As for the second prerequisite, recalling a judgment from Jacopo Sannazzaro (who described Poggio Bracciolini, who excessively praised the Florentines, as 'neither a bad citizen nor a good historian'), Campanella made a brief and bitter allusion to the unjust judgment of Tommaso Costo. As he put it, Costo was 'neither a good citizen nor a good historian' when he related the events of Calabria in an extremely hostile tone.[45] The need for veracity (in contrast to the 'lies' of the Greeks) was fundamental and Campanella railed against the judgment (which in truth he held to be unfounded) attributed to Paolo Giovio, according to whom the historian did not need to worry himself about lying, since 'a hundred years hence, lies will not be recognizable.' Those 'adulators of God' are wrong, however, who invent miracles that never took place. They are addressed in harsh tones: 'Thus, it is not enough for you to play games with men, so you dare to adulate God in a derisory fashion, as if he were a fraudster like you?' History can be divided into sacred, natural, and human. Natural history can be of a universal kind (as in Pliny) or of a particular kind (as in

---

[45] *Historiographia*, p. 1232.

Aristotle's history of animals or in modern authors such as Guillaume Ron-
delet and Georg Agricola, who had written of fish and metals). With regard to
the moderns, Galileo's *Sidereus nuncius* is recalled, of which it is said that 'it is
a historical work; indeed, it does not explain why around Jupiter four planets
orbit and two around Saturn, but it concerns itself with whether the matter
has been so confirmed. The mode of investigation was scientific; narrative was
the mode of rendering it. Yet on these facts, as on a new foundation, will be
built a wondrous astronomical doctrine of the heavenly systems.'[46]

Civil, or human, history is fundamental 'for politicians, moralists, orators,
and poets.' From histories of the past, we can in fact learn what is useful and
what is damaging, derive rules from so many experiences, and reform the
sciences and the law – 'so that he who knows well the history of all nations
from the origin of the world to our times can boast of having lived from the
primordial beginnings of the world right up until today and of having lived all
over the face of the earth.'[47] According to its extension in space and time, such
history can be universal or particular – of a single city, of an epoch, of individual
events, or a biography of a single life. Campanella underlined the importance
of an intelligent organization and selection of materials; it is important to
omit trivia, avoid digressions, the speeches of persons, and false celestial
prodigies. On the other hand, it is useful to refer, with clarity and brevity,
to some particulars: 'do not omit foods, medicines, arms, money, buildings,
or technical inventions.'[48] A biography ought to set out all the qualities of
its subject. It ought to 'describe the lineage, the day and hour of the birth,
under which dominant planet, and then physical appearance; thereafter the
subject's actions, one by one, the events, the most signal undertakings, both
good and bad.'[49] Excellent examples of brevity and clarity are Suetonius,
Diogenes Laertius, and Plutarch. Rather more suspect, however, is the life
of St. Francis of Paola narrated by Paolo Regio, which instead of offering
precise information to its readers, is limited to connecting 'a great number
of miracles almost with a single thread.'[50]

The New Metaphysics

At Paris, in the summer of 1638, less than a year before the death of its author,
the imposing folio of the *Metaphysics* would be published as the fourth tome

---

[46] Ibid., p. 1244.
[47] Ibid., p. 1246.
[48] Ibid., p. 1248.
[49] Ibid., p. 1250.
[50] Ibid. The work in question, by Paolo Regio (1541–1607), Bishop of Vico Equense,
was titled *La meravigliosa vita di San Francesco di Paola* (Naples, 1581).

in the series of projected *Opera omnia*. In the dedication to Claude Bullion de Bonolles, Superintendent of the Finances of France, Campanella displayed justified pride in his own principal work, presenting it as both a foundation and a crown for every kind of knowledge:

> Most honored Sir, ... one might call this book a Bible for the philosophers, wisdom of the sciences, treasure-chest of things human and divine, solution to every problem regarding all matters both actual and possible that can stimulate the minds of men, in such a way that each man is able to explore for himself the truth and errors of human sciences and laws from the ground up. ... I, who have never praised my own works, feel compelled to praise this work alone on account of its utility for all, for it will be discovered that in comparison to this work all other human books are nothing but puerile musings paling in comparison to a mature understanding, and that all those who put themselves to the test of metaphysics gave rise, more than to a metaphysics, merely to an insipid logic or grammar without order.[51]

Campanella showed the greatest satisfaction in finally seeing completed a work the redaction of which had occupied almost the entirety of his life.[52] In the work, in which almost all the themes that he had addressed in all his other works came together, he confronted all the doctrines of the entire philosophical and theological tradition, adopting an attitude of full liberality with respect to the diverse schools. Extremely rich, the *Metaphysica* has remained in large part unexplored and here it is possible to give only an extremely general idea of the structure of the work and to take note of some essential themes.

The proem begins by underlining that the fullness of *veracitas* is completed in God alone, while all men are mendacious in some measure and in some particular respects, either out of fear or ignorance. Or they may be mendacious on purpose, so that they lie in an 'officious' manner (for ends that are held to be useful) or because they are driven by passions such as ambition, avidity, jealousy, or hate. On the one hand, God is exempt from any passion whatsoever that can occlude or deform the truth that he communicates. On the other hand, as the creator, he is not ignorant of even the smallest thing. God alone is the true master, and it is to his school, and not to those of human

---

[51] *Lettere*, p. 395.

[52] According to the *Syntagma* (pp. 48f), the initial core of the work – which would eventually be divided into eighteen books in three parts (where the chapter list alone takes up around thirty pages) – goes back to the years of his youth. After that first draft was lost, Campanella, in the first years of his incarceration, prepared an Italian version. But that version, given to an unfaithful disciple was also lost and then Campanella began the Latin redaction, which, sequestered in 1610, was rewritten and continually enlarged and revised.

beings, that Campanella intends to recall men, with whom God communicates through two means – by creating things and through the medium of revelation. With reference to the first means, 'when God makes things, he makes or augments a living book, from the observation of which we learn,' on account of which the Church Fathers and saints called the world both "wisdom" and "the book of God." And they did so with reason, 'because God has written all his concepts in it and he explains them with his Word, so that there is nothing in the world that does not express something present in an ideal way in the divine mind. But the saying and the writing of God is his manner of making things real.' Men read this book with their senses, from which the successive moments of the cognitive processes take their beginning: memory, accumulation of multiple sensations, and gradually the *experimentum* to the point of reaching general principles and definitions. It is important never to forget the sensible origin of all understanding, and in case of doubt it is to sense that one must return in order to check and verify.

Regarding things that do not enter into our field of experience, because they are distant in time or space, we recourse to the senses of others, which are similar to ours. We put faith in those who base their doctrines on testimony, which is a product of the direct reading of the book of God, and not on opinions, which derive from a form of conjecture that can be mistaken. We believe in the experience of the sailor Columbus who with his voyages falsified the arguments of Augustine and Lactantius on the non-existence of the antipodes, even though Augustine and Lactantius were saints and learned men; as a general rule 'we measure certainty by how close or how distant something is from sense. The truth is indeed the extent of the thing, as it is and not as we imagine it for ourselves: sense testifies to things as they are; imagination, as we hold them to be.' From here comes the injunction to reject books that contradict the book of nature and to confront and correct human books in the light of the autograph script of God. One of the most problematic attitudes, from which neither theologians nor saints are exempt, consists in conferring unduly the dignity of God's autograph script upon fallible human 'copies,' an attitude that gives rise to divisions and controversies. This sets one school against another, Platonists against Aristotelians, Scotists against Thomists – for the Scotists consider St. Thomas 'rough and stupid, while Scotus is subtle' and the Thomists consider Scotus 'an enthusiast and vacuous' while only St. Thomas is 'solid and free from error.' It is in this way that one substitutes a common search for the truth with the partisanship of attachment to one's own masters. Similarly, the defects of the person loved appear to be beautiful to the enamored person. Conversely, he who is animated by malevolent and hostile feelings towards someone will always and only see defects in him. In general, in a green mirror everything will seem green.

Having studied all the philosophical and theological schools, all the laws, all the sciences, and all the arts – those that are true as well as those that are false or demonic – Campanella decided to write discourses on the true wisdom, in such a manner that anyone would be capable of examining the sciences from the book of God and to gather the deep connections between the sciences in the totality of the encyclopedia, and to distinguish truth and falsehood. Thus, this doctrine would deal with both the first principles and the ends of things as well as the foundations of the sciences, and we call it "metaphysics" on account of the fact that it goes beyond physical doctrines and common philosophy, on account of the fact that it embraces all the areas of philosophy and raises itself up to the first causes and to that supreme first cause in such a way as to permit us to see the causation and the cognition of everything little by little.[53]

The work begins with fourteen *dubitationes* (doubts) that, engaging with the renewed fortunes of scepticism, set out all the possible doubts concerning the value and the very possibility of human understanding in general (and that of the senses in particular), an understanding that is described as partial, uncertain, and contradictory.[54] The ninth doubt reveals how knowledge, if it consists in alienating oneself and becoming something other than oneself, is a form of madness. In the tenth doubt, it is reaffirmed that knowing is an "un-knowing" or self-forgetting, because the soul ignores itself and under such conditions how could the soul come to know other things? Enclosed in the body, the soul completes operations it does not know how to account for, and, in order to know its own nature and its own condition, it is constrained to search and to interrogate beyond itself. The soul is like the smith who works immersed in darkness, without seeing either himself or the work that he is completing, and then approaches the window and asks for news of what he is doing, about whether he finds himself in jail or not, about who he himself is and who it is that put him in that place. Or the soul is like the drunkard who upon awaking from his slumber asks for information about himself and what he has done while he was unconscious. The many opinions on the nature of the soul cannot but confirm these doubts. On this issue, the philosophers (each one believing he is right) fight furiously amongst themselves like madmen in the hospital of incurables at Naples – without taking into account that just as such men seem mad to us, we seem mad to them.[55]

---

[53] *Metaphysica*, part I, p. 4a.

[54] On the relationship between Campanella and the Scepticism see Gianni Paganini, *Skepsis. Le débat des modernes sur le Scepticisme Montaigne-Le Vayer-Campanella-Hobbes-Descartes-Bayle* (Paris, 2008); Id., 'Tommaso Campanella: The Reappraisal and Refutation of Scepticism', in Gianni Paganini and José R. Maia Neto (eds.), *Renaissance Scepticism* (Dordrecht, 2009), pp. 275–303.

[55] *Metaphysica*, part I, pp. 20–21.

Faced with such objections, Campanella adopted a Socratic attitude of learned ignorance, for which the awareness of limits, of difficulties, and of the inexhaustible infinity of true understanding represents the beginning of every genuine inquiry that wants to abstain both from presumptuous dogmatic certainties and from the sterile nay-saying of the skeptics. To the objections concerning the errors and uncertainties of sensible understanding, Campanella responded by affirming that the senses are able to correct themselves and that relativity lies not in the things themselves but rather in the mode in which they come to be learned – given that every piece of knowledge is tailored to every entity and only animals and the unlearned hold that things are precisely as they appear. Every being is affected by the same thing *pro mensura sua* (according to its own measure). Sounds, tastes, and smells are realities that come to be perceived in differentiated ways. But it is not the things themselves that are relative, but rather their mode of acting and being – that is always relative and proportionate to that which is acted upon. The same broom will seem sweet to the goat and bitter to a man; the same sound will be pleasing or displeasing according to the character of the spirit and the sense that undergoes the sensation.

But the responses of greater interest are those that concern understanding as alienation and undergoing and the paradox of the soul that understands all other things, but seems not to understand itself. Such apparent misunderstanding of itself derives in the first place from the fact that the soul understands itself in a way that is different from the way in which it knows all other things. Since it loves itself, it is beyond doubt that it knows itself, but it knows itself with an essential understanding that is not discursive (as Campanella had already indicated in the *Senso delle cose*): 'every soul knows itself, since it uses so many arts for the purpose of living, and loves itself; and that love is born from knowledge, but not knowledge of oneself with discourses, because discourse is a thing that is doubtful; instead, the soul knows itself by nature and by essence in that it senses itself in those transformations, whereas it knows all other things through discourse.'[56] Campanella distinguished thus between two kinds of knowledge, one essential that is the knowledge of itself, and another that is discursive and follows from the alterations induced by external objects. Understanding of oneself, *abdita* (hidden) and *innata* (innate), is intrinsic and coincides with the being of he who knows itself. It is what Augustine called *praesentia perennis* and Aquinas (referring to Augustine) called *notitia praesentialitatis*. Knowledge of oneself is the condition of that *addita*, which follows from the passions and all the modifications induced by objects:

> Wisdom is perception and judgment of passion and, consequently, of the
> object that induces the passion. Every being effuses its own proper entity,

---

[56] *Senso delle cose*, p. 109.

and certainly every being knows itself in the first place; otherwise, if it were ignorant of itself, it would not love its own being. But it knows itself because it is that which it is: it then senses other things in so far as it senses itself changed in those other things.[57]

When the eye sees an external stone, it sees it in the sense that 'first it senses the stone-like color received intrinsically by the pupil, and then it displaces that color at once onto the outside'; thus

> Passion is not the active cause of knowledge that is the cause of science, but the specifying occasion of science, which derives from an innate knowledge:... one does not acquire science, but rather knowable things. Knowledge is a primality like power and will and it does not have causes in objects, but rather specifications. Indeed, the ignorant stone does not teach me that it is a stone.... Knowledge is always a knowing of oneself and this is not understood by he who does not consider that every being loves itself, in that it senses itself through itself with a hidden sense; it knows other things with an explicit sense [*sensus additus*], in an accidental and reflex way.[58]

Understanding by way of alienation or modification is a consequence of the knowledge of self that is primary and innate, which is connected with the constitutive and essential principles of its being, 'beyond time, beyond effort, beyond passion and action.' In virtue of that understanding, all beings know themselves with an *abdita* notion, which is not acquired and coincides with knowledge itself, a constitutive primality comparable to power and love: 'if all things love their own being, then they know that being also with a kind of natural indication, just as they love it with a natural love. The soul, and likewise every being, knows itself before everything, in an essential way; and after that it knows all other things, in an accidental way, in that it knows itself to be changed and in a certain fashion changed into the things that it knows.'

This distinction between the two modes of knowing permits us to understand how it is that the soul appears to be ignorant of itself:

> It knows itself because it is what it is, but it then senses other things when it senses itself transformed through other things, and it is accustomed to knowing other things with such continuous transformations that it forgets itself or it transforms its understanding of itself: and it is on this account that the soul appears not to know itself.[59]

---

[57] *Metaphysica*, part I, p. 73a.

[58] Ibid., p. 73b.

[59] Ibid., p. 73a. On the relationship between Campanella and Descartes, see Gianni Paganini, 'Le Cogito et l'ame qui "se sent." Descartes lecteur de Campanella,' *B&C*, 14 (2008), pp. 11–29; see note 53.

The *superadditae* (added) understandings of external things and the incessant sequence of the passions and the modifications brought by external objects fade and induce a kind of forgetfulness of the original innate and hidden understanding: 'we are generated between contrary beings, we suffer continually from heat and cold and from innumerable objects, and in this way we transfer ourselves almost into the being of others: undergoing and being changed is becoming other, because the soul falls almost into a forgetfulness of itself and into ignorance, since it is always agitated by the forces of extraneous things.'[60]

Tobias Adami received a copy of the *Metaphysica*, but did not send it to press because Campanella had told him that he wished to work on it further. In a *Praefatio* addressed to German philosophers, however, Adami gave a very precise synthesis of the work, which suggests the hypothesis, quite probable, that these pages draw directly from Campanella's notes. He noted that in the first part of the work 'it is shown how small and meager is the human knowledge of things, how incomplete and partial; this is a knowledge not of things as they are in themselves but only according to the degree to which their being is understood by us.' He then offered a summary of the central part, which addresses difficult doctrines of the primalities and of the great influences. The summary is highly accurate and precise and doubtless echoes pages from Campanella:

> Created things are considered to be composed of Being and of Nothing. The author teaches that Being is constituted with the transcendental composition of the three primalities – namely, power, wisdom, and love – as if by a divine stamp; while Nothing is constituted by impotence, ignorance, and hate. Since every thing exists since it can be, knows how to be, and loves to be what it is, and since – losing the power of being, the knowledge of how to be, or the will to be – it at once loses its own being too (and dies when it is connected to that nothing, for indeed it was not every thing or the totality of being), it passes into another essence on account of the transformation and generation of things. Thus, only from the first and highest being – which produces all things from nothing and in which, in an ineffable manner, those primalities (with simplicity and infinitely higher and incomprehensible essential perfection, without participating in any way in nothingness) concur as in their own fount and they are the same thing, distinct only in reason – does the nature of creatures with such a composition derive. Essence, truth, and goodness are the objects of such primalities, on which they are sown and on which Necessity, Fate, and Harmony exercise their influence. In this way, the first and unitary being transports

---

[60] Ibid., p. 63a.

its inexhaustible ideas in various modes into the duration of things (which is time, image of the eternity that remains always equal to itself) thanks to its instruments and causal agents – heat and cold – in corporeal mass (matter) suspended in space (place) which is the basis of this world, which has in God its firmness and stability.[61]

In accordance with the doctrine of the primalities, the first Being is essentialized by the infinite principles of Power, Wisdom, and Love. Every finite being, qua being, is constituted and structured by these same primalities, which essentialize it according to different modes and proportions. Therefore, given that each being is distinct and limited, it is composed of finite degrees of existence and infinite degrees of non-existence. Nothingness does not exist (neither in God nor outside of him), but such nothingness serves to constitute the finitude and the distinctiveness of beings. After the exposition of the doctrine of the primalities, Campanella explains the three great influences (Necessity, Fate, and Harmony), to which is entrusted the role of bearing the infinite inflections of the divine mind in the world and in matter. In the light of such doctrines, he revisited much discussed and fundamental problems such as the relationships between necessity and contingency, between human freedom, fate, and providence, and problems related to evil and sin.

Particularly beautiful are the pages on harmony (an effect of love), in which Campanella depicted a universal coordination of ends. These pages constitute a strong rejection of philosophical positions, among which those of the Peripatetics and the Epicureans, that limit or deny divine providence, or (not recognizing nature as an expression of the intrinsic divine skill) hold that every thing happens by chance. For Campanella, however, divine wisdom radiates from even the most slender blade of grass or from a fly. Even the slightest feature or smallest fissures in the earth have a role to play in arranging matter so that it accepts the action of heat and light in a different way. Every atom of the world is arranged in such a way that one cannot add or subtract anything from it without altering the order of the whole. So as to reaffirm how nature is a multiplicity of ends, of which not all (or rather the minority) are known to us, Campanella recourses to a childhood memory, which appeared several times in the pages of his writings. When, as a small child, he would go into the workshops of smiths, or those of watchmakers and armsmiths, he would look with amazement at the number of objects and tools that to him seemed useless (because he was unaware of how they were used), and even dangerous because if he touched them in the wrong way they could hurt him. If a frog were to enter our house, the furnishings that it would

---

[61] *Ad philosophos Germaniae*, in *Opera Latina*, I, pp. 17–18; see ch. 4, note 14.

see would appear to it useless and without sense. When a mouse comes in, it twists the uses of our objects because it does not understand them. It nibbles at clothes, defaces books, and replaces food with excrement: 'this is how we are in the world, which is the house and the workshop of the prime craftsman – only much more ignorant – and on account of this we do not understand the function of things.'[62]

To the Epicureans, who deny divine art, and to those saying that divine art is incompatible with insects and pests or with evils such as wars and diseases, Campanella replied with the accusation that they were adopting egotistical and limited points of view. If one takes up the point of view of the total-ity instead, then beings (which to man appear to be useless or harmful) are revealed to have their own place and meaning with respect to the whole. Those beings that seem evil to us can in fact have a positive dimension: it is true not only that noxious things are integrated into the totality of the world, but also that if they did not exist then wisdom, knowledge, and vigilance would suffer. Each being, sunk deep in a continual laziness, would doze in the woods or in the fields and there would be no political association. Campanella recalled that flies and flees would often wake him and thereby call him back to study-ing, even as he also recalled rejoicing, as he does elsewhere, that among all of the evils that he had to endure he was not afflicted by the evil of lice.[63] Oppo-sitions between and distinctions among beings are necessary to the order of the world, and reality would be an undifferentiated chaos if they did not exist. Every thing, even the smallest (*vel tantilla*), radiates divine art. To Aristotle (who denied that God is concerned with the negligible events of the human world, a concern that for him would constitute a self-abasement on God's part), Campanella replied that God does not abase himself in caring for such things, because there is nothing in the world that is vile or base:

> I do not know what vileness Aristotle sees in things, from which he intends to preserve God. If he is referring to lice, to dung, to urine, to snakes, then he reveals himself to be a trifling philosopher, because they are base and vile things for us, but not for nature... In the world, vileness, like evil, is relative and not essential and such baseness exists relative to the parts but not with respect to the whole. Thus, nothing is vile or evil for God and the world, except non-being and sin. Therefore our universal God does not render himself base, whereas the partial God of Aristotle does. But what is more stupid than con-sidering God as a part and not as the whole?[64]

---

[62] *Metaphysica*, part II, p. 217.

[63] Ibid.; see note 32.

[64] Ibid., part II, p. 169b.

Rejecting the image of a divinity completely enclosed in a 'higher' and more perfect world and disdainful of the baseness of the human world, Campanella offered up the image of a God whose wisdom radiates in every being, from the smallest particle to the wonders of the heavenly bodies. This is a God that, according to what Hermes Trismegistus had affirmed, is not hidden, but radiates from every natural being, sign and testimony of divinity.[65]

The third part of the *Metaphysics* lingers on themes concerning abstract substances such as angels and demons; the government and the care of things, with a close study of the doctrines of Ficino and of the Hermetic and Neo-Platonic traditions; laws and legislators, offering an entire series of "signs" aimed at distinguishing laws sent by God, those that derive from cunning, and those sent by the devil; religion, distinguishing between the religion that is *indita* and natural and that which is *addita* and historical; questions regarding prophecy, every kind of divination and miracle, with relevant distinctions aiming at differentiating natural miracles and divine ones, those that are fictitious from those that are authentic; the purpose and renewal of laws, of ages, and of worlds, so that one might achieve the holiness 'to which one comes thanks to religion and to purity, in such a way that spirits are sustained and united in it. And outside of God one cannot search, for only He is the beginning and the end of every thing that has or desires being – He who is eternal, glorious and blessed forever.[66]

The fourteenth book is dedicated to the human soul and to the problem of its immortality. This is one of the most tortuous points that went back to that distant night of his adolescence, in which Campanella burst into tears realizing the weakness of Aristotle's arguments: 'Poor us, if the immortality of the soul were to depend on these arguments! One night in my youth, taking into consideration the fragility of these arguments, I began to cry and I turned with yearning to the philosophy of Plato and Telesio, and to the doctrines of the saints, which brought me great comfort – at that point, I abandoned Aristotle.'[67] In a beautiful passage in which he asked why divine soul is united to the opaque and terrestrial body, Campanella replied that God sent the soul down to the earth for his amusement (and so that the soul might have the chance to become worthy of merit). He said the soul is similar to celestial heat that, even as it fulfils its function and unites itself with the earth so as to produce every being, secretly hankers after the heavens, its origin: 'thus, the heat of the sun also hides itself on the earth and makes many beings forgetful of themselves on account of the passions that turn up. Yet, as if by a secret force, the heat of

---

[65] Ibid., part III, pp. 238, 239.
[66] *Ad philosophos Germaniae*, p. 18.
[67] *Quaest. phys.*, in *Phil. realis*, p. 513.

the sun senses and tends always towards that which is higher; just so, the soul of man, although ignorant of itself on account of the passions it undergoes, nevertheless senses God and tends towards him as if by a secret force.'[68]

The first book of the third part deals with cosmological and astronomical themes. The author reexamined all of the questions concerning the constitution of heavenly bodies and their motions, the duration of the *machina mundi* and the realignment of its hinges, the continual tightening of the solar obliquity, and the final transformation of the earth by fire. He who denies such transformations is similar to the ephemeral insect that does not even know the difference between day and night because it is born and dies in the course of a single day. He discussed the doctrines of Copernicus and Tycho Brahe and he addressed the new discoveries of Galileo. Several significant appendices attached to the text testify on several occasions to doubts, waverings, and reconsiderations with regard to Pythagorean doctrines, which he had discussed in his youth with the Brunian Colantonio Stigliola. Then, he had rejected them with the argument that it did not seem to him opportune to suppose the existence of other worlds and systems, multiplying the evils and sufferings of the earth. But now, those doubts seemed to reemerge and put in crisis his conception of the igneous nature of the heavenly bodies, residence of blessed spirits. In any case, whatever explanation or point of view one might adopt, there was no doubt that – in any case and above all – the variety and the harmony of celestial bodies manifested the wondrous wisdom of God. Natural principles, instruments of the divine art, 'execute the work of God, a work that they do not understand, even as they act for their own preservation,' and 'God makes use of the stars as the smith makes use of many hammers, raising them, lowering them, accelerating or slowing their motions, rendering some straight and some oblique in the workshop, so as to realize his idea. And God moves hammers of this kind not with a material hand, but with the pleasure and love of their preservation and the fear of their destruction.'[69]

Theologicorum Libri

Once again, the merit of having begun and carried forward the work of editing the gigantic *Theologia* (which consisted of thirty books that took more than a decade to complete) is due to Romano Amerio. In March 1614, Campanella told Galileo that he had gotten as far as the fourth book; only in

---

[68] *Metaphysica*, part III, p. 152b.
[69] Ibid., part III, p. 32b; on this issue, see Michel-Pierre Lerner, 'cosmologia,' in *Enciclopedia*, vol. 1, coll. 220–229.

1624 would he be able to say with satisfaction to Cassiano dal Pozzo: 'I have just finished the last and thirtieth book of the *Theologia* which is *de saeculis saeculorum*.'[70] The work remained unpublished during Campanella's lifetime. He was unable to get it published at Rome and unable also to get it published at Paris with a dedication to Cardinal Richelieu, as he would have liked. After being first mentioned by Spampanato, the publication of the volumes was undertaken in a systematic and sustained way by Amerio from the beginning of the 1940s. He published twenty-four books, setting the Latin text alongside an Italian version, and dedicated numerous essays to the theological thought of Campanella, in addition to an important book.[71]

The work, which had been presumed lost, was tracked down in two voluminous exemplars: one conserved in the General Archive of the Order of Preachers (AGOP) in Rome and the other in the Bibliothèque Mazarine at Paris.[72] The Roman codex is more complete, in that it encompasses almost the entirety of the work; but the manuscript is peppered with mistakes and is not completely reliable. The Parisian codex, on the other hand, is largely incomplete. The two volumes that remain from the original six contain only thirteen books. Yet it has the advantage of being a considerably more reliable exemplar, in that it bears numerous traces of emendations and insertions in the author's own hand. Some problems derive from the number and the enumeration of the books. In the *Syntagma* Campanella spoke of twenty-nine books, but in other passages he referred in a more reliable manner to thirty. The Roman codex (= R), indeed, lists thirty books, but of the fifteenth book it only gives the title (*De legibus speciatim*), and Amerio assumed that the book was never written, since the subject is treated elsewhere in the *Reminiscentur*. The Parisian codex (= P), for its part, introduces another variation with respect to the enumeration of books. In fact, from the massive first volume is excerpted the part that began with the seventeenth chapter, *De providentia*, which is rendered autonomous as book six. As a result of that insertion, in P the sequence of books from six to fifteen differs from that found in R.[73]

Starting in the 1990s, Maria Muccillo has resumed the work of bringing the *Theologia* to press. She has edited two of the five remaining unpublished

---

[70] Letter of 20 July 1624, in *Lettere*, p. 203.

[71] For a recent adjustment of the edition of the books on theology (and a detailed profile of Romano Amerio and his publications), see Maria Muccillo, *La pubblicazione della 'Theologia,'* in *Laboratorio Campanella*, pp. 213–234.

[72] Roma, AGOP, ser. XIV, 288–293, 6 vols.; Paris, Bibl. Mazarine, mss 1077, cc. 1031 (ll. VI–XV); 1078, cc. 884 (ll. XXI–XXIII); see Firpo, *Bibliografia*, pp. 159–162.

[73] In the other three books contained in the second Paris codex (ll. XXI, XXII, XXX-III), the enumeration comes back into alignment, in that the XV P (XIV R) fills the gap of the inexistent XV R. Such specification is necessary because the volumes edited by Amerio sometimes follow the numbering from R and sometimes the numbering from P.

books.[74] Thus, three books still need to be edited before the publication of the entire work can be brought to completion: *De virtute et vitio quibus felicitas et infelicitas conquiruntur* (which is book eight in R and book nine in P), *De legibus generatim* (book fourteen in R, fifteen in P), and *De dictis Christi legislatoris regisque* (book twenty-two in both R and P). It is obviously impossible here to even barely mention to the multiplicity of themes confronted in the *Theologia*. But we can at least take note of Campanella's explanation (included in the work's general introduction) of why he had been induced to confront the limitless field of theology. The first motive was identified in the enormous recent diffusion of heresies and in the diffusion of knowledge of religions that were not sufficiently confuted by the learned men of the scholastic tradition, such as the Islamic religion. The second motive derived from the discovery of new countries and new peoples, and above all new heavens, new stars, and new celestial systems – fields in which theologians do not have particular competence and in which they 'often speak as ignorant men, proceeding amidst the derision of those who philosophize on the basis of experience.' The third motive was the need for a radical reform of the sciences and the need to emancipate them from the yoke of Aristotelianism. The fourth reason consisted in the fact that the author intended to study not one science alone, but all sciences taking into account all authors, 'always comparing what I write and read with the book of the world, written by the wisdom of God in vivid and real letters.' The fifth and last of the motives was located in the desire to go beyond the 'carnal zeal of the modern scholastics' (on account of which each was attached to his own master and to his own school), so as to reconstruct an authentic solidarity beyond every particularism and conflict between science and sanctity, which ought not to be separated. The aim was to do this without forgetting that full and complete truth belongs to God alone, while men can achieve truths that are merely partial and provisional.

Campanella was able to demonstrate all of his own theological competence in the course of the work. He had already established such competence on other occasions (consider the *Apologia pro Galileo*), and this led to the much sought after title of *magister theologiae* to be bestowed upon him in June 1629. Campanella confronted theological problems of the greatest import in the various books contained in the work. And he did so in light of the entire tradition, which from time to time he reinterpreted and reread in order to offer more

---

[74] *De ceremonialibus Iesu Christo observatis* (Rome, 1993), l. XX (the book, trans. by Amerio, was completed with the transcription of the text and with a set of notes and an index by M. Muccillo); *De conservatione et gubernatione rerum* (l. VI R, VII P), ed. M. Muccillo (Rome, 2000).

satisfying solutions to the problems that were to him more heartfelt – from the primalitative structure of God in the creation and organization of the world to the economy of salvation. If some books are more conventional and display some signs of tiredness, others are more personal and are closely connected to the great arguments of his philosophical and metaphysical speculation – as, for example, when he addressed the question of original sin. At one level, the Christian doctrine of the fall of Adam offers an explanation and gives an account of the 'great confusion' (*scompiglio*) of the history of humanity – that is to say, of the shattering of the harmony between man and nature, between man and reason, which stems from the arrogance of Adam who perverted the just relation between reason and sensuality. But the deeper, more tormented and unresolved issue remained the question of why and to what end God, who is infinitely good, permitted such a massive corruption, from which would derive the damnation of the overwhelming majority of his own children. As usual, Campanella rejected the doctrine shared by Muhammad and the supporters of the Reformation (according to which God is the cause also of evil for the purpose of being able to punish us, and thereby manifest his own justice). In Campanella's opinion, God could in no way either wish or cause sin. On the contrary, sin had its origin in the fact that man is limited, prone to error, and free. But even the most subtle arguments of famous learned men such as Augustine, Chrysostom, and Ambrose – arguments that were analyzed and discussed in minute detail – were not able to resolve the basic problem: 'in any case, it is not yet made clear by these sacred doctors why God might have per-mitted sin (on account of which the world has been so much worsened), if the world would have been better without the reprobate and the damned, better without the punishment of hell and the calamity of the present life.' The ques-tion is so crucial because the eternal ruin of so many men is without remedy even following the Incarnation of God himself. Those who will be condemned to eternal torture actually outnumber those who will enjoy beatitude. This gives rise to a temptation to believe in the audacious solution of a progressive and universal salvation proposed by Origen, 'who teaches that the damned, returning in this world again and again, during another cycle of centuries, will obtain the merit necessary to ascend to glory and that even after so many evils the damned will all in the end be saved – men and devils alike.'[75] From here too comes the temptation to adopt solutions that might result in the most ample possibilities with regard to salvation.

---

[75] *Il peccato originale, Theologicorum l. XVI*, ed. R. Amerio (Rome, 1960), p. 69; see Germana Ernst, *Tommaso Campanella (1568–1639)*, in *Il peccato originale nel pensi-ero moderno*, ed. G. Riconda, M. Ravera, C. Ciancio, G. Cuozzo (Brescia, 2009), pp. 189–212.

Large parts of theology are dedicated to the birth, life, and works of Christ and to the sacraments instituted by him, which are often the object of harsh criticism from heretics or from other monotheistic religions. Some books echo and take up themes from other works. Thus, there are books on the virtues that expand upon the *Ethica*, while the final books on eschatological themes take up prophetic topics and treat the end of times in the manner of the *Articuli prophetales*. This theological work seems thus to reveal continuities in Campanella's thought, rather than points of rupture. One book, in particular, has attracted a lot of interest and bewilderment in this respect. Given the title of *Magia e grazia* by Amerio, the fourteenth book deals with the problematic nature of grace *gratis data* (as distinct from merited grace, which is treated in the preceding book, titled *Della grazia gratificante*). In contrast to grace that places man in a state of moral sanctity, rendering him in that way welcome in the eyes of God, grace *gratis data* consists in a gift bestowed by God independently of moral status. Here, one is dealing with a gift thanks to which man is able to undertake extraordinary deeds to the advantage of the community. Campanella's treatment is divided into nine parts, encompassing faith, discretion of the spirits, the capacity to speak and understand different languages. In truth, however, the aspects on which he focused most the longest are those that are particularly dear to him, such as prophecy and magic.[76] He argued with such argumentative exuberance that Amerio went as far as calling the text a second *De sensu rerum*.[77] The purpose, rigorously orthodox, was to avoid the radical naturalization of these operations and prerogatives, so as to preserve the divine charisma of the Church and so as to reaffirm that not every prophecy is natural and that miracles ought not to be considered in the same way as natural prodigies. Yet, so as to distinguish the various kinds of these arts and doctrines and so as to indicate the criteria according to which one can give order to such an extremely dense mass of phenomena, Campanella discussed with great attention all the kinds and forms of prophecy and magic. He recalled facts that were true and others that were false, illusory and truthful, strange and deceitful, scientific and diabolical; he offered an extraordinary repertoire of sources and points of interest, and referred also to his own personal experiences. He stressed that it is necessary to experience everything, because speculation is not valuable without practice, for the person who actually paints is to be counted a painter and not the person who knows all the abstract rules of the art.[78]

---

[76] On these topics, see Germana Ernst, *Magia, divinazione e segni in Tommaso Campanella*, in *La magia nell'Europa moderna. Tra antica sapienza e filosofia naturale*, ed. F. Meroi and E. Scapparone (Florence, 2007), vol. II, pp. 589–611.

[77] *Magia e grazia*, *Theologicorum l. XIV*, ed. R. Amerio (Rome, 1957), p. 7.

[78] Ibid., p. 153.

11. THE DISAPPOINTMENT OF LIBERTY

Politicians, Courtiers, and the Prophet's Fate

After extensive negotiations, unfulfilled promises, and worrying delays, a royal letter finally arrived in Naples from Madrid in March 1626 that asked the Viceroy to take a final decision regarding Campanella's case. The Collateral Council found that he should be freed, under caution, and on 23 May Campanella emerged from the Castel Nuovo after almost twenty-seven years in prison and returned to the convent of San Domenico. From there, a month later, the Holy Office ordered that he be delivered in secret to Rome, which he reached by sea, disguised as a secular priest under a false name.

The first period after the arrival in Rome constituted for Campanella the height of bitterness, and he could do nothing to hide his delusion and discomfort. Freed from the jails of Naples only to be closed up in those of the Holy Office, he not only found no sympathy for or solidarity with the sufferings that he had endured, but also had to confront renewed hostility and diffidence. The state of mind of despondency and irritation, unusual in him, appeared with utmost clarity in a letter from the beginning of April 1627 to Ippolito Lanci di Acquanegra, Commissioner of the Inquisition, who had requested an opinion from him on the question of titles. For some time previously, the aptness of bestowing the title of 'most eminent' on Cardinals had been discussed. Campanella replied to the prelate, who had shown benevolence and esteem towards him, with an explicitly and unusually annoyed tone:

> I write grudgingly. Until now I had avoided writing in this way restraining myself not only because I was unhappy at not having been able to obtain even the most minimal favor from these gentlemen (being given only trouble, and affliction from which after twenty-eight years I was hoping to get some relief), but also because I wrote a short work on this matter at the behest of Don Virginio Cesarini.... Thus, I now write in haste and out of necessity.

In the final lines, he affirmed that he no longer had any intention of putting his own knowledge at the service of those who clearly did not appreciate him: 'I am a worm, and I do not want to give advice in any matter where I am not commanded to obey, nor do I want any more to show that I know more than the ordinary courtier, since having philosophized in an uncommon manner in order to serve patrons has already cost me dearly.'[1]

Little more than a month earlier, on 21 February, he had sent a long letter to the Cardinal-Nephew Francesco Barberini, in which, once again, he had been forced to defend and explain himself, so as to confront the false accusations to which he had been subjected and so as to seek to overcome the deaf, tenacious hostility towards his person and his books. He attempted to specify the true reasons behind the persecutions against him, beyond the vain 'pretexts' given officially. Right from the beginning of the letter, he did not hide his painful astonishment at his own present condition, emphasizing the sad contrast between the last eight years at Castel Nuovo (when he had had the chance to give lectures on every subject to numerous 'Italian and Spanish gentlemen') and his present condition, 'which was being consumed and oppressed in this horrendous calamity in the hands of the Holy Father of the Christians.' In the light of this alarming paradox, he pointed out that although at Naples he had been among his enemies the Spanish had learned to appreciate him in time, and passed from reputing him 'a devil' to considering him 'a saint worthy of liberty and their favor.' Yet now, in the heart of Christianity itself, the devil – who sought continually to set 'the virtuous' against the Papacy 'with suspicions, jealousies, mistrust, and persecutions' – 'found a solution in some Judas so as to crucify me before the eyes of the wisest Pope in the world.'[2]

Campanella was particularly embittered by the hue and cry raised against his books, which his adversaries wanted to subject to a minute revision (an unjustified and absurd proposal), 'so as to take the pen out of the hands of all Christian minds, and so as to arm the tongues of heretics, and ban the sciences from Italy, and to lead every virtuous spirit into despair.' These same books had been read publicly at Castel Nuovo, and they were, in part, already published, while some of them were already known to the censors. They were books that had been in circulation for some time and were often requested, books that 'copyists and booksellers.... sold at high prices in Rome and at Naples and Padua,' without anyone finding a shadow of heresy; indeed, those who had craftily attempted to detect a heresy of some sort had remained disappointed.

---

[1] *Lettere*, p. 216. Campanella had addressed the issue in the elegant pamphlet *De' titoli*, sent on 4 April 1624 to Virginio Cesarini, who never got to see it, given that he died, at only twenty-nine years of age, precisely at that point. Published for the first time by Amabile, *Castelli*, II, doc. 201, pp. 138–147, there is a second edition in Germana Ernst, 'Segni, virtù e onore nell'opuscolo *De' titoli* di Tommaso Campanella,' *Filologia e Critica*, 15 (2000), pp. 281–301.

[2] See *Lettere 2*, pp. 85–94.

These books constituted the principal reason for pride in his life, his only chance to communicate his own truth and his own thought: 'I forthrightly sent my books all over the world in order to seek help for myself, and I thought that they would be helpful on account of the Christian truth that they contain and not for the heresies that my persecutors pretend to recognize in them.'[3]

To the persecution of his books were added the old accusations of rebellion and heresy. A recently discovered tract dating back to 1627[4] proposed once again the connection between his own biographical experience and the dramatic, but inevitable clash between the prophet and the politician. This clash took place within the context of the divine providential design and it was understood against the background of the difficult question that 'everyone finds mindboggling' – namely, the sufferings of the good and the triumphs of the bad.[5] Thus, a point of departure was as ever the difficult reflection on his own experience. In order to repel the accusations and to dispel suspicion, Campanella intended to show that the misfortunes of the philosopher should not be understood as the punishment of misdeeds or as a sign of having erred. The reasons for his suffering set down roots in a deeper terrain and were to be understood within a broader perspective. Since reality is nothing but the deployment of the infinite gradations and modulations of divine wisdom, the problem of the existence of evil is to be understood without ever putting in doubt the pervasive presence of divinity in every last corner of the human and natural world. From here came the polemics against doctrines (Epicurean, Aristotelian, or Manichean) which, so as to give reasons for evil, placed limits on God and on his providence. From the perspective of the whole, even that which appears to be the expression of negativity acquires a meaning and a purpose. Even evil comes to acquire a positive function with regard to the vicissitude of things and the totality of their relations, which is explicated in a sequence of clashes and contrasts:

---

[3]The censures were based on the still suspect doctrines of the *Senso delle cose* (which he would defend in a learned *Defensio*), and on the *Atheismus triumphatus*, which was accused of leaning towards Pelagianism.

[4]Tracked down in ms Chigi, F VI 137, cc. 31*r*-77*v* at the Biblioteca Apostolica Vaticana, the treatise ought perhaps to be identified with the *De technis aulicorum* (mentioned in the *Syntagma*, p. 64). It has been published with the title *Politici e cortigiani contro filosofi e profeti*, in Germana Ernst, 'L'opacità del male e il disincanto del profeta. Profezia, ragion di Stato e provvidenza divina in un testo inedito di Campanella (1627),' *B&C*, 2 (1996), pp. 89–155: 104–152 (and now as an appendix to Ead., *Il carcere, il politico, il profeta* (Pisa-Rome, 2002), pp. 143–179).

[5]*Poesie*, p. 354.

Every difficulty, both natural and artificial, is the school of God. If there were no hunger, war, thirst, evil beasts, hot and cold, then there would be no philosophy, no medicine, no mathematics, no mechanics, no art of peace and no art of war, no art of navigation, no science of the stars, of the elements, or of those things that are harmful or helpful. Nor would good be cherished, there would be neither forethought nor prudence, nor any virtue among those who disdain and defeat evil and attain good. Therefore, only as beasts do we lament that there are evil men, whereas first we ought to lament the existence of thorns, heat and cold, ferocious beasts and tiny fleas, as well as the sky, the earth, and the sea – and in this way we would lose everything.[6]

Campanella did not hesitate to find a positive meaning even in his own long detention, which had offered him the opportunity to reform all the sciences, and in his sufferings, which had forced him to meditate on the central problem of the immortality of the soul and had allowed him to offer to posterity, citing his own example, 'the security and the certainty of another life because of which I endured every affliction and discomfort.' There were evil men who like demons had chosen the point of view of partiality and personal interest, and the 'good of oneself alone' and 'not the good of all or of the human race.' Such men lived imprisoned in particularity in an illusory and blinded condition, which made them ever more arrogant, and sure of themselves:

And they laugh at religion and at those who fear to sin, and they rejoice at the thought of knowing more than anyone else, because they learn to deceive or deny citizenship, family, and friends and make use of the loyalty of others with their own duplicity and false promises to achieve their ends. Finally all their prudence is nothing but the knowledge that they can sin without fear of punishment and that they can make use of everything according to their own liking – thereby making fun of scientists and recondite doctrines as donkeys loaded with letters driven by them astutely towards burdensome work.[7]

To the politician, bearer of a vision of the world that adopted the point of view of partiality and personal interest, are opposed once again the figures of the philosopher and the prophet, who are conscious of the correct relationship of the parts with the whole. With disconcerting temerity, Campanella did not hesitate to affirm that just as among the twelve apostles there was Judas, so there was no lack of emissaries from the forces of the devil even among the bishops and within the College of Cardinals. Naturally, their triumphs too are illusory, in that they too (unwittingly) are nothing but the docile instruments of a higher divine will. The exemplary places of the political arts are the

---

[6]'L'opacità del male,' p. 120.

[7]Ibid., p. 127.

courts, which he describes as puerile microcosms dominated by the licentious desire to achieve self-interest, where adulation triumphs. All of this involves a constant work of keeping distant from the prince anyone who might be able to reveal intrigues and deceits. The autobiographical allusions that pervade this work culminate in a passage that lays bare the subtle web of slanders, denigrations, hypocrisies, and mistrust towards every novelty, seen as a threat, in which Campanella felt himself involved:

> When a great literary figure appears, all the little literary types fear him. So among themselves they make jokes about him, and at the beginning they pass small comments in the presence of the prince. Pretending to praise him they say that he lacks something, that he is foolish, that he does not know how to live, that he is not polished in matters of grammar or speaking; they assiduously pick on little defects in some work or sonnet, or they find in him some other faults of this kind. They do so to the extent that is required for them to be able to sow further lies, because they then make out of him a heretic on account of the dissimilitude of customs or on account of some serious proposition that has been badly understood. They say that it is dangerous to have anything to do with such people, and especially so for a prince, because large brains come up with new things and they feign that every novelty is contrary to the state and religion. This is a most bestial assertion, since novelty adorns the world and augments and enlarges the state. And these adulating scoundrels feign that all those things that do not come from them are harmful to the state and to religion or that they render the prince somehow suspect: they do not even speak to these philosophers by night – as Nicodemus did while facing the same fear.[8]

In this way, the prince is deprived of the reliable help of the virtuous and is forced to make use of these base courtiers, who are depicted in an ever more precise and unforgiving way: the courtier 'sullies the court, the people, and the kingdom with vices,' seeing that his chief virtues consist in his own servility to the master, by 'showing himself to be the first to fetch the chamber-pot for the master, moan with shouts and cries when he says that his foot or his tooth is giving him trouble, flattering him, greasing him, and duping him.' In the sinister light of the mechanisms of power and the court, the true reasons for which prophets are persecuted by politicians and bad advisers become easier to understand. These are politicians and bad advisers who 'intoxicate the princes with this love of oneself alone, and they blind them such that when they hear that someone says or does something good that is not immediately advantageous to his own condition (as it is to the common good), they become

---

[8] Ibid., p. 131.

consumed by an anger more implacable than that of a lover when he is told that others love or desire the object of his love.'

Campanella was exasperated because he felt himself to be the object of a tenacious hostility even more at Rome – the heart of Christianity – than in the prisons of Naples. At Rome, he felt immersed in an environment that was saturated with ambitions and calculations, full of pettiness and hypocrisy. In the *Dialogo politico tra un Veneziano, Spagnuolo e Francese* several years later, with an all too transparent allusion to the persecution suffered by the nephews of the Pope, Campanella would not fail to mention

> the hatred that the nephews of the great Prelates bear towards all those who are distinguished by virtue, for which they are usually loved by their uncles – and so they are always looking for opportunities to disgrace them [philosophers and prophets]. When they see the prelate speaking secretly with someone more than once, confiding in that individual, they at once suggest on their own accounts or on behalf of others that the Prelate has tarnished his reputation or risks the jealousy of other princes by acting in this manner. They suggest that the individual is not in fact so very learned, or that actually he is not held in very high esteem by others, so that in the world it is said to be shameful to deal with his sort; then they make it seem that he spreads lies, and deceives, and they change, as one says, the cards he holds in his hand. [9]

The Astrological Affair and the Pope's Horoscope

There can be little doubt that the most sensational episode in this period at Rome was one linked to Campanella's astrological skill and the desire of Urban VIII to make use of it in order to combat the rumors of his own imminent death in view of unfavorable celestial signs. Rumors of this kind had been in circulation from 1626, and they would become ever more insistent in the years that followed. The gloomy predictions would reach the level of a genuine international event, culminating in 1630 with preparations and maneuvers by the Spanish, who were angling for a new conclave as if there were already a 'vacant seat.' This was an episode that constituted an infamous example of the ambiguous marriage of astrology, politics, and propaganda.

Urban VIII was also rather alarmed because he did indeed have a secret interest in astrology, and he intuited that there could be something true in such insistent predictions. He turned therefore to Campanella, who reassured him on the basis of an attentive investigation into his birth. Called to the Papal palace,

---

[9]*Dialogo politico tra un Veneziano, Spagnuolo e Francese,* in Amabile, *Castelli,* II, doc. 244, pp. 185–214; there is also a more correct version (from which I am citing) in *Tommaso Campanella,* pp. 955–993: 963.

Campanella, from the beginning of the summer of 1628, set about putting into practice the theories of natural magic described in the short treatise *De siderali fato vitando*.[10] In the *Avvisi* from Rome came frequent reports of secret meetings between the Pope who was intent more than ever on protecting his own life in every way possible and a friar who was 'extremely gifted and unique in astrology.' It was said that thanks to nocturnal rituals (illuminated by the glow of torches and candles) and thanks also to 'certain medicines against bad humors and melancholy,' this friar was able to placate the illustrious man's anxieties, persuading him that 'he would live a long and quiet life.'[11] One of the best chapters of Walker's *Spiritual and Demonic Magic from Ficino to Campanella* is dedicated to the episode.[12] Revealing the affinities and debts of Campanella's suggestions to those of Ficino's *De vita coelitus comparanda*, Walker expertly focused on the most famous page of the work, which suggests remedies against the dangers posed by eclipses and which reveals the practices used by the Pope. When the heavens are corrupted and the air is contaminated by noxious seeds, it is necessary – so as to protect oneself from infection and just as one does for the plague – to halt the diffusion of infected seeds, purifying the air and the environment. Campanella advised action that would ensure 'right from the beginning that scattered seeds cannot set down roots in you; just like the seed that comes from fruit or from mustard (or any other kind of seed), which if it does not find a suitable terrain cannot set down its roots.' Campanella recalled that during the terrible plague in Athens, Socrates remained immune, thanks to the temperance with which he had neutralized the aggression of the disease. So as to confront the threat of the danger, it is thus necessary to mark out a separate space and to reconstruct a favorable environment, combating the obscuring of the heavens with white clothes and adornments and purifying the infected air with fires of aromatic wood, sprinklings of essences and distilled waters, together with the use of relaxing music. But above all, thanks to the lighting of seven torches representing the sun and the planets, it is necessary to prepare a representation of a symbolic sky, which substituted in miniature form the obscured and threatening real sky:

> First, make an effort to live in a temperate manner, conforming to religion and the greatest possible vicinity to God, dedicating yourself to him with orations and ceremonies.

---

[10] The *De siderali fato vitando*, in *Opuscoli astrologici*, pp. 64–133.

[11] Amabile, *Castelli*, I, pp. 325 ff.; II, doc. 203, 210, 211, 216, pp. 148, 153ff.

[12] Daniel P. Walker, *Spiritual and Demonic Magic from Ficino to Campanella* (London, 1958), pp. 203–236, now with an introduction by B. Copenhaver (Pennsylvania State U. P., 2000).

Second, you ought to sprinkle your house (once it had been well-sealed so that no air could enter from outside) with rose vinegar and aromatic perfumes; you ought to set a fire with laurel, myrtle, rosemary, cypress, and other aromatic woods. Nothing is more effective for dissipating toxic influences from the sky, even those sent by a demon.

Third, you ought to adorn the edifice with white silk clothes and leafy boughs.

Fourth, you ought to set two lamps and five torches, which represent the planets of the sky, in such a way that, when they are obscured in the heavens, there is not lack of substitutes on the earth, just like at night, when the sun is at a distance, a lamp may substitute for it, so that the day that is far away is not actually missed. Let there be candles emitting an aromatic blend, and, were you to imitate the twelve signs, you ought to proceed in a philosophical manner and not superstitiously as ordinary people do.

Fifth, among your friends frequent those whose aphetic areas in their respective nativities do not seem prone to being harmed by the eclipse...

Sixth, you ought to listen to jovial and venereal music, so that the malignity of the air might be shattered and so that helpful symbols might be opposed to the evil influences of the stars.

Seventh, since for every star there are adequate correspondences to stones, plants, colors, odors, forms of music and motions (as I argued in the fifth book of my *Medicina*), you ought to adopt those baits that attract positive forces and repel negative ones.[13]

The Pope seemed to make use of such counsel, and the scandal would erupt in the autumn of 1629. At that point, the tract *De fato* – which had been imprudently given to a 'treacherous confrere' (*insidiosus frater*)[14] and which according to Campanella had been brought to press without his knowing – was published as the seventh and final book of the *Astrologicorum libri*.[15] The circumstances surrounding the publishing of this work are not entirely clear, but it is beyond doubt that the printing of the work was carried out with the

---

[13]*Opuscoli astrologici*, pp. 92–94.

[14]*Syntagma*, p. 60; the allusion is to Niccolò Riccardi O.P., an instigator of the plot along with the General of the Dominican Order, Niccolò Ridolfi. On this second figure and on the 'violent and rapacious way with which he rules,' see the letter that Campanella sent from Paris to Urban VIII on 9 April 1635, in *Lettere*, pp. 282–295.

[15]In the first edition of the *Astrologicorum* (Lyon, 1629), the short treatise *De fato* was added at the end of the book by the printer, who in an introductory note declared that he had received it when the printing of the other six books had already been completed and that he had wanted to add it, even so late in the day, so as not to deprive the reader of the chance to read it.

aim of robbing its author of a growing benevolence from the Pope and of stopping abruptly his ascent in Roman circles.[16] At the beginning of 1629, he had been definitively cleared of every charge and on 2 June the general chapter of the Dominicans had bestowed upon him the coveted title of *magister theologiae*. At the same time, there were rumors circulating of his nomination as consultor to the Holy Office, and perhaps even higher honors. The despicable maneuver of the printing of the *De fato* achieved its aims. The nomination as consultor was suspended. The solicited presentation of the *Astrologicorum* to the Pontiff was accompanied by insinuating accusations that the author was lapsing into disobedience because he had printed his work without the required authorizations. All of this (combined with other accusations of heresy and superstition) unleashed an extremely violent anger in the Pope, who was worried by the risk of being publicly compromised and suspected of superstitious practices. Understanding too well the dire straits into which he had fallen, Campanella hurried to set down an *Apologeticus* in defense of the work. Having easily cleared the field of the accusations of heresy, he tried to prove how the suggested practices ought not to be understood as a ceremonial and superstitious ritual, but rather as a completely licit natural remedy, which did not imply any pact with the devil, either implicit or explicit.[17] But if Campanella's self-defence was easy with regard to the need to purify infected air and surroundings (as physicians recommended and as Ficino too had recommended in his work on the *Consilio contro la pestilentia*),[18] he had to turn to the entirety of his own doctrines in order to reply to the more insidious objections regarding the influence of numbers, the symbolic value of representation, and the power of astrological images.

---

[16]Firpo, who was also a passionate bibliophile, provides a close reconstruction of the four editions that followed between 1629 and 1630 (for which, see the chapter 'La stampa clandestina degli *Astrologicorum libri*,' in *Ricerche*, pp. 155–169): two authentic printings from Lyon and a third counterfeited for the purpose of confronting the competition of the Frankfurt edition of 1630. Picking up on cues from Amabile and on the basis of passages from letters, re-elaborated in an approximate and unconvincing fashion, Francesco Grillo, *Questioni campanelliane. La stampa fraudolenta e clandestina degli* Astrologicorum libri (Cosenza, 1961), maintains that the first edition was published not at Lyon, but at Rome, at the printing press of Andrea Brugiotti.

[17]See Germana Ernst, 'Il cielo in una stanza. L'*Apologeticus* di Campanella in difesa dell'opuscolo *De siderali fato vitando*,' *B&C*, 3 (1997), pp. 303–334; the work is now in *Opuscoli astrologici*, pp. 136–173; there is an English translation by Noga Arikha in *Culture and Cosmos*, 6 (2002), pp. 45–71.

[18]On this work, see Teodoro Katinis, *Medicina e filosofia in Marsilio Ficino. Il Consilio contro la pestilentia* (Rome, 2007).

Remembering that there were no bans and condemnations on Pythagorean doctrines regarding the influence of numbers, Campanella recalled the oft-cited verse from the Book of Wisdom, according to which God made everything 'in number, weight, and measure' as well as passages from Scripture in which recourse to numerological symbolism is relatively frequent. Indeed, Scripture pays particular attention to the number seven; it is enough to think of the vortex-like whirlwind of the seven angels, phials, thunder claps, trumpets, and seals of the Apocalypse. Extremely apt, then, were the references to the Church Fathers, from Origen to Jerome to Augustine to Richard of Saint Victor, and to texts from modern authors such as the Flemish physician Cornelius Gemma, author of the *De arte ciclognomica* and Fabio Paolini from Udine, whose *Hebdomades* consisted in a highly learned, vertiginous variation on Orphic theology and the value of the number seven and took its cue from a verse in the *Aeneid*.[19] As for the value of symbols, the Bible often recommended the reproduction of exemplary models and Campanella, recalling the learned Jewish convert Sixtus of Siena, noted the representative power of the Aaron's priestly robes, which depicted the entire world in miniature. Beyond having a peculiar efficacy, according to Sixtus such images called for a certain kind of explanation ('sciographic'), in which the reproduction of an image is essential. Relating the illustration of Aaron's solemn garments, Sixtus followed it up with a highly interesting discussion on which, without doubt, Campanella must have meditated at length. In this kind of 'shadowy and pictorial exposition,' an image puts under one's eyes things that cannot be expressed adequately by words alone. In the absence of a figure, objects such as Noah's ark, the Mosaic Tabernacle, and the temple of Solomon are graspable only badly and with effort. Yet with the help of representations they are understood easily and can be remembered for a long time.[20] Beyond a symbolic or mystical meaning, the seven torches that represent the heavenly bodies also take on a *vis physica* from the stars. In order to sustain this claim, Campanella did not hesitate to grapple with the delicate question of astrological images. He again took up the authorities to which he had previously appealed: Ficino in the most discussed and problematic pages of the books *De vita*;[21] Albert the Great in the *Speculum astronomiae* that

---

[19] Regarding Gemma, see *Cornelius Gemma. Cosmology, Medicine, and Natural Philosophy in Renaissance Louvain*, ed. H. Hirai (Pisa-Rome, 2008); on Paolini, see Walker, *Spiritual and Demonic Magic*, pp. 126–144.

[20] Sixtus Senensis, *Bibliotheca sancta*, l. III (Lyon, 1575), pp. 184f.

[21] See Marsilio Ficino, *Three Books on Life*, III, 18, crit. ed. and Latin text with English transl. by C. V. Kaske and J. R. Clark (New York, 1989).

was attributed to him;[22] and St. Thomas in texts that were more toned-down and cautious. Campanella added an extremely adept reference from Cajetan's commentary on Aquinas' *Summa*, in which the Cardinal succeeded, with a subtle piece of hermeneutical skill, in showing how some of Aquinas's affirmations, which appeared to be contradictory, were in truth reconcilable. He therefore concluded that astronomical images were not to be condemned, provided that they were stripped of letters, which were the only manifestly superstitious elements.[23]

Beyond risking the loss of the Pope's favor, Campanella understood the gathering of the storm over astrology that would be unleashed shortly thereafter. The growing, exasperated, anti-astrological intransigence of Urban VIII – a Pope who in private boasted of knowing the birth charts of all the cardinals and who consulted the horoscope of the old Duke of Urbino in order to identify when he would finally quit the scene so that he could take possession of his state – would culminate in the trial of astrologers in the summer of 1630. Along with this came the incarceration and death (in a case of suspected poisoning) of Don Orazio Morandi, the Abbot of the convent of Santa Prassede, which was one of the most active centers for prognostication and private meetings and where astrological practices were closely bound up with political intrigue.[24] In the spring of 1631, there would follow the promulgation of the extremely severe Bull *Inscrutabilis*, which banned every kind of divination and threatened harsh punishments (from the confiscation of property to capital punishment) for the authors of predictions pertaining to the life of the Pope and his relatives.

Embittered and worried by these events, Campanella wrote an ingenious and convoluted *Disputatio* on the Bull. Under the pretense of replying to the criticisms of hypothesized adversaries, he did everything he could to provide a mitigating interpretation. He denounced the possibility that it might be said that the Pope was showing greater rigor against astrologers than against heretics

---

[22] See P. Zambelli, *The 'Speculum astronomiae' and its Enigma* (Dordrect-Boston-London, 1991); A. Paravicini Bagliani, *Le 'Speculum astronomiae': un énigme? Enquête sur les manuscrits* (Florence, 2001).

[23] *Summa th.*, II IIae, q. 96, art. 2 in S. Thomae Aquinatis *Opera omnia*, with commentary by Cardinal Gaetanus, vol. IX (Rome, 1897), pp. 331–333. On images, see Nicolas Weill-Parot, *Les 'Images astrologiques' au Moyen Age et à la Renaissance. Spéculations intellectuelles et pratiques magiques (XIIIᵉ–XVᵉ siècle)* (Paris, 2001).

[24] On the event, see Germana Ernst, 'Scienza, astrologia e politica nella Roma barocca. La biblioteca di don Orazio Morandi,' in *Bibliothecae selectae. Da Cusano a Leopardi*, ed. E. Canone (Florence, 1993), pp. 217–252; B. Dooley, *Morandi's Last Prophecy and the End of Renaissance Politics* (Princeton, 2002).

and schismatics or that the Pope might be thinking more of his own personal interest (and that of his family) than the common good.[25] Aware that the banning of astrology was a political condemnation, Campanella asserted that the wisdom of the father of all can condemn not only false doctrines but also the dangerous ones that are capable of causing unrest. Such dangerous doctrines had appeared in the previous year, when vain predictions and superstitions pertaining to the Pope and the Church, unscrupulously diffused and utilized by politicians and princes, had sparked serious disorder.[26]

In the final 1637 revision of his most famous text (the *Civitas Solis* in which correspondences between the terrestrial world and aspects of the celestial world play a central role), he introduced a long digression, precisely so as to respond to the perplexities of the Hospitaller, to whom it seemed that the Solarians 'use astrology too much' (*nimis astrologizant*). Having reaffirmed the full philosophical licitness of astrology, given the undeniable role of mediation played by the heavens, and having recalled the diverse levels of causality and the limits on the effects of the stars, the Genoese sailor did not hesitate to accentuate proudly the Solarian invention of a remarkable remedy against astral threats. When threatening celestial events are pending, they suggested recreating a closed, separated, and protected space, a room with white walls, in which aromas, jovial music, and happy conversations might combat the infected seeds that were being diffused from the outside. They also suggested the lighting of seven torches so as to create a private sky, a domestic theater of the world. Even this rapid description was so convincing that the interlocutor could not but recognize the utility and admire the wisdom of the remedy: 'Oh, all these are medical remedies and applied with such wisdom!'[27]

Living and Writing in Rome

The events connected to the publication of the *De siderali fato* meant the end, at least officially, of the short period of Papal favor that Campanella enjoyed. It confirmed once again the fierce hostility towards his books, a fact that had left him profoundly embittered since his arrival in Rome. In the months straddling 1627 and 1628, a real trial was initiated against one of the works that was most dear to him, the *Atheismus triumphatus*.

---

[25] The *Disputatio an Bullae Sixti V et Urbani VIII contra iudiciarios calumniam in aliquo patiantur*, which was published in the volume that also included the *Atheismus triumphatus* (Paris, 1636), pp. 255–273, in *Opuscoli astrologici*, pp. 178–241.

[26] Ibid., pp. 218–220.

[27] See *Civitas Solis*, in Tommaso Campanella, *Città del Sole*, ed. N. Bobbio (Turin, 1941), pp. 160ff.: 162.

The never quite neutralized criticisms against the doctrines of the *De sensu rerum* were renewed. Campanella replied with an able and learned *Defensio*, which would appear with the Parisian republication of the original text. The laborious, but certainly not cold or merely encomiastic, *Commentaria* to the Latin poetry of Urban VIII, completed around 1632, were never published. As Lina Bolzoni (who is in the process of preparing a complete edition) has demonstrated in a persuasive way, they are of interest for several reasons, particularly because they reveal the limitations of judgments that consider the commentaries a work dictated solely by the desire to please the vanity of the Pope. Conducted on several levels, the commentary on the poetry of Urban VIII (which he hoped would be used as a textbook in schools) effects a "deconstruction," of the text that permits the author to enter into ample digressions and insert his own naturalistic, philosophic and theological doctrines – even those that were most doubtful from the point of view of orthodoxy.[28] Within a few years, the *Atheismus* ended up being confiscated. Having arrived at the press between 1630 and 1631 (after overcoming a whole series of obstacles) and even after it had been corrected and reviewed according to the indications of the censors, the text was withdrawn hardly six months after it first appeared. Also very quickly sequestered was the *Monarchia Messiae*, which had been published at Iesi in 1633.

One of the most singular results to derive from Campanella's exasperation at the uproar against his books was a very particular, little known text of the 1630s. Amabile had published some extracts from it,[29] but only recently was it edited in its entirety. The text in question is the *Censure sopra il libro del Padre*

---

[28] Lina Bolzoni, 'La restaurazione della poesia nella Prefazione dei *Commentaria* campanelliani,' *Annali della Scuola Normale Superiore di Pisa*, ser. III (1971), pp. 307–344; Ead., 'I *Commentaria* di Campanella ai *Poëmata* di Urbano VIII. Un uso infedele del commento umanistico,' *Rinascimento*, ser. II, 28 (1988), pp.113–132. Published only in part, the *Commentaria super poëmatibus Urbani VIII* are conserved in mss., Barb. Lat. 1918, 2037, 2048 of the Vatican Library. The *Praefatio* (Barb. Lat. 1918) and the *Commentum in Elegia 'Poësis probis et piis documentis primaevo decori restituenda'* (Barb. Lat. 2048) have been published in Tommaso Campanella, *Opere letterarie*, ed. L. Bolzoni (Turin, 1977), pp. 666–889 (with a facing-page translation); sections of Barb. Lat. 1918 have been published by R. Tirindelli Sferra-Carini in *Letteratura e critica. Studi in onore di Natalino Sapegno*, vol. III (Rome, 1976), pp. 287–316, and C. Ferri, in Tommaso Campanella, *De Sancto Ludovico* (Rome, 1990); the texts of the Barb. Lat. 2037 are contained in Gianfranco Formichetti, *Campanella critico letterario* (Rome, 1983), pp. 47–109; the same author published a section of Barb. Lat. 1918 in G. Formichetti, *I testi e la scrittura* (Rome, 1990), pp. 19-66.

[29] Amabile, *Castelli*, II, doc. 243, pp. 179–185; Firpo, *Bibliografia*, n. 38, pp. 148–149.

Mostro 'Ragionamenti sopra le litanie di Nostra Signora.'[30] The Master of the Sacred Palace, Niccolò Riccardi (or as everyone called him *Padre Mostro*, literally 'Father Monster') was always involved in the persecutions to which Campanella was subjected. Campanella therefore contemplated a kind of retaliation, directed more against the rage of censorship than against the person of his adversary. He decided to proceed in a manner comparable to his enemies. Having extracted a lengthy list of propositions that he held to be erroneous, ridiculous, or decidedly heretical from Riccardi's book entitled *Ragionamenti sopra le litanie di Nostra Signora* (Genoa, 1626), he commented on them and subjected them to a rigorous censure. The result is unnerving. On the one hand, the passages extracted from the original text cannot help but strike us, even after making allowances for baroque taste, for their insipidness and awkwardness. On the other hand, Campanella replied to them with seriousness and punctiliousness – and with a complete absence of lightness and irony. He unmasked the rhetorical tricks employed by the Monster, denouncing its equivocations, its improper metaphors and paradoxes, together with its affected and histrionic language, accusing him of expressing himself like a comedian and of taking pleasure in jokes worthy of a 'buffoon' on the stage. We should recall that Riccardi was a famous preacher, proud of his own 'dexterous' oratory, with which he was able to bring those who listened to him to tears or make them laugh. But Campanella did not permit joking 'about saints.' Right from the proem, he condemned 'the preacher's excuse that it is convenient for him to tell lies with grace and make fun of the sacred for the sake of his listeners' amusement.' In general, he did not hide his own intolerance towards authors such as Lucian or Erasmus, or literary figures such as Boccaccio or Aretino (denouncing also 'the nonsense' with which 'the buffoon Francis Rabelais introduced heresy into France'), when they play games with religion and sacred things – things about which one can argue, certainly, but not joke.[31] The frigid comparisons of Riccardi between paradise and Mary's uterus did not amuse him. He also replied to philosophical errors: glass when it breaks does not break 'into nothing,' but rather 'into pieces'; ideas are not at all illusory, but rather extremely real; one ought not to 'praise' but rather 'honor' virtue.[32] He did not hide his impatience with the exaggeration of 'false honors'

---

[30]Tommaso Campanella, *Censure sopra il libro del Padre Mostro 'Ragionamenti sopra le litanie di Nostra Signora,'* ed. A. Terminelli (Rome, 1998); the edition of the text suffers from many oversights and is questionable in several respects. Among other things, the editor claims improperly to have 'discovered' a manuscript that was already known, cited, and partly published. On the text, see Michele Miele, 'Tommaso Campanella e le *Censure al padre Mostro*,' in *Laboratorio Campanella*, pp. 197–211.

[31] *Censure sopra il libro del Padre Mostro*, pp. 39–40.

[32] Ibid., pp. 88; 67; 104.

attributed to the Virgin, who, even in the exceptionality of her role, continued in her own condition as creature. And he did not fail to put 'maternity' back in the context of 'paternity,' recalling that for Aquinas 'Deus masculinis, non femininis vocabulis est nominandus' ('one should use masculine terms when referring to God, not feminine ones.')

He became even more indignant when Riccardi implied the most serious theological errors in completely inappropriate language, calling Mary 'Maness, Christ-ess, or Goddess,' tending to set her up as a divinity, considering her superior to Christ, making out of her a kind of fourth person in the Trinity.[33] Campanella was equally incensed at the linguistic expedients to which the Monster recoursed. He accused him of attenuating his own audacious affirmations with expressions such as 'very nearly' and 'to put the matter thus.' Campanella made him the butt of a rare and witty joke: 'although he might say, out of fear for the Inquisition, that it is a blasphemy to consider Mary as a fourth person of the Trinity, nevertheless he adds that *being very nearly divine and treated as if she were divine* – such that therefore it is *very nearly blasphemy, as if he were really blaspheming*.'[34] Campanella's text circulated in manuscript to some extent, but never reached the press. In its own way this achieved his aims, by raising some doubts in Roman circles and above all by alarming Riccardi. That Riccardi was indeed alarmed is obvious from the conciliatory – rather unctuous – tones of a famous letter that he wrote to Campanella on 28 November 1638. In that letter, he asserted that he had always had him in his heart, and protested against the improper and arbitrary extrapolation of his propositions, which were 'taken out' of context. This was, of course, precisely the kind of treatment to which Campanella's texts had been subject.[35]

In the autumn of 1631 and 1632, Campanella was able to stay at Frascati, in the institution of the Pious Schools, founded by José of Calasanz, offering lessons to around ten 'clerical students.'[36] Connected to these contacts and this teaching activity was a small work of great elegance. Taking up the defense of the Pious Schools (which intended to extend higher education even among the lower classes), the work responded to a double series of objections, both political and religious, and dealt with a theme that was particularly dear to the

---

[33] Ibid., pp. 68,70.

[34] Ibid., p. 75.

[35] The text of the letter is in an appendix in Ambrosius Eszer, 'Niccolò Riccardi, O.P.- 'Padre Mostro' (1585–1639),' *Angelicum*, 60 (1989), pp. 458–461.

[36] In 1597, the Spaniard José of Calasanz (1558–1648) had founded the Pious Schools at Rome. Their aim was to offer a free education to all, and they were (especially after recognition in 1621 as a regular religious order) highly successful.

author – namely, the education and diffusion of knowledge to every level of society in the broadest possible way.[37]

In the opening lines of the work, Campanella returned once again to a theme that had been a constant in his writing and on which he was now forced to reflect again – namely, the attacks against those who are divinely inspired, do their best, and work for the benefit of men. That extremely useful institutions, such as the Pious Schools, should be criticized from political and religious quarters should come as no surprise, when one considers that when philosophers and prophets, the apostles and even Christ himself, were all victims of accusations and persecution. Campanella had experienced it enough in his own life to know that one was dealing with real slander. He recalled having confronted the issue in a specific treatise that had been dedicated to proving that those who bear witness to the truth and operate for the benefit of other people are persecuted and put to death. Yet later they rise again to fame and glory, and so it was that the world that had assailed them with scourges when they were alive honored them once they were dead.

Politicians insisted on the social harm caused by religious orders in general, accusing them of consuming goods and resources without offering anything in return. More precisely they accused popular schools of subverting the social order. In point of fact, the extension of knowledge to the most humble risked altering the relationship between the working classes and the nobles – for now the nobles would be forced to work in their turn, losing their privileged roles and functions. Before replying to the objections, Campanella launched into a passionate plea in favor of the sciences, to which all we are called and which grow and are perfected as they amplify and expand. The diffusion of knowledge to every level of society cannot but be useful to society as a whole and every government ought to encourage and favor it, rather than putting obstacles in its way. Even he who dedicates himself to practical activity will do it much better if he knows the principles of his own art and his own trade. A painter will be more able if he learns mathematics, and a peasant will be more capable if he knows the rules of agriculture – something, it was worth noting, that had been held in high esteem by the Romans. Generally speaking, it is

---

[37]The work was tracked down and published by Leodegario Picanyol as Tommaso Campanella, *Liber apologeticus contra impugnantes institutum Scholarum Piarum, Ephemerides Calasanctianae* (1932), pp. 170–177, 217–223, 253–258; subsequently, it appeared in L. Picanyol, *Le Scuole Pie e Galileo Galilei* (Rome, 1942), pp. 229–239. There is an Italian translation in Cesare Gamba, *Il pensiero pedagogico della Controriforma*, ed. L. Volpicelli (Florence, 1960), pp. 571–585, and it was translated into English by K. Jensen and A. K. Liebreich, *Archivum Scholarum Piarum*, 8 (1984), pp. 29–76.

advantageous that artisans and workers – from sailors to builders, from cobblers to barbers – understand properly the principles of their own activities and are not only in possession of a merely empirical expertise. Insisting on a very important theme, to which he returned on other occasions, Campanella did not hesitate to assert that only tyrants sustain and support ignorance, for they do so deluded into thinking that it will permit them to dominate their subjects all the more effectively. From that perspective even idolatry and false superstition are arms that work in favor of unjust princes, while belief in the true God and in his wisdom has an emancipatory function.

The responses all proceed along these general lines. The supposed social cost of religious orders is non-existent, in that the religious orders that practice a communitarian life give society much more than the little that they subtract for their own maintenance. The intention of the Pious Schools to invite all, irrespective of their class, to the convivium of the sciences is worthy of the highest praise. With regard to the worries about social order, even Machiavelli admitted that the contests between the plebs and the nobility turned out to be useful when they raise the plebs up to higher office. He admitted likewise that the Roman Republic made great use of this raising up of the lower strata of citizens, even as the opposite happened at Florence – where the nobles abased themselves into the lower orders. It is therefore just that poor pupils should achieve cultural distinction if they are naturally talented. It is a boon for the state that not only nobles occupy the socially most elevated positions, because some of those nobles 'are endowed with obtuse minds that are made worse by negligence.' Laziness is always harmful, on account of which it is a positive thing that the nobility should work. In any case, 'it is just that those who by nature are better be preferred to those who are better only in opinion, in that the plebs of good, natural character are of greater utility than obtuse, negligent nobles.' A shining example of this tendency is provided by (St.) Carlo Borromeo, who admitted both noblemen and the poor into the seminaries that he founded. These pages are yet another example of the polemic against Aristotle and his theorization of a society that legitimizes inequality:

> Aristotle bestows only a temporal happiness and only to a few, almost as if the human genus were divided into different species, one capable of happiness, the other not. But God made the entire human race from one progenitor and promised eternal happiness to all (as the apostle [St. Paul] says) and declared that temporal goods are not enough for the vastness of the human soul. He chooses also those who labor in poverty and in other works; they have a better hope, in fact, in that they are fighting more for victory in this world.

With regard to the religious objections, Campanella contended that they seemed motivated by rivalries between different religious orders, particularly on the part of the Jesuits, who were fearful of an unwelcome competitor in the field of teaching. Those objections perhaps reflected an internal debate on the possible risks of transforming the duties, purposes, and call to poverty of the 'Calasanzians.' On this point too, Campanella could not but reply by reaffirming his praise for knowledge and its diffusion. Those who prohibit the study of the sciences or consider such study useless are not to be listened to – and, furthermore, they are to be rejected entirely. Since Christ is the wisdom of God and all the sciences are rays of the divine Word, Campanella concluded with a happy and synthetic formula (fairly close to the sense of the *Apologia pro Galileo*) according to which 'he who opposes the sciences, opposes Christ.' Aristotle did not permit peasants, artisans, or anyone else who worked for a living to be involved in philosophy, because they were all considered to be servants of society. In making this assertion, Aristotle not only took up a position that was cruel; he also took up a position that was impious and bestial. Anyone who upholds similar doctrines 'abases, obscures, depresses the human race and transforms it into livestock.'[38]

From the Fall of La Rochelle to the Flight to France

While in the prison of Holy Office at Rome, in the spring of 1628, Campanella received a visit from the learned orientalist Jacques Gaffarel (1601–1681), scholar of the cabala and occult doctrines. Having defended the *De sensu rerum* against the attacks of Marin Mersenne, Gaffarel displayed a constancy of friendship and esteem towards Campanella. In 1633, at Venice, he published Campanella's *De reformatione scientiarum Index*. With enthusiasm, he emphasized the novelty of every doctrine from logic to natural philosophy to medicine, from politics to astrology to ethics. He thus highlighted the novelty of an author who, 'for the acuity and almost divine splendor of his spirit, sets out doctrines so varied and remarkable that no one can do anything but admire and exalt the wondrous power of his mind.'[39] Two years later he would have the *Medicina* printed with similar praise at Lyon and dedicate it to Prince Odoardo Farnese. But it was perhaps Gaffarel's account of his encounter with Campanella in prison that contributed most to the diffusion in Europe of the

---

[38] *Ephemerides Calasanctianae,* pp. 176–177, 217–219, 223. Two other theological works date back to the Roman period: the *De conceptione beatae Virginis,* ed. L. Firpo, *Sapienza,* 22 (1969), pp. 82–248; there is also an Italian translation: *Apologia dell'Immacolata Concezione,* ed. A. Langella (Palermo, 2004). The second tract is *De praecedentia, praesertim religiosorum* ed. by Michele Miele in 'Un opuscolo inedito ritenuto perduto di Tommaso Campanella,' *Archivum Fratrum Praedicatorum,* 52 (1982), pp. 267–322.

[39] *De reformatione scientiarum Index* (Venice: Andrea Baba, 1633).

name and condition of Campanella; he reported the episode in a famous page of the *Curiositez inouyes* (1629). Gaffarel evoked the meeting, stressing two points that were closely related and that would both strike the reader. On the one hand, there was the curious process of mimetic identification in the prisoner. Intent on writing a letter, Campanella would reproduce the grimaces and facial expressions of the recipient of the letter, so as to make present to himself the state of mind of that person. On the other hand, there was the horror and emotion of the visitor upon seeing the effects of the tortures. Even years later, the torture sessions had left indelible signs on the body and on the lacerated thighs of the philosopher: 'ayant le gras des jambes toutes meurtries et les fesses presque sans chair, la lui ayant arraché par morceux, afin de tirer de lui la confession des crimes dont on l'accusait.' The wounds were so striking that, at first, they give Gaffarel the incorrect impression that Campanella's facial grimaces were the result of madness and sufferings connected to those events![40]

In the 1630s, Campanella struck up friendships, epistolary or personal, with other French scholars. Particularly important were those with Gabriel Naudé and Pierre Gassendi. Before meeting him at Rome, Naudé had been a precocious reader and admirer of Campanella. Already in 1623, he had praised Tobias Adami, who, in the capacity of a midwife ('sage femme'), had between 1617 and 1623 published a significant number of texts by Campanella, who was called 'phoenix de tous les philosophes et politiques.'[41] A couple of years later, in the *Apologie pour tous les grands personnages qui ont été faussement soupconnés de magie* (1625), Campanella was cited, together with Socrates, Apollonius Tyaneus, Cecco d'Ascoli, and Cardano, among those who, in order to reinforce their own credit with the people, have spread the supposition that the gods take a special interest in their person 'par la continuelle assistance de quelque génie tutelaire et directeur de toutes leurs principales actions.' Reference was being made to the passage in the *De sensu rerum* (3.10) where the author confessed having heard voices in particular instances of danger and to the passage (2.25) in which he alluded, in a rather obscure and reticent way, to the effect of

---

[40] Jacques Gaffarel, *Curiositez inouyes sur la sculpture talismanique des Persanes, horoscope des patriarches et lecture des estoilles* (Paris: H. du Mesnil, 1629), pp. 267–274.

[41] *Instruction à la France sur la verité de l'histoire des Frères de la Rose-Croix* (Paris, 1623), p. 79; at the end of the work (pp. 116–117), translating it into French, Naudé cites a lengthy excerpt polemicizing against the Rosacrucians that he thought belonged to Campanella but that actually is taken from the appendix (anonymous, but in fact the work of the text's translator, Christoph Besold) added to the second German translation of the *Monarchia di Spagna*.

demonic apparitions on his life and his thought.[42] In the *Bibliographia politica* Campanella was numbered among those 'imaginative spirits who endeavored to show us the form, or rather the idea, of a true and most perfect republic.'[43] Having recalled the 'learned' and 'wise' Thomas More, 'whose *Utopia* will live and will be esteemed so long as justice, modesty, and piety are not entirely banished from the spirits and the hearts of men,' Naudé cited the *Civitas Solis*, praising the 'ardent and prodigious spirit' of its author and 'the novelty of its thoughts' as well as 'the sublimity of the feeling' of the work written 'amidst the shadows and squalor of prison.' In the *Considérations politiques sur les coups d'État* (a text largely shot through with Campanellian conceits that are not always explicit), Campanella would be remembered once more for that kind of "secrecy" and astuteness on account of which some thinkers – from Pico to Postel and Cardano – were credited with receiving special assistance from demons. In a further passage, Campanella's name would return in a context that stressed the importance of preaching and eloquence in politics. According to Naudé, the people – which for its irrationality and inconstancy is subject to all the storms of the passions, but which retains its strength – can be deceived and seduced by recourse to visions and prophecies, but above all to the persuasive capacity of the word.[44] In his political works, Campanella too had underlined the power of words, which bind spirits together. The power of words is the first link on which all the other chains of the body and of the goods of fortune depend. In the *De sensu rerum* as well as in the *Rhetorica*, Campanella insisted on the magical force that words exert on the imagination and the passions of he who is listening.[45]

Naudé was able to visit Campanella frequently in the course of his stay in Rome in 1631 and 1632. He showed himself to be an admirer of his erudition and very devoted to his writings, to the point of conserving even notes and rough copies. Under the pressing insistence of his friend, Campanella dictated to him that precious intellectual autobiography that is the *Syntagma de libris propriis* and he passed on to him many pieces of biographical information.[46] Although the *Vita Campanellae* would be lost before it was published, many

---

[42] *Apologie pour tous les grands personnages qui ont été faussement soupçonnés de magie* (Paris: F. Targa, 1625), ch. 3, p. 55; the text (there were various editions and translations in the course of the seventeenth and eighteenth centuries) also appears in the volume *Libertins du XVIIe siècle*, ed. J. Prévot (Paris, 1998); the passage cited appears at p. 166.

[43] (Venice: F. Baba, 1633), p. 35.

[44] *Considérations politiques sur les coups d'Estat* (Rome, 1639; Paris, 1673), pp. 606, 711.

[45] *Rhetorica*, pp. 742–45; see ch. 10, pp. 197–198.

[46] See ch. 1, note 2.

steps in the life of the philosopher can be identified from that emphatic *Panegyricus* addressed to Urban VIII that Naudé published in Paris in 1644.[47] In the midst of erudite citations and excessive adulation directed at the Pope, one encounters passages and information that are of great interest, regarding the failed conspiracy in Calabria and pertaining to the years of imprisonment at Naples. Naudé described these things in a grim and gruesome manner but not without efficacy and emotion, presenting the philosopher against the background of shadowy places, infested with mice and snakes, echoing with the cries of owls and bats. The bleak depiction (unfortunately not so far from the truth) served to confer a greater emphasis on the moral power of the philosopher and on the originality of his thought, born as it was in a condition of extreme isolation and concentration. Unlike birds that fly in the open air and that can make use of the most varied materials for constructing their nests, the philosopher was forced to reach exclusively inwards for his own life-blood – in a manner similar to the spider, which (enclosed in a tower or a cell) constructs its own wondrous thread and by extracting the most deeply hidden juices from its own interior.

Among the *Epigrammata* that Naudé wrote for the philosophers and men of letters of his time (which would accompany the portraits in the collection of Cassiano del Pozzo), there is one that is dedicated to Campanella.[48] In these verses, he emphasized the 'extraordinary appearance of this extraordinary man,' who was characterized by a flamboyant gaze and by an unusually shaped head. This look corresponded well to the originality of his thought; and it was said that 'he who was superior to all in talent/was different from all others in appearance.'[49] Some years after the meeting at Rome, the intense friendship between Campanella and Naudé would be overshadowed by misunderstandings and polemics that Fabri de Peiresc, a friend to both, would

[47] G. Naudé, *Panegyricus dictus Urbano VIII Pont. Max. ob beneficia ab ipso in M. Thom. Campanellam collata* (Parisiis: apud S. et G. Cramoisy, 1644). See Michel-Pierre Lerner, 'Le Panégyrique différé ou les aléas de la notice "Thomas Campanella" des *Apes Urbanae*,' *B&C*, 7 (2001), pp. 413–451.

[48] On the iconography of Campanella, other than the fundamental study by L. Firpo, *L'iconografia di Tommaso Campanella* (Florence, 1964), see Eugenio Canone, 'Il volto di Campanella. Dipinti e incisioni,' in *Laboratorio Campanella*, pp. 241–251.

[49] Gabriel Naudé, *Epigrammata in virorum literatorum imagines* (Rome, 1641), p. 13: 'Effigies miranda viri mirabilis ista est,/si modo naturae par fuit artis opus. /Nam geminas torquent oculi sub vertice tedas/et caput in septem scinditur areolas:/scilicet ingenio potuit qui vincere cunctos/diversam a cunctis possidet effigiem.' There is a new edition of this extremely rare book in Gabriel Naudé, *Epigrammi per i ritratti della biblioteca di Cassiano dal Pozzo,* ed. E. Canone and G. Ernst (Pisa-Rome, 2009).

seek to mediate with some irritation and effort.[50] To the recriminations from Campanella, who accused his friend not only of not having given to the press some writings that he had entrusted to him, but also of having used them to compose his own, Naudé replied with resentful personal attacks, accusing him of being a charlatan and a cheat. In any case, the episode merits being reconsidered in a more balanced and precise way.[51]

If the issues in Campanella that seemed to interest Naudé most pertained to some aspects of his political thought (and in particular those that had to do with rhetoric and religion as powerful forms of magic that work on the passions and imagination of the common people), the intellectual dialogue with Gassendi centered on the problem of atomism and its impossibility – to Campanella's way of thinking – of giving an exhaustive account of reality. Evidence attesting to relations between the two scholars is contained in several letters that date back to the beginning of the 1630s. On 7 May 1632, Campanella – praising Gassendi for having contributed to disclosing the *arcana coeli* that had already in part been disclosed by Copernicus and Galileo – remarked that the schools were occupied by traditional philosophers, who measured everything not according to what nature teaches *(duce natura)*, but according to their own choices *(proprio arbitratu)*, such that they kept the minds of people in the dark, slumbering. Campanella added the most important point towards the end of the letter: if he could not but rejoice that his friend had chased away the 'clouds of Aristotle,' he also could not approve of the way in which he had turned towards the delusions of Epicurus. He warned him that the world was not ruled by chance but was rather guided by wisdom and reason, referring him to his own *Atheismus triumphatus*. In a letter written some time later, Campanella once again emphasized the limitations of the atomist position: in his opinion exceptional celestial phenomena could not be accounted for "in a accidental manner, without the intervention of the author or all things and

---

[50]See Nicolas-Claude Fabri de Peiresc, *Lettres a Naudé (1629–37)*, ed. Ph. Wolfe (Paris-Seattle-Tübingen, 1983).

[51]The reconstruction put forward by René Pintard ought to be reconsidered on many points, *Le Libertinage érudit dans la première moitié du XVIIe siècle* (1943; new ed. Geneva-Paris, 1983). On the relationship between Campanella and Naudé, see Anna Lisa Schino, 'Campanella tra magia naturale e scienza nel giudizio di Gabriel Naudé,' *Physis*, 22 (1980), pp. 393–431; Michel-Pierre Lerner, *Tommaso Campanella en France au XVIIe siècle* (Naples, 1995), pp. 33–36; Lorenzo Bianchi, *Rinascimento e libertinismo. Studi su Gabriel Naudé* (Naples, 1996), pp. 62–70; Id., '*Libertas philosophandi* et République des Lettres: France et Italie à travers les relations entre Naudé et Campanella,' in *Les premiers siècles de la République Européenne des Lettres (1368–1638)*, ed. M. Fumaroli (Paris, 2005), pp. 342–363.

without him doing or saying anything in some way.' He went on to say 'how then can you, such a learned man, ... think that comets and phenomena of such great size come to pass in a purposeless manner on their own account only, without God being their author? Or perhaps you hold that he attends to some things only and not to others?' The scientific explanation of a celestial event cannot exclude the possibility that it also has some value as a sign. The fact that the thought of man can turn itself towards the infinite proves that it is not the result of the clash of material corpuscles. Furthermore, the wondrous 'structure of the world and of animals and of plants and the use of their parts and their force and their understanding – all these things manifest with complete clarity this first power that we call God.' Simply because we are ignorant of the ends and the meanings of many things does not mean that we ought to deny them in the manner of a child who, upon entering the workshop of a blacksmith, is amazed at the sight of objects and instruments that he does not know and that seem to him useless or dangerous. Replying to the letter, Gassendi (having described his interlocutor as *praecipuus* (most excellent) among the philosophers of the day) reassured him on the question of divine providence. He too argued against the Epicureans and he too was 'a Christian and a theologian.' Indeed, he praised the *Atheismus triumphatus*, even if he did not fail to express a degree of concern that malicious persons could make evil use of the antireligious arguments listed in the text.[52]

In a political sense, the years at Rome were a period of repositioning. At first cautiously and then ever more openly, Campanella moved towards the position of France – also defended by Urban VIII. Immediately after the defeat of the Huguenots at La Rochelle by the Most Christian Sovereign on 15 October 1628 (an event marked at Rome by garish celebrations that profoundly irritated the Spanish), Campanella exalted the event in a *Oratio pro Rupella recepta* that has not survived. The work was read aloud in public, however, by someone other than the author – on 1 December 1628, in the Church of San Luigi dei Francesi, the historical church of the French community in Rome, in the presence of the Pope.[53] Another short work followed with the long title

---

[52] *Lettere*, p. 236f; Pierre Gassendi, *Opera omnia* (Lyon, 1658), VI, p. 54. There is a French translation by S. Taussig, in Pierre Gassendi, *Lettres latines* (Turnhout, 2004), I, pp. 95–96. On the relationship between the two scholars, see Germana Ernst, 'Atomes, Providence, signes célestes. Le dialogue epistolaire entre Campanella et Gassendi,' in *Gassendi et la modernité,* ed. S. Taussig (Turnhout, 2008), pp. 61–82.

[53] Regarding the dating of the speech, see Rodolfo De Mattei, 'Note sul pensiero politico di T. Campanella (con tre lettere inedite),' in *Campanella e Vico* (Rome: Accademia Nazionale dei Lincei, 1969), pp. 100–101. On the relationship between Campanella and French circles, both in Italy and in Paris, see Michel-Pierre Lerner, *Tommaso Campanella en France au XVIIe siècle.*

of *Avvertimento al Re di Francia, al Re di Spagna e al Sommo Pontefice circa alli presenti e passati mali d'Italia*. In that work, Campanella distanced himself from the pro-Spanish position and aligned himself cautiously with the French position upheld by the Pontiff. This short treatise probably dates to 1629, when, following the fall of La Rochelle, France felt free enough to return to occupying itself with Italian issues in the most direct way, set itself against the pretenses of Spain, and took an active role in events connected to the intricate affair pertaining to the succession of the Duchy of Mantua. In these pages, Campanella once again energetically deplored the squabbles of the Italian princes, which did nothing but advance the interests and the territorial acquisitions of the enemies of the faith. Thus, the Turkish sovereigns had reinforced and extended greatly their power, taking advantage, with great political astuteness, of the in-fighting with Christendom. Campanella expressed the fear that the renewal of the clash between the French and the Spanish in Italian territory could endanger the security and the very survival of the Kingdom of Naples, which had always been a prize in the sights of foreign powers. Lest it fall victim to their opposing ambitions, Campanella proposed putting the Kingdom in the hands of the Pontiff once again, a solution that obviously would have been warmly welcomed by Urban VIII, who had already for years hoped to add the Kingdom to his own estate and to have his much loved nephew Taddeo govern it after an eventual territorial reorganization following from the weakening of Spain. Beyond contingent events, however, Campanella brought up points that were very important to him and that he had upheld since the years of his youth. He stressed that the Pope was 'a common father' and that princes had nothing to lose in that 'giving to the Church is not giving, but investing in the community.' Campanella insisted on the importance of eliminating the dangerous reasons for conflict between foreign princes by removing from the mouths of the two warring dogs their bone of contention, for this preoccupation prevented them from concentrating on the defense of the Christian flock in a more profitable manner.[54]

Campanella's interest in and understanding of French politics became deeper and more precise thanks to an assiduous frequenting of the circles centered on the French embassy. To the Count of Brassac, Campanella dedicated an important theological treatise (the *De praedestinatione*). At his request, he wrote a commentary on the ninth chapter of the Letter to the Romans, which was one of the hottest points of contention with the Reformers. Indeed, it would be another French ambassador, François de Noailles,

---

[54]The text – published for the first time in Amabile, *Castelli*, II, doc. 241, pp. 168–171– is now in *Tommaso Campanella*, pp. 945–949.

who would organize Campanella's flight to France in the autumn of 1634.[55] The most conspicuous result of this change of position was the lively *Dialogo politico tra un Veneziano, Spagnolo e Francese* composed at Rome towards the end of 1632. In that text, the clash between the positions of the 'Spaniard' and the 'Frenchman' was compared to the more detached and rational position of the Venetian (who was the author's spokesman).[56] It is not improbable that the reading, in the previous summer, of Galileo's *Dialogo sopra i due massimi sistemi del mondo* had had some influence on this stylistic choice. The political discourse was punctuated by repeated naturalistic references. The Spaniard maintains that the efforts of Louis XIII to return France 'to its pristine state of its ancient glory' were vain. The French kingdom was already 800 years old, it was argued. As is true in all organisms, 'the old cannot become young once again,' and whatever 'attempt is made at rejuvenation cannot last.' France had already completed its cycle and could never return to the grandeur of the age of Charlemagne, since it had reached 'the arid period of its arc.' And it is precisely on this account that France is afflicted with discord inside the royal family itself, given that 'in an old body the old parts are not well coordinated, with humors disagreeing and the blood becoming dry.' Furthermore, it has difficulty restoring itself to health. In fact, only a young organism can easily recuperate after 'it suffers some violent scourge, such as war, or internal malady like sedition.' To these arguments, the Frenchman replies by making reference to another naturalistic image: with the passage to the house of the Bourbons, the kingdom of France has begun again 'under new auspices' and has initiated a new cycle in its own history. The same happens when 'onto the trunk of an old plant we graft the sprig of a new and young plant, creating thereby a new age and allowing for growth, together with plentiful fruit.'[57]

With the possibility assured in a preliminary way that the French monarchy might play a decisive role in European politics, the Venetian will ably demonstrate in the course of the dialogue that France, despite its difficulties and disagreements,

---

[55] *Expositio super cap. IX Epistulae Sancti Pauli ad Romanos*, in *Atheismus triumphatus* (Paris, 1636), pp. 327–344; there is a modern edition in Paolo Ponzio, 'Predestinazione divina e volontà umana. L'*Expositio super Cap. IX Epistulae Sancti Pauli ecc.* di Tommaso Campanella,' in *Verum et Certum. Studi di storiografia filosofica in onore di Ada Lamacchia*, ed. C. Esposito et al. (Bari, 1998), pp. 369–413, 389–413.

[56] Rodolfo De Mattei, in 'Intorno al *Discorso* (o *Dialogo*) *sui rumori di Francia* attribuito a T. Campanella,' *Atti dell'Accademia Nazionale dei Lincei*, Rendiconti, s. VIII, 26 (1972), pp. 583–588, has cast doubt on the authenticity of the *Dialogo*. In his opinion, the understanding of French personalities and affairs is too detailed. But Campanella could have obtained such precise information from the diplomatic circles that he frequented – diplomatic circles that might have prompted him to draft the *Dialogo*, furnishing him with appropriate material.

[57] *Dialogo politico tra un Veneziano*, p. 955f.

is entering into an ascendant phase, while Spain displays all the symptoms of crisis and decline. With these positions, Campanella announced themes that would be central in the following years. He revealed with clarity (and not without risk) that the years were now long gone in which he identified the Spanish sovereign with the mystical Cyrus, from whom the work of rebuilding a new Jerusalem and gathering together the peoples of the world into a single flock was expected. The chief motive of the work is a defense of the person and the actions of Cardinal Richelieu against the accusations of the Queen mother, Marie de' Medici, and her son Gaston d'Orléans, the younger brother of the King and next in line for the throne. On account of their intense hostility towards the growing power of the Cardinal, they had put themselves at the forefront of a politics of opposition to and confrontation with the sovereign. Deploring this dangerous discord (which, dismembering the ruling family itself, risked paralyzing the energies of the entire nation), Campanella showed how the initiatives of Richelieu were all directed not egotistically at the acquisition of personal power, but rather at reinforcing the state against the forces that attacked its unity and at the constitution of an ever more unified 'political body.' In his interventions, the Venetian rebutted the accusations against the Cardinal with precision, both on the Spanish side and on the French. He demonstrated how his politics of centralizing and consolidating power was inspired by a desire to return France to its ancient glory and splendor. In this way, Richelieu was acting as a faithful instrument of the King and was not motivated, as his enemies insinuated, by an unbridled personal ambition that aimed at excluding him from power. But this project, which privileges 'the common good' over the good of the individual, unleashed suspicions and resentments. As Campanella pointed out in a page of acute psychological analysis, one of the most difficult things for man consists in 'rejecting love of self in preference for the common good.' This is so much more true in those who set themselves one against another so as to acquire the same prize. If 'natural similitude induces love, similitude in claims on goods leads to hatred'; heat fights against cold precisely because both would like to occupy the same matter. One can witness such things within the family too, where 'the children all envy one another with each claiming the attention of the father and his patrimony.' Above all, such things are evident 'at court, where all are chasing the goodwill of the lord in order to acquire those goods that are customarily given to courtiers, and yet among them one finds the greatest jealousy and inextinguishable thirst.' Wives hate those who are loved by their husbands and they hate most intensely their direct rivals, and despise with 'a most rabid hatred' the ruffians 'who share the love of the husband about or alienate it to others.'[58] One ought not to be surprised, therefore, that Richelieu was hated by the relatives of the King. The more a counselor is a virtuous person and exhorts the prince to high and honorable undertakings, the more he is unpopular with the relatives of the prince, who aim only at their own good. And it is for this reason that 'powerful men have no greater enemies for their own glory than their own blood-relations.' These sympathies for France would be reaffirmed some months later, when Campanella replied by means of a Latin couplet to another couplet that accused the French sovereign of being as cruel as Nero and the Turk put together (the first a matricide, the second a murderer of his siblings). If the crimes of Nero and the Turk were so much more odious because they were perpetrated against innocents, then on the contrary the French sovereign showed the greatest piety and generosity in forgiving his own family members even though they were guilty.[59]

But between 1633 and 1634 dramatic new events would bring the period at Rome brusquely to a close. In August of 1633 Tommaso Pignatelli was jailed at Naples. Pignatelli was a young Calabrian Dominican who was accused of having plotted a conspiracy against the Spanish. Since he had been a disciple of Campanella, renewed suspicions began to take shape, together with threats from the Spanish authorities. When, in the Autumn of 1634, Pignatelli was condemned to death (and was in fact strangled in prison on 6 October), the situation escalated to such an extent that it was deemed opportune, even by the Pope, to expatriate Campanella to France. Campanella was aided by Ambassador François de Noailles, in whose carriage – at night, disguised as a Minim friar, and under a false name – Campanella fled on 21 October 1634 from Rome to Livorno, where he boarded ship, bound for France.

---

[58] Ibid., p. 962f.
[59] *Poesie*, p. 609f.

12. THE PARIS YEARS

The Arrival in France and the Stay in Paris

After disembarking at Marseilles, Campanella wrote a letter in Latin to the Provençal scholar Nicolas-Claude Fabri de Peiresc on 29 October 1634, informing him of his arrival on French soil and alluding in a laconic manner to the grave matters that had forced him to abandon Rome so precipitously – without even having had time to bid farewell to his friends.[1] Peiresc had contacted Campanella by letter the previous year, in order to ask for his opinion of Herbert of Cherbury's *De veritate*, a letter in which Peiresc had expressed his admiration to the Dominican friar for 'such exquisite work and such sublime thoughts.'[2] Having received the letter in which Campanella manifested his own lively desire to meet as soon as possible with such a patron and protector of the learned, Peiresc hurried to send him a litter that brought him to his home in Aix, where he hosted him for about ten days. As Gassendi (who would himself also be invited to Aix for the purpose of meeting the Dominican) would later recall, Peiresc welcomed the exile with a generosity and affection that elicited from Campanella the deepest emotion and gratitude. When, after several days, Campanella resumed his journey to Paris, he was overcome with emotion upon receiving a sum of money. He confessed that, if in the past he had had the capacity to hold himself back from tears even during the most cruel tortures, he could not hold them back now after

---

[1] *Lettere*, pp. 247–248. Érudit and collector of books and ancient objects, Nicolas-Claude Fabri de Peiresc (1580–1637) was a counselor to the Parlement of Aix-en-Provence and correspondent to all the scholars of Europe; see Peter N. Miller, *Peiresc's Europe. Learning and Virtue in the Seventeenth Century* (New Haven and London, 2000); on his connections with Italy, see Cecilia Rizza, *Peiresc e l'Italia* (Turin, 1965), esp. pp. 239–273.

[2] Amabile, *Castelli*, II, doc. 313, pp. 248–249. From 1626, Peiresc hurried to acquire all the works of the Dominican available on the market. There is evidence of this desire to collect Campanella's works in a volume, recently identified, which brings together four of his works rebound with Peiresc's monogram; see, Michel-Pierre Lerner, 'Un recueil d'oeuvres de Campanella dans la bibliothèque de Peiresc,' *B&C*, 11 (2005), pp. 101–110.

G. Ernst, *Tommaso Campanella*, International Archives of the History of Ideas / Archives internationales d'histoire des idées 200, DOI 10.1007/978-90-481-3126-6_12, © Springer Science + Business Media B.V. 2010

such a generous gesture from a friend.[3] In a passage from the *Oeconomica*, he would later affirm that he who gives his own money ought to be thought of as a greater friend than he who offers his own life. This is what Peiresc, glory of the French as well as of philosophers and patron of famous men, had done.[4]

After a brief stop at Lyon, where he checked the printing of the *Medicina* (which was underway), Campanella resumed his journey to Paris and arrived there on 1 December. During the first weeks, he stayed in the home of the Bishop of Saint Flour. Thereafter, he set himself up in the reformed Dominican convent, in the rue St. Honoré. In his first letter to Peiresc from the capital, while reporting to him the warm welcome he had received ('I am the beneficiary of continual acts of care, beneficence, loving duties and visits from great men and scholars'), Campanella announced a meeting with Richelieu set for the next day, while also showing a great satisfaction at the pleasant nature of place, climate, and persons:

> I admired the scale of France, its mountains and its plains ... together with the fecundity of the hills and the usefulness of the ranges, the bountifulness of the plains that can provide bread for four kingdoms – and I have not yet felt cold. In fact, one finds all the lands right up to Paris verdant and flourishing, a sign of the wonderful temperateness. One notes the variety of land in its texture, color, and manner of being worked. For its abundance of meats and butters, it is superior; and all of its people are happy. I do not find either complaints or sadness, except among those boys who emerge from every village, hamlet, and tavern pleading for charity – but then immediately they proceed to laugh.[5]

On the following 9 February, he would be received by the Most Christian King, Louis XIII, who embraced him twice, welcomed him to France, and displayed a joy at the encounter and an empathy for the misfortunes that had befallen the exile: 'he laughed with happiness and at the same time showed compassion for my troubles,' said Campanella, 'and empathized with a kingly decorum.'[6]

In the years spent in Paris, Campanella's literary activity flourished to a surprising degree. He took part in philosophical and scientific debates, such as that on the size of the mathematical point, composing the *Quaestio singularis*

---

[3]Pierre Gassendi, *Viri illustris Nicolai Claudii Fabricii de Peiresc... Vita* (Paris, 1641), pp. 289–290: '...sed accepit etiam discedens quinquaginta aureos, adeo ut tanta beneficentia obrutus, et quasi suffusus, testatus fuerit se prius quidem habuisse satis constantiae, ut per tormenta saevissima continere lacrymas posset, at non habuisse, quando est virum adeo munificum expertus.'

[4]*Oeconomica*, in *Phil. realis*, p. 210.

[5]Letter dated 11 December 1634, in *Lettere*, pp. 261–263.

[6]Letter to Peiresc dated 9 March 1635, *Lettere*, p. 272.

in reply to the question circulated among the learned by Jean-Baptiste Poysson d'Angers.[7] He added a fulsome appendix to the sixth article of the twentieth physiological question on the causes of the flooding of the Nile following a reading of the text by Marin Cureau de la Chambre, who years later would publish a volume of his own in response to the argument contained in Campanella's fragment.[8] He maintained a regular correspondence with Rome, in which he complained to the Pope and the Cardinals about old intrigues and new persecutions.[9] He sent vivid letters to the French sovereign and to the King's sister Henrietta Maria, married to Charles I of England. He composed eloquent dedicatory epistles for the volumes of his own *Opera*, which – amid myriad difficulties – began to appear, to his great satisfaction. Furthermore, we see a significant reprise of Campanella's political thought and a renewal of his poetic voice after a long silence. On the occasion of the long-awaited birth of the Dauphin (at the first news of the event Campanella had written: 'here one experiences a great joy and celebration on account of the Queen's miraculous pregnancy'),[10] he composed an inspired Latin *Ecloga* in which he took up once again astrological and prophetic themes that had always been dear to him. Conscious that even being exiled on French soil had its own significance and aware that at Paris he was completing the cycle of his extraordinary human and philosophical experience, Campanella did not hesitate to interpret even the long detention in the prisons of Naples in terms of a divine wisdom as he dedicated the huge tome of the *Philosophia realis* to the Grand Chancellor Pierre Séguier. Likewise, the arrival in France – homeland of liberty – was read as the result of a 'prodigious fate.' Cast into solitude, stripped of normal contacts with the world and with men, far from any everyday happiness, he found the kind of concentration that was necessary for bringing to completion the great project of reforming the entire encyclopedia of knowledge, a project that he had envisioned even in the years of his youth:

> My mind, a terrain well prepared by persecution, had nourished deep roots. But it would never have been able to bear fruit if God had not liberated me with a miracle far more wondrous than the cunning stratagem that permitted Ulysses to escape from the cave of Polyphemus, when I was able

---

[7]See Paolo Ponzio, 'Tommaso Campanella e la *Quaestio singularis* di Jean-Baptiste Poysson,' *Physis*, 34 (1997), pp. 71–97; the text of the *quaestio* is to be found in Amabile, *Castelli*, II, pp. 297–299; it is reproduced in *Mathematica*, ed. A. Brissoni (Rome-Reggio Calabria, 1989), pp. 92–94.

[8]*Phil. realis*, pp. 200–204; see Firpo, *Bibliografia*, p. 94.

[9]See especially the letter in which he sketched a portrait of General Niccolò Ridolfi, unmasking his plots, in *Lettere*, pp. 282–295 (see ch. 11, note 14).

[10]Letter to Filippo Colonna dated 10 January 1638, in *Lettere 2*, p. 138.

to complete the book on the ages of ages, crowning achievement of every science. And while at Rome again, with the benevolence of the most wise Pontiff, I wore myself out bringing to light works completed with divine inspiration – divinely, I say, since I summon men to God as the master, and not to me or any other man. Then once again, innocent though I was (as everyone agreed), disaster struck and I was forced, by a kind of prodigious fate, to come to the most Christian kingdom of France, homeland of liberty.[11]

Through his letters, Campanella maintained relations with scholars, such as Cassiano dal Pozzo, Fabri de Peiresc, and the chancellor Pierre Séguier. Of particular importance is the correspondence with the Provençal érudit, which continued after the meeting in Aix. In such letters, Campanella replied to questions that had been put to him by his kind and learned correspondent. Campanella would inform him of his own encounters with the most illustrious personages of the capital and volunteer information on the publication of his works, sending him exemplars at the first opportunity and communicating to him his desire to dedicate one of them to him, so as to demonstrate thereby his gratitude to a man he called 'a great light for his speculative and moral powers.'[12] But his friend would refuse the offers of a dedication, saying that he did not seek 'such vanities,' and that for him 'the love of friends without such pomp' sufficed.[13]

These reciprocal professions of esteem and sympathy suffered a sudden rupture in the summer of 1635, when Peiresc felt himself duty-bound to write a very severe letter to Campanella after receiving some troubling information. Already in a letter to Naudé that dated from the end of June, Peiresc had had very harsh words to say about the friar, who – he felt – failed to practice the precepts of his own moral philosophy. In a letter to Campanella dated 3 July, he criticized the Dominican, on account of alleged derision for the atomistic doctrines held by Gassendi, warning him that 'from principles that may appear ridiculous one can sometimes recognize the most weighty and exquisite things.' Peiresc asked Campanella to weigh with greater caution his own judgments when conversing with French scholars, reminding him that in France there is 'the greatest freedom for one man to choose one opinion and another man another.' In a subsequent letter, he argued that, given the brevity of human life, it was not worth the trouble to invest one's own energies in refuting the doctrines of others. It was more profitable to prize the good that

---

[11] Letter dated 6 August 1637 to Chancellor Séguier, in *Lettere*, pp. 379–380.

[12] Letter dated 11 December 1634, in *Lettere*, p. 261. The letters of Peiresc to Campanella are in Amabile, *Castelli*, II, doc. 313–324, pp. 248–259.

[13] Amabile, *Castelli*, II, doc. 321, p. 257.

one could find in every philosophy and, leaving aside inopportune and tiresome polemics, it was better to limit oneself 'to teaching that which the light of nature has been able to make clear to you.'[14]

Very much embittered, Campanella rushed to reply, defending himself with passion and dignity against the criticisms that were leveled against him and that seemed to him to be derived from intolerable slanders. Emphasizing the coherence of his own doctrines with his way of living ('I observe whatever I wrote in the new *Ethics*'), he reaffirmed his admiration and esteem for his friend Gassendi, even as he said once again that atomism seemed insufficient to him on many counts, in that it limited itself to a consideration of the 'matter of the universe' without taking into account 'the wondrous skill' exhibited in the cosmos. With regard to liberty, Campanella noted, he who has been brutally deprived of liberty for so many years not only respects it but also prizes it to the point that he comes to France precisely because he 'thirsts' for liberty 'after so many troubles.' He declared himself fully in agreement with regard to the respect one owes to philosophical positions different from one's own. Echoing images from a famous letter to Monsignor Querenghi written many years earlier, Campanella reaffirmed the principles that inspired his new philosophy and at the same time expressed an interesting judgment on Galileo and the Copernican system:

> I never fail to learn something from ants, from flies and from all the minute creatures of nature, and yet as Your Lordship can see I hate to learn from men ... And I see that in the most disdained sects of philosophy there are wonderful thoughts. And when I examine those doctrines it is necessary that I move on to confute them, as Galileo did with Copernicus – and one should note that in this matter simple caution did not suffice for him. But I place these sects in the theater of the world for the good of all ... I call all to the school of God, in the book of the universe, where God writes his concepts and dogmas in living form. I call them away from the schools of men (and indeed from my own school), and I beseech them not to mistake me for some master – *unus magister vester qui in coelis est* ('your one master who is in heaven') – but rather to dedicate themselves to the school of God.[15]

The regret that Campanella displayed was so sincere and heartfelt that Peiresc could not help concluding that the matter was closed. A month later, Campanella could put his mind at rest in the knowledge that he had not lost a friend.[16] In the first half of the nineteenth century, three letters to Peiresc from 1636

---

[14] Ibid., doc. 321, p. 255–257; doc. 322, p. 258.
[15] Letter to Peiresc dated 17 July 1635, in *Lettere*, pp. 316–321: 318–319; see Mt 23, 8.
[16] Letter to Peiresc dated 22 August 1635, *Lettere*, p. 322.

kept in the Biliothèque Nationale in Paris were removed by Guglielmo Libri, the adventurous and unscrupulous count of Florentine origin, whose unbridled passion for manuscripts and rare books induced him to ransack the libraries of France and remove great quantities of precious materials. The third letter (cited above, dated 19 June), the most sought after, has been traced in recent years and added to the first two letters tracked down and published by Firpo. In this way, the wound inflicted by Libri on the correspondence between Campanella and Peiresc has been healed completely.[17]

The renewal of political interests of the French years is also reflected in the letters, as in the eloquent appeal to Henrietta Maria of Bourbon, married to Charles I, in which Campanella – returning to a theme that he held close to his heart (namely, the denunciation of the negative consequences for political life stemming from the Protestant doctrine of predestination) – encouraged the Queen to work on her consort so as to advance the cause of the Catholic religion, which, in his opinion, was the only faith compatible with a peaceful political organization.[18]

Also connected to the lively political interests of Campanella's last years were the two tracts of 1636, found by Firpo in a codex containing seven political writings from the period. Firpo himself vividly described his adventurous trip to Paris hot on the heels of a codex that was pursued, lost, and finally recovered.[19] In the first tract, Campanella answered the request of an unknown gentleman who was asking for explanations of 'the prodigy and paradox' by virtue of which the empire of Spain (by then exhausted and in economic collapse) continued to extend itself throughout the world, while the dominion of the French – which was clearly 'superior in population, riches, military valor, and armaments' – struggled to maintain its natural borders. The second is a passionate appeal to the sovereign Louis XIII, which – as Firpo emphasized – is more than a private communication and is written as a 'genuinely political pamphlet,' directed at influencing public opinion. Campanella intended to dissuade the

---

[17] See ch. 1, note 14; ch. 2, note 41.

[18] See the letter dated 10 January 1637 (and 2 June 1638), in *Lettere 2*, pp. 126–136, 151–157.

[19] Firpo gave notice of the rediscovery and the acquisition of the codex, publishing three of the seven manuscripts it contained, in 'Gli ultimi scritti politici del Campanella,' *Rivista Storica Italiana*, 63 (1961), pp. 772–801. The two tracts of 1636 are published in Id., 'Idee politiche di Tommaso Campanella nel 1636 (Due memoriali inediti),' *Il Pensiero politico*, 19 (1986), pp. 197-221: 207-221; see also Id., 'Gli "Opuscoli" del Campanella,' in *Tommaso Campanella (1568-1639). Miscellanea di Studi nel IV centenario della sua nascita* (Naples, 1969), pp. 301–337: 312ff. Regarding the journey to Paris, see Enzo Baldini's vivid reconstruction, 'Luigi Firpo e Campanella: cinquant'anni di ricerche e pubblicazioni,' *B&C*, 2 (1996), pp. 325–358: 336–337; on the publication of the last two unpublished writings, see note 26 below.

sovereign from signing a peace treaty with Spain, which he presented as ruinous and humiliating even as many others hoped for its ratification after the repeated defeats of the French army. Firpo believed these to be among the most beautiful pages in the rediscovered political writings, in which 'the humble foreign friar' put himself forward as the authentic moral conscience of the country that was hosting him. Firpo emphasized the particular oratorical power of the letter's peroration, in which the French sovereign is exhorted to take up decisively the role of *liberator orbis* (liberator of the world) against the tyranny of the Spanish (who are characterized as oppressors and destroyers of the human race). And, in an eloquent passage, Firpo pointed out that here it is not simply the political advisor who speaks, the shrewd purveyor of themes of anti-Habsburg propaganda. Instead it is the old Calabrian conspirator, witness to the oppression of the kingdom and prisoner in Neapolitan castles, who gives voice to his bursting indignation and fights lest a great opportunity for liberation be wasted.[20]

From Spanish Decline to French Hegemony

Campanella did not fail to return the warm welcome he had received from scholars and from the court, taking up political reflection again with a renewed passion. Thus, we see, in the course of the two-year period from early 1635 to late 1636, a surprising flowering of works of varying lengths, styles, and persuasiveness that are nevertheless united by a reaffirmation of consistent themes and by the exhortation directed at France to see itself as the paladin of liberty against the tyranny of the Hispanic-Habsburg power, the inexorable decline of which Campanella pointed out with lucidity.

Already in the spring of 1635, he sent to the Pope the quick-witted *Aforismi politici per le presenti necessità di Francia*, which would later be translated into Latin and amplified, informing the Pope that he had 'given [the *Aforismi*] in secret to the Cardinal.'[21] In the following year, Richelieu himself would commission a discourse entitled *De auctoritate Pontificis supra imperio instituendo et mutando* from Campanella. The philosopher had the honor of presenting this discourse at a lecture on 8 June 1636, at Conflans, in the presence of leading dignitaries of the realm and the Cardinal himself.[22] Campanella paid homage to Richelieu in the new edition of the *De sensu rerum*, dedicated to

---

[20] Firpo, 'Idee politiche,' p. 20; the letter to the King is also in *Lettere 2*, pp. 126–130, 151–154.

[21] See the letter to Urban VIII dated 23 April 1635, in *Lettere*, p. 297.

[22] For the Conflans discouse, see the letter to Francesco Barberini dated 15 July 1636, in *Lettere*, p. 349; John M. Headley, 'Tommaso Campanella's Military Sermon before Richelieu at Conflans – 8 June 1636,' *Archiv für Reformationgeschichte*, special issue *Die Reformation in Deutschland und Europa: Interpretationen und Debatten*, 84 (1993), pp. 553–574.

him with the highest praise as someone who 'out of a divided, dismembered realm that was infested with nests of impious and rebellious men' had made 'a united kingdom, home to the good, scourge of the bad, secure bulwark for the Christian Church, and refuge of the Muses' thanks to his own remarkable prudence and to the power of a most pious and most strong king.[23] The year 1635 also saw the appearance of the *Documenta ad Gallorum nationem*, a treatise in which it was imagined that Charlemagne himself had returned to his own nation, so as to underscore the merits of the present sovereign and his ministers, together with the insidiousness of the Spanish political agenda.[24]

To these years dates the drafting of a vast work, untitled and incomplete, that we may refer to as the *Monarchia di Francia* and the texts of 1636 recovered by Luigi Firpo.[25] The last two unpublished writings of the codex have appeared recently. We are dealing here with two groups of brief texts, in which the style and argumentation seem at points to grow obscure, but they testify to the renewed energy of these years. The first group includes the three discourses that the author directed towards the Christian princes, so as to exhort them to reconsider once again their relationships with the papacy and so as to demonstrate to them how it might be advantageous and necessary to enter into relations of alliance and full accord with the Pontiff, who is put forward as the guarantor of peace and justice, defender of their rights, and the cause of union and defense against enemies of the faith. The final cluster of texts bears the title *Avvertimenti a Venezia*, and it deals, in a lucid synthesis, with various points of prime and constant importance in Campanella's thought concerning the connections between theological and political beliefs.[26]

At the core of the political reflection of this period we find a comparative analysis of the two great European powers, from which it was inferred that France found itself in an ascendant phase of 'increasing fortunes,' while Spain was experiencing an inexorable decline, as can be seen in the comparison of the two powers sketched in an effective and direct style in the exordium to the *Aforismi politici per le presenti necessità di Francia*:

1. In all wars, ventures, and negotiations that are done with speed and promptness, the French win and the Spanish lose.
2. In all wars and matters that are done slowly or by procrastinating, the Spanish win.
3. When undertakings and negotiations are conducted in secret, the Spanish win.

---

[23] The dedication is also to be found in *Lettere*, pp. 372–374: 373.

[24] The text of the *Documenti* is in *Opuscoli inediti*, pp. 57–103.

[25] See note 19.

[26] See Germana Ernst, 'Ancora sugli ultimi scritti politici di Campanella. I. Gli inediti *Discorsi ai principi* in favore del Papato,' *B&C*, 5 (1999), pp. 131–153: 137–153; 'II. Gli *Avvertimenti a Venezia* del 1636,' ibid., pp. 447–465: 452–465.

4. When such matters are brought out into the open, the French win.
5. It is said that, for the most part, the Spanish are by nature cunning; the French, courageous. But sometimes, by accident, these characteristics can be inverted.
6. He who plays his own game wins; he who plays the game of others loses – as when one plays strap with gypsies, which is their stock in trade.
7. Thus, when the Spanish play in the open and with speed, they lose; and the French lose when the game is played in secret and slowly.
8. The Spaniard is more apt to conserve; the Frenchman, to conquer.
9. Thus, all the great acquisitions of the Spanish have come from intrigue or marriage, and under the guidance of Italian captains; the preservation of French gains ought to be done in the same manner.
10. Engaging in combat with someone whose fortune is on the rise is extremely dangerous, even though he who is attacked is not powerful. And attacking he who is without fortune renders victory easy, even though he who is attacked is more powerful.
11. One recognizes the ebb and flow of fortune from events, stars, and from the nature of similar cases – and likewise from the origin, present state, and decline of principalities.
12. A principality that is dying under its own, old auspices can renew itself by using foreign, young auspices.
13. One ought to reckon that the aged power of the French under the house of Valois is being rejuvenated under the house of Bourbon, just as when a new branch is grafted onto an old one.
14. And one ought to reckon also that the power of Spain, dying under the royal houses of Castile and Lusitania, has been rejuvenated by the House of Austria, which has been tied to it.
15. Things that grow quickly, die quickly, as one sees in mushrooms, melons, grains, and the like, whereas on the contrary those trees that bear fruit only with time live long – as one sees with oaks, orange trees, and the like.
16. The monarchy of Spain grew with great speed; in 100 years it occupied more lands than the Romans occupied in 700 – whence one can conclude that it is by now in a state of decline.[27]

The formation itself of the empire – which had come to pass remarkably quickly (thanks to exceptionally favorable external conditions such as marriages, successions, heredity, and the aggregations of states) – could not but cause astonishment. Indeed, 'all false things that have more appearance than reality are quick to grow and quick to fail,' as one sees in torrents that, gener-

---

[27]The *Aforismi* (composed in 1635 and published for the first time by Amabile, *Castelli*, II, doc. 344, pp. 291–297) now in *Tommaso Campanella*, pp. 999–1007: the passage cited is at p. 1000.

ated by sudden rains, rise and disappear with great speed, while 'great rivers that have their own source of water are perpetual.' Products such as 'marrows, melons, and oats grow quickly and bear fruit in the first year, and then die in the summer,' while trees such as the oak and the beech that bear fruit only with time live a long life.[28]

But for Campanella there were two points above all that more dramatically announced the fatal decline of Spain: it knew neither how to 'hispanisize' nor how to accumulate savings. If the Romans were masters of assimilating populations piecemeal, rendering them participants in the empire (such that the larger it became territorially, the more its population of citizens grew), the Spanish, on account of their immense arrogance, disdained any integration with other populations whatsoever. Thus, as their empire grew they came to 'lack citizens and forces.' Having failed to adopt the wise politics of mixed marriages proposed in the *Monarchia di Spagna*, the Spanish Empire experienced an alarming demographic contraction, due to the losses of troops in war and on account of the sterility of its women, who were subject to excessive heat. Thus, the Spanish, from the eight million that they had been, were now reduced by half and 'just as marrows and grains send all of their substance, juice, and spirit outwards without setting down roots (such that luxuriating and dilating they deflate and grow old), so Spain had sent all its power and life-blood beyond its borders and was left without inhabitants and without value – left only with clergy, friars, priests, monks, and whores.'[29] Owing to the scarcity of inhabitants they are forced (and in Campanella's opinion it was a very grave consequence) to depopulate the countries in which they arrived, 'such that there are no longer any indigenous peoples in Cuba, in Hispaniola, nor in South America; they are called destroyers of the human race, and they make themselves the object of hatred.' Chosen by occult divine providence to evangelize the entire globe, the Spanish have betrayed their own mission so as to transform themselves into executioners and instruments of divine wrath. Incapable of governing nations with laws adapted to their own particular nature, 'they depopulate and destroy them, such that wherever they have gone, they have made a desert of the earth … and are hated by every nation for their cruelty and immense arrogance.'[30] They 'destroy the nations that are not able to adjust to their customs, as they did in the New World, which was rendered desolate on their account.' They leave nothing behind them but desolation and death: 'you go to the Americans and in those immense lands you

---

[28] *Mon. Francia*, pp. 461–462.

[29] Ibid., p. 463.

[30] Ibid., pp. 451, 395.

will not find living beings any more, but rather only bones and ashes, and the land grown fat on the blood of its inhabitants.'[31]

The second point, which condemns the politics of Spain even more gravely, is its incapacity to accumulate savings and its ruinous economic policy. Its enormous income is badly administered, and infinite sums of money are wasted on 'buffoons, women, *piazze morte* (deadheads), clergymen, and a treacherous people.'[32] As early as the *Monarchia di Spagna* Campanella had asserted that 'we can say that in truth the gold of the New World has in part ruined the old world, because it created avarice in our minds and broke the reciprocal love between men.' In the later works, Campanella reaffirmed that the influx of riches had rendered social inequality (and the vices that come along with it) more extreme.[33] That influx had contributed to the abandoning of agriculture and the trades, activities already gravely compromised due to the banishments of the Moors and the Jews, such that all preferred to give themselves over to 'business deals involving money and serving rich men' rather than work itself.[34] Valuable coins passed into France, for the purchasing of foodstuffs, or so as to corrupt political leaders. Thus, while the rival nation abounded with people, with money, and with goods of all kinds, Spain offered to the visitor an ever more miserable spectacle. Men were forced to enlist, so as to have something to eat and a pair of shoes to put on their feet (and only the most fortunate also had laces to tie them) and 'the homes are few, either deserted or fallen into disrepair. Even where the population is low, there is nothing to eat and sometimes things get to the point that blinded by hunger they kill each other so that the one may rob the other of a piece of bread.'[35]

The most dramatic results of this unwise economic policy could be confirmed precisely in southern Italy, of which Campanella repeatedly painted a desolate picture. He had not spared Spanish misgovernment from harsh criticism in some pages of the *Monarchia di Spagna*. In the first of the *Arbitri sopra le entrate del Regno* from many years earlier he had exhorted the sovereign to assume the true and natural function of father and pastor to his people by eliminating at its roots the most odious of speculative businesses: the commerce of grain, which subjected citizens to hunger and desperation. Dearth, Campanella asserted, does not come from nature or God, who gives to each country a supply of grain sufficient to keep it from hunger. It comes instead

---

[31] Ibid., p. 459; *Documenta ad Gallorum nationem*, in *Opuscoli inediti*, p. 95.

[32] *Mon. Francia*, p. 447. In mercenary armies, the post of a purely nominal soldier who was paid but did not exist was called a *piazza morta*.

[33] Ibid., p. 161.

[34] Ibid.

[35] *Documenta*, pp. 91–92.

from merchants and from usurers, who acquire the whole supply in order to store it and resell it at triple the price. When 'they do not find the profit their greed lusts after,' they prefer storing it and let it rot:

> And then they sell it putrefying or mixed with other grains and invite in this way not only famine but also pestilence. This has the effect of depopulating the country, because some flee the Kingdom altogether, while others become robbers and bandits simply in order to eat, and still others die from that noxious food, or from eating poisonous plants. Oppressed by usurers, hunger, disease, and troubles, many do not take wives so as not to pass on such miseries to their children, while women become whores in return for a piece of bread.[36]

References to the Kingdom of Naples return in the later political writings too. In the ninth chapter of the *Documenta*, a particularly striking image of southern Italy is conjured. The French subjects, who complain of incessant tributes (which are in truth used for the purpose of augmenting the strength and glory of the nation), ought to consider what happens in the unhappy Kingdom of Naples, where 'the greed and arrogance of the Spanish set the standards for what is just and what is permissible.' In Naples, more taxes are paid than goods are possessed; there, every last person – even the poorest, without home, without field, who lives from his own labor – pays twenty ducats simply 'to carry his own head on his neck.' There, every month, taxes go up indiscriminately on every good, both natural and manufactured, both bought and sold. He who earns fifteen 'carlino' coins by extracting the thread of silk from cocoons with great effort has to hand over eleven to the tax collector. There, one pays both for real goods and for imaginary ones too. In Apulia, the king buys land from peasants in order to sell it to pastoralists and then sells it back to the peasants at a much higher price arguing that it has been fertilized by the pastoralists' sheep. By now, almost no one is the owner of the house he lives in or the field he ploughs, and even other goods are sold for small amounts of money to usurers or the Genoese, who collect the taxes:

> Therefore unfortunate souls are forced to work the fields of others so as to be able to eat and so as to pay their personal tribute; and if that is not enough, they are forced to emigrate to other regions or to enlist themselves as soldiers, abandoning wives and children. Yet they never receive the pay they are promised, and they die desperate men. What is more, if a man has

---

[36] *Arbitrio primo*, in *Discorsi ai principi d'Italia*, pp. 168–169; the three *Arbitrii sopra l'aumento delle entrate del Regno di Napoli* date back to 1607.

something to say about all of this, he is at once condemned to death as the perpetrator of an act of treason.'[37]

But the degradation of the country is nothing but a mirror in which is reflected the general decadence of Spain itself, which, while it lacks any of the virtues present in a nation on the rise, abounds in the vices belonging to countries in decline. It displays an extremely rapacious avarice, both in the old world and in the new, where, according to the Milanese Girolamo Benzoni, indigenous people gave a Spanish captain gold to drink. It displays the most arrogant disdain for other peoples, all of them treated as if they are slaves, and it displays the foulest ingratitude towards its benefactors. No one is ignorant of the sad end of Christopher Columbus, discoverer of the New World, and among those who had been persecuted Campanella did not hesitate to count himself – he who, although he had written admirable works for Spain, had suffered years of imprisonment. Moreover, the Spanish monarchy appeared as a monstrous organism, devoid of compactness and intrinsic unity. It was similar to a gigantic serpent with three heads (that of its essence, which was empire; that of existence, which was Spain; and that of value, which was Italy), the body of which was made up of parts that were disunited and far from one another. Stronger and more prosperous and ready to take over the role of hegemonic power from its adversary, France ought not to fear Spain and ought in fact to undertake bold initiatives suited to accelerating the fall of a power that was no longer able to hide its own fragility and inadequacy. Given that one ought never to play the games of others, the French ought to counterbalance their own strength with the cleverness of the Spanish, hitting them quickly without giving them time to recover and recourse to delaying and secret maneuvers. Thus, 'it is necessary, as is proper for the lion, to begin the war in the French manner, that is with ceaseless rapidity, and openly, not in the manner of Spain, by delaying and operating in secret, as is characteristic of the wily fox.'[38] The French ought to denounce the Spanish and unmask their religious hypocrisy, hitting the most vulnerable points of the monstrous Geryon, so as to shatter it and liberate people from such odious Spanish tyranny.

Campanella's attention was focused above all on two things: the authority of the empire and the Italian peninsula. To the first of these questions he dedicated the so-called *Comparsa regia*, a legal speech written in Latin and addressed by the French king to the Pope. He sought to argue that on account of its tyranny and heresy the house of Austria no longer had a just

---

[37] *Documenta*, p. 94.
[38] *Mon. Francia*, p. 582.

claim on the prerogatives of empire and that the pope should appoint the king of the Romans *motu proprio*, since the empire had become the property and an exclusive prerogative of the house of Austria and since it had lost any universal pretension whatsoever and lost also the specific purpose of defending Christianity. Just like all timid nations, the Spanish maintain themselves with hypocrisy, 'pretending to be highly religious and reliant on God and zealous in the faith.' On the pretext of fighting in defense of Christianity, they arrogate to themselves huge sums of money, offering in return nothing but vain titles, 'for the purpose of cheating people.' They accuse all other nations, France included, of being heretics; the Spanish cardinals in Rome are nothing by spies for their sovereign. So as to enforce belief, they have discovered the tribunal of the Inquisition, 'the true instrument of their power.' They have destroyed the populations of the New World, and, in order to justify their actions, they have cast into doubt the very membership of those peoples in the human race. They excuse every misdeed with religion, in the name of which they have 'depopulated, occupied, killed, and acted like sharks towards people.'[39]

Even if Campanella had plenty to work with in his demonstration of the completely political nature of the appeal to religion on the part of the Spanish, this did not mean that for him politics might be detached from religion. On the contrary, he reaffirmed that religion 'in all nations at all times has dominated politics, regardless of whether that religion was true or false' and that 'political leaders are able to rule insofar as they can show themselves derived from God, lord of lords.' Campanella concluded that 'thus, dominion consists in the will of people, bound with the chain of religion among themselves and to the prince.'[40] To the instrumentalization of religion carried out by Spain, Campanella opposed the exhortation to follow the politics that was practiced and espoused by Charlemagne, who, turning to his own nation, combined in the following fashion the directives to which he conformed his own political actions, with a highly interesting allusion to 'living' faith and to the powers of the imagination and persuasion:

> I, raising up the good and casting down the bad, have gained such a great glory for my fellow Franks that, owing also to the help of the virtue of the Apostles Peter and Paul, I have transferred to you the Roman Empire, master of the world, when I built my kingdom subject to God and not against him, not with a false and simulated faith (that renders the heart cowardly and vile, deprived of all hope of divine recompense and eternal immortality, a faith that is on that account attached only to the terrestrial life), but rather with a

---

[39] Ibid., p. 427, 505, 503.
[40] Ibid., p. 484.

true and living faith, a faith that renders the heart steady and true and ready to act with courage in the face of any undertaking, in that it is animated by the hope of divine help that is present (although imagined in the case that it be denied that it is authentic, but it is unnecessary to prove how great is the power of the imagination) and at the same time boosted by the desire of the prize of eternal life. Believe me, o my sons, the pseudo-politicians fight with a dead heart, while pious princes fight with a living heart.[41]

But the most vulnerable point of the empire, that against which one ought to move quickly if one wanted to accelerate its dismemberment, was precisely the kingdom of Naples and Italy itself. Campanella was convinced that the Italian princes – even those who displayed submissiveness and friendship towards Spain – hated it in their hearts, but dared not state it publically out of fear. Above all, France ought to make it her business to reassure them, undoing the web of prejudices and fears that Spain had put about deliberately with respect to the French and make those princes understand that they do not present themselves as new masters (wishing only to displace the old rulers) but rather as liberators from a tyrannical domination. They ought to clarify that they did not aspire to territorial enlargement, and reassure the Pope and the clergy, who were fearful of what they presumed was the French desire to restrict the prerogatives and jurisdictions of the Church. On that issue, Campanella addressed three eloquent speeches to Genoa, to the Duke of Savoy, and to the Grand Duke of Tuscany, for the purpose of inviting them to sever without delay every political and economic tie with Spain, a nation from which they could receive no real advantage, but rather only ruin and shame. The reversal from the early *Discorsi ai principi d'Italia*, which exhorted the princes of Italy to support the universalist project of the Spanish empire, thought to be clearly 'founded on the hidden providence of God ... dedicated to the purpose of unifying the world under a single law,' could not have been more complete.

In the appeal to Genoa, the reference to a glorious past served to emphasize the present condition of voluntary slavery to which it had been reduced, blinded by greed for a profit more imaginary than real. Genoa was forced to hand over to Spain the money that it received from the Kingdom of Naples, as a kind of loan that would never be repaid. Paying the price for taking upon itself the hatred and the disdain of its tormented vassals, the republic became impoverished and lost prestige from the point that the Genoese made themselves the 'publicans of Spain.' With regard to Vittorio Amedeo I, Duke of Savoy, Campanella reminded him of the false promises, the unbridled ambition,

---

[41] *Documenta*, pp. 59–60.

the senseless cruelty of the Spanish, dissuading him from following the ambiguous politics of his father, who, maneuvering between Spain and France, had made of their conflicts 'a hugely profitable business.' That double game would now be merely dangerous, because 'now is not the time to play the fool, but rather the time either to lose all or to acquire a kingdom.' The Grand Duke of Tuscany, Ferdinand II, was also brusquely invited to open his eyes to the reality of his submission to Spain – a nation that 'is like a griffin,' with claws planted in the ports and the fortresses of Tuscany. He was invited to abandon every illusion of alliance and friendship with anyone who takes him to be 'a hare or a dove in his hands.'

Determined to awaken the Italian princes from a kind of spell (as a result of which they give money and soldiers to reinforce a power that would devour them, acting like 'a goat who gives succor to a wolf, when it enters its herd in order to hunt' or like the man who gives money to the executioner who will hang him), Campanella spurred them to become conscious of their own power, to emancipate themselves from the tyranny of a power in decline and by now exhausted, so as to recover – with their liberty – their own dignity. At the same time, he certainly knew that these steps required commitment, courage and sacrifice, as one can confirm contrarily from the worrying behavior of some galley slaves, who prefer to live and die as slaves when the period of their forced labor is over, because 'they do not know the goodness of liberty, and they return to jail over and over, until they die.'[42]

So as to dispel the hypnotic attraction of power, it is necessary for a 'wise philosopher' to unmask it in front of those who are being deceived and reveal the intrinsic fragility of a power in decline. The exile Campanella – notwithstanding the disappointments, the weariness of years, the bitter experiences – took this role upon himself energetically, both for the purpose of reawakening the Italian princes and also so as to exhort the French to take on the responsibility of being liberators of the globe having become conscious of their own superiority. After all, 'it is shameful that France, more powerful in arms, in fleets, in soldiers, in captains, in valor, and in population, is overshadowed by the Spanish, who are timid, few in number, poor, beggars, without leaders, without troops, and who have to resort to subterfuge and foreign valor and the appearance of being what, in fact, they are not.'[43]

---

[42] Firpo, 'Gli ultimi scritti politici,' pp. 784, 796, 798, 793, 800.

[43] *Mon. Francia*, p. 591. The first letter of 1636 – in Firpo, 'Idee politiche,' pp. 207–211 – is also dedicated to this paradox.

Last Writings

During the Paris years, Campanella dedicated a great deal of energy to editing his writings for publication. Many of those writings successfully obtained the necessary permissions and were published, despite the obdurate hostility of cliques and individuals at Rome. The projected *Opera omnia* opened, at the beginning of 1636, with a volume comprised of the *Atheismus triumphatus*, the *De gentilismo non retinendo*, the *Disputatio* on the Papal bulls condemning astrology, and the *De praedestinatione*. Then it was the turn of the new edition of the *De sensu rerum*, dedicated to Richelieu, preceded by a *Defensio* that supported the doctrine of the animation of all beings by employing the authority of many theologians and philosophers. On 6 August 1637, Campanella dedicated the imposing tome of the new edition of the *Philosophia realis* to the Chancellor Pierre Séguier, 'second sun' of France and third patron to the author (after the King and Richelieu), to whom he noted that with the sound of his 'bell' he had intended to recall men to the book of nature and to the infallible school of God, the sole true master worthy of a faith free from doubt. In 1638 the *Philosophia rationalis* was published preceded by a dedicatory letter to the brothers François and Charles de Noailles, signed on 15 March 1635, in which the author expressed the deepest gratitude both to François (to whom he owed 'liberty, honor, and life' for helping him flee to France) and to Charles who had welcomed him with affection upon his arrival in Paris. Thereafter followed the *Metaphysica*, dedicated on 15 August 1638 to Claude Bullion, General Superintendent of Finances of the Kingdom, who generously supported the publication of Campanella's books and his very life. Campanella praised him for his political and administrative gifts, calling him the architect of the prosperity of a nation that thanks to his work enjoyed incomes greater than those of the Turk, Spain, and England put together. Recalling a visit to his home (which, as Campanella put it, had occasioned an astonishment greater than that experienced by the Queen of Sheba as she admired the house of Solomon on account of its structure, its objects, and its order), Campanella was happy to dedicate to him the most important of his books, the true 'Bible of philosophers.'[44]

As for theology, during the final years in Paris Campanella would rework his doctrines on predestination, articulated and discussed in various places in particular books of the *Theologia* and in the *De praedestinatione*, into a limpid synthesis in the deft *Compendium*.[45] He sent it to the Chancellor Pierre

---

[44]Letter dated 15 August 1638, in *Lettere*, p. 395; see ch. 10, p. 201.

[45]*Compendium de praedestinatione, reprobatione et gratiae divinae auxiliis*, in *Opuscoli inediti*, pp. 123–142.

Séguier, for the purpose of clarifying once more his own positions and seeking to rebut the criticisms and the censures that he knew came from the theologians of the Dominican convent at Santa Maria sopra Minerva in Rome and that he had not been able to see, despite repeated protests and supplications.[46] Campanella's doctrine was strongly characterized by the principle of the double will of God, according to which God, as a father who created men as his own children and in his own image, extended to all without favor the natural and supernatural gifts apt to lead to salvation. *Antecedenter*, that is to say as part of this first will, men were loved equally and were thus all equally predestined, so that no one was doomed to damnation. As Campanella effectively underscored, 'no father gives birth to his own children so as to send them to the gallows; a father may destine some for lesser goods, but certainly not for evil.'[47] But to this first divine will is added a second will subsequent to the first, one in which God is a righteous judge, beyond being simply a loving father. It is from this second point of view that, with a determination that follows from the foreseeing of merits and demerits in men, God does not predestine all for glory, but condemns to punishment those who have 'defiled' the image of and the similitude with the father and those who have persisted in sin, rejecting all divine help.

With regard to the incarnation, God – foreseeing that man, a free creature, would deviate from the end for which he had been created – knew also that the Word, by means of which he had originally created everything, would become incarnate in order to heal the wound inflicted by sin. Once again, that remedy was offered indiscriminately to all, *gratiose et copiose et affluenter et efficaciter ex parte sui* ('graciously and copiously and abundantly and effectively on his part') and not only to some. Human beings might render the remedy ineffectual, if they were to reject it and close their eyes to the light. In this way, grace (both natural and supernatural) was for all abundant and effective. But, as John Chrysostom (one of Campanella's favorite authors and an authority he often cited in order to smooth the harsher edges of Augustine) had pointed out, such grace *non salvat te sine te* ('cannot save you without you').[48] Grace, which came to all abundantly extended by God, absented itself from no one. It was man, through his indigence and rejection, who absented himself from grace.

In this way, Campanella distanced himself decisively from the doctrine of an indiscriminate (*indiscrete ad libitum*) condemnation on God's part, before considering the demerits and the final impenitence of man. This would

---

[46] See Luigi Firpo's Note, in *Opuscoli inediti*, pp. 174–175.

[47] Ibid., p. 124: 'nullus enim pater generat filios propter furcam, et si quosdam ad minora bona, non tamen ad mala.'

[48] Ibid., pp. 124–125.

prove either the original evil of men or of God, who who thus hate the good. The Spanish theologians, such as the Dominican friars Diego Alvarez and Domingo Bañes, in turn maintained that predestination for glory or damnation was irrevocable, without respect to the good or evil use of free will. They emphasized instead the absoluteness of the decree of God, who would have decided the matter thus, so as to demonstrate his generosity to some and his power and anger to many.[49] Campanella, who analyzed and discussed the subtle distinctions of such doctrine, did not hesitate to define it *nugax et sine fructu* ('clumsy and fruitless') and contrary to the entire tradition of the Fathers. He saw it as a doctrine that was instead in accordance with the anti-Christian positions of those who according to the prediction of Daniel would worship the god Maozim, who would operate in all things with power and not with wisdom and goodness, designating a few for heaven and the majority for hell not on the basis of justice or mercy, but only in order to show his own power in accordance with a decree that did not depend on the goodness or badness of works and that was instead an absolute and, on that account, diabolical decree. This was a god who would abandon without being first abandoned, a god who would make evil those who he had already decided to condemn in order be able to punish them and 'to give vent to his irrational anger' (*saturare iram suam irrationalem*). To these positions, Campanella did not tire of opposing those of John Chrysostom, according to whom the 'mercy of God is given to all without exception,' so that 'just as fire always heats and the sun always illuminates, so God always does good and does not stop doing good on account of our sins or of some passion of God.' This is a God that does not forsake even if he has been forsaken in the manner of a lover who runs after his beloved, as one reads in one of Chrysostom's most beautiful passages that is often cited: 'God did not create us in order to damn us: he never forsakes us, even when we forsake him, as a lover does who is delirious for the beloved; damnation is due to us alone and not to some defect in grace.'[50]

Beyond simply his political advice, however, Campanella was appreciated in court circles for his astrological knowledge and understanding of the occult. A short work of chiromancy has recently been located that was composed at the fervent request (*ardenter expostulavisti*) of Richelieu, a man who harbored interests in such doctrines.[51] In the 1630s, the Cardinal had not remained

---

[49] Such opinions Campanella blamed on the long cohabitation of the Spanish with the Muslims, upholders of fatalistic doctrines, conducive to their politics of military conflict.

[50] Tommaso Campanella, *Della grazia gratificante, Theologicorum l. XIII*, ed. R. Amerio (Rome, 1959), pp. 103–105.

[51] Germana Ernst, 'Note campanelliane. I. L'inedita *Chiroscopia* a Richelieu,' *B&C*, 1 (1995), pp. 83–94: 90–94; also in Tommaso Campanella, *Dalla Metaphysica. Profezia, divinazione, estasi*, ed. G. Ernst (Soveria Mannelli, Cz, 2008).

above the astrological–political affair regarding the Pope's horoscope, and his curiosity in this field is confirmed by numerous pieces that were dedicated to him. Jacques Gaffarel – his chaplain, sent to Italy to search for the rarest Hebrew, Siriac, and Chaldean manuscripts – offered to him the *Abdita divinae cabalae mysteria* in 1625. Furthermore, in 1635 a young boy of twelve years of age dedicated to him his own translation from the Greek of the physiognomic work by Adamantius, which contained maxims very similar to 'those that you have happily practiced for the purpose of discovering the strengths and weaknesses of enemies of this crown.'[52] The Lyonais physician Lazare Meysonnier, translator of della Porta and author of texts imbued with mysticism and natural magic, dedicated to the Cardinal the *Nova et arcana doctrina febrium* (Lyon, 1641). Likewise, the Venetian Dominicus De Rubeis sent him his own *Tabulae physiognomicae* (Venice, 1639), emphasizing the utility of the science that aids the understanding of the inclinations and the affections of men judging from their exterior features and habits. Campanella certainly could not refuse the imperious desire of such a personage, and he composed a slender tract, conventional but not vulgar, asking for the protection of this famous dedicatee. If already in the introductory epistle to the *De sensu* Campanella had noted how a single look from the powerful minister could be enough to dissolve the malevolent clouds of slander and persecutions that afflicted him, he noted in the brief words of dedication for the short work that treated the lines of the palm that his own destiny lay in the hands of the Cardinal – only then to add that all matters remain in the hands of God.

After the bull *Inscrutabilis*, which had reiterated and intensified the condemnation of the divinatory doctrines of the *Coeli et terrae* of Sixtus V, Campanella adopted an attitude of extreme caution with regard to divination. He was attentive to distinctions and specifications, but did fight to preserve some space (even if meager) for predictive doctrines. The real aim of this *Disputatio* on the Bulls was that of specifying the limits of astrology for the purpose of salvaging from it at least its 'natural' aspect and, in this way, a degree of legitimacy. Distinguishing therefore the doctrines that derive from an authentic *studiositas* from those that make appeal to a vain *curiositas* and distinguishing likewise the sciences that proceed on the basis of signs placed by nature or by God from those that are based on artificial or arbitrary signs, Campanella condemned geomancy as vain and baseless along with practices such as aeromancy, hydromancy, and pyromancy. Chiromancy, however, was to be saved, because it was limited to observation of physical signs and to the expression of opinions on

---

[52] Henry de Boyvin du Vaurouy, *La Physionomie ou les indices que la Nature a mis au corps humain par ou l'on peut descouvrir les moeurs et les inclinations* (Paris: Toussaint Du Bray, 1635).

tendencies and aspects of character, without presuming to pronounce definitively on future events.

The minute treatise on chiromancy was limited to several general considerations on three principal lines of the hand. It made references to a successful and continuous tradition that had begun at the outset of the century with the *Anastasis chiromantica*, in which Bartolomeo Cocles boasted, following a motif typical of the Renaissance, of having brought back to light a doctrine that had become buried and neglected and restoring it to the dignity of a science. The art had enjoyed a wide diffusion in the first half of the sixteenth century and authors such as Cardano had dealt with it. Indeed, Cardano dedicated a chapter of his *De varietate* to the subject, and Giambattista della Porta wrote a detailed Latin treatise, which remained unpublished (probably because of censors) and was only published in 1677 in a beautiful Italian translation by Pompeo Sarnelli with the title of *Chirophysiognomy*. This is a work that is famous for its splendid autobiographical piece in which the author remembers his own association with the Neapolitan hangman, a certain Antonello Cocozza, so as to have the chance to analyze the hands and feet of those who had been hanged, convinced as he was that the doctrine could make use of observations of persons in whom the passions had prevailed and in whom rational control had proven fragile:

> When he took down from the gallows those who had been hanged and carried them to the Ricciardo bridge (this is a place about a thousand yards from the city of Naples, where the wretched are left hanging, so as to terrorize those scoundrels who might pass by, until they rot, and are consumed by wind and rain), he would inform me of the hour of those transportations. Going to that place, I observed the markings on the hands and feet, and drew them with a stylus on paper made for that purpose, or took their forms in plaster so that I might apply wax later and have their prints at home. And in this way I had the chance to study them by night at home and to compare them with others. I would piece together all the signs that might reveal the truth, doing always the same thing, until I found all the signs that pointed towards a person being strung up. In this way, I satisfied my desire of knowing.[53]

Upon the birth of the future Sun King, which finally came to pass after long years of disappointment on Sunday, 5 September 1638 (the same day on which, seventy years earlier, he himself had been born), Campanella was called to the palace, because the Queen wanted a horoscope for the new-born. Having

---

[53] *Della Chirofisonomia* (Naples: A. Bulifon, 1677), p. 23; the Italian translation by Sarnelli is reproduced after the Latin text edited in Giambattista della Porta, *De ea naturalis physiognomoniae parte quae ad manuum lineas spectat libri duo*, ed. O. Trabucco (Naples, 2003).

examined the naked child with care and having considered the matter for several days, the friar announced a synthetic and not adulatory prognostication. He emphasized the future sovereign's inclinations to luxury and to arrogance, his long reign, together with the unhappiness and confusion of his last years.[54] In the next weeks, he composed the Latin hexameters of the *Ecloga in nativitatem Delphini*.[55] In the last verses of this piece, there emerged, once again, a convergence between utopia, astrology, and prophecy. Already, the dedicatory epistle to Richelieu for the *De sensu rerum* had concluded with an invitation to the Cardinal to build the city of the sun that the author had described (with the wish that its splendor would never diminish). Then, in the eclogue the citation of the exordium from Virgil's verses on the return of the reign of Saturn is followed by a call to the celestial signs and to the prophecy that announced the advent of a new age, which the 'portentous child' was called to instaurate. He called upon the Muses of Calabria to shake off old age so as to demonstrate once again signs of divine judgments and to communicate faith in the approaching of an age in which 'somber colors, signs of grief and ignorance' would be rejected, so as to put luminous clothing over pure hearts, an epoch in which impiety, fraud, lies, and quarrels will be over and done with; lambs will no longer fear the wolf, nor the herds the lion; tyrants will learn to rule for the good of the people; idleness will cease and painful toil will come to an end. Indeed, labor will be a game shared amicably between many, since all will recognize a single father and god.[56]

Almost anticipating the approaching of the end, on 6 July 1638, Campanella had sent to Ferdinand II de' Medici, along with a copy of the *Philosophia realis*, a letter in which some of the most important themes of his own life seem to come together and constitute a genuine spiritual testament: praise for the house of Medici for having favored the rebirth of Platonism and an emancipation from the yoke of Aristotle; the youthful hopes of finding a place under the protection of the Medici, wrecked by his adherence to the philosophy of Telesio; the reform of knowledge in the light of the two divine books of nature and Scripture; the 'fatal secret' of the arrival in French territory, for the purpose of bringing his own works to press, among which he would not fail to remember the early and still much loved *Civitas Solis*; the remote, but indelible encounter in his youth with Galileo at Padua, which had signaled the beginning of a constant friendship and esteem, despite the lack of agreement on some issues:

---

[54] See Lerner, *Tommaso Campanella en France*, pp. 83–84.

[55] See Germana Ernst, "'Redeunt Saturnia regna." Profezia e poesia in Tommaso Campanella,' *B&C*, 11 (2005), pp. 429–449. The term *nativitas* in the title indicates that one is dealing with a genuine horoscope.

[56] *Poesie*, p. 650.

Your Highness will see in this book that in some things I am not in agreement with the admirable Galileo, your Highness's philosopher and my dear friend and master since the time in Padua when he brought me a letter from the Grand Duke Ferdinand. Intellectual discord can co-exist with a concord of the wills of each party, and I know that he is a man so sincere and perfect that he will take more pleasure from my criticisms – for which each of us has given permission to the other – than from the approval of others.

And finally, there is also Campanella's reflection on the destiny of prophets who, defeated and persecuted, rise on the third day – or in the third age. As he said, 'the next age will judge us, because the present always crucifies its benefactors, who then rise again on the third day or in the third age.'[57] Worried by the approach of a solar eclipse, he sought in vain to ward off the threat with astral remedies well known to him and already practiced in the past with Pope Urban VIII. Campanella died some hours before dawn on 21 May 1639.

On 28 May, Théophraste Renaudot's *Gazette* announced the sad event.[58] On July 3, Naudé wrote a long letter from Rome to Schoppe at Padua, hoping to feel himself united in grief with him at the loss of their mutual friend.[59] Amplifying both the merits of Schoppe in relation to the deceased and the conditions of his life at Paris, he related that Campanella – hit suddenly by strong colic pains that lasted for twenty days (the result perhaps of the erroneous administration of a drug) – died three or four hours before daybreak, serenely, in his sleep. As he went over the writings and the teachings of the man, the arcane doctrines and the meditation on eternal things, Naudé was pleased that Campanella had died satisfied that many of his own works had been published, works 'in which he had stretched the nerves of his genius to their breaking point.' Assuring his reader of his profound esteem for Campanella, Naudé asked Schoppe to hold alive the memory of their friend and asked him likewise to defend him against slander.

Rather than end with the solemn moment in which Campanella realized the impossibility of brightening the gloom and the shadows that were about to engulf him and to put an end to the life that he well knew was nothing but 'a child's game played in the dusk before dinner,'[60] it is better to recall a gentle anecdote, relayed by Nicolas Chorier, that testifies to his love for life and nature. Chorier had met Campanella in Paris, and he tells us that the old philosopher, with the ingenuity and happiness of a child, would run after small birds, imitating their twittering – Campanella had always been fascinated by

---

[57] Letter to Ferdinand II de' Medici dated 6 July 1638, in *Lettere*, pp. 388–390.
[58] Lerner, *Tommaso Campanella en France*, p. 91.
[59] Gabriel Naudé, *Epistulae* (Geneva: I. H. Widerhold, 1647), pp. 614–629.
[60] *Ath. triumph.*, VIII, p. 93.

the varied voices and languages of creation. He would throw his hat in the air, and, running with a certain ungainliness that testified to a body weighed down by the years, he would invite whoever was with him to breathe deeply in the pure air, because (as he would say) it was the soul of the world: '"Let us draw life from the life of the world." He would call air the life of the world – air, which is the soul of nature.'[61]

---

[61]Luigi Firpo, 'Apppunti campanelliani. XIX. L'amicizia con Christoph von Forstner, Pierre de Boissat e Nicolas Chorier,' *GCFI*, 29 (1950), p. 91: "Hauriamus, hauriamus vitam de vita mundi." Aërem vitam mundi vocabat, qui naturae anima est.'

LIST OF ABBREVIATIONS

Works of Campanella

Aforismi pol.: *Aforismi politici*, ed. Luigi Firpo (Turin: Istituto Giuridico dell'Università, 1941)

Apologia: *Apologia pro Galileo/Apologie pour Galilée*, ed. Michel-Pierre Lerner (Latin text with French trans.; Paris : Les Belles Lettres, 2001)

Art. proph.: *Articuli prophetales*, ed. Germana Ernst (Florence: La Nuova Italia, 1977)

Astrologia: Astrologicorum libri VII (Francofurti: sumptibus Godefridi Tampachii), in *Opera Latina*, II, pp. 1081–1346

Ateismo trionfato: *L'ateismo trionfato*, ed. Germana Ernst, 2 vols. (Pisa: Edizioni della Normale, 2004)

Ath. triumph.: Atheismus triumphatus (Parisiis: apud T. Dubray, 1636)

Città del Sole: *La città del Sole*, ed. Luigi Firpo, new. ed. by Germana Ernst and Laura Salvetti Firpo (Bari-Rome: Laterza, 1997)

Città del Sole (1996): *La città del Sole - Questione quarta sull'ottima repubblica*, ed. Germana Ernst (Milan: Rizzoli, 1996)

Dialogo politico: Dialogo politico contro Luterani, Calvinisti e altri eretici, ed. Domenico Ciampoli (Lanciano: Carabba, 1911)

Dichiarazione: Dichiarazione di Castelvetere in Firpo, *Processi*, pp. 99–117

Discorsi ai principi d'Italia: Discorsi ai principi d'Italia e altri scritti filo-ispanici, ed. Luigi Firpo (Turin: Chiantore, 1945)

Discorsi universali: Discorsi universali del governo ecclesiastico, in Giordano Bruno-Tommaso Campanella, *Scritti scelti*, ed. Luigi Firpo (Turin: UTET, 1968), pp. 467-523

Discorso sulla cometa: Germana Ernst and Laura Salvetti Firpo, 'Tommaso Campanella e la cometa del 1618. Due lettere e un opuscolo epistolare inediti,' *B&C*, 2 (1996), pp. 57–88

Disputatio: Disputatio in prologum instauratarum scientiarum, in *Phil. realis*, ff. B-F$_{4v}$

Epilogo magno: *Epilogo magno*, ed. Carmelo Ottaviano (Rome: Reale Accademia d'Italia, 1939)

Informazione: Informazione sopra la lettura delli processi fatti l'anno 1599 in Calabria, in Firpo, *Processi,* pp. 273–287

Lettere: Lettere, ed. Vincenzo Spampanato (Bari: Laterza, 1927)

Lettere 2: Lettere 1595–1938, ed. Germana Ernst (Pisa-Rome: Istituti Editoriali e Poligrafici Internazionali, 2000)

Medicina: Medicinalium libri VII (Lugduni: ex officina I. Pillehotte, sumptibus I. Caffin et F. Plaignard, 1635)

Metaphysica: Metaphysica (Parisiis: [D. Langlois], 1638); anast. repr. by Luigi Firpo (Turin: La Bottega d'Erasmo, 1961)

Mon. Messia: La monarchia del Messia, ed. Vittorio Frajese (Rome: Edizioni di Storia e Letteratura, 1995)

Mon. Messiae (2002): Monarchie du Messie, ed. Paolo Ponzio, French trans. by Véronique Bourdette (Paris: Presses Universitaires de France, 2002)

Mon. Francia: Monarchia di Francia, in *Monarchie d'Espagne et Monarchie de France,* ed. Germana Ernst, French trans. by Nathalie Fabry (Paris: Presses Universitaires de France, 1997), pp. 373–597

Mon. Spagna: Monarchia di Spagna, in *Monarchie d'Espagne et Monarchie de France,* by Germana Ernst, French trans. by Serge Waldbaum (Paris: Presses Universitaires de France, 1997), pp. 1–371

Narrazione: Narrazione della istoria sopra cui fu appoggiata la favola della ribellione, in Firpo, *Processi,* pp. 289–313

Oeconomica: Oeconomica, in *Opera Latina,* II, pp. 1037–1080

Opera Latina: Opera Latina Francofurti impressa annis 1617–1630, ed. Luigi Firpo, 2 vols. (Turin: La Bottega d'Erasmo, 1975)

Opuscoli astrologici: Opuscoli astrologici. Come evitare il fato astrale, Apologetico, Disputa sulle Bolle, ed. Germana Ernst (Latin texts with Italian trans.; Milan: Rizzoli, 2003)

Opuscoli inediti: Opuscoli inediti, ed. Luigi Firpo (Florence: Olschki, 1951)

Phil. realis: Disputationum in quatuor partes suae philosophiae realis libri quatuor (Parisiis: ex typographia D. Houssaye, 1637)

Phil. sens. dem.: Philosophia sensibus demonstrata, ed. Luigi De Franco (Naples: Vivarium, 1992)

Poesie: Le poesie, ed. Francesco Giancotti (Turin: Einaudi, 1998)

Poetica, in *Scritti letterari,* pp. 317-430

Prima delineatio: Prima delineatio defensionum, in Firpo, *Processi,* pp. 122–169 (Latin text with Italian trans.)

Quaest. mor.: Quaestiones morales, in *Phil. realis,* pp. 1–60

Quaest. phys.: Quaestiones physiologicae, in *Phil. realis,* pp. 1–570

Quaest. pol.: Quaestiones politicae, in *Phil. realis,* pp. 71–112

Quod reminiscentur: Quod reminiscentur et convertentur ad Dominum universi fines terrae, ed. Romano Amerio (books I-II, Padua: Cedam 1939);

(book III, with the title *Per la conversione degli Ebrei,* Florence: Olschki, 1955); (book IV, with the title *Legazioni ai Maomettani,* Florence: Olschki, 1960)

Rhetorica: Rhetorica, in *Scritti letterari,* pp. 715–903 (Latin text with Italian trans.)

Scritti letterari: Tutte le opere di Tommaso Campanella. I. Scritti letterari, ed. Luigi Firpo (Milan: Mondadori, 1954)

Secunda delineatio: Secunda delineatio defensionum, in Firpo, *Processi,* pp. 172–213 (Latin text with Italian trans.)

Senso delle cose: Del senso delle cose e della magia, ed. Germana Ernst (Bari-Rome: Laterza, 2007)

Syntagma: De libris propriis et recta ratione studendi syntagma, ed. Germana Ernst (Latin text with Italian trans.; Pisa-Rome: Fabrizio Serra, 2007)

Tommaso Campanella: Tommaso Campanella, ed. Germana Ernst, intr. by Nicola Badaloni (Rome: Il Poligrafico e Zecca dello Stato, 1999)

Other Works

Amabile, *Congiura:* Luigi Amabile, *Fra Tommaso Campanella, la sua congiura, i suoi processi e la sua pazzia,* 3 vols. (Naples: Morano, 1882)

Amabile, *Castelli:* Luigi Amabile, *Fra Tommaso Campanella ne' castelli di Napoli, in Roma e in Parigi,* 2 vols. (Naples: Morano, 1887)

B&C: Bruniana & Campanelliana, Pisa-Rome, 1995–

Baldini and Spruit: Ugo Baldini, Leen Spruit, 'Campanella tra il processo romano e la congiura di Calabria. A proposito di due lettere inedite a Santori,' *B&C,* 7 (2001), pp. 179–187

Congiura di Calabria: Tommaso Campanella e la congiura di Calabria, ed. Germana Ernst (Stilo: Comune di Stilo, 2001)

Enciclopedia: Enciclopedia Bruniana e Campanelliana, ed. Eugenio Canone and Germana Ernst (Pisa-Rome: Istituti Editoriali e Poligrafici Internazionali, vol. 1, 2006; vol. 2, forthcoming)

DBI: Dizionario Biografico degli Italiani (Rome: Istituto della Enciclopedia Italiana, 1960–)

Laboratorio Campanella: Laboratorio Campanella. Biografia. Contesti. Iniziative in corso, ed. Germana Ernst and Caterina Fiorani (Rome: L'Erma di Bretschneider, 2008)

Ernst, *Religione:* Germana Ernst, *Religione, ragione e natura. Ricerche su Tommaso Campanella e il tardo Rinascimento* (Milan: Fanco Angeli, 1991)

Firpo, *Bibliografia:* Luigi Firpo, *Bibliografia degli scritti di Tommaso Campanella* (Turin: Giappichelli, 1940)

Firpo, *Processi*: Luigi Firpo, *I processi di Tommaso Campanella,* ed. Eugenio
   Canone (Rome: Salerno editrice, 1998)
Firpo, *Ricerche*: Luigi Firpo, *Ricerche campanelliane* (Florence: Olschki, 1947)
Galilei, *Opere*: Galileo Galilei, *Opere,* Edizione Nazionale, by Antonio Favaro,
   20 vols. (Florence: Barbera 1890–1909)
GCFI: *Giornale critico della filosofia italiana*, Florence, 1920–

INDEX OF NAMES

SUBJECT INDEX

Aristotelianism, anti-Aristotelianism, 4–10, 13, 23, 26, 42, 86, 96, 100, 115, 122, 145, 161, 163, 164, 168–171, 186–188, 208–209, 212, 231–232

astrology, 11–12, 71, 86, 124, 127, 172–180, 220–221, 225–226, 259, 262, 264

astronomy, *see* cosmology

atheism, 26, 77, 92, 136, 140

atomism, 26, 115–116, 159, 165, 184, 236, 246–247

authority, 6, 63, 142–144, 255

brain, 10, 27, 100, 119, 121, 191

breath, 12–13, 118

Christianity, 60, 85, 87, 93, 102, 128, 130–133, 141, 146, 148–149, 152–158, 216, 256; and science 162–164, 167–169, 171

cold, 10, 11, 13, 47, 48, 49, 63, 111, 115, 116, 123, 161, 187, 190, 198, 206, 207, 218, 240

conception, *see* generation

cosmos, cosmology, 9–11, 17, 47, 86, 111, 113, 158, 162, 163, 210, 224.

devil, 2, 19, 20, 55, 112, 125, 133, 144, 194, 209, 218, 223

dominion, 60, 90, 141–142, 146, 185, 187, 256; *see also* authority

education, 51, 229–230; and poetry, 41–43

elements, 10, 14, 17, 47, 48, 115–117, 121, 154, 187, 189

ens rationis, 10

equality, inequality, 90, 91, 187, 231, 253

equity, *see* justice

evil, 81, 83, 92, 99, 103, 110, 113, 131, 144, 152, 185, 197, 208, 217–218, 253, 261

fate, 12, 30, 48, 60, 206, 207

fortune, 62, 90, 92, 109, 142, 234, 251

freedom, 6, 36, 63, 68, 71, 75, 87, 111, 138, 150, 151, 158, 173, 184, 246–247, 258; *see also libertas philosophandi*

free will, 82, 173–174, 176, 177

government, 90, 92, 94, 140, 143, 145, 147, 151

geomancy, 31, 262

generation, 10, 11, 51, 100–101, 119, 183

God, 13, 38–40, 48, 54, 57, 60, 88, 92, 101, 104, 112–113, 117, 121, 123, 124, 131, 141, 142, 144, 148, 154, 156–158, 167, 172, 201–202, 208–210, 213–214, 229, 237, 256, 260–261

good, 37, 50–51, 54, 81, 90–92, 99, 103, 111, 122, 158, 185, 186, 197, 218, 254, 261; chief good, 53, 56, 184, 185–186, 187; common or public good, 91, 93,

Breinigsville, PA USA
21 March 2010
234568BV00003B/3/P